T0312086

The Failure of Judges and the Rise of Regulators

The Failure of Judges and the Rise of Regulators

Andrei Shleifer

[Walras-Pareto Lectures]
The MIT Press
Cambridge, Massachusetts
London, England

© 2012 Massachusetts Institute of Technology

All rights reserved. No part of this book may be reproduced in any form by any electronic or mechanical means (including photocopying, recording, or information storage and retrieval) without permission in writing from the publisher.

This book was set in Palatino by Toppan Best-set Premedia Limited.

Library of Congress Cataloging-in-Publication Data

Shleifer, Andrei.
The failure of judges and the rise of regulators / Andrei Shleifer.
    p.   cm.—(Walras-Pareto lectures)
Includes bibliographical references and index.
ISBN 978-0-262-01695-7 (hc. : alk. paper)—978-0-262-52952-5 (pbk. : alk. paper)
1. Trade regulation—Economic aspects. 2. Judicial process. 3. Administrative procedure. I. Title.
K3842.S55   2012
342′.066—dc23
                                                                                                    2011021320
The MIT Press is pleased to keep this title available in print by manufacturing single copies, on demand, via digital printing technology.

Contents

Acknowledgments

The ideas presented in this book have been developed with several collaborators, as reflected in joint authorship of all but the introductory chapter. Most importantly, the central idea of this book—that regulation emerges as an alternative strategy of social control of economic life in response to the failure of courts—was developed together with Edward L. Glaeser. This idea of course is not entirely new: both Woodrow Wilson in his *New Freedom* program and James Landis in his classic 1938 defense of regulation *The Administrative Process* emphasized the failures of courts to deal with the problems of modern society. Yet the insight appears to have been lost in modern regulatory economics, and we attempted to bring it back, theoretically, historically, and (with Simon Johnson) empirically.

A key part of the argument is the failure of courts to deal with modern problems, which has led me to an effort to understand judicial behavior. The notion that judges exercise enormous discretion leading to unpredictability of litigation is again not new; it has long been known in American jurisprudence as *Legal Realism* and has recently been beautifully articulated by Judge Richard A. Posner (2008) in his *How Judges Think*. Nicola Gennaioli and I tried to revisit some of the fundamental questions of legal realism formally in the chapters presented in this book. Judge Posner, Anthony Niblett, and I then joined forces to examine empirically whether the widely accepted belief in the long-run convergence and predictability of common law is accurate. We found that it is not, at least in one key area of tort law.

One way to understand how litigation or regulation is chosen is to look across jurisdictions. Some of the most exciting evidence on regulatory styles comes from comparing patterns of regulation and litigation across countries from different legal traditions. For over a decade, I have been involved in research in this area with Simeon Djankov,

Rafael La Porta, and Florencio Lopez de Silanes, which continued earlier work with Robert Vishny on *Law and Finance*. Some of the research on comparative regulation appears in this volume. More recently, Casey Mulligan and I have argued that there are increasing returns to regulation, so that more populous jurisdictions should have more of it.

I am extremely grateful to all of my coauthors for allowing me to reprint our joint work in this book. I am also grateful to Nicolas Ciarcia, Virginia Crossman, Lori Reck, and Benjamin Schoefer for help with producing this volume. Last but not least, I am grateful to my hosts for the Walras-Pareto Lectures at the University of Lausanne, Professor Alberto Holly and Claudine Delapierre Saudan, for hospitality in their beautiful city.

1   The Enforcement Theory of Regulation

1   Ubiquitous Regulation

The American and European societies are much richer today than they were 100 years ago, yet they are also vastly more regulated. Today, we work in jobs extensively regulated by the government, from hiring procedures, to working hours and conditions, to rules for joining unions, to dismissal practices. We live in houses and apartment buildings whose construction—from zoning, to use of materials, to fire codes—is heavily regulated. We eat food grown with approved fertilizers and hormones, processed in regulated factories, and sold in licensed outlets with mandatory labels and warnings. Our cars, buses, and airplanes are made, sold, driven, and maintained under heavy government regulation. Our children attend schools that teach material authorized by the state, visit doctors following regulated procedures, and play on playgrounds built under government-mandated safety standards.

Government regulation is extensive in all rich and middle-income countries. It transcends not only levels of economic development, but also cultures, legal traditions, levels of democratization, and all other factors economists use to explain differences among countries. There is surely a lot of variation across countries, but it pales by comparison with the raw fact of ubiquity. Why is there so much government regulation? Why has it grown?

I begin this chapter by reviewing the standard theories of economic regulation, and arguing that they fail to account for the basic facts of regulation. I then propose "The Enforcement Theory of Regulation," which sees regulation as one of several alternative strategies of social control of business, of which the most prominent is dispute resolution by courts. Because such resolution is often costly, unpredictable, and ineffective, regulation, with all its faults, emerges as the more efficient strategy for enforcing desirable conduct.

2 Theories of Regulation

The standard Pigouvian, "public interest" or "helping hand" theory of regulation is based on two assumptions. First, unhindered markets often fail because of the problems of monopoly or externalities. Second, governments are benign and capable of correcting these market failures through regulation. This theory of regulation has been used both as a prescription of what governments should do, and as a description of what they actually do, at least in democratic countries. According to this theory, governments control prices so that monopolies do not overcharge, impose safety standards to prevent accidents such as fires or poisonings, regulate jobs to counter the employer's monopsony power over the employee, regulate security issuances so investors are not cheated, and so on. The public interest theory of regulation has become the cornerstone of modern public economics, as well as the bible of socialist and other left-leaning politicians. It has been used to justify much of the growth of public ownership and regulation over the twentieth century (Allais 1947; Meade 1948; Lewis 1949). It has also been the bedrock of modern anti-market rhetoric (Stiglitz 1989).

The public interest theory of regulation has been subjected to a number of criticisms, associated mostly with the Chicago School of Law and Economics. These criticisms proceed in three intellectual steps. First, contracts and private orderings can take care of most market failures without any government intervention at all, let alone regulation. Second, in the few cases where markets might not work perfectly, private litigation can address whatever conflicts market participants might have. And third, even if markets and courts cannot solve all problems perfectly, government regulators are incompetent, corrupt, and captured, so regulation would make things even worse. Consider these three lines of argument in order.

The first line of attack criticizes the public interest theory for exaggerating the extent of market failure, and for failing to recognize the ability of competition and private orderings to address many of the alleged problems. Competition for labor, the argument goes, itself assures that employers provide safety and good working conditions for employees. If an employer failed to do so, his competitors would offer the more efficient packages, and thereby attract better workers at lower wages. Likewise, private markets assure the efficient safety levels in a variety of products and services, such as trains, houses, or cars. Sellers who fail to deliver such levels of safety lose market share to competitors who run safer trains, build safer houses, or produce safer cars. The competition criticism also maintains that what looks like a monopoly to would-be regulators is subject to potential entry and competition. Moreover, cartels typically break up after a short time because their participants cheat to make windfall profits.

Even when competitive forces are not strong enough, private orderings work to address potential market failures. Neighbors resolve disputes among themselves, without any government intervention, because they need to get along with each other over long stretches of time (Ellickson 1991). Industries form associations that guarantee quality, and penalize cheaters among themselves to assure that, in the long run, customers continue their patronage (Greif 1989; Bernstein 1992). Families, cities, and ethnic groups establish reputations in the marketplace, and thereby control any possible misconduct by their members.

The thrust of these arguments is that the domain of market failure or socially harmful conduct that is not automatically controlled by impersonal forces of competition is extremely limited, and therefore so is the scope for any desirable intervention by the state. But this, of course, is only the first step in a much broader assault on regulation.

The second step, originating in the work of Coase (1960), maintains further that, in the few cases where competition and private orderings do not successfully address market failures, impartial courts can do so by enforcing contracts and common law rules for torts. Employers can offer workers employment contracts that specify what happens in the event of an accident, security issuers can voluntarily disclose information to potential investors and guarantee its accuracy, and so on. As long as courts enforce these contracts, market outcomes are efficient. Indeed, even when there are no contracts, efficient adjudication by courts restores efficiency through appropriate tort rules. When courts award damages to harmed plaintiffs correctly, potential tortfeasors face exactly the right incentives to take the efficient level of precaution (Posner 1972). With well-functioning courts enforcing property rights and contracts, the scope for desirable regulation—even by a "helping hand" government—is minimal.

Coase's logic has proved extremely powerful, both as a technical critique of regulation and as a libertarian manifesto. Following Coase, the Chicago School has gone much further. The third, and crucial step in its critique of regulation is to question the assumptions of a benevolent and competent government. This is the essence of Stigler's capture theory (Stigler 1971; Posner 1974). As forcefully summarized by Peltzman (1989), this theory consists of two basic propositions. First, the political process of regulation is typically captured by the regulated industry itself. Regulation not only fails to counter monopoly pricing, but is to the contrary used to sustain it through state intervention. Second, even in the cases where, under the influence of organized consumer groups, regulators try to promote social welfare, they are incompetent and rarely succeed. Thus the scope for government regulation is minimal at best, and such intervention is futile and dangerous even in the rare cases where there is scope.

The Chicago critique of public interest regulatory theory is one of the finest moments of twentieth-century economics. The pioneers of this critique not only provided new theories for thinking about the role of government, but also delivered predictions that in many cases have been supported by the evidence—particularly the evidence of pervasive regulatory failure. Yet the Chicago critique cannot be the final answer, for at least two important reasons.

At the most basic level, the Chicago tradition has failed to come to grips with the fundamental facts described in the first paragraph of this chapter, namely that today we live in a much richer, more benign, but also more regulated society, and that as consumers we are generally happy with most of the regulations that protect us. We are happier knowing that trains and airplanes are safe than we would be savoring the thought of a fortune that our loved ones would collect in a lawsuit should we die in a fiery crash. In securities markets, investors prefer a regulated, level playing field to the prospect of loss recovery through litigation. Indeed, there is strong evidence that regulation benefits the development of financial markets and public participation in them (chapter 7; La Porta et al. 2008). A more nuanced theory, which incorporates the powerful Chicago critiques of the public interest approach to government, but also recognizes the benefits of regulation in some circumstances, is clearly needed to keep the logic and the facts together.

Second, the Coasian logic runs into contradictions as a description of reality. In Coase's view, contracts are a substitute for regulation. If potential externalities are contracted around, no regulation is necessary. Yet, contrary to this prediction, we see extensive government regulation of *contracts themselves*. Employment terms are delineated in contracts, yet these contracts are heavily regulated by the government. Purchases of various goods, from homes, to appliances, to stocks, are governed by detailed contracts, yet these contracts too are restricted by government mandates. The regulation of contracts goes much beyond mandatory disclosure, which suggests that asymmetric information is not at the heart of the problem. The fact that contracting itself is so heavily regulated undermines both the public interest theory of regulation and its Coasian critique. The public interest theory is undermined because market failures or information asymmetries do not seem to be necessary for regulation, yet those are seen by the theory as the prerequisites for government intervention. The Coasian position is undermined because free contracts are expected to remedy market failures and eliminate the need for regulation, yet regulation often intervenes in and restricts contracts themselves, including contracts with no third party effects. The puzzle of ubiquitous regulation remains.

This book argues that to understand ubiquitous regulation, one needs to take a broader perspective on how societies enforce desirable conduct by their members. This perspective recognizes that enforcement is not free, but instead requires resources (Becker and Stigler 1974). Private orderings, litigation, and regulation are all examples of strategies of enforcing desirable conduct. Over time, there is some pressure for societies to gravitate toward the more efficient, or less expensive, strategies of enforcing socially desirable conduct. In some spheres of activity, these efficient strategies require minimal government involvement: private orderings work extremely well. In other instances, nothing but the full control of the activity by the government would meet social goals: imagine the contracting out of keeping nuclear weapons. Away from these extremes, an intermediate form of government involvement is necessary, with two principal forms being litigation and regulation. Litigation, central to the Coasian logic, emphasizes dispute resolution by courts; regulation emphasizes the enforcement of rules by the executive. Of course, in many instances, the two are combined.

The key point of the enforcement theory is that the choice between regulation and litigation often depends on which one is the more efficient strategy of addressing externalities and torts. The fundamental assumption of Coase's argument is that courts, as a rule, effectively enforce contracts and efficient tort remedies, creating a strong presumption against regulation. Because courts are needed both to enforce contracts and to provide remedies for torts, they are central to the basic private mechanisms for curing market failures. In so far as courts resolve disputes cheaply, predictably, and impartially, the efficiency case for regulation is difficult to make in most areas. Efficient regulation would be an exception, not the rule. But when litigation is expensive, unpredictable, or biased, the efficiency case for regulation opens up. Contracts accomplish less when their interpretation is unpredictable and their enforcement is expensive. Liability rules do not cure market failures if compensation of the victims is vulnerable to the vagaries of courts. The choice between regulation, litigation, or a mixture of the two is then a choice of the efficient strategy of enforcement of socially desirable conduct. In this book, I argue that the superiority of courts is far from clear cut. And when courts fail, regulation emerges as the more efficient approach.

In what follows, I show that this theory explains not only the ubiquity of regulation, but also its growth over the last century. The enforcement theory also helps shed light on the patterns of regulation and litigation across activities, as well as across jurisdictions. I am not suggesting that regulation is universally desirable; regulators often suffer from far deeper problems than judges. The point is that there are tradeoffs between the two. Indeed, if this theory is correct, it suggests that the growth of regulation reflects an efficient institutional adaptation to a more complex world.

3   Perfect Courts

To fix ideas and to illustrate the arguments, consider the example of workplace safety regulation, an important area of government intervention in markets. Workplace safety is especially informative because the traditional transaction-cost objection to the Coase Theorem, namely that contracting is impractical because many parties are involved (as with pollution), does not apply. Nor is it plausible that asymmetric information between firms and their workers, who are specialists and interact over time, limits contracts (or has third party effects). Indeed, the puzzle of ubiquitous and growing regulation is most dramatic in areas, such as workplace safety, where there are no obvious limitations on or externalities from contracts and tort law is well developed.

The explosion of workplace safety regulation is indeed puzzling from the Coasian perspective. To begin, market forces should work in this area, even with spot labor markets and without complex contracts.

Because wages adjust in risky occupations, employers have an economic incentive to control accident risks so as to reduce the wage premium they have to pay. Firms would also want to establish reputations as safe employers to attract better workers, and to pay them less. Competition for labor provides strong incentives to maintain a safe workplace.

Extensive contracting opportunities are available as well. Employees, through collective bargaining agreements or even individual employment contracts, can require firms to take safety precautions. Firms can likewise require certain levels of care from their employees by specifying that they follow safety procedures. Private insurance is available to both workers and firms to insure the damages to health and property resulting from accidents. Insurance companies can then demand, as part of the insurance contract, that firms and workers take specific precautions. With knowledgeable firms, knowledgeable workers, and knowledgeable insurance companies, one would think correct incentives could be worked out. Moreover, the parties interact over time, and are able to learn where the risks are, mitigate them, and adjust their contracts accordingly. It seems compelling, in this context, that private solutions provide parties with correct incentives to take efficient precautions.

Should one of the parties fail to follow the terms of the contract, the other can go to court. Indeed, it can do so even before an accident occurs if contractual terms regarding precautions are violated. After an accident, likewise, the victim can demand in a lawsuit a contractually specified compensation for damages. Courts can then enforce the contracts, by requiring the insurance company or the firm to pay, or alternatively by finding that the worker had not taken contractually agreed upon precautions. No governmental authority beyond courts is needed.

If the necessary contracts are too elaborate to negotiate up front, insurance companies and industry associations can produce recommendations for safety standards, and contracts can incorporate those. An individual firm, a union, or even a worker bears few incremental costs of figuring out what is appropriate by opting into industry standards. Standardization also reduces the costs of compliance by specifying standard safety equipment or safety procedures.

Finally, even if contracts do not cover some eventualities, tort law deals with accidents not covered by contracts. Courts develop precedents and guidelines for addressing questions of liability and damages, and can also rely on industry standards for reaching conclusions. As the law develops over time, these precedents and other rules developed by courts cover more and more situations, leaving ever smaller uncertainties. Indeed, as courts complete the law, they eliminate the need for actual litigation since parties know what to expect and settle without it.

With so many protective mechanisms for both workers and firms available through markets and courts, and so many incentives for efficient precautions provided by these mechanisms, why would anyone need regulation?

Once the puzzle is framed in this way, it becomes clear where to look for the answer. Start with the forces of competition on the spot markets, without contracts or insurance. It is probably true that, in the world of well-heeled and well-established firms, with access to capital markets and expectation of long-run survival, the savings from taking efficient precautions outweigh the immediate costs. But many firms operate in a very different world, in which capital is scarce, downward pressure on prices is relentless, and incentives to cut costs today are strong. In such a competitive world, the firm may face huge pressure to undersupply precautions relative to the efficient level and to accept incremental accident risks. Should an accident happen, the firm might be able to fight its liability in court, settle for a small sum with a desperate victim, or go bankrupt. To hold the firm accountable for causing accidents, there need to be effective courts. Competition without courts and contracts does not do much for safety.

If competition does not lead firms to take efficient precautions, it must be contracts, including insurance contracts, as well as tort rules, that do the job. But contracts and torts fundamentally rely on enforcement by courts. Suppose for concreteness that the firm and its employees have agreed on a contract that delineates the precautions that need to be taken, and suppose further that the firm has taken out an insurance policy compensating workers who are harmed. After that, an accident happens. Neither the insurance company nor the firm wants to pay the victim, so the victim has to sue for damages. Most accidents occur because of some combination of bad luck and lack of precautions on the parts of both the employer and employee (or, to make it more complex, an employee other than the one who got hurt). Each litigant blames the other, often sincerely. And even if the "true" facts of the case are clear to an omniscient observer, and even if the litigants know what happened, they each have a story for why it is not their fault, but the other party's. The insurance company likewise has a story for why the particular accident is not covered, or if covered not to the full extent of the damages. A court, or some substitute such as an arbitration board, has to ascertain the facts and interpret the contract or apply the law. The question then becomes how cheaply, predictably, and impartially the court can do so.

Consider this question in steps. Begin with courts as assumed in law and economics. In those courts, 1) judges are motivated to exert effort to enforce contracts and laws, 2) judges are knowledgeable enough to verify the facts, and 3) judges are impartial. I argue later that all three of these assumptions are dubious descriptions of reality, and that the failure of each gives rise to a distinct argument for regulation. But for now consider this extreme example of knowledgeable, motivated, and impartial judges.

One might think that, in this case, courts could easily deal with a workplace accident. But even here several issues hamper adjudication and make it uncertain. First, judges do not witness the accident and need to figure out what happened. They can only do so imperfectly. The litigants have different perceptions of what happened, even if they are honest, and the judge needs to piece the story together. Litigants, or their lawyers, often lie, or at least shade the truth in their own favor. With conflicting testimony, even ideal judges would have trouble figuring out what actually happened.

To protect the system from manipulation by the litigants, legal procedure is itself heavily regulated and burdensome. Discovery is extensive, invasive, and expensive, including both the collection of records and the examination of witnesses. Chapter 5 examines the regulation of legal procedure and efficiency of courts in 109 countries by focusing on the simplest cases: the eviction of a non-paying tenant and the collection of a bounced check. Based on surveys of legal experts in these countries, the evidence shows that the judicial procedures governing such litigation are extremely cumbersome and time consuming, yielding highly uncertain payoffs to plaintiffs.

Second, the contract may not cover the exact facts of the dispute: in an accident, both litigants are often at fault. Moreover, language is often unclear and vulnerable to alternative interpretations. What are best efforts, for example? With incomplete contracts, the litigants disagree on how the contract allocates the costs of an accident. The judge has to decide what the contract means.

Third, both contractual interpretation and tort liability are governed by multiple conflicting principles, and judges need to pick which ones to apply. Judges reason by analogy to precedents, and a case is often analogous to multiple precedents with conflicting results. Lawyers argue that the precedent favoring their clients is the closest one. Judges then decide. It might be difficult to tell in advance which of the potentially governing precedents the judge will pick, especially when the facts are close to the line.

With factual, contractual, and legal uncertainty, the judge must exercise at least some discretion in resolving a dispute. Aspects of such discretion have been called fact discretion, referring to the judge's flexibility in interpreting facts, and legal discretion, referring to room to maneuver in applying the law to the facts. Pistor and Xu (2003) aptly call this "incomplete law." Posner (2008) refers to this as "open area" uncertainty. Posner recognizes the existence of such uncertainty, but seems to believe that this open area is usually small.

The bottom line is that, even assuming that judges are unbiased, knowledgeable, and properly motivated, judicial discretion imposes risk on the litigants. Judicial discretion, which follows from legal, contractual, and factual uncertainty, is an essential feature of litigation, and one from which many consequences follow.

Recent research has begun to uncover systematic evidence of judicial discretion. A large empirical literature discussed by Posner (2008) documents the effect of the judges' political party affiliations on their decisions. Chang and Schoar (2007) use a sample of 5,000 Chapter 11 filings by private companies in the U.S., and find that in their motion granting practices, some bankruptcy judges are systematically more pro-creditor than others. Niblett (2009) examines interpretation of very standard arbitration clauses in contracts by California appellate courts. He finds that judges make arbitrary distinctions in their contract interpretation even in the simplest of cases, for instance focusing on the size of the print or the location of the arbitration clause in the contract. This evidence is noteworthy because the cases Niblett selects are so similar.

Beyond judicial decision making, there is also the problem of enforcing decisions. A firm, especially a small firm, might not have the money to pay to compensate the employee, might not have bought insurance, and might even go bankrupt. In fact, such a firm might ex ante choose to skimp on precautions and go bankrupt after an accident occurs. This problem, identified by Summers (1983) and Shavell (1984a), plagues contract and tort law enforcement. Even without bankruptcy, damage payments for negligence might be high, especially when they are jacked up to compensate for imperfect detection (Becker 1968). Although such penalties may provide strong incentives for firms to take precautions, they may also deter socially useful activity when courts make unavoidable mistakes in assigning liability. Firms reluctant to bear such risks may exit, or not enter in the first place. This aspect of imperfect enforcement leads to inefficiency because it reduces desirable business activity (Schwartzstein and Shleifer 2010).

These aspects of the legal process interact prominently with the strength of competition. A firm facing significant price competition seeks to reduce costs. It knows that, should an accident occur, the trial may take some time and it may wiggle out of paying under either contract or tort. It can also settle with the victim of an accident, who may need money and be less patient. If all goes badly in court, it can go bankrupt and still avoid paying. Facing competitive pressure today, such a firm might take fewer precautions or buy less insurance. When justice is not certain, competition in the product market leads firms to economize on worker safety measures.

All these problems arise in even the simplest of circumstances. Their effect is to make contract enforcement expensive and unpredictable, leading workers and firms to bear unnecessary risks. This of course is just the beginning of the story: we need to return to our three assumptions about judges.

4   What Do Judges Do?

I have argued that judicial work is quite complex, and judicial outcomes uncertain, even in relatively simple circumstances, and with unbiased, knowledgeable, and motivated judges. Reality, of course, is less idyllic. Several of these assumptions must be revisited.

Begin with the assumption that judges are motivated to understand the issues of the case. In reality, judges face weak incentives (see Posner 2008). Judges cannot be fired. They do not receive promotions with sufficient likelihood to elicit effort, and promotion need not depend on diligence. Judges are not paid for performance. Some judges are elected, but it may be not diligence but humoring the community that improves their election chances. The weak incentives of judges to work hard are particularly important when the cost of verification is high, as when the facts are complex. And when judges do not bother to verify facts, litigants bear the risk of judicial error. Firms might fail to take precautions, for example, hoping to confuse the judge.

The second assumption about judges is that they are knowledgeable enough, at least with the assistance of court experts, to get to the bottom of the relevant issues. This is a tall order, especially in the modern world. Judges are trained as lawyers, not safety experts. Their work is fundamentally general: they consider large numbers of cases in multiple areas of law. In a complex case, judges must rely on lawyers and experts. The goal of lawyers and experts, however, is to seek judicial favor, not enlightenment. It would often take a rather brilliant judge to get to the bottom of the issue when persuasion takes this form.

The third assumption is the most interesting, namely that judges are impartial. Judicial partiality may derive from many sources, including political biases, intrinsic preferences over litigants, incentives such as those coming from reelection, or vulnerability to persuasion by the litigants, appropriate or not. Partiality would not be problematic if judicial discretion were minimal. But when discretion in finding fact, interpreting contract, or applying legal rules is substantial, it can massively amplify the effects of partiality.

Start with judicial preferences over litigants, or over their lawyers. Legal realists such as Frank (1930) considered these crucial in shaping the outcomes of trials. These preferences might be over individuals, but also over issues, perhaps because of the political preferences of judges. Some judges sympathize with workers injured in accidents and believe that, absent overwhelming evidence of worker malfeasance, companies should pay. Other judges feel that workers employed in dangerous occupations accept the risks and are put on notice to be extra careful, so absent overwhelming evidence of company malfeasance, they should not collect. When the facts of the case are uncertain and judges exercise discretion over which testimony or expert analysis to accept, these biases, even if relatively minor and even unconscious, can translate into substantially biased decisions.

Recent research has begun to unravel, at least theoretically, the crucial interaction between judicial preferences and fact discretion. Chapter 2 argues that the selection of "relevant" facts is the crucial mechanism by which judges satisfy their biases, especially because the finding of fact is rarely vulnerable to appeal. Once the facts are found, the application of the law to the facts is typically uncontroversial. Likewise, when contractual terms are uncertain, judges can interpret contracts to favor the party, or the issue, to which they are sympathetic, perhaps by choosing one of the several conflicting principles of contractual interpretation (Gennaioli 2011). In either case, adjudication is biased. And when the contracting parties do not know the judge's preferences up front, they bear substantial risks which they can mitigate by taking inefficient actions and signing inefficient contracts that protect them from judicial discretion in the first place.

Many legal scholars do not like this kind of argument. Some, like Posner (2008), see judicial biases as relatively minor (except on the highly political Supreme Court) because judges are selected from a relatively uniform population: "The pool from which our judges are chosen is not homogeneous, though neither is it fully representative; it is limited as a practical matter to upper-echelon lawyers, almost all of whom are well-socialized, well-behaved, conventionally minded members of the upper middle class" (p. 155). Posner is surely correct, but it is far from clear how much such selection limits the variety of views. Politicians who appoint judges wish to be confident that judges agree with them on particular issues. Such selection may well bias away from moderation. For example, a politician moderately concerned with worker safety might choose not a judge who is centrist on that issue but rather one who is far left of center, just to be sure. Similarly, lawyers who accept judgeships often give up considerable income as private attorneys. In part, they do so to win the respect of their peers, but also in part because, like academics, they have strong beliefs about influencing the world. As with academics, such beliefs are not always conducive to moderation.

Another argument is that review by appellate courts constrains trial judges. If judges were automata applying unambiguous law to unambiguous facts, this argument would compel. But, as I already indicated, much of the time judges are interpreting incomplete contracts in light of uncertain facts, or else applying uncertain law. In such circumstances, the role for appeal is more limited, especially since appellate courts do not typically review the facts. Fact discretion gives trial judges enormous flexibility. Indeed, appellate review may cause a trial judge to further distort his rendition of facts, so as to render the application of the law to those facts uncontroversial and thus invulnerable to appeal (chapter 2).

In some jurisdictions, judges are elected, which raises the question of whether this mechanism bolsters impartiality. The electoral process for judges, like that for other local officials, selects individuals whose views are representative of the communities they serve. Berdejo and Yuchtman (2009) examine judicial elections in the State of Washington, and find that judges increase sentences prior to elections, in line with voter preferences for harsher criminal sanctions. More generally, if the community is large and diverse, the median voter is likely to be fairly centrist. On the other hand, when a community is neither large nor diverse, the views of its median voter might be quite biased relative to a broader group. The United States Congress is full of representatives diligently articulating the parochial views of their constituents.

The final source of judicial bias is historically the most important one, and that is judicial vulnerability to persuasion or subversion. Such vulnerability follows from litigants having different access to resources (Galanter 1974). Defendants in workplace accident cases have access to substantial financial resources, including better lawyers, while the victims might be poor, in part because they are injured. Some adaptations, such as contingency fees for attorneys, ameliorate this problem, but probably only in selected cases. If judges do not correct for the inequality of weapons, litigants with more resources have a substantial advantage in court.

Better resources may take the form of better lawyers and court tactics, of delay when plaintiffs cannot wait and therefore must settle for less, but they may also take the form of bribes or even threats of violence. Corruption may be only modestly relevant for the U.S. courts today (how one thinks of this depends in part on the distinction between bribes and campaign contributions), but bribing judges was common in nineteenth-century America, and is pervasive in large parts of the world today (chapter 6). Indeed, as documented by Dal Bo et al. (2006), judges in developing countries are not only bribed to rule for the strong, but also threatened with violence if they rule against them. Corruption helps the richer litigants, and obviously distorts incentives to act efficiently.

Judicial bias interacts with the evolution of law over time, and the consequent predictability of the legal rules themselves. It is one of the core beliefs of law and economics that common law is fairly complete and provides unique legal answers to most patterns of case facts. A stronger version of this thesis holds that common law converges to efficient legal rules so that these answers encourage efficient behavior. Yet recent scholarship begins to question the belief in convergence to efficiency, both theoretically and empirically. Plausible models do not suggest that sequential decision making by appellate courts with preferences over the shape of the law brings the law to efficient rules (see chapter 3). From time to time, judges overrule existing precedents because their preferences are different from those of their predecessors. Such overruling undermines convergence (Gennaioli and Shleifer

2007). More frequently, judges do not overrule the existing precedents, but rather distinguish cases from precedents, based on possibly material, and sometimes immaterial, facts. They then reach different conclusions, which of course reflect their own preferences, based on these new facts. As chapter 3 shows, such distinguishing refines and completes the law over time. But even though the quality of the law improves on average over time, there is no convergence to efficiency.

Recent empirical evidence casts doubt on the proposition that common law converges to efficient rules over time, even in relatively simple situations. Chapter 4 looks at the evolution of the Economic Loss Rule, a well-known common law doctrine limiting tort claims when plaintiffs only suffer financial losses, using the universe of state appellate court decisions in a very homogeneous group of construction disputes. Over the last 30 years, different U.S. states have treated the Economic Loss Rule in construction disputes very differently, and have achieved no agreement on the scope of its applicability and exceptions. Nor is there evidence of convergence over time in the acceptance of this rule or of its exceptions. Legal certainty looks like a myth even in standard situations after decades of legal evolution.

Posner (2008) recognizes all these concerns with the exercise of judicial discretion, but in the end appeals to judicial professionalism to explain why the "open area uncertainty" is minimal. "To regard oneself and be regarded by others, especially one's peers, as a good judge requires conformity to the accepted norms of judging. One cannot be regarded as a good judge if one takes bribes, decides cases by flipping a coin, falls asleep in the courtroom, ignores legal doctrine, cannot make up one's mind, bases decisions on the personal attractiveness or unattractiveness of litigants or their lawyers, or decides cases on the basis of 'politics' (depending on how that slippery word is defined)" (p. 61). I think that Posner is exactly right. So long as a judge does not take bribes, acts deliberately, refers to precedents and legal principles, renders decisions with only modest delays, does not flirt with lawyers, and is not overtly and exorbitantly political, he will be regarded as professional and remain unchecked. The open area uncertainty referred to by Posner is therefore vast.

5 The Enforcement Theory of Regulation

When courts are expensive, unpredictable, and biased, the public will seek alternatives to dispute resolution in courts. The form this alternative has taken throughout the world is regulation. Indeed, each of the problems with litigation discussed in the previous section gives rise to a separate argument for efficient regulation as a response to the failure of courts.

Begin as before with the case of motivated, knowledgeable, and impartial judges who are adjudicating idiosyncratic disputes, so the facts relevant to the establishment of contract violation on tort liability are costly to verify. Perhaps the most fundamental feature of regulation is that it tends to homogenize the requirements for appropriate conduct by both employees and firms. Such homogenization is often excessively rigid, but it reduces enforcement costs because the items that need to be verified are standardized. Does the factory floor have the required number of fire exits? Is there proper spacing between machines? Are the workers wearing helmets? Even if the determination of violation and of damages is left to courts, regulation reduces the costs of litigation because it effectively provides a judge with a checklist of items that need to be verified, as opposed to leaving open to the litigants the scope of issues to be debated. By narrowing the scope for disagreement, regulation may render outcomes, and hence behavior, more predictable.

One important instance of regulatory rules that are relatively cheaper to enforce are quantity regulations, such as blue laws prohibiting liquor sales on Sundays or fishing and hunting laws restricting the activity to a few days a year. Viewed from the perspective of standard economics, such rules appear inferior to Pigouvian taxes, for example. Yet, as Glaeser and I (2001) argue, from the perspective of efficient enforcement these rules make perfect sense precisely because the government can co-opt the private sector to facilitate enforcement. With fishing laws, for example, competitors would turn in a fisherman who goes out to catch fish on prohibited days. The relative cheapness of enforcing bright line rules explains the attractiveness of regulation.

Next, what about the judges who might lack incentives, knowledge, or impartiality? Begin with incentives. In contrast to judges, the incentives of regulators can be manipulated by their superiors, or even by legislation. Regulators can be forced to specify precautions, to verify whether they are taken, and to investigate in detail after an accident occurs. Unlike judges, regulators can be asked to go through checklists of items to be verified, and incentivized to follow these rules. This possibility of compelling the regulators to investigate and check, perhaps by rewarding them for finding violations, was one of the crucial New Deal arguments for regulation (see Landis 1938; chapter 7).

Unlike the generalist judges, regulators also tend to be specialized. Courts, of course, can also be specialized (Posner 2008), but perhaps not to the same extent as regulators. In principle, such specialization lowers the costs of understanding the facts in a given situation, as well as of applying the rules to the facts. Specialization of the regulators is a central efficiency argument in their favor, particularly in areas such as finance and the environment where the issues are enormously complex (Landis 1938).

Finally, one can make a case for regulation as a mechanism for reducing the vulnerability of law enforcers to subversion. Unlike judges, regulators are experts, and hence might be less vulnerable to persuasion by the skilled but disingenuous litigants. Historically, inequality of weapons has been the crucial factor behind the rise of the regulatory state in the United States. The mechanism was democratic politics at the end of the nineteenth and the beginning of the twentieth centuries. As industrialization changed the economic landscape, the country saw a sharp rise in industrial and railroad injuries. Evidently, workers could not find adequate compensation for these injuries in courts, because companies exercised what many saw as undue influence on judges. As muckraking journalists exposed the problem, it became a political issue in several presidential campaigns, including those of Theodore Roosevelt and Woodrow Wilson. Regulation became a central feature of Wilson's *New Freedom* program. Chapter 6 summarizes these historical developments, and argues that the rise of regulation was indeed a political—and efficient—response to the failure of courts to adjust to economic changes in the country.

Regulation can take a variety of forms (at the extreme, the government can take ownership of firms if it believes nothing short of complete control can get around the consequence of market or contractual failure—think about the ownership of Air Force One). In some instances, the government can lay down the rules for required precautions, conduct inspections, and impose penalties both upfront for failure to comply before an accident occurs and after an accident happens if the failure to comply is recognized only then. In other instances, the government can lay down the regulations, such as disclosure rules and procedures for dealing with conflicts of interest, but then leave the enforcement to private action in court, as in the case of many financial regulations. The purpose of such regulations, very much in the spirit of the present argument, is to reduce the costs of litigation, because both courts and litigants know more precisely what constitutes liability.

A particular version of this approach is the regulation of contracts, which makes perfect sense as a strategy for facilitating enforcement by courts when judges exercise discretion, but not if all contracts are interpreted equally predictably.

This, in sum, is the argument. I should stress that the analysis is not in any way intended as an endorsement of all regulation and of its expansion. At the level of implementation, all the complaints leveled at judges apply to regulators as well. Enforcement effort, expertise, and absence of bias among the regulators can all be fairly questioned. Regulators are public sector employees, and as such often lack incentives for hard work, know less than they ought to, exhibit policy preferences inconsistent with efficiency, and are vulnerable to subversion by those they regulate. Academic studies and news stories are replete with accounts of regulatory failures.

There is one particularly important way in which regulation might be substantially inferior to litigation. Specifically, regulators have far greater opportunity to create rules that are not only politically motivated, but actually serve principally to benefit themselves by creating opportunities for bribe taking. Licenses and permits are the clearest examples of such regulations. Chapter 10 examines what has become the proverbial example of such predatory regulation—the regulation of entry by new firms—by focusing on the rules of entry regulation in 85 countries. The chapter finds no evidence of the benefits of extensive entry regulation, but a strong correlation between entry regulation, poor government performance, and corruption. Chapter 10 illustrates how the regulators' behavior can end up severely biased against consumers.

The choice between regulators and courts, then, is one between imperfect alternatives, in which the virtues and failings of each must be compared. But this in no way detracts from my basic point: the case for efficient regulation rests on that against courts. And historical trends in the best-governed countries suggest that this efficiency case often wins the day for regulation.

6 Institutional Choices

An informative way of shedding light on the relative merits of regulation and litigation in different circumstances is to compare the two modes of social control of business across activities and jurisdictions. The comparative perspective on regulation and litigation yields a range of empirical predictions. Some of these turn on the comparative efficiency of the two approaches to enforcing socially desirable conduct. Other predictions focus on institutional choices shaped by considerations other than efficiency, such as politics, history, and culture.

To begin, the analysis may shed some light on the choice between courts and regulators for a given activity in a country. Courts appear to be particularly appropriate in relatively nontechnical yet idiosyncratic situations, such as the interpretation of individual contracts (even if some aspects of these contracts are restricted by regulation) or the determination of liability in torts or fault in crimes. In these situations, flexibility is of great value ex ante, and application of reasonably broad standards is of value ex post. Such situations are difficult to homogenize through regulation, and indeed they are typically addressed by courts (see Posner 2008).

On the other hand, when similar problems recur often enough that repeated utilization of courts is too expensive or unpredictable, regulation might be a socially cheaper alternative. Whether the regulator is the ultimate decision maker, or in the end the judge must decide, regulation can delineate the issues that must be addressed. It might be more efficient to specify the rules than for courts to sort out the threshold of liability in distinct situations. This argument implies that regulation is more efficient in the more common situations.

Chapter 9 tests this prediction. It shows that, in cross-sections of both U.S. states and around the world, higher populations are associated with more extensive regulation. The regulation of a particular area requires a fixed setup cost, which can be amortized over a higher number of disputes that comes with more people. With small populations, litigation, while idiosyncratic, is rare enough that fixed costs are not worth paying. This approach might also explain why we see regulation in areas such as workplace safety, where contracts and torts are readily available: disputes occur often enough that standardized regulation is cheaper, and more predictable, than idiosyncratic litigation.

Regulation would also be more common in situations where facts are complex and fact finding requires expertise and incentives. As the society develops, this criterion might apply to a growing range of activities. This observation might explain the basic fact of growing regulation over time. It might also explain why we see regulation in financial markets or in complex industrial activities. Indeed, expertise and motivation of the regulators were the crucial arguments for the expansion of regulation in the U.S. (Landis 1938).

Finally, regulation might be particularly relevant in situations of inequality between the injured plaintiffs and the injurer. The rise of regulation might be intimately tied to specialization and the rise of large corporations as organizational forms. Thus, while courts or similar methods of dispute resolution might work when disputants have comparable resources, they fail when inequality of weapons becomes overwhelming. This, too, might account for the ubiquity of regulation, including the regulation of contracts between parties with different resources, in the modern world, as chapter 6 argues. In fact, if we go back to the introductory paragraph, this might be the reason for the regulation of so many basic aspects of consumption and employment.

Perhaps the most remarkable differences in the patterns of social control of economic life become apparent in comparing countries (Djankov et al. 2003). Different societies have different levels of expertise, and hence comparative advantage, at regulation, litigation, or perhaps other forms of social control. For example, as chapter 6 argues, poor countries might experience severe failures of all public administration, including both regulation and litigation. In these countries, free markets might be the best approach, even when market failure is pervasive. In more developed countries, in which the capacity to administer laws and regulations is higher, stronger government intervention, whether through courts or regulators, becomes more attractive.

One crucial determinant of the actual patterns of regulation and litigation is specialization intimately related to the legal origin of a country's laws. In a series of empirical papers written with Simeon Djankov, Rafael La Porta, and Florencio Lopez de Silanes, and summarized in La Porta et al. (2008), I have argued that countries from common and civil law legal traditions exhibit different regulatory styles. Relatively speaking, common law countries tend to rely on private orderings and courts, while civil law countries, particularly French civil law ones, rely more heavily on regulation. We see these differences empirically across a broad range of activities, from the regulation of product (chapter 10) and labor markets, to the regulation of legal procedure (chapter 5), to the military draft (chapter 9). Such specialization in the forms of social control might be efficient, as each legal tradition perfects its approach, or it might be just a consequence of hysteresis. Whatever the ultimate cause, we see substantial variation in the reliance on regulation and litigation across legal traditions. The data leave no doubt that history plays a key role in patterns of social control.

Chapter 8 analyzes the historical origins of this variation by focusing on England and France starting in the twelfth and thirteenth centuries. It argues that England was a relatively peaceful country, and as such could sustain dispute resolution through trials, including trials by jury, without a concern that adjudicators would be coerced by powerful litigants. This experience laid the foundation for reliance on enforcement of good conduct through courts in common law systems. France, in contrast, was a country of powerful local lords who could subvert adjudication by trial unless judges were employed and protected by the crown. This experience laid the foundation of the civil law system, with its more centralized and administrative approach to law enforcement. There is a striking parallel between the pressure for administrative solutions in the U.S. in the early twentieth century, described in chapter 6, and the pressure for centralized law enforcement in France over the last millennium. Both were driven by the failure of decentralized justice.

In summary, the enforcement theory of regulation holds that all methods of public enforcement of socially desirable conduct are imperfect, and that the choice of the methods being used is at least in part driven by efficiency. Regulation and litigation are the two principal strategies of public enforcement. Societies will choose regulation in part when litigation proves to be expensive, unpredictable, and biased. With all the faults of regulation recognized by a generation of scholars, it can emerge as the more efficient form of social control. Regulators rise when judges fail.

2 Judicial Fact Discretion

with Nicola Gennaioli

1 Introduction

Does the identity of a judge matter for the outcome of a trial? Since the advent of legal realism, it has been generally understood that the answer is yes, in part because of the considerable discretion that trial courts have in finding fact. While constrained by law, trial courts can select, describe, and characterize the facts to which the law is applied with some freedom. When a judge exercises such fact discretion, his identity begins to matter.

Jerome Frank (1951, p. 57) defines judicial fact discretion as follows:

When the oral testimony is in conflict as to a pivotal fact-issue, the trial judge is at liberty to choose to believe one witness rather than another. In other words, in most cases the trial judges have an amazingly wide "discretion" in finding the facts, a discretion with which upper courts, on appeals, seldom interfere, so that, in most instances, this "fact discretion" is almost boundless.

Frank recognized that some fact discretion is unavoidable, since judges necessarily have to decide which witness accounts to trust. But Frank (and later Posner 2005) also recognized that fact discretion creates significant leeways for the expression of judicial preferences, which derive from political, social, or economic views, or even from a judge's career concerns. Such expression need not be conscious or unethical. Judges may unconsciously interpret the evidence, or disregard some inconvenient truths, through the lens of their experiences, beliefs, or ideologies, or perhaps even something as mundane as attitudes toward specific litigants or lawyers.[1] Yet discretion leads to unpredictability of judicial decisions from the objective facts of a case, and elevates the importance of knowing "who the judge is" for predicting the outcome of a trial.

This paper introduces judicial fact discretion into a formal analysis of trial court decision making, and examines its consequences.[2] We identify two distinct motives for the exercise of fact discretion. The first, emphasized by legal realists, is judicial bias. As Posner (2005, p. 14)—echoing Frank (1930, 1932)—writes about federal district (i.e., trial) judges: "But [deciding a particular case in a particular way might increase the judge's utility] by advancing a political or ideological goal, economizing on the judge's time and effort, inviting commendation from people whom the judge admires, benefiting the local community, getting the judge's name in the newspaper, pleasing a spouse or other family member or a friend, galling a lawyer whom the judge dislikes, expressing affection for or hostility toward one of the parties—the list goes on and on."

The second motive, specific to trial judges, is the dislike of being overruled by appellate courts. As Posner (2005, p.16) comments: "Judges also don't like to be reversed, even though a reversal has no tangible effect on a judge's career if he is unlikely to be promoted to the court of appeals in any event." Appellate courts typically do not revisit facts found by trial courts, but only the application of the existing law to those facts.[3] When such application is uncertain, a trial court has an incentive to "fit" the facts into the settled precedent, so that from the point of view of the appellate court, the application of the law to the facts is uncontroversial.

We consider each of these motives for the exercise of judicial fact discretion in a standard model of a tort. In this model, the first best efficient legal rule is strict liability with all harms being legally cognizable for the calculation of damages. In section 3 we assume that trial courts follow this rule, but can distort facts about harm. We show that the damages awarded by judges are unpredictable from true facts of the case, but predictable from knowledge of judicial preferences. We show how precautions, accidents, and welfare losses depend on factors such as the polarization of judicial preferences, the relative proportion of pro-injurer judges, the sensitivity of judicial preferences to the case's facts, and the factual complexity of a dispute.

Section 4 enriches this model by allowing for appellate review. In our model, when all harms are legally cognizable, appellate review is irrelevant, as trial courts avoid reversal by simply finding the level of harm triggering their preferred damages. When instead the law is unsettled, appellate review *increases* trial courts' incentive to distort harm. This is due to trial courts' uncertainty over appellate bias.

Because different appellate courts address new factual circumstances differently, trial courts can avoid being overruled by fitting their finding of harm into a settled precedent, that is, by finding facts to which the law has already been applied. Crucially, this implies that under unsettled law even *unbiased* judges distort harm so as to avoid reversal by biased appellate courts.

In section 5, we consider whether this conclusion holds in a model of adversarial litigation. When the law is unsettled, competition among litigants—often seen as beneficial (e.g., Milgrom and Roberts 1986)—encourages them to take extreme (and uninformative) positions catering to judges' desire to find facts insulating their decisions from reversal. Such litigant extremism also increases the incidence of litigation as opposed to settlement.

These predictions are consistent with the empirical findings of Schanzenbach and Tiller (2007), who document that, in spite of the U.S. Sentencing Guidelines, significant disparities in the sentencing of federal criminal defendants remain, with Democrat-appointed judges giving shorter sentences than Republican-appointed judges for street crimes involving violence, theft, and drugs. The evidence shows that judges meet their goals by distorting fact finding, especially if their preferences conflict with those of the reviewing circuit court. Consistent with our model, since fact finding has little precedent value, trial courts engage in fact discretion so as to avoid being reversed on appeal by a court with different preferences.

In sum, fact discretion not only creates leeway for the expression of judicial biases but also undermines the appeals process and adversarial litigation. Although these mechanisms are sometimes believed to put a beneficial check on trial courts, under fact discretion they lose their effectiveness. Taken together, our results suggest that trials are likely to perform poorly in the areas of law that are fact-intensive, relatively new (so precedents are undeveloped), and vulnerable to judicial bias. The controversial product accident litigation may fit this description.

Our paper follows a large literature on the consequences of court errors. Calfee and Craswell (1984), Craswell and Calfee (1986), Kaplow (1994), and Kaplow and Shavell (1994, 1996) examine the effects of both random and non-random judicial errors on precautions. Although we also consider precautions, we start with judicial preferences and biases, and derive court errors from those. This allows us to ask additional questions. Milgrom and Roberts (1986), Froeb and Kobayashi (1996), and Daughety and Reinganum (2000) examine the effects of adversarial litigation for revelation of information at trial. Since we begin with judicial preferences, we can ask when judges are unwilling to use information, rather than just process it in a biased way. We compare our results to those from these studies throughout the paper, but here emphasize only that none of these papers model explicitly purposeful judicial behavior.

1.1   An Example of Judicial Fact Discretion

Before turning to the formal analysis, we present an example of the exercise of judicial fact discretion in one famous case. We note, first, that fact discretion has been studied in the context of appellate courts, where the idea has been that appellate judges sometimes "simplify" the facts to elucidate a legal principle. A very clean example of this is Cardozo's extreme mischaracterization of facts in *MacPherson v. Buick* (Henderson 2003), but Cardozo appears to have altered the facts at least marginally in *Palsgraf* as well (Posner 1990). Dershowitz and Ely (1971) denounce the Burger Supreme Court for its extreme mischaracterization of facts in *Harris v. New York*, an exercise of fact discretion that the authors call "the failure of candor."

Our example of judicial fact discretion in action comes from one of the first cases in the standard torts textbook (Keeton, Sargentich, and Keating 2004), *Garratt v. Dailey*. In textbooks, the case stands for the proposition that knowledge of possible harm is sufficient to find intent in battery, so the plaintiff does not need to show purpose to harm to establish the defendant's liability. But the case is also a clear instance of judicial fact discretion. Although it does not deal with the exact situation we study, *Garratt v. Dailey* shows a trial judge completely changing his *fact finding* after an appellate court remands the case to him on a matter of law.

Brian Dailey, a five-year-old boy, accompanied his mother on a visit to his aunt, Ruth Garratt, in the garden of Garratt's house. The boy allegedly pulled a chair from under his aunt as she started to sit down. She fell and injured herself, and subsequently sued Brian. According to the appellate court review of the evidence, "the trial court accepted the boy's statement that he had moved chair and seated himself therein, but, when he discovered that plaintiff was about to sit at place where chair had been, *attempted to move chair toward plaintiff, and was unable to get it under plaintiff in time.*" Having accepted the boy's view that he was trying to help his aunt rather than hurt her, the trial court ruled for the boy on the grounds that he did not have the purpose—and therefore intent—to harm her.

The appellate court ruled that purpose to harm is not required to prove intent in battery, and that knowledge of possible harm is sufficient, and remanded the case to the trial judge (in this case, superior court). "Upon remand for clarification on the issue of the defendant's knowledge, the superior court reviewed the evidence, listened to additional arguments and studied briefs of counsel, and entered a finding to the effect that the defendant knew, with substantial certainty, at the time he removed the chair, that the plaintiff would attempt to sit down where the chair had been, since *she was in the act of seating herself when he removed the chair.*" The trial court shifted all the way from the finding that the boy was moving the chair *toward* the aunt as she was sitting down to the finding that he was pulling it *from under* her.

There may be a number of explanations, some innocent, for how the trial court found such entirely different facts after the case was remanded. But there are two simple stories. First, the judge might have been initially annoyed with the aunt for bringing a case against her five-year-old nephew, presumably to collect insurance, and so accepted the boy's somewhat bizarre testimony to reach his initial verdict. He could have, and of course eventually did, accept the other testimony instead. This judicial bias view of fact discretion is analyzed in section 3.

Alternatively, the trial judge might have feared reversal. When he thought that the standard of intent in battery was purpose, he found the facts under which the boy could have hardly had the purpose to harm his aunt, namely that he was moving the chair *toward* her. Under the legal rule, the judge believed the factual finding that the boy was pulling the chair from under his aunt would have raised the question of his purpose, and exposed the judge to the risk of reversal if the appeals court ruled that pranks are not purposeful. To the judge's surprise, the appellate court took a radically different view of the standard of intent in battery. So when the trial judge learned that the standard of intent was merely knowledge of possible harm, and not purpose to harm, he found the facts under which knowledge was pretty much obvious, even to a five-year-old. Had he stuck to his old finding of facts that the boy was trying to put the chair back, the question of knowledge would have been legally controversial. In both of his decisions, the trial judge found the facts that render the application of the law that he believed to be in place utterly straightforward. We consider this motivation for fact discretion in section 4.

2 The Model

Consider a tort where injurer I harms victim V. I could be a company using explosives and V a resident whose person or property is damaged in an accident with explosives. V's harm from the injury, denoted by h, is uniformly distributed on $[0,1]$. We assume that I knows the victim's harm h before he engages in the potentially harmful action.[4]

At a cost $c(p) = (1/2)p^2$, I can take precautions $p \in [0,1]$ and avoid the injury with probability p. For example, p could represent the company's effort to transport explosives more securely or to store them further away from V's property. Since the level of harm h is known in advance to I, expected social losses from taking precautions p are given by:

$$(1-p)h + (1/2)p^2 \tag{1}$$

First best precautions are then equal to $p_{fb}(h) = h$. Aggregate social losses in the first best (L_{fb}) when I takes optimal precautions are equal to:

$$L_{fb} = \int_0^1 [(1-h)h + (1/2)h^2]dh = 1/3 \tag{2}$$

We study torts where there is no contract, or alternatively where it is too costly for the parties to specify precautions contractually. As in the standard model of torts (Posner 1972; Shavell 1987), I's precautions are shaped by the damages set by courts in light of the prevailing legal rule. For simplicity and in line with the explosives example, we study the strict liability regime, but distinguish two situations within that regime. The first, "settled law," is defined as $d(h) = h$ for all possible kinds or levels of harm.[5] This definition of settled law includes both strict liability *and* the assumption that all harms are legally cognizable—the situation that yields first best precautions under standard assumptions. In the second situation we consider, "unsettled law," not all factual scenarios have been previously considered by courts, so the function $d(h)$ has been defined only for some fact situations h. In the explosives example, it might not have been settled by precedent whether mental anguish is a legally cognizable form of harm. Unsettled law tends to be the standard situation in new or complex areas of law (Llewellyn 1960; Stone 1985).

The timing of the model is as follows: at $t = 0$, I observes h and takes precautions; at $t = 1/2$, V is injured; at $t = 1$, a trial judge is randomly selected from the population of judges. The selected judge observes h (we drop this assumption in section 5), finds h' that is potentially different from h, and awards damages $d(h')$ to the victim.

A judge's fact finding policy is thus summarized by the function $h'(h)$, assigning to every true harm level h the utility maximizing harm level actually found by the judge. In our definition, the judge engages in fact discretion when the facts found $h'(h)$ differ from those revealed at trial h. Fact discretion is possible because, to verify harm, courts must evaluate soft evidence, whose interpretation is vulnerable to distortion. Some of the evidence presented to them may be oral, and so they may choose whom to believe. The documents in the evidence may include ambiguous language, which judges are free to interpret. The victim's harm may depend on a multitude of conflicting factors. By emphasizing certain pieces of evidence and neglecting others, a judge may discretionally alter the facts of the case to meet his desired level of harm.

To find h' when true harm is h, the judge bears the cost $c(h' - h)^2/2$. A larger discrepancy between estimated and true harm is more costly to the judge. A smaller c reflects a lower cost of fact discretion. Empirically, a low c may capture factual complexity. The higher is the number of material dimensions determining h, the greater is judicial discretion in estimating it.[6]

A study of fact discretion requires that we specify judicial preferences. We define judicial preferences over damages, so that judge j's loss from setting damages d in case h is equal to:

$$L_j = \left[d - d_j^*(h) \right]^2 / 2 \tag{3}$$

Here $d_j^*(h)$ is the judge's ideal level of damages when true harm is h. A measure one of judges is distributed according to their ideal damages. Share u of judges is *unbiased*, with $d_j^*(h) = h$, share ι of judges is biased for the injurer (*pro-I*), with $d_j^*(h) < h$, and share v is pro-victim (*pro-V*), with $d_j^*(h) > h$. The distribution of judicial biases is common knowledge. Notice that u measures judicial polarization: the smaller is u, the greater is the share of biased judges in the population. Empirically, u may measure the political or social sensitivity of a dispute. For example, environmental torts or discrimination disputes are likely to have a smaller u.

3   Enforcement of Settled Law under Judicial Fact Discretion

Consider how trial courts enforce settled law. At any harm level h, judge j finds h'_j and sets $d_j = h'_j$ so as to minimize $[d - d_j^*(h)]^2 / 2 + c(h' - h)^2 / 2$. This judge j sets:

$$d_j(h) = \frac{d_j^*(h) + ch}{1 + c} \tag{4}$$

Judge j's choice of damages is a weighted average of his ideal damages $d_j^*(h)$ and true harm h. *Unbiased* judges set the first best damages, the damages of *pro-I* (*pro-V*) judges are lower (higher) than true harm h. The discrepancy between biased judges' damages and true harm decreases in c. If judges can freely distort facts ($c = 0$), they set their ideal damages. If instead fact discretion is impossible ($c = \infty$), adjudication is entirely driven by the case facts.

3.1   Unpredictability of Damages and Social Welfare

Before moving to the *observable* implications of fact discretion for trial courts' behavior, expression (4) allows us to examine how fact discretion affects precautions and welfare. Since I chooses p before knowing the judge's type, his choice of precautions at h is:

$$p_{sl}(h) = E_j(d_j(h)|h) = \frac{E_j\left(d_j^*(h)\right) + ch}{1 + c}, \tag{5}$$

which averages the damages set by *pro-V*, *pro-I*, and *unbiased* judges. The pattern of precautions at a given harm h depends entirely on the average judicial bias at h. If $E_j(d_j^*(h)) > h$, judges are on average *pro-V* and the injurer takes over-precautions. If $E_j(d_j^*(h)) < h$, judges are on average *pro-I* and the injurer takes under-precautions. Correct precautions are only taken if judges are on average *unbiased*, that is, when $E_j(d_j^*(h)) = h$. Section 3.2 provides conditions under which adjudication is on average *unbiased*. For now, we take the average bias as given and find:

Proposition 1   Under settled law, if for some h, $E_j(d_j^*(h)) \neq h$, then first best social welfare is attained if and only if $c \to \infty$. Social losses relative to the first best fall as c or u increase. The marginal social cost of a decrease in c is larger when u is smaller.

Intuitively, judicial bias is responsible for the welfare loss from fact discretion. As pointed out by Kaplow and Shavell (1996), if damages are on average equal to true harm, then the first best is attained irrespective of judicial errors. If instead average damages are sometimes different from true harm, the first best is no longer attained. The deviation of precautions (and welfare) from the first best depends on c and u. An increase in judges' ability to misrepresent harm (i.e., a decrease in c) distorts precautions, thereby reducing welfare. A similar effect is triggered, for a given c, by an increase in the proportion of biased judges (a decrease in u). The extent of fact discretion and judicial bias interact: as c falls, biased judges are better able to distort the setting of damages, so judicial polarization has a more detrimental impact on precautions.

Aside from the welfare cost of fact discretion, what might be some of the *observed* consequences of this behavior of trial judges? First, the outcome of a dispute in this model is obviously determined by who the judge is. More specifically, the analysis has implications for statistical predictability of judicial decisions *from case facts*. By "unpredictability" we mean the variability of damages for given facts (i.e., true harm h). That is, at harm h we define:

$$\text{unpredictability } (h) \equiv V_j(d_j(h)) = \frac{V_j(d_j^*(h))}{(1+c)^2}, \tag{6}$$

where $V_j(d_j(h))$ is the variance of damages at harm level h and $V_j(d_j^*(h))$ is the variance of judicial ideal damages at harm h. We have:

Corollary 1 Under settled law, unpredictability increases with $V_j(d_j^*(h))$ and falls with c.

Under fact discretion (i.e., if $c < \infty$), dispersion of judicial views fosters unpredictability in damages, even when legal rules are fixed. We expect more variability of outcomes in politically sensitive cases where the dispersion of judicial biases is large. In addition, unpredictability falls when it is harder for judges to engage in fact discretion (when c is higher).

3.2 Average Damages and the Number and Severity of Accidents

To obtain predictions on average damages and on the number and severity of accidents, we must consider how $E_j(d_j^*(h))$ varies with harm. We do so by presenting a flexible specification of judicial biases that allows us to stress the role of two key factors: the relative proportion of *pro-I* and *pro-V* judges and the slope of bias with respect to harm. We assume that all *pro-V* and *pro-I* judges have ideal damage schedules $d_V^*(h)$ and $d_I^*(h)$ respectively, given by:

$$d_V^*(h) = h + h^\alpha(1-h) \text{ and } d_I^*(h) = h - h(1-h)^\alpha, \tag{7}$$

with $\alpha \geq 0$. To understand these expressions, consider the *pro-V* bias $h^\alpha(1-h)$. This bias can be thought of as the product of two factors. The first factor, h^α, means that a *pro-V* judge tends to be more biased when harm is higher. The second factor, $(1-h)$, means that the *pro-V* bias cannot exceed the distance between current and maximum harm $(1-h)$; due to this physical constraint, *pro-V* bias tends to get smaller with h. Thus, the *pro-V* bias $h^\alpha(1-h)$ initially rises but eventually falls with h. Similarly, with respect to *pro-I* bias, $(1-h)^\alpha$ implies that a *pro-I* judge is more biased when harm is lower, while h is the maximal bias he is allowed to entertain.

As we show below, by shaping the sensitivity of bias to the case's facts, the parameter α determines whether and when adjudication is on average *pro-I*, *pro-V*, or *unbiased*. When α is high, the bias actually exercised by a judge relative to its maximum possible level is higher the more the evidence favors his preferred party. *Pro-V* judges exercise greater bias when harm is high and *pro-I* judges do so when harm is low. If instead α is small, judicial bias is insensitive to evidence. At any harm h, the *pro-V* bias mainly depends on the maximum harshness $(1-h)$ a judge is allowed to entertain, the *pro-I* bias on the maximum leniency h a judge is allowed to entertain. In addition, the larger is α, the more judges pay attention to the case's facts and the less ideological they are (i.e., the smaller is their bias). As $\alpha \to \infty$, all judges become *unbiased*.[7]

To study the shape of average damages under the functional forms in (7), consider the slope of the former at their interior intersection with first best damages $h^* \equiv (\iota/\nu)^{1/(\alpha-1)}/[1 + (\iota/\nu)^{1/(\alpha-1)}]$ (the other intersections are $h = 0$ and $h = 1$). We then have:

Corollary 2 When $\alpha > 1$, average damages are too steep at h^*. When $\alpha < 1$, average damages are too flat at h^*. When $\alpha = 1$ and $\iota = \nu$, average damages are first best.

The key parameter determining the location of over and under precautions is α. Figure 2.1 below plots the case with $\alpha = 2$:

The bold line plots average damages under fact discretion and the diagonal plots the first best level of damages. Since $\alpha > 1$, average

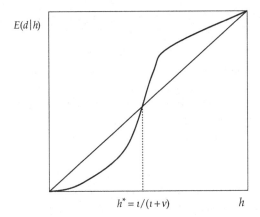

Figure 2.1
Average damages under fact discretion: $\alpha = 2$.

damages are too steep at h^*. In practice, this means that the *pro-V* bias is stronger at high levels of harm while the *pro-I* bias is stronger at low levels of harm. As a consequence, average damages are too low at low h and too high at high h.

What about the opposite case, with $\alpha < 1$? Figure 2.2 plots the case $\alpha = 0$ where ideal damages do not depend on actual harm: $d_V^*(h) = 1$, $d_I^*(h) = 0$:

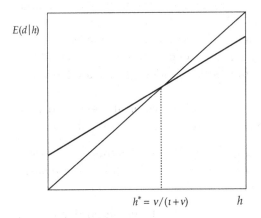

Figure 2.2
Average damages under fact discretion: $\alpha = 0$.

Once more, the bold line plots average damages under fact discretion. Unlike in the previous case, expected damages are too flat when $\alpha < 1$ (in this specific example, this is true globally). Indeed, for small α, the key factor is the physical constraint on bias: at low levels of harm pro-V judges have the greatest leeway to distort damages and the pro-V bias is stronger; at high levels of harm pro-I judges have the greatest leeway to distort damages and the pro-I bias is stronger. As a result, when $h < h^*$ average damages are too high; when $h > h^*$, they are too low.

In this respect, α shapes the extent of moral fault (Bauer 1933). When α is high, judicial bias is sensitive to the case facts. As a result, adjudication is more pro-V precisely when the victim's harm is higher. This flexible formulation of judicial biases also allows for the possibility that pro-V and pro-I biases exactly cancel out, so that average damages are *unbiased* and the first best is attained. This case requires not only $\alpha = 1$, but also $\iota = \nu$, namely there should be an equal proportion of pro-I and pro-V judges. This knife-edge result shows that, when legal errors are not purely random, as in Kaplow and Shavell (1996), but rather a product of the deliberate decisions of utility-maximizing judges, it is unlikely that opposite errors cancel out on average.

Having considered average damages, we can examine how fact discretion affects the observed number and severity of accidents. If average damages are too flat (i.e., if $\alpha < 1$), under-precautions and thus accidents prevail at high levels of h. For a given total number of accidents, there are too many major accidents. If instead average damages are too steep (i.e., if $\alpha > 1$), under-precautions and thus accidents prevail at low levels of h. For a given total number of accidents, there are too many minor accidents.

Consider next the impact of judicial biases on the expected total number of accidents, which is equal to $1 - E[E(d_j(h) \mid h)]$. We find:

Corollary 3 Under settled law, the number of accidents is first best if and only if $\iota = \nu$. The number of accidents increases in the relative proportion of pro-I judges, ι / ν.

The number of accidents depends on the relative proportion of pro-I and pro-V judges. If pro-I judges are relatively more prevalent, the average level of damages and thus precautions are too low, and there are too many accidents. The converse is true if pro-V judges are relatively more prevalent. The number of accidents should be higher in the areas of law where relatively more judges are biased in favor of the injurer.[8]

These results relate to the research on accuracy in adjudication (e.g., Kaplow 1994). This literature stresses that, when different errors do not wash out on average, otherwise optimal legal rules such as strict liability or negligence may distort precautions and lead to welfare losses (Craswell and Calfee 1986). By modeling legal error as the deliberate decision of utility-maximizing judges, we predict how the patterns of precautions, accidents, and welfare losses depend on factors such as the polarization of judicial preferences, the relative share of *pro-I* judges, the sensitivity of judicial bias to case facts, and the factual complexity of a dispute. These comparative statics may help compare legal rules across different areas of law.

More broadly, while fact discretion makes facts less helpful in predicting trial outcomes, it makes judicial preferences more helpful for such predictions. Independent measures of judicial bias should predict resolution of identical disputes. Knowing who the judge is should be useful to researchers, and not just to litigants. There is by now an enormous literature indicating that race, gender, and the party of the nominating President affects the decisions of appellate judges, especially in politically sensitive cases. Some of the key studies are George and Epstein (1992), Brenner and Spaeth (1995), Revesz (1997), Pinello (1999), Klein (2002), Sunstein, Schkade, and Ellman (2004), and Hansford and Spriggs (2006). For trial courts, some studies find significant exercise of discretion in criminal sentencing (Partridge and Eldridge 1974; Abrams, Bertrand, and Mullainathan 2011) and in bankruptcy decisions (Chang and Schoar 2007). Most relevant to the current study, Schanzenbach and Tiller (2007) find that in spite of the Sentencing Guidelines, fact discretion allows judicial ideology to matter in the context of street crimes involving violence, theft, and drugs, with Democrat-appointed judges giving shorter sentences than Republican-appointed ones.

4   Fact Discretion and Appellate Review

A second possible determinant of fact discretion—pertinent to judges but not juries—is appellate review. Our model of appellate review relies on the generally accepted idea that appellate courts take the trial courts' fact finding as given (except in the cases of "clear error"), but can reverse trial courts if the law was misapplied to the found facts.

Although there are some exceptions, the acceptance of trial courts' fact finding by appellate courts is a central feature of common law, which distinguishes it from the civil law tradition. One explanation is the greater reliance of common law adjudication on open trials and on oral examination of witnesses at trial as a strategy of gathering evidence, which is not easily compatible with appellate review of fact finding (see Merryman 2007; chapter 8).

For concreteness, suppose that a (randomly selected) trial court solves dispute h by choosing $(d', h'(h))$, where $h'(h) \in [0,1]$ is the trial court's (potentially distorted) finding of facts and $d' \in [0,1]$ is the corresponding level of damages set by the judge. After the trial, the case is automatically appealed.[9] The appellate court can either affirm or reverse the trial court's ruling. We assume that trial judges dislike being reversed and incur a psychic or reputational loss $r > 0$ when this happens. To simplify the analysis, we also assume that $\alpha = 0$, so that ideal damages are equal to 0 for *pro-I* judges and 1 for *pro-V* judges, regardless of h. As before, the exercise of fact discretion is assumed to be costly to the trial judge.

An appeals court is randomly selected from the population of such courts. Crucially, appeals courts' preferences are identically distributed to those of the trial courts. In contrast to Bueno de Mesquita and Stephenson (2002) and Shavell (2006), we thus allow appellate courts to also be biased. In deciding whether to affirm or to reverse, the appellate court maximizes its utility but is compelled to apply the prevailing legal rule. If—given the trial court's fact finding $h'(h)$—the trial court's damages d' are consistent with the prevailing legal rule, then the appellate court must affirm even if its bias tempts it to set a different level of damages.[10] In contrast, if the law specifies that a level of damages $d'' \neq d'$ should be set at $h'(h)$, then—irrespective of its preferences—the appellate court must reverse and award d''. The more interesting case arises when the law is unsettled, in that for some facts $h'(h)$ the prevailing legal rule does not specify what level of damages should be correctly applied. In the explosion example, suppose that precedents have not settled whether victims should be compensated for mental suffering. Then our assumption implies that a trial court finding no mental suffering cannot be reversed, while a court introducing or denying compensation for mental suffering can be reversed on appeal.[11] In the latter case, section 4.2 shows that the decision to affirm or to reverse crucially depends on the appellate court's bias.

4.1   Appellate Review under Settled Law

An immediate consequence of the working of judicial review in our model is that, under settled law, judicial review is irrelevant: trial courts can avoid reversal and still be able to set their preferred damages by simply distorting the facts. For example, when true harm is h_0 but the trial judge wants to set $d' = h_1 \neq h_0$, he just needs to find $h'(h_0) = h_1$. Because the appellate court takes h_1 as given, it cannot reverse $d' = h_1$: this ruling is precisely the one mandated by strict liability for the facts found. Reversal would only occur if the trial court finds h_0 but sets $d = h_1$, since then $d = h_1$ is a misapplication of the law to the facts. Yet, the trial court never chooses the latter strategy: reversal can be simply avoided by engaging in fact discretion. We are back to the findings of section 3. Note that, because in our model appellate courts are just as biased as trial courts, allowing the former to review the latter's fact finding would not change our results: it would only transfer to the appellate courts the ultimate control over fact discretion.

4.2   Appellate Review under Unsettled Law

Trial courts often deal with cases in which the mapping from true harm to damages remains unsettled by previous legal rulings. Because such gaps in the law are filled by appellate courts, a trial judge's freedom to set damages is limited by the appellate review of his decision.

This situation, which we call unsettled law, is typical in common law, where legal rules are a by-product of judges resolving specific disputes. When existing precedents fail to exhaust all factual circumstances, and new facts arise in a case, a trial judge who reports these facts truthfully must consider which precedent is controlling. After he renders his decision, the losing party may appeal his ruling by insisting that a more favorable precedent should be applied to the facts found by the trial court. An appellate court must then decide whether, given these facts, the current case as a matter of law is "closer" to the plaintiff's or the defendant's preferred precedent.

We capture the idea of unsettled law by studying the case with two precedents governing damages in the tort between I and V: one of them is the case $(h = 0, d = 0)$; the other is the case $(h = 1, d = 1)$. For harm levels away from the existing precedents, that is, for $h' \in (0,1)$, the law is silent. This situation is represented in figure 2.3, with the two precedents highlighted in bold.

To choose damages, an appellate court interprets the current case in light of existing precedents. It may deem h' sufficiently analogous to

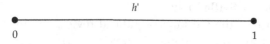

Figure 2.3
Precedents and unsettled cases.

$h = 0$ and resolve the legal ambiguity in favor of $d = 0$. Alternatively, the appellate court may deem h' analogous to the precedent $h = 1$ and set $d = 1$. Finally, the appellate court may distinguish h from both precedents and award a third (new) level of damages. The choices of different appeals courts among these alternatives are key to understanding how judicial review affects trial judges' incentives to engage in fact discretion. Consider the appellate courts' reaction to a trial ruling (we are still assuming that $\alpha = 0$):

Lemma 1   At $h' = 0$ and $h' = 1$, the trial court is affirmed if and only if $d' = 0$ and $d' = 1$, respectively. If $h' \in (0,1)$, *pro-V* appeals courts reverse any $d' < 1$, *pro-I* appeals courts reverse any $d' > 0$, while *unbiased* appeals courts reverse any $d' \neq h'$.

Not surprisingly, appellate courts exploit legal ambiguities to affirm their biases. If the facts fit into existing precedents (i.e., $h' = 0$ or 1), there is no legal ambiguity and appellate courts affirm trial court rulings, consistent with those precedents (i.e., $d' = 0$ or 1, respectively). But if $h' \in (0,1)$, the resolution of legal uncertainty over damages depends on the bias of the appellate court reviewing the case.

To illustrate, suppose that the victim contends that to properly estimate harm $h \in (0,1)$ the judge should also consider mental suffering, which was not considered in existing precedents. From the standpoint of appellate review, a trial court's finding of no mental suffering is radically different from the finding that mental suffering should be excluded from the damage calculation. The former decision simply cannot be reversed, but the latter one can. Indeed, suppose the only harm at stake is mental suffering h, and the trial court finds it correctly, but rules that it is not cognizable for the damage calculation, so $d = 0$. In this case, a *pro-I* appellate court affirms the ruling that mental suffering is not cognizable, but a *pro-V* one reverses and sets $d = 1$, by analogy with the existing precedent of severe harm.[12] An *unbiased* appellate court also reverses, rules that mental suffering is an admissible harm, but sets damages $d = h$. The trial court can avoid this appellate scrutiny, and possible reversal, by simply distorting the facts of the case so that one of the precedents applies exactly. By finding no mental suffering, the trial court can avoid any legal ambiguity in the setting of damages. In this case, fact discretion is no longer a prerogative of biased judges (cf. *Garratt v. Dailey*).

How does appellate review affect an *unbiased* trial judge's fact-finding policy $h'(h)$? Suppose that $h \in (0,1)$. If the *unbiased* trial judge engages in fact discretion and rules $(d' = 0, h' = 0)$, he loses $(1 + c)h^2/2$; if he rules $(d' = 1, h' = 1)$, he loses $(1 + c)(1 - h)^2/2$. In neither case he gets reversed. If instead the *unbiased* trial judge finds $h'(h) \in (0,1)$, by lemma 1 he optimally finds the truth and rules $(d' = h, h' = h)$. In this case, his expected loss is:

$$\iota(h^2/2+r)+u0+v[(1-h)^2/2+r].\tag{8}$$

The first term is the trial judge's loss from reversal by a *pro-I* appeals court that sets $d' = 0$. The third term is the trial judges' loss from reversal by a *pro-V* appeals court that sets $d' = 1$. If the appeals court is *unbiased*, it affirms the *unbiased* trial judge's ruling, who then loses nothing.

By comparing a trial court's loss from alternative strategies, we see that *unbiased* judges trade off the gain from setting first best damages against the total reversal cost. Reversal is costly to the trial judge for two reasons. First, the appellate court may set damages too far away from the trial judge's ideal points. Second, the trial judge bears the psychic or reputational cost r. Taking into account the behavior of all trial courts, we find:

Proposition 2 If $c \leq 1$ and $r \geq 1$, there are two thresholds $\overline{h}_V, \underline{h}_I$ such that *pro-I* trial judges set $h' = d' = 0$ for $h \leq \overline{h}_I$ and $h' = d' = ch/(u + c)$ otherwise, and *pro-V* judges set $h' = d' = 1$ for $h \geq \underline{h}_V$ and $h' = d' = (u + ch)/(u + c)$ otherwise. There are two thresholds $\overline{h}_U, \underline{h}_U$ ($\underline{h}_U < 1/2 \leq \overline{h}_U$) such that *unbiased* judges set $h' = d' = 0$ for $h < \underline{h}_U$, $h' = d' = 1$ for $h > \overline{h}_U$ and $h' = d' = h$ otherwise.

As long as the cost of fact discretion is not too high (i.e., if $c \leq 1$) and the reversal cost is sufficiently high (i.e., if $r \geq 1$), biased trial courts try to follow the precedent that is closest to their bias. They refrain from doing so (and moderate their exercise of fact discretion) only if the current facts are sufficiently far from their preferred precedent (relative to the reversal cost r).

More importantly, and in contrast with the previous section, under unsettled law even *unbiased* judges engage in fact discretion. *Unbiased*

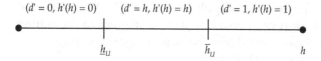

Figure 2.4
Adjudication by *unbiased* judges.

judges would ideally avoid fact discretion. However, with unsettled law, fear of reversal by a biased appellate court encourages them to distort fact finding so as to fit the current case into settled precedents. If all appellate courts are *unbiased*, then *unbiased* trial courts never risk reversal, refrain from fact discretion, and rule ($d' = h$, $h'(h) = h$). If instead some appellate courts are biased, the adjudication by *unbiased* trial courts is represented in figure 2.4 in terms of the cutoff points $\underline{h}$, $\overline{h}$ for various decisions.

Corollary 4 $\overline{h}_U - \underline{h}_U$ increases in u, c and decreases in r. There exists a $\hat{u}$ such that, for $u \le \hat{u}$, $\overline{h}_U = \underline{h}_U = 1/2$ and $\underline{h}_V = 0$, $\overline{h}_l = 1$.

The size of the region where *unbiased* trial courts do not engage in fact discretion increases in c but falls in the proportion of biased judges ($1-u$) and in the pain of reversal r. The same is true for the region where biased courts prefer not to fit the case in their preferred precedents. In particular, when $u \le \hat{u}$, the cost of reversal is so high that trial courts always fit the case into existing precedents and even *unbiased* judges *always* engage in fact discretion.

What is the impact of *unbiased* courts' fact discretion on precautions and welfare? We answer this question by focusing on the case of corollary 4 where $u \le \hat{u}$. Besides being analytically more tractable, this case allows a sharper evaluation of how judicial review affects fact discretion. Figure 2.5 below plots average damages in this case.

Compared to settled law, where average damages smoothly increase with harm, under unsettled law damages jump sharply at $h = 1/2$. Now biased judges rule, irrespective of harm, according to their preferred precedent, while *unbiased* judges condition adjudication only on whether h is above or below $1/2$. In this case, social welfare has the following properties:

Proposition 3 Under unsettled law, if $c \le 1$, $r \ge 1$ and $u \le \hat{u}$, welfare is lower than in the first best. There exists a $u^* \in [\hat{u}, 1]$ such that social welfare increases in u if and only if $u < u^*$.

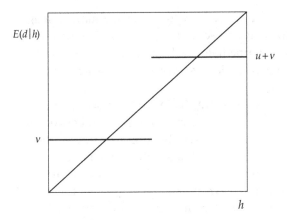

Figure 2.5
Damages and precautions under unsettled law.

Under unsettled law, fact discretion lowers social welfare relative to the first best. When $u < u^*$, as with settled law, judicial bias reduces the extent to which damages vary with harm, thereby inducing over- and under-precautions. Yet, in contrast to settled law, under unsettled law greater polarization is beneficial for $u \geq u^*$. Under unsettled law, an increase in the share of biased judges reduces the jump in damages and thus in precautions at $h = 1/2$. Because the marginal cost of precautions is increasing, this beneficially reduces the average cost of precautions by smoothing them across harm levels. In contrast to proposition 2, under the assumed parametric conditions the cost of fact discretion c does not affect welfare at the margin.

More importantly, the main observable implications of fact discretion arising from judicial review line up with those arising from judicial bias. It is obviously still the case that the identity of the trial judge matters, and that measurable judicial bias affects trial outcomes, though now even *unbiased* judges make biased decisions. It is still the case that damages are unpredictable from true harm, the more so the greater the polarization of judicial biases. Specifically, we have:

Corollary 5 If $c \leq 1$, $r \geq 1$ and $u \leq \hat{u}$, under unsettled law $V_j(d_j(h)) = v(1 - v)$ for $h \leq 1/2$, and $V_j(d_j(h)) = \iota(1 - \iota)$ otherwise. Unpredictability increases in v and ι.

With respect to the number of accidents, it is still the case that too many accidents occur if and only if $\iota > v$. With respect to the severity of accidents, it is still the case that at very high levels of harm damages are flat and there are too many bad accidents. However, the sharp jump in damages occurring at intermediate levels of harm implies that there are also too many moderate accidents, which is consistent with the steepness of incentives in that region.

Two predicted consequences of judicial fact discretion arising from appellate review are new. First, the lower the congruence between the preferences of trial and appellate courts, the more the former should engage in fact discretion. Schanzenbach and Tiller (2007) find that the behavior of U.S. courts under the Sentencing Guidelines is consistent with this prediction. Second, we expect that in complex and unsettled areas of law, where determination of liability requires answers to a variety of factual questions, the exercise of fact discretion would be more pronounced. If a researcher had an independent ability to observe the facts (perhaps from the documentary record), and compare them to the judge's summary of the evidence, it is precisely in these unsettled and fact-intensive areas of law that we expect the greatest mismatch between the true facts and the judge's representation of those facts. For it is precisely in these areas of law that mischaracterization of the evidence best protects the judge from reversal.

5   Fact Discretion and Adversarial Litigation

So far we have focused on judicial behavior, neglecting the role of litigants. However, it has been argued that adversarial litigation may improve fact finding by increasing information revealed in trials (Milgrom and Roberts 1986; Froeb and Kobayashi 1996). In this section, we consider a model of adversarial litigation to study whether competition among litigants can limit fact discretion and improve fact finding (section 5.1). We also ask whether fact discretion affects the incidence of litigation as opposed to settlement (section 5.2).[13]

5.1   Fact Discretion and Fact Finding
Can adversarial litigation reduce the extent of fact discretion and improve fact finding? To answer this question, consider the following game played by the litigants and the judge. Suppose the parties failed to settle and end up in a trial before a judge with a *known* bias (we discuss settlement later). Each party $P = I, V$ sends to the judge a message h_P concerning the level of harm. A litigant's message about harm represents his position in court and summarizes a possibly exten-

sive characterization of evidence that the litigant submits to the judge. A litigant's position is thus the more partisan the closer it is to his desired level of damages.

We continue to assume that judicial preferences are given by (7), with $\alpha = 0$. Instead of assuming that the judge finds out h without cost, we assume that, after receiving the parties' messages, the judge decides whether to find out h at the cost of $k(h_V - h_I)^2/2$, with $0 < k < 1/3$. One should think of $k(h_V - h_I)^2/2$ as an effort cost incurred by the judge in order to gather the evidence that, in addition to the parties' reports, is necessary to establish the true h.[14] If the judge does not search and remains uninformed, he effectively updates the posterior distribution of harm to be uniform on $[h_I, h_V]$. In this sense, the judge is Bayesian.

If the judge does not find out the truth, he rules according to one of the parties' messages (the cost of that is assumed to be zero). Thus, a judge choosing not to search cannot set his optimal level of damages given the posterior distribution of harm estimated on the basis of the parties' reports.[15] If instead the judge becomes informed, he has the additional possibility of finding a new level of harm that is a combination of true harm and the judge's preferred message among h_I, h_V. For algebraic simplicity, we study the case where the weight attributed to the preferred party's message is positive but negligible. The possibility for the judge to find out the truth renders the litigants accountable ex post. If the judge is expected to search, a litigant refrains from misrepresentation to prevent the judge from shading the decision against him. Unlike in the models of Milgrom and Roberts (1986) and Froeb and Kobayashi (1996), the judge here plays a key role in shaping the willingness of litigants to submit truthful reports.

5.1.1 Fact Finding under Settled Law Suppose that the law is settled. When appearing before a judge with a known bias, the party that the judge favors sends a message equal to the judge's ideal damages. The other party's message is irrelevant: in front of a *pro-V* judge, V sends $h = 1$ and the judge sets $d = 1$, irrespective of I's message; in front of a *pro-I* judge, I presents $h = 0$ and the judge sets $d = 0$. In this setting, the cost of fact discretion does not affect adjudication because the litigants themselves provide distorted facts to biased judges. As a consequence, when judges are biased, adversarial litigation does not improve adjudication.

Suppose, in contrast, that the judge is *unbiased*. Let the litigants' messages be h_I, h_V, with $h_I \le h \le h_V$, where h is true harm. (This is always true in equilibrium.) Then, if the judge decides to find out the truth, he rules ($d' = h$, $h' = h$), bearing a loss of $k(h_V - h_I)^2/2$. If instead the judge does not find out h, his loss is identical if he sets either $d = h_I$ or $d = h_V$ and is equal to $(h_V - h_I)^2/6$. Because $k < 1/3$, the judge is always better off finding h. What is the impact of such judicial strategy on the parties' optimal choice of h_I, h_V?

Proposition 4   Under settled law, if the judge is *unbiased* $h_I = h_V = h$ for any h, and $d = h$. If the judge is *pro-V*, then $h_V = 1$, h_I can take any value and $d = 1$. If the judge is *pro-I*, then $h_I = 0$, h_V can take any value and $d = 0$.

By allowing *unbiased* judges to accurately fine tune damages to harm, settled law gives *unbiased* judges a strong incentive to verify harm. As a result, each litigant tries to move closer and closer to the actual h so as to avoid having the judge shade damages against him. Settled law dampens partisanship by giving *unbiased* judges a strong incentive to scrutinize the litigants' positions in court. When $k \geq 1/3$, judges never find out the truth and proposition 4 no longer holds. We assume that $k < 1/3$ to illustrate the difference between settled and unsettled law in shaping litigants' partisanship. In sum, under settled law, we confirm that, with *unbiased* judges, adversarial litigation yields perfect fact finding, in the spirit of Milgrom and Roberts (1986).

5.1.2 Fact Finding under Unsettled Law   What happens under unsettled law? Section 4 showed that when the law is unsettled even *unbiased* judges may set damages at the extremes. In our model of litigation, this finding has two implications. First, *unbiased* judges may prefer to remain uninformed, because—in contrast to settled law—unsettled law does not allow them to set their preferred damages anyway. Second, litigants may take partisan positions to cater to even an *unbiased* judge's need to fit the facts into the existing law. Hence, under unsettled law, adversarial litigation may not improve adjudication.

To see how this works, suppose that $u \leq \hat{u}$, so *unbiased* judges only consider whether harm is larger or smaller than $1/2$ to choose between $d = 0$ and $d = 1$ (see corollary 4). Then, irrespective of the parties' messages, if the judge becomes informed, he obtains:

$$\int_0^{1/2} \frac{h^2}{2} dh + \int_{1/2}^1 \frac{(1-h)^2}{2} dh + k/2 = \frac{1}{24} + \frac{k}{2} \tag{9}$$

This expected loss equals the judge's average loss from setting $d = 0$ when $h \leq 1/2$ and $d=1$ when $h > 1/2$, plus the search cost $k/2$. Although the judge is fully informed, he rules according to the parties' extreme messages to avoid reversal. If instead the judge does not find out harm, his expected loss is the same if he sets $d=0$ and $d=1$ and is equal to $1/6$. Overall, we find:

Proposition 5 If $k > 1/4$, under unsettled law even if the judge is *unbiased* the parties' messages are $h_I = 0$, $h_V = 1$ and the judge randomizes between $d = 0$ and $d = 1$. If the judge is biased, then the outcome is the same as under settled law.

The key difference between settled and unsettled law concerns trials before an *unbiased* judge. With unsettled law, *unbiased* judges sometimes remain uninformed and choose to fit the case into an existing precedent. As a consequence, competition between parties is radically different from that prevailing under settled law. Now competition leads to extreme partisanship, not to convergence to the truth. To avoid reversal, even an *unbiased* judge may (randomly) endorse a partisan message such as $h_I = 0$ or $h_V = 1$ as opposed to a message claiming that h is in the middle. Litigants then compete by proposing extreme views so as to cater to the judge's demand for precedent-fitting narratives that render reversal less likely. In court, plaintiffs overreach and over-claim, while defendants refuse to acknowledge even the slightest liability for harm, each hoping that the judge simply buys their story.

One feature of this equilibrium is that no information trickles up to appellate courts, which slows down legal evolution. Trials fail to lead to accurate fact finding not only due to differential incentives of the litigants to gather information (Daugherty and Reinganum 2000), but also to the incentives created by the appellate review, especially when the law is unsettled.

5.2   Litigation vs. Settlement

Suppose now that, before learning the judge's type, the disputants have an opportunity to settle. What is the impact of fact discretion for the incidence of litigation under settled law? If settlement is cheaper than litigation, then parties litigate only in the presence of bargaining frictions, which may result from litigants' over-optimism (Landes 1971; Posner 1972) or private information (Bebchuk 1984) about the merits of the case. Although in our model the parties fully agree on the facts of the case, they may still fail to settle if each party is optimistic about the possibility of getting a favorable judge. This latter scenario is even more plausible when, as argued by Frank (1930), a judge's bias reflects his idiosyncratic sympathy or antipathy toward specific litigants rather than more stable, and therefore predictable in advance, policy preferences. A judge may be annoyed with a lawyer from an earlier case, sympathetic to one who previously clerked for him, or deferential to a government attorney who works in the same building.

For simplicity, we follow Yildiz (2004) and study the situation where the parties' failure to settle is due to heterogeneous beliefs rather than to asymmetric information. Suppose that there is an equal proportion of *pro-I* and *pro-V* judges and that *I* believes that the share of *pro-I* judges is inflated by a factor $(1 + \delta)$ and that of *pro-V* judges is deflated by a factor $(1 - \delta)$, while *V* misperceives the share of *pro-I* and *pro-V* judges the other way around. $\delta \geq 0$ captures the divergence in litigants' beliefs: when δ is higher, both parties are more optimistic about the case being tried by a favorable judge. The individual litigation cost is assumed to be $C > 0$.

5.2.1 Litigation vs. Settlement under Settled Law

Consider the parties' decision to settle or litigate a case h when the law is settled. The previous assumption implies that litigants' expected payoffs from litigating case h are:

$$Eu_{injurer} = -(1/2)(1-u)(1+\delta)0 - uh - (1/2)(1-u)(1-\delta) - C$$
$$Eu_{victim} = (1/2)(1-u)(1-\delta)0 + uh + (1/2)(1-u)(1+\delta) - C \tag{10}$$

With these payoffs, the parties fail to find a mutually profitable settlement amount paid by the injurer to the victim and thus litigate if and only if:

$$(1/2)(1-u)\,\delta \geq C \tag{11}$$

From this expression, we immediately obtain:

Proposition 6   Under fact discretion, there exists a $\underline{\delta} \in [0,1]$ such that the parties litigate if and only if $\delta > \underline{\delta}$; $\underline{\delta}$ increases in u.

Because under fact discretion judicial bias affects the setting of damages, the parties litigate when they are sufficiently optimistic about the chance of getting a favorable judge (i.e., when δ is high enough). The required level of optimism is smaller when the proportion of biased judges is higher. By introducing extrinsic factors such as judicial bias into trials, judicial fact discretion may lead to wasteful litigation.

5.2.2 Litigation vs. Settlement under Unsettled Law Under unsettled law, litigation is more likely, as disagreement over the judge's bias is not even necessary to obtain litigation. Key to this finding is the result (proposition 5) that, under unsettled law, even *unbiased* judges might remain uninformed and thus indifferent among extreme outcomes (as long as u is low enough). In such a case, litigants can hope to sway adjudication to their side through courtroom tactics, persuasion techniques, and so on. As a consequence, litigants' optimism about their ability to sway and influence the decision of an indifferent judge can lead them to litigate, irrespective of their optimism about judicial favor.

For concreteness, parameterize the parties' overconfidence about their ability to sway an *unbiased* judge with $\sigma > 0$. The injurer (victim) believes that he will be able to influence *unbiased* judges to set $d = 0$ ($d = 1$) with probability $(1/2 + \sigma)$. Then, much in the spirit of expression (11), settlement fails when:

$$[(1/2)(1-u)\delta + u\sigma] \geq C \tag{12}$$

Just as under settled law, divergence in beliefs as to the proportion of biased judges (δ) in the population fosters litigation. However, under unsettled law, the litigants' optimism (σ) about their ability to move an *unbiased* and therefore indifferent judge to their side also promotes litigation. Under settled law, the impact of σ is downplayed because *unbiased* judges become informed and have strict preferences over damages. While under settled law, then, the parties readily settle after knowing the judge's type; under unsettled law they may fail to do so even if the judge is *unbiased* because disagreement remains until the ruling is released. Fact discretion promotes litigation to a greater extent when the law is unsettled.

This analysis of litigation under fact discretion yields two empirical predictions. First, litigation should be more prevalent in the politically or socially charged areas of law, where judicial views are more likely to be polarized. Likewise, litigation should be more prevalent in complex areas of law, where the application of legal rules requires the verification of many factual issues, even when the law is clear but especially when the law is unsettled. Second, when parties hold similar beliefs on the distribution of judicial bias and litigation does not occur, we predict that—due to fact discretion—pre-trial settlement amounts in different cases would cluster around the mean settlement, especially if judicial polarization is high. This finding stands in contrast with the standard prediction of Priest and Klein (1984) that pre-trial settlements are especially likely to occur when the facts of a dispute are clear. In their model, settlement amounts should reflect the disparate facts of individual cases and presumably display considerable variance rather than converge to the mean. On the other hand, as do Priest and Klein, our model predicts that settlement amounts should spread out once the identity of the judge, and therefore presumably his type, is revealed. In such settlements, the party whose position the judge is expected to favor should receive most of the benefit in the settlement.

More broadly, section 5.2 suggests that the common law system of dispute resolution will perform particularly poorly when the cases are factually complex, the law is unsettled, and fact-finder preferences are important for the determination of damages (or for that matter of liability). These conditions seem to describe adequately the determination of damages for pain and suffering, as well as of punitive damages, in product accident cases. Law and economics scholarship has been highly critical of how damages are set in these situations (Viscusi 1988, 1998; Cooter 1988), blaming the randomness of observed outcomes on the lack of clarity in the law, the sentiments of judges and juries, and the actual complexity of finding the correct answer. These conditions are, of course, a recipe for trouble in our model.

6 Conclusion

We have presented two models of judicial fact discretion. In the first, the motivation for the exercise of fact discretion is a trial judge's preference over the outcomes of litigation. This model is probably most relevant for politicized or otherwise emotionally charged disputes. In the second model, the motivation for the exercise of fact discretion is trial judges' aversion to reversal by appellate courts, which leads them to fit the facts of the current dispute into available precedents. This model is probably most relevant for new and developing areas of law, with significant factual complexity and relatively few precedents. For both models, we have shown that the outcome of a trial is determined at least in part by who the judge is. Fact discretion leads to judicial behavior that is unpredictable from the facts of the case, but predictable from the knowledge of judicial preferences. We have also shown that the exercise of fact discretion leads to systematic distortions in individual behavior, to excessive and acrimonious litigation, and also to welfare losses.

In conclusion, we briefly mention some issues suggested by our model that we did not analyze. First, the model implies clearly and perhaps significantly that summaries of relevant facts that accompany written judicial opinions cannot be trusted. As we saw in *Garratt v. Dailey* and discussed throughout the paper, when judges summarize the facts, they do so to justify their legal conclusions. When a judge exercises fact discretion, this summary need not reflect the true facts of the case, even as seen and believed by the judge. In some instances, the summary of the facts might be possible to check against other available documents. Unfortunately, from the viewpoint of a researcher, a journalist, or a law student, the judge's summary is often all that is available. This aspect of judicial opinions does not necessarily undermine the study of legal principles, but may shed only a dim light on the actual facts of any given case.

Second, without conducting a full analysis, our model suggests some possible strategies for using legal procedure to contain the effects of fact discretion. One strategy is to limit the range of legally cognizable harms. The economic loss rule might be one example of this general principle. Another strategy is to introduce procedural rules concerning admissibility of evidence or even, as in civil law systems, more extensive appellate review of fact finding. When judicial fact discretion becomes extreme, dispute resolution in court may become socially inefficient. In those instances, adjudication can be replaced by ex ante regulation based on bright line rules. By relying on few cheap-to-verify facts, these rules are less vulnerable to fact discretion.

Third, we have focused our analysis on the exercise of fact discretion by judges, although of course the same phenomenon might be as or more prevalent among juries (Kalven and Zeisel 1966). In the case of juries, legal strategies aiming to control fact discretion tend to focus on the rules of evidence rather than on re-specifications of legal rules that might not impress juries.

Appendix: Proofs

Proof of Proposition 1 Social losses are $\int_0^1 [(1 - p_{sl}(h))h + p_{sl}(h)^2 / 2]dh$. For each h, optimal precautions are $p_{fb}(h) = h$. If for some h, $p_{sl}(h) \neq h$, social losses are larger than in the first best. Hence, if for some h $E[d_j^*(h)] \neq h$, the first best is attained iff $c \to \infty$. A marginal change $p_{sl}'(h)$ triggers a change $L' = \int_0^1 p_{sl}'(h)[p_{sl}(h) - h]dh$ in social losses. It is immediately apparent that $\partial p_{sl}(h)/\partial c = [h - p_{sl}(h)]/(1 + c)$ and $\partial p_{sl}(h)/\partial u = [h - p_{sl}(h)]/(1 - u)$. This implies that $\partial L/\partial c < 0$, $\partial L/\partial u < 0$, $\partial^2 L/\partial c\partial u > 0$. ♠

Proof of Corollary 1 By inspection. ♠

Proof of Corollary 2 Consider $\alpha > 1$. Damages are first best at $h = 0$, $h = 1$ and at $h^* = (\iota/v)^{1/(\alpha-1)}/[1 + (\iota/v)^{1/(\alpha-1)}]$. Damages are too steep iff $\partial Ed_j^*(h^*)/\partial h > 1$ because damages are too low iff $h > h^*$. This is always true for $\alpha > 1$. Consider $\alpha < 1$. Damages are first best at $h = 0$, $h = 1$ and at $h^* = (v/\iota)^{1/(1-\alpha)}/[1 + (v/\iota)^{1/(1-\alpha)}]$. Damages are too flat iff $\partial Ed_j^*(h^*)/\partial h < 1$ because damages are too low iff $h > h^*$. This is always true iff $\alpha < 1$. Consider $\alpha = 1$. If $\iota = v$ damages are optimal at any h. If $\iota \neq v$ damages are only optimal at $h = 0$ and $h = 1$. For $h \in (0,1)$ damages are too low if $\iota > v$ and too high if $\iota < v$. ♠

Proof of Corollary 3 First of all, note that the expected bias is $h + [vh^\alpha(1 - h) - \iota h(1 - h)^\alpha]$. In addition, $\int_0^1 h^\alpha(1-h)dh = \int_0^1 h(1-h)^\alpha dh = \dfrac{1}{(\alpha+1)(\alpha+2)}$.

Thus, $1 - E[d_j(h)] = 1/2 - \dfrac{(v-\iota)}{(1+c)(\alpha+1)(\alpha+2)}$. ♠

Proof of Proposition 2 We must consider three cases. A) *Unbiased judges*. For $h = 0$ and $h = 1$ the trial judge finds the truth, sets $d = 0$ and $d = 1$ respectively, and is not reversed. If $h \in (0,1)$ and the trial judge rules $(d' = 0, h' = 0)$, he loses $(1 + c)h^2/2$; if he rules $(d' = 1, h' = 1)$, he loses $(1 + c)(1 - h)h^2/2$. If the judge rules $(d' = h, h' = h)$, his loss is $(1 - u)r + \iota h^2/2 + v(1 - h)^2/2$. Call $h_{u^*} \equiv \dfrac{\sqrt{v^2 + 2(u+c)[(1-u)r + v/2]} - v}{u+c}$

and $\underline{h}_u = \min[1/2, h_{u^*}]$. If $h \leq 1/2$, the judge find the truth for $h > \underline{h}_u$, $(d' = 0, h' = 0)$ otherwise. If $h > 1/2$, the judge finds the truth for $h < \overline{h}_u \equiv 1 - \underline{h}_u$, $(d' = 1, h' = 1)$ otherwise. B) *pro-I judges*. If the judge rules $(d' = 1, h' = 1)$, he loses $1/2 + c(1 - h)^2/2$; if he rules $(d' = 0, h' = 0)$, he loses $ch^2/2$. For $c \leq 1$ the *pro-I* trial judge always prefers $(d' = 0, h' = 0)$ to $(d' = 1, h' = 1)$. If the judge sets $d' = h' \in (0,1)$, he solves $\min_{h'}(1-u)r + v/2 + u(h')^2/2 + c(h-h')^2/2$, thereby setting $h' = ch/(u + c)$ and bearing a loss of $(1 - u)r + v/2 + uch^2/2(u + c)$. Define $h_{I^*} \equiv \dfrac{1}{c}\sqrt{2(u+c)[(1-u)r + v/2]}$ and $\overline{h}_I = \min[1, h_{I^*}]$. Then, the judge rules $(d' = 0, h' = 0)$ for $h < \overline{h}_I$ and sets $d' = h' = ch/(u + c)$ otherwise. C) *pro-V* judges. If the judge rules $(d' = 1, h' = 1)$, he loses $c(1 - h)^2/2$; if he rules $(d' = 0, h' = 0)$, he loses $1/2 + ch^2/2$. For $c \leq 1$ the *pro-I* trial judge always prefers $(d' = 1, h' = 1)$ to $(d' = 0, h' = 0)$. For $d' = h' \in (0,1)$ the judge solves $\min_{h'}(1-u)r + \iota/2 + u(1-h')^2/2 + c(h-h')^2/2$, thereby setting $h' = (u+ch)/(u+c)$ and bearing a loss of $(1-u)r + \iota/2 + uc(1-h)^2/2(u+c)$. Define $h_{V^*} \equiv 1 - \frac{1}{c}\sqrt{2(u+c)[(1-u)r+\iota/2]}$ and $\underline{h}_V = \max[0, h_{V^*}]$. Then, the judge rules $(d' = 1, h' = 1)$ for $h > \underline{h}_V$ and sets $d' = h' = (u+ch)/(u+c)$ otherwise. $r \geq 1$ ensures that $\overline{h}_I > 0$, $\underline{h}_V < 1$. ♠

Proof of Corollary 4 $\overline{h}_U - \underline{h}_U = 1 - 2\underline{h}_U$, where $\underline{h}_U = \min[1/2, h_{U^*}]$ and h_{U^*} is defined by $(1-u)r + \iota h_{U^*}^2/2 + v(1-h_{U^*})^2/2 = (1+c)h_{U^*}^2/2$. By using the implicit function theorem, one can verify that h_{U^*} (and thus $\underline{h}_U$) decreases in u, c and increases in r. Similarly, one can prove that h_{V^*} (and thus $\underline{h}_V$) increases in u, c and decreases in r while h_{I^*} (and thus $\overline{h}_I$) decreases in u, c and increases in r. If $u \leq \ddot{u} \equiv (8r-c)/(1+8r)$, then $h_{U^*} \geq 1/2$ which implies $\underline{h}_U = 1/2$. Furthermore, there exists a $\tilde{u}$ such that, for $u \leq \tilde{u}, \overline{h}_I = 1, \underline{h}_V = 0$. Define $\hat{u} = \min[\tilde{u}, \ddot{u}]$. ♠

Proof of Proposition 3 If $c \leq 1, r \geq 1, u \leq \hat{u}$, precautions are $p(h) = v$ for $h \leq 1/2$, $p(h) = 1 - \iota$ otherwise. Social losses are $L = [1 - v + 2v^2 + 3\iota + 2(1 - \iota)^2]/8$, which is always larger than $1/3$, that is, social losses in the first best. Set $\iota/v = \theta$ and rewrite $\iota(u) = (1 - u)/(1 + \theta)$, $v(u) = (1 - u)/(1 + \theta)$. Then, $\partial L/\partial u = (-1 + 4v)v'(u)/8 + [3 - 4(1 - \iota)]\iota'(u)/8$. It is easy to see that $\partial L/\partial u \leq 0$ iff $u \leq \bar{u} = (3 + 3\theta^2 - 2\theta)/4(1+\theta^2)$. Define $u^* = \max[\bar{u}, \hat{u}]$. ♠

Proof of Corollary 5 By inspection. ♠

Proof of Proposition 4 If the trial judge is *pro-V*, $h_V < 1$ is not an equilibrium. If $h_V < 1$ and $h_I < 1$, for any "search" strategy of the judge, V deviates to $h_V = 1$ as the judge endorses (at least partly) such higher message. If $h_V < 1$ and $h_I = 1$, then—for any "search" strategy of the judge - I deviates to a lower h_I to prevent the judge from increasing damages. Hence, a *pro-V* judge induces $h_V = 1, h_I \in [0,1], d = 1$. The judge does not search. Similarly, the equilibrium in front of a *pro-V* judge has $h_V \in [0,1], h_I = 0$, $d = 0$ and the judge does not search. In front of an *unbiased* judge, for any two reports h_I, h_V, with $h_I \leq h \leq h_V$, if the judge searches he rules $(d' = h, h' = h)$, bearing cost $k(h_V - h_I)^2/2$. If the judge does not search, his loss is identical if he sets either $d = h_I$ or $d = h_V$ and is equal to $\int_{h_V}^{h_I}[(d-h)^2/2][1/(h_V - h_I)]dh = (h_V - h_I)^2/6$, $d = h_I, h_V$. Because $k < 1/3$, the judge always searches. When the *unbiased* judge searches, he negligibly shades damages toward the message that was closer to h. What about the parties' messages? First, parties' messages are never worse than the truth, that is, $h_l \leq h \leq h_V$. Second, if the judge searches, the parties' competition to win the shading induces $h_l = h_V = h$ for every h. As a result, the equilibrium in front of an *unbiased* judge has $h_V = h_l = h$ and $d = h$. ♠

Proof of Proposition 5 In front of biased judges, the behavior of the parties does not change. Suppose the judge is *unbiased* and $u \leq \hat{u}$. Even after observing the truth, an *unbiased* judge chooses between $d=0$ and $d=1$ depending on whether h is larger or smaller than $1/2$. Thus, if the parties expect the judge to search, it is optimal for them to send $h_l = 0$, $h_V = 1$. By searching, the judge obtains $\int_0^{1/2} (h^2 / 2) dh + \int_{1/2}^1 [(1-h)^2 / 2] dh + k / 2 = 1/24 + k/2$. If the judge does not observe h, he is indifferent between $d=0$ and $d=1$: his expected loss is $1/6$ in both cases. Thus, even if the judge is *unbiased*, under unsettled law the parties send $h_l = 0$, $h_V = 1$. Furthermore, for $k \in [1/4, 1/3]$, under unsettled law *unbiased* judges decide not to observe harm. As a result, the parties send $h_l = 0$, $h_V = 1$ and the judge randomizes between $d = 0$ and $d = 1$. ♠

Proof of Proposition 6 By inspection. ♠

3 The Evolution of Common Law

with Nicola Gennaioli

1 Introduction

In a common law legal system, such as that of the U.S. and the U.K., many important legal rules are made not by legislatures, but by appellate courts deciding specific cases and thus creating precedents. Judge-made law is dominant in commercial areas of law, such as contract, property, and tort. Judge-made legal rules promote or undermine economic efficiency when the Coase (1960) theorem does not apply. Yet compared to the vast body of research on legislative lawmaking, judicial lawmaking has been relatively neglected by economists.

We present a simple model of precedent setting, which emphasizes the role of judicial preferences. Our model addresses both positive and normative questions about the evolution of judge-made law. Under what circumstances does legal evolution occur? What form does it take? Is it on average beneficial? What is the relationship between polarization of judicial preferences, volatility of legal rules, and welfare? Does the law ultimately converge to efficiency?

At least three areas of scholarship have tackled these issues. First, free market philosophers such as Hayek (1960, 1973) and Leoni (1961) praised judge-made law for its role in preserving freedom. To them, decentralized evolution of law through primarily apolitical judicial decisions is vastly preferable to centralized yet arbitrary lawmaking by legislatures. Consistent with these ideas, La Porta et al. (2004) find a positive relationship in a cross-section of countries between economic freedom and a proxy for recognition of judicial decisions, as opposed to just legislation, as a source of law. Beck, Demirguc-Kunt, and Levine (2003, 2005) argue in the Hayek tradition that judge-made law is more adaptable than statutes. They suggest that such adaptability benefits financial markets, and find evidence that recognition of judge-made law predicts financial development and might account for the La Porta et al. (1998) finding of the superior development of financial markets in common law compared to the civil law countries.

Second, the legal realist tradition in American jurisprudence, which in contrast to the free market philosophers emphasizes that judges make decisions based on their political and other beliefs, nonetheless concludes that judge-made law evolves for the better (e.g., Llewellyn 1960, p. 402).[1] Perhaps the most famous assessment of this evolutionary process is Judge Cardozo's (1921, p. 177): "The eccentricities of judges balance one another. One judge looks at problems from the point of view of history, another from that of philosophy, another from that of social utility, one is a formalist, another a latitudinarian, one is timorous of change, another dissatisfied with the present; out of the attrition of diverse minds there is beaten something which has a constancy and uniformity and average value greater than its component elements."

Third, the evolution of common law rules and their convergence to efficiency has been taken up in law and economics. In his *Economic Analysis of Law* (2003, 1st ed. 1973), Posner hypothesizes that common law tends toward efficiency, based largely on the argument that judges maximize efficiency. Cooter, Kornhauser, and Lane (1979) find that decision making by welfare-maximizing but imperfectly informed judges improves the law over time. Rubin (1977) and Priest (1977) further suggest that disputes involving inefficient legal rules are more likely to be taken to court rather than settled, leading to the replacement of such rules by better ones over time. Cooter and Kornhauser (1979) formally show that the law tends to improve if inefficient rules are more likely to be replaced than the efficient ones.[2]

These diverse strands of research do not share a common framework for studying the evolution of judge-made legal rules and evaluating their efficiency. In such a framework, there must be judges, these judges must be able to make decisions based on their preferences, and questions about the evolution and the quality of law must still be possible to address. For even if judicial decisions are governed by ideologies and biases rather than maximization of efficiency, the evolutionary process may still improve the law. When does legal evolution warrant the optimistic assessments of free market philosophers, legal realists, and law and economics scholars?

To address these issues, we present a model in which precedents evolve though a series of decisions by appellate judges. Our model relies on three assumptions. First, following the legal realists and a modeling strategy of Gennaioli (2011), we assume that judges hold biases favoring different types of disputants, and that these biases vary across the population of judges. Political scientists document the importance of judicial attitudes in shaping appellate rulings. The U.S. Supreme Court judges sometimes vote based on their ideological preferences and distinguish precedents incompatible with their political orientation (George and Epstein 1992; Brenner and Spaeth 1995; Songer and Lindquist 1996). Extreme judges are more likely to vote against the precedent than the centrist ones (Brenner and Stier 1996). Hansford and Spriggs (2006) conclude that the decision to follow a precedent depends on the ideological distance between the preferences of the deciding Supreme Court and the precedent itself.[3]

Second, following Radin (1925) and Posner (2003), we assume that changing precedent is personally costly to judges: it requires extra investigation of facts, extra writing, extra work of persuading colleagues when judges sit in panels, extra risk of being criticized, and so on. "Judges are people and the economizing of mental effort is a characteristic of people, even if censorious persons call it by a less fine name" (Radin 1925, p. 362). The assumption that, other things equal, judges would rather not change the law implies that only the judges who disagree with the current legal rule strongly enough actually change it. Posner (2003, p. 544) sees what he calls "judicial preference for leisure" as a source of stability in the law; we revisit this issue.

Third, we assume that the law evolves when judges distinguish cases from precedents, rather than just overrule precedents. By distinguishing we mean the introduction of a new legal rule that endorses the existing precedent, but adds a new material dimension to adjudication, and holds that the judicial decision must depend on both the previously recognized dimension and the new one. Distinguishing cases is the central mechanism, or leeway, through which common law evolves despite binding precedents (Llewellyn 1960; Stone 1985).

Using a model relying on these three assumptions, we examine the evolution of legal rules in the case of a simple tort: a dog bites a man (e.g., Landes and Posner 1987). In this analysis, two general principles stand out. First, legal change enables judges to implement their own biases, and to undo those of their predecessors. Second, such change occurs more often when judges' preferences are polarized because judges are more likely to strongly disagree with the current precedent. Putting these principles to work, we find a cost and a benefit of judicial polarization. On the one hand, biased judges distort the law away from efficiency. On the other hand, by fostering legal evolution, diversity of judicial views improves the quality of the law because, irrespective of whether the judge changing the law is biased or efficiency-oriented, distinguishing brings new data into dispute resolution, thereby increasing the precision of legal rules. Consistent with this trade-off, we find that greater polarization of judicial opinions may lead to better law. Although the cost of judicial bias renders the conditions for full efficiency of judge-made law implausibly strict, in our model legal evolution is beneficial *on average*, even if judges are extremely biased. In line with Cardozo's optimism, judicial biases wash out *on average* and the informational benefit of distinguishing improves the quality of the law.

These findings provide a theoretical foundation for the evolutionary adaptability of common law. They further suggest that such adaptability is more beneficial in the areas of law where there is room for change and updating, but the disagreement among judges is not extreme. The relatively apolitical yet still changing areas of law, such as contract and corporate law, are the likely candidates for reaping the benefits from the decentralized evolution of judge-made law.

2   A Model of Legal Precedent

There are two parties, a dog owner O and a bite victim V, as well as a dog. The dog bit V, who seeks to recover damages from O. The dog was not on a leash, so to assess O's liability one should determine whether O was negligent (and so is liable) or not (and so is not).

Let P_{NP} be the probability that the dog bites V if O does not take precautions (he does not put it on a leash) and P_P the probability that the dog bites V if precautions are taken. Let C be the owner's cost of precautions (e.g., the costs of putting the dog on a leash). First best social efficiency requires that the dog owner takes precautions if and only if their cost C is lower than the reduction in the probability of a bite (weighted by V's harm, which we normalize to 1).

We assume that damages are always set high enough to enforce precautions whenever the law holds O liable.[4] As a result, as indicated by the Hand formula, the first best is implemented by holding O negligent and thus liable if $P_{NP} - P_P \geq C$ and not liable if $P_{NP} - P_P < C$. In this context, the question for the law is how to determine negligence from the facts of a case.

Many factual situations may influence the probability of a bite and thus whether O was negligent. We assume that only two empirical dimensions—the dog's aggressiveness and the location of the interaction between O and V—are *material* to determine liability in this legal dispute.

Variable $a \in [0,1]$ measures the dog's aggressiveness. A dog with $a = 0$ is very peaceful (a golden retriever) and less likely to bite V than a dog with $a = 1$ (a pit bull). Variable $d \in [0,1]$ measures the density of people in the location where the dog is walked: if $d = 0$ the bite occurred in a forest; if $d = 1$, it occurred on a playground. We assume that a and d are independently and uniformly distributed over the population of interactions between O and V.

We further assume that:

$$P_{NP} - P_P = \begin{cases} \overline{\Delta P} & \text{for } a + d \geq 1 \\ \underline{\Delta P} & \text{for } a + d < 1 \end{cases} \tag{1}$$

where $\overline{\Delta P} > C > \underline{\Delta P}$. Thus, O is optimally held liable if and only if $a + d \geq 1$. Even owners of peaceful dogs are optimally held liable if they did not take precautions on a playground ($d = 1$); even owners of violent dogs are optimally excused if the dog was unleashed in a forest ($d = 0$).

In general, the social benefit of putting the dog on a leash is a function $\Delta P(a, d)$ increasing in a and d. We could allow for more general functions, but to clarify our analysis of legal change we assume that $\Delta P(a, d)$ only depends on $a+d$ and "jumps" at $a + d = 1$. The first restriction makes a and d symmetric for determining liability, which allows us to isolate the effect of legal change per se, abstracting from the particular dimension introduced into the law. The second restriction allows us to separate the *probabilities* of the different errors induced by a legal rule from their welfare *cost*.

A legal rule in this environment attaches a legal consequence (O liable, O not liable) to every case (a, d). In a sense, different legal rules put different substantive content into Hand's formula by specifying how $P_{NP} - P_P$ must be determined from a case's empirical attributes (a, d).

How do appellate judges make legal rules? We assume that, when no legal rule deals with dog bites at the beginning, the only factual issue that comes up through trial is the aggressiveness of the dog. As a result, the appellate judge who reviews the case sets the rule by choosing a threshold on a, which we call A. Owners of dogs more aggressive than A are held liable; owners of dogs less aggressive than A are not. We can think of A as the *ratio decidendi*—the principle of decision—of the case (Goodhart 1930, Stone 1985). The judge cannot at this point set a rule in which liability also depends on d, since a well-established principle of common law holds that judges only consider cases and factual dimensions that come before them (Llewellyn 1951).

Once A is set, a later judge dealing with a dog bite must respect *stare decisis* or adherence to precedent, and so accept A. However, as soon as the issue of location of a bite is brought on appeal, the judge can still radically change the law by *distinguishing* the case from the precedent based on this previously neglected dimension d. True this golden retriever is gentle, but it was unleashed on a playground. True this pit bull is dangerous, but who would reasonably keep it on a leash in a forest? Effectively, the judge introduces d into adjudication, applying the previous precedent to only some of the cases in the (a, d) space, but not others. Such distinguishing is the main source of legal change in common law systems (Llewellyn 1960; Stone 1985).

Because the judge respects the initial precedent, the best he can do is to choose two thresholds on density D_0 and D_1. The rule he establishes thus takes a two-dimensional threshold form, as illustrated in figure 3.1 below.

In figure 3.1, O is held liable in regions denoted by L, but non-liable in those denoted by NL. Relative to a one-dimensional rule, a two-dimensional rule allows for liability of owners of peaceful dogs ($a \le A$) in crowded locations ($d \ge D_0$), and non-liability of owners of aggressive dogs ($a > A$) in deserted locations ($d < D_1$). We expect $D_0 \ge D_1$. To take an extreme example of the power of distinguishing, if the first judge sets $A = 0$, the second judge can reverse it completely by saying that liability exists only in the most crowded locations, that is, by setting $D_0 = D_1 = 1$, which eliminates owner liability entirely. Although

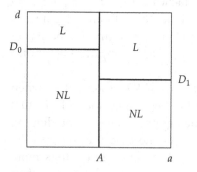

Figure 3.1

distinguishing by the second judge may allow him to render the law more precise (as when he sets $D_0 = D_1 = 1/2$), the second judge can also distinguish strategically for the sole purpose of implementing his bias.

Sequential decision making by judges gives legal rules their threshold structure. Because only the dog's aggressiveness comes up through initial fact finding, the first judge sets the threshold on aggressiveness beyond which O is liable. When future judges distinguish the case, they accept this initial threshold but, by bringing d into the law, create a two-dimensional threshold rule.

We assume that a judge distinguishing the case from precedent incurs a personal (fixed) effort cost k. The model's timing is as follows. At $t = 0$, the first judge establishes the aggressiveness threshold A. This precedent guides adjudication until another judge (if any) changes the rule at some time t'. If at $t = t'$ a judge changes the rule, he sets two density thresholds D_0 and D_1. In that case, the law is permanently fixed, as there are no further material dimensions to introduce.

We now investigate the efficient—welfare-maximizing—rules that provide the normative benchmark for our analysis of legal change and judge-made law in sections 4–6.

3 Optimal Legal Rules

A dog owner finding himself in situation (a, d) decides whether to put the dog on a leash by considering the risk of liability under the prevailing legal rule at (a, d). First best welfare, achieved under optimal precautions (i.e., O puts the dog on a leash whenever $a + d \geq 1$), is equal to:

$$W^{F.B.} = -(1/2)\underline{\Delta P} - (1/2)C , \tag{2}$$

where the probability of a bite when precautions are taken is normalized to 0. In half the cases, precautions are not efficient and the parties bear the extra risk $\underline{\Delta P}$ of the dog biting the man; in the other half, precautions are efficient but cost C to society.

Judge-made law cannot achieve such high welfare because legal rules arrived at sequentially take threshold form. Consider a one-dimensional threshold rule A, which holds O liable if and only if $a \geq A$. Figure 3.2 represents it as a vertical bold line together with the first best in the (a, d) space.

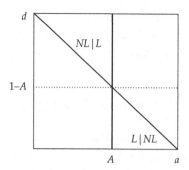

Figure 3.2

In the first best, O is liable above the diagonal $a+d=1$ but not below. The one-dimensional rule A holds O mistakenly liable in region $L \mid NL$ and mistakenly not liable in region $NL \mid L$. In the former region, O takes excessive precautions, which cost $\Lambda^{over} = C - \underline{\Delta P}$ to society. In the latter region, O takes too few precautions, which cost $\Lambda^{under} = \overline{\Delta P} - C$ to society. We take these costs of over- and under-precautions as given, and focus on how different legal rules affect the likelihood of different errors in adjudication. Also define $\lambda = \Lambda^{over} / \Lambda^{under}$ as the relative cost of over-precautions. For a given A, the error probabilities are given by $\Pr(L \mid NL) = (1/2)(1 - A)^2$ and $\Pr(NL \mid L) = (1/2)A^2$. The corresponding loss of social welfare (relative to the first best) is:

$$\Lambda(A) = (1/2)\Lambda^{under}[A^2 + \lambda(1 - A)^2] \tag{3}$$

If A is the initial precedent, social losses are $\Lambda(A)$—an average of over and under-precautions costs under the error probabilities that A introduces. The higher is A (the more the initial rule favors O), the larger is the loss from under-precautions but the smaller is the loss from over-precautions.

Figure 3.3 depicts the two-dimensional legal rule with thresholds A, D_0, and D_1. O is over-punished in region $L \mid NL$, with area $\Pr(L \mid NL) = (1/2)[(1 - D_0)^2 + (1 - A - D_1)^2]$, and under punished in region $NL \mid L$, with area $\Pr(NL \mid L) = (1/2)[(A + D_0 - 1)^2 + D_1^2]$.

The social loss from the use of the two-dimensional legal rule is given by:

$$\Lambda(A, D_0, D_1) = \Lambda^{under}(1/2)\{[(A + D_0 - 1)^2 + D_1^2] \\ + \lambda[(1 - D_0)^2 + (1 - A - D_1)^2]\} \tag{4}$$

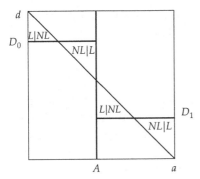

Figure 3.3

By minimizing (3) with respect to A and (4) with respect to A, D_0, D_1, we find the optimal one- and two-dimensional threshold rules, which are the normative benchmarks for our analysis.

Proposition 1   i) The optimal one-dimensional legal rule is given by $A_L = \lambda/(1 + \lambda)$; ii) The optimal two-dimensional legal rule is given by $A_F = 1/2$, $D_{0,F} = (1 + A_L)/2$, $D_{1,F} = A_L/2$.

The optimal one-dimensional rule responds to social costs. The higher is the relative cost of over-precautions λ, the more lenient is the optimal rule (the higher is A_L). This is also true for the optimal two-dimensional rule. Going back to figure 3.3, if the cost of over-precautions is higher, then $D_{0,F}$ and $D_{1,F}$ should be raised so as to reduce the size of $L \mid NL$, the region where O is mistakenly held liable. In addition, in the optimal two-dimensional rule, $A_F = 1/2$ maximizes the precision benefit of introducing population density into the law. For extreme A_F (1 or 0), the added dimension d is worthless: a single threshold on d (D_0 or D_1) describes liability over the entire (a, d) space, just like in a one-dimensional rule.

In our model, the efficiency of a rule depends on two factors: its overall imprecision $\Pr(NL \mid L) + \Pr(L \mid NL)$, and the ratio of different errors $\Pr(NL \mid L)/\Pr(L \mid NL)$. The optimal initial precedent and the optimal two-dimensional rule fare equally well in terms of this second factor (i.e., they induce the same $\Pr(NL \mid L)/\Pr(L \mid NL)$). Yet, by including d in adjudication, the optimal two-dimensional rule is more precise, and thus more efficient.

With the results of this section in mind, we can move on to study judicial lawmaking. We ask when and how judge-made law evolves over time, and evaluate the efficiency of legal evolution. By efficiency we mean ex ante efficiency, before judge types are revealed.

4 Distinguishing

Like social welfare, the utility of a judge settling a dispute between O and V depends on the precision of the rule and on the ratio of different mistakes. We assume that a judge's objective diverges from efficiency because of his bias, which reflects his preference for V or O and induces him to sacrifice efficiency for a pattern of mistakes more favorable to the preferred party. Specifically, we assume that the utility of judge j is given by:

$$U_j = -\beta_{V,j} \Pr(NL \mid L) - \beta_{O,j} \Pr(L \mid NL) \tag{5}$$

Judges dislike making mistakes, but they do not dislike the two types of mistakes equally. $\beta_{O,j}$ and $\beta_{V,j}$ ($\beta_{V,j}, \beta_{O,j} \geq 0$) capture the preference of judge j for O and V, respectively: the larger is $\beta_{O,j}$, the more he is eager to hold O not liable, the larger is $\beta_{V,j}$, the more he is willing to hold O liable.

Under the assumed utility function, judges are unhappy with any error they make (albeit differentially for different errors). This judicial aversion to making mistakes leads to judicial self-restraint that is crucial for our results: even a judge heavily biased against dog owners would not introduce the most anti-owner liability rule available if this rule leads to mistakes he can avoid, including mistakes favoring bite victims. Such preferences allow us to emphasize—in line with the legal realists—that judicial bias is more problematic in the presence of uncertainty, when judges trade off different errors. We do not model the more extreme kind of favoritism where the judge rules against dog owners who he knows for sure should not be efficiently held liable.

In our specification of judicial preferences, a judge's utility depends on the expected outcome arising from the application of a given rule, not from the resolution of a particular case. Such a judge would consider replacing a legal rule he dislikes even if the outcome of the specific case before him is the same under the new rule. A judge cares about having a rule in place that meets his idea of justice, rather than about delivering a desired outcome in a specific dispute before him. This assumption is particularly appropriate for appellate judges, who establish legal rules.

There is a measure 1 of judges, who can be of three types: share γ of judges are *unbiased*, with bias $\beta_{O,j}/\beta_{V,j} = \lambda$ reflecting social welfare; the rest are equally divided among *pro-O* judges, with bias $\beta_{O,j}/\beta_{V,j} = \lambda\pi$ and *pro-V* judges, with bias $\beta_{O,j}/\beta_{V,j} = \lambda/\pi$. Parameter π ($\pi \geq 1$), measures the polarization of judges' preferences: with a higher π, the preferences of *pro-O* and *pro-V* judges are more extreme (there is more disagreement among them). We assume that all judges have the same preference intensity and normalize it to 1 ($\beta_{V,j} + \beta_{O,j} = 1$, $\forall_j$).

4.1 The Initial Precedent

The first judge adjudicating a dispute between O and V establishes the initial precedent. We have assumed that, in this dispute, the issue of location never arises (and the judge cannot entertain legal issues that do not arise in the dispute). Suppose that this initial dispute comes up before judge i, with preferences $\beta_{V,i}$ and $\beta_{O,i}$. This judge then selects a threshold A_i to maximize:[5]

$$-(1/2)\beta_{V,i}[A^2 + \beta_i(1-A)^2] ,\qquad (6)$$

where $\beta_i = \beta_{O,i}/\beta_{V,i}$ measures the *pro-O* bias of this judge. Judge i then sets:

$$A_i = \frac{\beta_i}{1+\beta_i} \qquad (7)$$

The subscript indicates that A_i is the initial precedent set with *pro-O* bias β_i. The result is intuitive: the more *pro-O* is the judge, the more lenient he is (the higher is A_i). A_i coincides with the efficient one-dimensional rule A_L only if $\beta_i = \lambda = \Lambda^{over}/\Lambda^{under}$, that is, if the judge's bias toward O reflects the relative social cost of over-precautions. If the case ends up in front of a *pro-O* judge ($\beta_i > \lambda$), too many aggressive dogs roam and bite with impunity; if instead the case ends up in front of a *pro-V* judge ($\beta_i < \lambda$), too many peaceful dogs are put on a leash. Depending on β_i, the initial precedent may turn out to be severely inefficient.

4.2 The New Precedent

Suppose that after some time, a judge j has an opportunity to distinguish the initial precedent A_i by introducing d into the legal rule. Judge j's utility from setting thresholds $D_{0,j}$ and $D_{1,j}$ is:

$$-(1/2)\beta_{V,j}\{[(A_i + D_{0,j} - 1)^2 + D_{1,j}^2] + \beta_j[(1 - D_{0,j})^2 + (1 - A_i - D_{1,j})^2]\} \qquad (8)$$

The first term of the expression represents the cost for judge j of mistakenly holding O not liable (i.e., ruling against V), while the second term is the cost for judge j of erroneously holding O liable. Let $A_j = \beta_j / (1 + \beta_j)$ be the ideal threshold on the dog's aggressiveness that would be chosen by judge j if he were setting the initial precedent. From first order conditions, we obtain

$$D_{0,j}(A_i) = 1 - (1 - A_j)A_i \tag{9}$$

$$D_{1,j}(A_i) = A_j(1 - A_i) \tag{10}$$

These reaction functions tell us that distinguishing exhibits path dependence: because of *stare decisis*, the way judge j introduces $D_{0,j}$ and $D_{1,j}$ into the law depends on the initial precedent A_i. To gauge the impact of such distinguishing, it is helpful to look at the probabilities of different errors after legal change has occurred:

$$\Pr(L \mid NL) = (1/2)(1 - A_j)^2[A_i^2 + (1 - A_i)^2] \; ; \tag{11}$$

$$\Pr(NL \mid L) = (1/2)A_j^2[A_i^2 + (1 - A_i)^2] \tag{12}$$

As discussed in section 3, the efficiency of a legal rule depends on the ratio of the two errors $\Pr(NL \mid L)/\Pr(L \mid NL)$, and on the overall imprecision $\Pr(NL \mid L) + \Pr(L \mid NL)$ it induces. Expressions (11) and (12) show that after distinguishing $\Pr(NL \mid L)/\Pr(L \mid NL) = A_j^2/(1 - A_j)^2$, the ratio between errors is fully determined, through A_j, by the *desired* bias of the second judge! When judge j introduces d into adjudication, he discretionally sets $D_{0,j}$ and $D_{1,j}$ so as to favor the party he prefers. As a result, there is no presumption that the final configuration of the law is less biased than the initial precedent. Due to the very discretion embodied in distinguishing cases, legal change cannot eliminate this first effect of judicial bias: it cannot correct the ratio of different errors. In this sense, the eccentricities of judges do *not* balance one another and legal evolution does not reduce the ability of biased judges to distort the ratio of errors away from efficiency.

On the other hand, the imprecision of the legal rule shows the potential of distinguishing:

$$\Pr(NL \mid L) + \Pr(L \mid NL) = (1/2)[A_j^2 + (1 - A_j)^2][A_i^2 + (1 - A_i)^2] \tag{13}$$

Because $[A_j^2 + (1 - A_j)^2] \leq 1$, distinguishing (weakly) *reduces* the imprecision of the law, which is equal to $(1/2)[A_i^2 + (1 - A_i)^2]$ under the initial precedent. This has two implications. First, even if judges are biased, legal evolution can beneficially increase the precision of the law. Notice, however, that expression (13) indicates that even from the standpoint of the law's precision, judicial bias is costly as it increases the *overall* likelihood of judicial error. The bias of the first judge reduces the precision of the initial precedent; that of the second judge reduces the precision benefit of distinguishing. For example, when $A_j = 1$, the precision benefit of distinguishing is nil.

Second, and in contrast to the finding on the ratio of errors, the *path dependence* resulting from sequential decision making now matters: the final legal rule is more precise the greater the precision of the initial precedent A_i. Expression (13) shows that the initial precedent dampens the impact of the second judge's bias on the precision of the law. Although a very *pro-O* judge may wish to introduce location just to excuse dog owners, he does not want to totally discard the information embodied into the initial legal rule. As a result, the waste of information associated with his exercise of discretion is limited. To see why this is the case, suppose that judge i sets legal rule $A_i = 1/2$, whose imprecision is $1/4$. Then, a very *pro-O* judge j still *can* set $D_{0,j} = D_{1,j} = 1$, which would make imprecision jump to $1/2$, but he does not want to. The reason is that he can set $D_{0,j} = 1$, and $D_{1,j} = 1/2$, and in this way avoid the error of excusing the owners of vicious dogs unleashed on a playground. He still keeps the area of false liability down to zero, but because he does not like making *any* errors, his decision is more efficient. In this way, the initial precedent helps constrain the impact of the bias of the second judge on the precision of the law. This discussion also shows that our assumption about judicial preferences actually matters; if judge j only cared about favoring dog owners without regard for making errors, he would set $D_{0,j} = D_{1,j} = 1$ regardless of what judge i did before him.

The ability of the initial precedent to soften the impact of the bias of the second judge depends on the bias of the first judge, as the moderation of the first judge i entails the relative moderation of judge j. If the first judge was extremist (i.e., if $A_i = 0$ or 1), then the second judge behaves *as if* no precedent is in place. For example, in light of precedent $A_i = 0$, a very *pro-O* second judge sets $D_{0,j} = D_{1,j} = 1$. Since judge j only cares about not erroneously holding dog owners liable, his introduction of d fully eliminates dog owner's liability. When judge i is so extreme, judge j is both able *and willing* to move from the regime of strict liability to the regime of virtually no liability by distinguishing the case based on location. To summarize this argument, we formally define extremism as the distance of a judge's preferred threshold A from $1/2$ and can show:

Proposition 2 Distinguishing increases the law's precision, but less so the more extreme the second judge is. The initial precedent softens the adverse impact of the second judge's extremism on the law's precision, and the more so the less extremist the first judge is.

4.3 Welfare Effects of a Precedent Change

After judge j distinguishes the initial precedent A_i, social losses are:

$$\Lambda(A_i, D_{0,j}, D_{1,j}) = [A_i^2 + (1 - A_i)^2]\Lambda(A_j) \tag{14}$$

The term $\Lambda(A_j)$ stands for the social loss under the hypothetical assumption that the initial rule is chosen by judge j (and subsequently not distinguished), and captures the idea that legal change allows judges to regain their discretion. The term $[A_i^2 + (1 - A_i)^2]$ captures the precision benefit of distinguishing. If the initial threshold A_i were not binding in virtue of *stare decisis*, the social loss would be entirely determined by the preferences of judge j, as reflected in the hypothetical A_j.

Because distinguishing allows very biased judges to regain discretion, legal change is not *always* good. To see why, notice that under the initial precedent social losses are equal to $\Lambda(A_i)$. When the bias of the second judge is more costly to society than the bias of the first judge (if $\Lambda(A_j) > \Lambda(A_i)$), legal change *reduces* welfare when the precision benefit of distinguishing is small. To illustrate, consider the extreme case where judge i is infinitely *pro-V*, and judge j is infinitely *pro-O*. The precision benefit of distinguishing is now absent and legal change effectively allows the second judge to replace the initial rule of strict liability ($A_i = 0$) with his preferred rule of no liability ($A_j = 1$). If under-precautions are socially costlier than over-precautions ($\lambda < 1$), such legal change is harmful because it enables the *pro-O* judge to excuse careless owners of very aggressive dogs. More broadly, legal change is most likely to be detrimental when both the judge setting the initial precedent and the one distinguishing it are extremists, and when the latter judge's extremism is more detrimental to social welfare than that of the former.

5 Judge-Made Law in the Long Run

Although judicial activism may make matters worse, to evaluate legal change overall we need to a) study when and how it occurs and b) average over all the possible paths of the law.

By comparing the utility judge j derives from retaining A_i completely (expression (6)) with the utility he obtains by introducing his preferred thresholds $D_{0j}(A_i)$ and $D_{1j}(A_i)$ into the law (expression (8)), we find that judge j distinguishes A_i when:

$$(A_i - A_j)^2 + 2A_j(1 - A_j)A_i(1 - A_i) \geq 2k \tag{15}$$

Intuitively, the smaller the cost k of changing the law, the higher the chance that legal change occurs. More importantly, the left hand side of (15) illustrates that a judge changing the law obtains two benefits. First, legal change allows him to replace the precedent's bias with his own preferred bias. This benefit is captured by the term $(A_j - A_i)^2$ and suggests that greater disagreement between judges j and i leads the former to distinguish A_i more often. Second, there is an informational gain from distinguishing, namely $2A_j(1 - A_j)A_i(1 - A_i)$. This gain is stronger for moderate judges ($A_j = 1/2$) who care most about the precision of the law, but is small or absent if the first judge was an extremist (i.e., if $A_i = 0$ or 1). This gain may induce a judge to distinguish even a precedent set by a predecessor with identical preferences.

The idea that the extent to which a judge disagrees with the existing precedent shapes his incentive to change the law suggests that the polarization of judges' views is a key determinant of the long-run configuration of judge-made law. Indeed, the more polarized are judges' views (i.e., the larger is π), the greater the likelihood that a judge inherits a precedent he strongly disagrees with. The case of $\lambda = 1$ illustrates this intuition.

Proposition 3 If $\lambda = 1$, there exist two polarization levels $\tilde{\pi}_1$ and $\tilde{\pi}_2$ ($\tilde{\pi}_1 \leq \tilde{\pi}_2$) such that: i) If $\pi < \tilde{\pi}_1$ the initial precedent is never distinguished; ii) If $\pi \in [\tilde{\pi}_1, \tilde{\pi}_2)$ only *pro-O* and *pro-V* initial precedents are distinguished; iii) If $\pi \geq \tilde{\pi}_2$ all initial precedents are distinguished.

Polarization of judicial preferences determines whether d is eventually introduced into the law. If π is low, judge-made law immediately converges to the one-dimensional threshold on aggressiveness set by the first judge. At intermediate levels of polarization, *pro-O* and *pro-V* judges distinguish each other's precedents. The law converges to a two-dimensional legal rule unless an *unbiased* judge sets the initial threshold A, which then becomes permanent. At high levels of polarization, even *unbiased* precedents are distinguished.[6,7]

Our model yields the empirical prediction that legal change occurs more often the higher is the dispersion of judicial preferences. Looking across areas of law, those areas with greater dispersion of judicial views (perhaps because they are more political) would see more legal change. These results are broadly consistent with the main finding of the political science literature, namely that the Supreme Court distinguishes precedents incompatible with its political orientation and that extreme judges are more likely to vote against the precedent than the centrist ones (Brenner and Stier 1996). But proposition 3 delivers another novel empirical prediction, namely that legal rules are more complex (include more empirical dimensions) when judicial views are more dispersed.

The only novel feature arising when $\lambda < 1$ is that the *unbiased* initial precedents may no longer be the hardest to distinguish. For example, at intermediate levels of polarization, *pro-O* judges may prefer to distinguish an *unbiased* precedent to a *pro-V* one, because the informational benefit of distinguishing the latter is too small when λ is very low. Still, the main thrust of proposition 3 is maintained: distinguishing increases with the polarization of judicial preferences.

6 The Efficiency of Legal Evolution under Distinguishing

Having studied when and how legal evolution occurs, we now evaluate the efficiency properties of judge-made law. We start by asking when judge made law converges to the optimal two-dimensional legal rule. We find:

Proposition 4 Judge-made law converges to efficiency if and only if all judges are *unbiased*, k is sufficiently small, and $\lambda = 1$.

Because biased judges distort the ratio between different errors away from efficiency, a population of fully unbiased judges is necessary for judge-made law to converge to the efficient two-dimensional rule. But two other conditions must be met. First, judges must be interventionist enough to introduce d into the law; otherwise a two-dimensional rule cannot even be reached. That is, k must be sufficiently low for *unbiased* judges to distinguish the initial precedent A_L.

Second, and more importantly, even with two unbiased judges ruling sequentially, it must be that $\lambda = 1$, that is, the optimal ratio between different errors is 1. This is due to the law's path dependence, which introduces an externality across judges. The initial precedent is set at A_L and not at $1/2$ (as in the optimal legal rule) because the first judge disregards the adverse impact of his choice on the long-run precision of the law. By virtue of *stare decisis*, the initial precedent is then respected, thus keeping the long-run law from full efficiency. Forward-looking behavior on this judge's part does not remove this inefficiency unless he is infinitely patient.

The key role of efficiency-seeking judges in the convergence of common law to efficiency is recognized by Posner (2003), although he does not explain just how stringent the conditions for full efficiency are. Nor does Posner (2003) discuss how path dependence of judge-made legal rules may prevent them from attaining full efficiency, even if all judges are unbiased.

How does social welfare depend on polarization? We find:

Proposition 5 For every k, there exists a $\pi^*(k) \geq 1$ such that social welfare decreases with π if $\pi < \pi^*(k)$ or $\pi > \pi^*(k)$, but social welfare is maximized at $\pi = \pi^*(k)$ and $\pi^*(k) > 1$ for some k.

Proposition 5 points to a cost but also a benefit of judicial polarization. The cost of greater polarization of judicial views to the long-run efficiency of judge-made law comes from two effects. First, when judges are more biased, legal rules are less precise. Second, when judges are more biased, legal rules induce a ratio between different errors that is further away from efficiency. Both of these costs of polarization hold for both one- and two-dimensional legal rules.

However, proposition 5 also highlights a benefit of judicial disagreement, because the efficiency of judge-made legal rules often jumps up at polarization level $\pi^*(k) > 1$. The intuition for this result hinges on our finding in proposition 4 that judges are more likely to distinguish a precedent when the disagreement among them is greater. If polarization is low, judges lack an important incentive to change the law, namely the benefit of replacing the bias of their predecessor with their own. The law then does not evolve from its initial one-dimensional configuration. If judicial views are sufficiently polarized, judges find it worthwhile to distinguish the initial precedent, allowing the introduction of d into the law to improve its "precision." In a sense, polarization is the price to pay for judge-made law to adapt and become ever more precise. Of course, as proposition 5 shows, the "precision" benefit of distinguishing becomes smaller as polarization increases. Our model thus predicts an inverted U-shaped relationship between polarization and the efficiency of judge-made law.

Although proposition 5 indicates that some judicial polarization can improve the long-run efficiency of judge-made law, it does not tell whether legal change is generally good. For example, at high levels of polarization the introduction of d into the law may reduce welfare. When π is large, the precision benefit of distinguishing is small and the adverse impact of judicial bias on the ratio between different errors may undermine the desirability of legal change.

This observation leads to a key result of our paper. In line with Cardozo's intuition, we find that if we consider all possible paths of the law, then distinguishing is *on average* beneficial in many circumstances, even when judicial polarization is very high.

Proposition 6 (Cardozo Theorem)   There exists a $\bar{k} > 0$ such that, for $k \le \bar{k}$ distinguishing of precedents is on average beneficial. As a result, at every π, $k = 0$ is socially preferred to $k = \infty$.

Irrespective of judicial polarization π, judicial activism (i.e., a low k) renders legal change desirable on average. To see why judicial activism (and thus legal change) is beneficial even in the presence of biased judges, compare the ex-ante social loss attained at $k = 0$ with that attained at $k = \infty$. If $k = 0$, judges are so activist that they always distinguish any initial precedent A_i, thereby leading to a second period expected loss of $[A_i^2 + (1 - A_i)^2]E_j[\Lambda(A_j)]$. Averaging such losses across all paths of legal change (i.e., across initial precedents), we find an ex-ante loss of:

$$E_i[A_i^2 + (1 - A_i)^2]E_j[\Lambda(A_j)] \tag{16}$$

If instead $k = \infty$, judges are passive and never distinguish the initial precedent, thereby leading to an ex-ante loss of $E_i[\Lambda(A_i)]$. Since $E_i[A_i^2 + (1 - A_i)^2] \le 1$, legal change is beneficial at every level of judicial polarization and $k = 0$ is socially preferred to $k = \infty$. This is because the introduction of d into the law brings an informational benefit that *on average* overpowers the cost of bias.

This result vindicates Cardozo's intuition for the presence of a "technological" force driving the evolution of precedent toward efficiency despite the vagaries of individual judges. When judges embrace legal change (as in the case of $k = 0$), their biases "wash out" on average and the net gain for the law comes from the more accurate information (greater number of empirical dimensions) embodied into legal rules. At high levels of polarization, legal change may be detrimental along some paths, such as when a *pro-O* judge distinguishes away a *pro-V* precedent thereby imposing on society a worse scenario of under-precautions. However, when judges embrace legal change, this event is just as likely as the one where a *pro-V* judge distinguishes a *pro-O* precedent, thereby sparing society the cost of under-precautions for the lesser cost of over-precautions. From an ex-ante standpoint, the influence of bias along these two paths cancels out and what remains on net is the greater precision of the law, which now uses two material dimensions rather than one. This creates a *tendency* for the law to become more efficient over time.[8]

Propositions 5 and 6 suggest that the evolution of common law would produce most socially efficient results in the areas of law where there is room for change and updating, but where the disagreement among the judges is not extreme. The relatively apolitical yet still changing areas of law, such as contract and corporate, are the likely candidates for relatively efficient outcomes resulting from the decentralized evolution of judge-made law. In the extremely political areas of law, in contrast, the likelihood that the law gets stuck on a wrong trajectory is higher.

7 Conclusion

When and how does the evolution of judge-made law take place? When does such evolution improve the law on average? Does it lead to convergence to efficient legal rules? We addressed these questions in a legal-realist model, in which deciding judges face opportunities to distinguish the precedent from the case before them, but may be both biased and averse to changing the law.

We found that the conditions for ultimate efficiency of judge-made law are implausibly stringent. Moreover, a legal rule governing a particular situation may start off in a very inefficient place, and because of path dependence in judge-made law, remain highly inefficient despite future refinements. Yet even though full efficiency is hard to attain and some legal rules remain bad, there is a presumption that legal change raises welfare as it improves the informational quality of judicial decision making, at least when the cost of changing the law is low. Although common law judges do not seek to improve the efficiency of legal rules but rather pursue their own agendas, their independent decentralized decisions have a benign side effect. The law better adapts to the underlying transactions (and to new circumstances) when activist judges distinguish cases. This basic finding on the evolution of common law is very supportive of the ideas of free market philosophers, such as Hayek and Leoni, of legal realists such as

Llewellyn and Cardozo, and of law and economics scholars following Posner.

The benefit of legal change implies that, compared to the case of no judicial disagreement, some judicial disagreement is beneficial. Indeed, we found that judicial disagreement is an important factor fostering legal change and volatility in the law. The model predicts a faster pace of legal change in the more politically (or otherwise) divisive areas of law. On average with such change, legal rules become more efficient by becoming more complex, as measured by the number of tests or considerations entering into a legal decision. These predictions on the volatility and complexity of different areas of law can be tested using data on appellate court decisions.

Our model is a first step in the analysis of judge-made law, and omits some important aspects of legal evolution. First, we consider legal change though distinguishing, and disregard the possibility that courts occasionally simply overrule precedents. We examine the case of overruling in Gennaioli and Shleifer (2007), but the basic point is simple. Since overruling, unlike distinguishing, does not bring new material dimensions into the law, it leads to the volatility of legal rules without a tendency to improve the law over time. With overruling, there is no benefit of legal evolution.

Second, we have ignored several institutional features of appellate review, which might affect our results. Unlike the previous research, we neglect the selection of disputes for judicial resolution rather than settlement. In addition, appellate judges sit in panels and make decisions collectively. These factors might be a force for moderation, although—precisely by inducing moderation—they might also slow down the pace of legal change, which is not necessarily efficient.

As a final note, we emphasize that ours is a theoretical analysis of the proposition that the evolution of common law is beneficial. We have tried to develop several testable implications of our analysis, which suggest the areas of the law where this benign conclusion is more likely to hold, in particular connecting efficiency to the volatility and complexity of legal rules. In chapter 4, we examine the evolution over time of one important common law rule.

Appendix: Proofs

Proof of Proposition 1   The optimal one-dimensional threshold rule A_L is defined as

$$A_L = \arg\min_{A \in [0,1]} A^2 + \lambda(1-A)^2$$

The objective function is convex and $A_L = \lambda/(1 + \lambda)$ ($A_L \in [0,1]$) is found by solving the f.o.c. $A_L - \lambda(1 - A_L) = 0$. The optimal two-dimensional threshold rule (A_F, D_0, D_1) is defined as

$$(A_F, D_0, D_1) = \arg\min_{A, D_0', D_1' \in [0,1]^3} [(A + D_0' - 1)^2 + (D_1')^2] + \lambda[(1 - D_0')^2 + (1 - A - D_1')^2]$$

Again, the above objective function is convex in (A, D_0', D_1') (its Hessian is positive definite). Thus, solving the first order conditions for A_F, D_0, D_1, namely

$$\partial\Lambda/\partial A_F = (A_F + D_0 - 1) - \lambda(1 - A_F - D_1) = 0$$

$$\partial\Lambda/\partial D_0 = (A_F + D_0 - 1) - \lambda(1 - D_0) = 0$$

$$\partial\Lambda/\partial D_1 = D_1 - \lambda(1 - A_F - D_1) = 0$$

yields $A_F = 1/2$, $D_0 = (1 + A_L)/2$, $D_1 = A_L/2$. Notice that A_F, D_0, $D_1 \in [0,1]^3$.♠

Proof of Proposition 3 Judge j distinguishes precedent A_i when:

$$h_{j,i}(\pi) \equiv \frac{\beta_i^2 + \beta_j^2}{(1 + \beta_i)^2(1 + \beta_j)^2} \geq 2k$$

Given symmetry, we must only consider the following cases:

a) *pro-O* ($\beta_i = \pi\lambda$); *pro-O* ($\beta_j = \pi\lambda$). $h_{O,O}(\pi) \equiv 2\dfrac{\pi^2\lambda^2}{(1 + \pi\lambda)^4}$.

b) *pro-V* ($\beta_i = \lambda/\pi$); *pro-V* ($\beta_j = \lambda/\pi$). $h_{V,V}(\pi) \equiv 2\dfrac{\lambda^2\pi^2}{(\pi + \lambda)^4}$.

c) *unbiased* ($\beta_i = \lambda$); *unbiased* ($\beta_j = \lambda$). $h_{U,U}(\pi) \equiv 2\dfrac{\lambda^2}{(1 + \lambda)^4}$.

d) *pro-O* ($\beta_i = \pi\lambda$); *pro-V* ($\beta_j = \lambda/\pi$). $h_{O,V}(\pi) \equiv h_{V,O}(\pi) \equiv \dfrac{\lambda^2(\pi^4 + 1)}{(1 + \lambda\pi)^2(\pi + \lambda)^2}$.

e) *pro-O* ($\beta_i = \pi\lambda$); *unbiased* ($\beta_j = \lambda$). $h_{O,U}(\pi) \equiv h_{U,O}(\pi) \equiv \dfrac{\lambda^2(\pi^2 + 1)}{(1 + \pi\lambda)^2(1 + \lambda)^2}$.

f) *pro-V* ($\beta_i = \lambda/\pi$); *unbiased* ($\beta_j = \lambda$). $h_{V,U}(\pi) \equiv h_{U,V}(\pi) \equiv \dfrac{\lambda^2(1 + \pi^2)}{(\pi + \lambda)^2(1 + \lambda)^2}$.

Call $\pi_{j,i} \in [1, +\infty) \cup \{+\infty\}$ the level of π such that, for $\pi \geq \pi_{j,i}$ j distinguishes i (and vice versa). In this proof, we set $\pi_{i,j} = +\infty$ when i and j never distinguish each other for any level of π. This way, we can accommodate in proposition 3 also the special case where $k > 1/2$. Because $\lim_{\pi \to \infty} h_{O,V}(\pi) = 1$, for $k > 1/2$ there is no π at which the initial precedent is distinguished. In this case, we set $\bar{\pi}_{O,V} = \tilde{\pi}_1 = \bar{\pi}_{O,U} = \tilde{\pi}_2 = \infty$ and proposition 3 correctly yields the result that the initial precedent sticks forever. At the same time, because $h_{O,U} = h_{V,U} \geq 1/8$, then for $k < 1/16$ every initial precedent (pro-V, pro-O, or unbiased) is distinguished. This case is accommodated by setting $\bar{\pi}_{O,V} = \tilde{\pi}_1 = \bar{\pi}_{O,U} = \tilde{\pi}_2 = 1$. More generally, because of the ranking in the incentive to distinguish, we have that, for every k, $\bar{\pi}_{O,V} \leq \bar{\pi}_{O,U} = \bar{\pi}_{V,U} \leq \bar{\pi}_{U,U} \leq \bar{\pi}_{O,O} \leq \bar{\pi}_{V,V}$. Call $\bar{\pi}_{O,V} = \tilde{\pi}_1$; $\bar{\pi}_{O,U} = \tilde{\pi}_2$. Then, the long-run configuration of precedent behaves as in proposition 3.♠

Proof of Propositions 4 and 5 Unless $\gamma = 1$, judge-made law necessarily leads to an inefficient bias. However, with distinguishing, even $\gamma = 1$ is not enough for efficiency. This is, first, because if $\gamma = 1$ and $k = 0$, the law converges to $A = \lambda/(1 + \lambda)$, $D_0 = 1 - D_1$, $D_1 = \lambda/(1 + \lambda)^2$, which is efficient only if $\lambda = 1$. Second, it must be that judges are willing to distinguish, that is, that $k \leq \tilde{k} \equiv (1/2)h_{u,u}$. To see the differential welfare effects of polarization, consider $k \leq \tilde{k}$. In this case, *unbiased* judges are sufficiently motivated to distinguish even if $\pi = 1$, so polarization here is likely to reduce welfare. In contrast, when $k > \tilde{k}$, if $\pi = 1$ the law sticks at A_L and d is never introduced. For every k, define $\hat{\pi}(k)$ as the level of polarization such that $\min_{i \neq j} h_{i,j}(\hat{\pi}(k)) = 2k$. In words, $\hat{\pi}(k)$ is the minimal level of polarization at which all judges j distinguish A_i for $i \neq j$. Clearly, as $k \to \tilde{k}$, $\hat{\pi}(k)$ can be made close to 1 (but greater than 1) and the expected social losses at $\hat{\pi}(k)$ can be made arbitrarily close to $[A_L^2 + (1 - A_L)^2]\Lambda(A_L) < \Lambda(A_L)$. Thus, for some $k > \tilde{k}$, there exists a $\pi^*(k) > 1$ such that social losses at $\pi^*(k)$ are smaller than social losses at 1. Hence, under distinguishing some polarization can be strictly beneficial.♠

Proof of Proposition 6 Define $\bar{k} = h_{i,j}(1) = 2\lambda^2/(1 + \lambda)^4$. If $k \leq \bar{k}$, judges $j \neq i$ and $j = i = U$, distinguish A_i (they would do it at $\pi = 1$). For $j = i$, $i = O, V$ judges can distinguish or not. If *pro-O* distinguish, welfare may go down if $\Lambda(A_O) \geq E_i(\Lambda(A_i))$, which we assume w.l.o.g. Hence, for $k \leq \bar{k}$, legal change is good if it is good when only *pro-O* judges distinguish their precedent. In this respect, two cases must be considered. If $\Lambda(A_V) \geq E_i(\Lambda(A_i))$ (i.e., the activism of *pro-V* on their precedent reduces welfare), then legal change is good for $k \leq \bar{k}$ because, even if we add to the activism of *pro-O* judges the harmful activism of *pro-V* judges on their own precedents, social losses are exactly the same as under $k = 0$. If $\Lambda(A_V) < E_i(\Lambda(A_i))$, then legal change is good if: $[(1/2)(1 - \gamma)\theta_O + \gamma\theta_U + (1 - \gamma)\theta_V - 1]E(\Lambda(A_i)) \leq (1/2)(1 - \gamma)^2\theta_V\Lambda(A_V)$ (where $\theta_i = A_i^2 + (1 - A_i)^2$). This inequality holds if legal change is good when $\Lambda(A_V) = E_i(\Lambda(A_i))$ and thus a fortiori if $\Lambda(A_V) < E_i(\Lambda(A_i))$. This is true because if $\Lambda_V = E(\Lambda_i)$, social losses are the same as at $k = 0$. As a result, under both circumstances, for $k \leq \bar{k}$ legal change is on average beneficial even if *pro-O* judges but not *pro-V* ones distinguish their own precedent. This immediately implies that the same holds in all other cases. As a result, for $k \leq \bar{k}$ legal change is on average beneficial for every π. It immediately follows that at every π, $k = 0$ is socially preferred to $k = \infty$.

4 The Evolution of a Legal Rule

with Anthony Niblett and Richard A. Posner

1 Introduction

We investigate the evolution of a particular common law rule pertaining to the construction industry, as developed by state appellate courts in the United States over the last three and a half decades. The evolution and efficiency of legal rules governing commercial activity are central to understanding a market economy. As long as property rights are well defined and private parties whose behavior affects each other can freely contract over their conduct at low cost, they will agree to act efficiently (Coase 1960). Efficient behavior maximizes total surplus, which parties can agree to divide between themselves via contract. But when negotiating explicit contracts is costly, efficient resource allocation may require that the law creates rules that give parties incentives to act efficiently—rules that steer parties to outcomes that mimic those that the market would produce if transaction costs were low. Hence the need for efficient legal rules.

In a common law system such as that of the United States, many legal rules are created by judges as a byproduct of deciding appeals. Scholars in law and economics have sought to understand why common law rules might be efficient. Posner (1973) recognized the importance of this question and argued that appellate judges have career or other personal incentives to maximize efficiency. Rubin (1977) and Priest (1977) argued that because inefficient legal rules lead to inefficient outcomes, they are more likely to be challenged in court. Such litigation is likely to drive them out in favor of efficient rules, even when judges do not consciously pursue efficiency (see also Cooter, Kornhauser, and Lane 1979).

These arguments do not come to grips with the legal realist criticism that judges have policy preferences other than social welfare or disagree about what serves social welfare. A considerable empirical literature concludes that judges often pursue political objectives (George and Epstein 1992; Brenner and Spaeth 1995; Songer and Lindquist 1996; Hansford and Spriggs 2006; Landes and Posner 2008), and when they do, the case for the efficiency of common law is harder to make. Nevertheless, one can still argue, in the spirit of Cardozo (1921), that the law evolves toward better rules through sequential decisions of judges with diverse preferences (see also: Holmes 1897; Frank 1930; Llewellyn 1951; Stone 1985; chapter 3).

Yet most of the discussion of the efficiency of legal rules remains theoretical, with few empirical studies of how the law evolves in commercial fields that particularly matter for the efficiency of resource allocation. That is the gap we try to fill. The doctrine we have chosen for our study is the "economic loss rule" (ELR), and the context is its application to a homogeneous universe of construction disputes. We ask whether the courts have adhered to the ELR (with some standard exceptions that might be necessary to make the rule efficient) in that industry, and, if not, how the pattern of adherence and nonadherence has evolved.

Stated at its broadest, the ELR excludes tort liability for "economic loss" unless that loss is accompanied by personal injury or property damage. "Economic loss" means a loss that is not a personal injury or property damage. So if the builder of a house installs windows negligently, with the result that they do not keep out the rain, the owner cannot sue the builder in tort for the cost of re-installing the windows carefully, because the loss is purely "economic."[1] In contrast, if the water that seeps into the house because of the badly installed windows damages furniture (i.e., causes damage to property other than what the builder sold you), the owner can sue the builder in tort.

The antecedents of the ELR are old,[2] but in the context of liability resulting from a product defect the doctrine was first clearly articulated in the 1960s by the Supreme Court of California in *Seely v. White Motor Co.*[3] The plaintiff had bought a truck with defective brakes. The truck overturned, but the plaintiff was not hurt; nor was there damage to any other property. He sued in both contract and tort to recover repair costs and lost profits. The court held that the plaintiff was limited to suing for breach of warranty, essentially a contractual remedy.[4]

The ELR was first applied to construction disputes in the 1970s; we have found no earlier precedents.[5] Most construction activity is governed by contract, but there are two principal types of cases in which tort claims, and therefore the ELR, become relevant. In the first, a property owner sues in tort for economic loss when he has no contract claim or when he wants to make additional claims, exploiting procedural or remedial advantages of tort over contract suits. In the second type of case, a builder sues other builders, architects, engineers, inspectors, or manufacturers for damages resulting from negligence. We investigate how state appellate courts have dealt with such cases.[6] Our sample contains all the 461 state appellate decisions between 1970 and 2005 that we could find: enough to reach some conclusions on how the law evolves but not so many as to make the project unmanageable.

We emphasize that our sample of cases—cases involving the application of the ELR to construction disputes in the United States—is homogeneous. Research in law and economics, including comparative work by Bussani and Palmer, eds. (2003a), Bussani, Palmer, and Parisi (2003b), Dari-Mattiacci and Schafer (2007), Gomez and Schafer (2007), and Parisi, Palmer, and Bussani (2007), confirms that the ELR covers diverse situations in which courts consider whether to allow recovery in tort for "economic loss." Examples include a store owner who loses customers because of an accident in front of his store, and a business having to shut down because of accidental damage to electric lines resulting from construction activity several miles away (Posner 2006). Many of these are situations in which a contractual resolution is infeasible because of prohibitive transaction costs. We confine our study to one industry, and in all but 11 cases in our sample the plaintiff either is or could be in a contractual relationship with the defendant. In many ELR cases, the efficiency justification for the ELR is that it protects parties engaged in normal business conduct from unpredictable tort claims from strangers if an accident occurs. In construction disputes, the plaintiffs and the defendants are not strangers, so this argument does not apply. Our sample is focused on the product liability sphere of application of the ELR on the border of contract and tort emanating from *Seely*.

The theoretical case for the efficiency of the ELR in contractual settings rests on the feasibility of anticipating such disputes through explicit contracting. As Posner (1973) pointed out, courts prefer parties to govern their relationships through privately negotiated contracts rather than through tort suits whenever transaction costs are low enough, because the parties know their business better than the judges can. He reiterated this logic as a judge in applying a bright-line ELR in *Miller v. United States Steel Corp.*: "tort law is a superfluous and inapt tool for resolving purely commercial disputes. We have a body of law designed for such disputes. It is called contract law."[7] Because we are studying the ELR in cases in which parties do have an opportunity to contract, the refusal to allow the parties to bypass contract and thrust the allocative decision on the courts by invoking tort law is probably efficient. But this logic behind the ELR implies denial of monetary recovery to some persons harmed by wrongful acts, and that troubles some courts.[8]

Even in a homogeneous field, such as the application of the ELR to construction disputes, we need to specify what is an "efficient" ELR doctrine. One possibility is that efficiency requires applying the ELR with no exceptions at all (call this the strict view). On this view, if the law converges to efficiency, appellate courts should increasingly be refusing to allow any exceptions to the ELR. Another view is that efficiency admits several exceptions, specifically the ones that are generally recognized by most courts (call this the middle view). One such exception is fraud (the deliberate infliction of economic loss), and another is economic loss that accompanies a personal injury or physical damage; these situations are difficult to anticipate and make provision for by contract. The generally recognized exceptions essentially add standard default terms to private agreements and by doing so economize on transaction costs. Under the middle view, if the law converges to efficiency, over time courts should be refusing to make exceptions to the ELR other than the generally recognized ones. Thus, if we find that, over time, appellate courts not only fail to reduce the use of exceptions to the ELR but also fail to reduce the use of those exceptions that are not generally recognized, we will have evidence against convergence to efficiency, according to the middle view.

A third view of efficiency is that courts have more information about cases than researchers do, and so the application of the ELR and its exceptions is contingent on specific facts of the case (call this the broad view) invisible to research based on aggregated data. Our data allow us to test both the strict and the middle view, but the broad view flexibly enough interpreted is untestable by the methods we use. Having said this, we will show in our empirical analysis just how elastic the broad view must be to be consistent with the data: different state appellate courts (or the same courts at different times) issue contradictory rulings in cases that appear to be nearly identical. We also present evidence of unusually high rates of dissent when courts adopt exceptions that courts in other states do not recognize.

In studying the evolution of the ELR in construction disputes, we first consider both the bright-line ELR (strict view) and the ELR with generally recognized exceptions (middle view) as candidates for the efficient rule, and ask whether the law achieves or moves toward either of them. Then we ask more generally whether the law converges over time to any resting point. If it does not, in an environment that is basically stationary, it becomes harder to argue that the law tends toward efficiency.

We also look at the evolution of the law in different jurisdictions. Under the assumption that legal rules relating to construction should not efficiently vary across jurisdictions, large differences in the patterns of legal evolution across jurisdictions would argue against an inference of efficient judicial rulemaking under all three of our conceptions of efficiency.

To summarize the results, over our sample period the law did not converge to the bright-line (strict) ELR, to the ELR with generally recognized exceptions, or to any other resting point. While there is some tendency to convergence in the first 25 years of the sample, in the last decade courts increasingly have created idiosyncratic exceptions to the ELR—exceptions adopted in only a few jurisdictions and rejected in others. Moreover, while adherence to the ELR in some form has grown in some states in others it has shrunk. These results are inconsistent with theories of efficient judicial lawmaking as well as with other theories that would predict that laws across states should converge. A tendency of judges to imitate decisions in other jurisdictions, for example, would bias against any finding of nonconvergence.

The ELR in construction deals with the important but fuzzy border between contract and tort, and legal scholars debate which field should cover particular situations in the border region (see Rubin 1993; Edlin and Schwartz 2000). For less controversial doctrines, courts would find it easier to agree on what would be efficient outcomes, and so there would be faster and more complete convergence. But no one doubts that efficiency has *some* domain in law; the interesting question is whether courts can converge to stable rules in the numerous areas of law in which there is room for disagreement about efficiency or equity. The ELR is one such area.

The next section describes the data. In section 3, we present basic trends in the use of exceptions to the ELR by state appellate courts. Section 4 looks behind the trends to ask whether they reflect changes in plaintiffs' claims, the presence of explicit contracts, the economic power of the parties, or leadership by the U.S. Supreme Court. We also check how much variation there is across states.

2 Data

2.1 Overview of the Database

We gathered data on state appellate decisions in all the construction cases involving the ELR that we were able to find, a total of 461 cases (see appendix for details). Even though appellate cases represent a tiny minority of all disputes, they contain the only authoritative statements of legal doctrine. There is no other body of data on which to base a study of the evolution of the rule.[9]

We have read the 461 cases in our sample and extracted our variables from the judicial opinion in each case. We coded the state in which each decision in our sample was rendered, the date of the decision, and the level of the court (whether the state's highest court or a lower appellate court). We did not include information about individual judges. We classified the parties as (1) property owner; (2) builder (such as general contractors and subcontractors); (3) architect, engineer, or inspector; (4) manufacturer; and (5) other (real estate agent, insurance company, or bank). We noted whether the plaintiff and the defendant were parties to a contract and whether any contractual claims were made by the plaintiff (breach of contract, breach of express warranty, or breach of implied warranty), as well as the outcomes of such claims on trial and on appeal.

Our primary interest, however, is in the use of exceptions to the ELR by the court in tort claims. We use data about the specifics of such claims to investigate whether the appellate court applied an exception to the ELR to permit a tort claim to be made. That is a test for adherence to the strict view. The nature of the exceptions applied provides the test for the middle view.[10]

2.2 Coding the Reasons for Not Applying the ELR

The different types of exception are summarized in table 4.1. We recorded only the primary exception to the ELR applied by the court. We distinguish between two categories of exceptions: (1) generally recognized exceptions; and (2) idiosyncratic exceptions. The term "generally recognized exception" means that the exception is found in the vast majority of jurisdictions but does not necessarily mean that all

Table 4.1
Distinction Between Generally Recognized Exceptions and Exceptions That Are Idiosyncratic.

Generally recognized exceptions	• *Other property*
	• *Independent torts*
	• *Generally recognized independent duties*
	  ○ Statutory independent duties
	  ○ Architect's independent duty to a general contractor under the *Restatement on Torts*

Idiosyncratic exceptions	• *Idiosyncratic independent duties*
	  ○ Builders owing an independent duty to property owners
	  ○ Builders owing an independent duty to other builders
	  ○ Architects owing an independent duty to property owners
	  ○ Architects owing an independent duty to subcontractors
	  ○ Manufacturers owing an independent duty to property owners
	• *Other reasons*
	  ○ The plaintiff does not have a contractual remedy
	  ○ The economic loss rule applies only to commercial plaintiffs
	  ○ The economic loss rule does not apply to negligence claims
	  ○ Sudden and calamitous event poses unreasonable risk of injury

cases from all jurisdictions have accepted it.[11] Under the middle view of efficiency, courts should apply only generally recognized exceptions to defeat invocation of the ELR.

There are three kinds of generally recognized exception:

Independent Torts   Intentional wrongdoing is a generally recognized exception to the ELR. For example, when the defendant fraudulently induces the plaintiff to sign a contract, the ELR does not bar him from suing the defendant in tort for fraud.

Other Property   The ELR precludes only recovery of economic loss unaccompanied by any other form of injury. Plaintiffs may be permitted to recover economic loss in tort if they also suffer personal injury or property damage. So if a defective product causes injury to the plaintiff or damage to his property, he can sue in tort for the damage to the defective product itself, invoking the other-property exception.[12]

Generally Recognized Independent Duties Courts have recognized exceptions to ELR when defendants owe a duty that is independent of any contract. Many of these exceptions are idiosyncratic, but two are generally recognized. First, as noted in section 552 of the *Restatement (Second) of Torts*, architects have an independent tort duty to avoid inflicting economic loss on a general contractor. This seems an efficient way of avoiding making architects contract separately with builders when both have already contracted with the owner. Second, several states have imposed statutory duties on these and other participants in construction, thus curtailing the common law ELR. For example, Florida has imposed a number of statutory duties on builders, architects, and inspectors. Section 553.84 of Florida Statutes (1995) provides a cause of action for economic loss when a builder has caused a loss to a property owner by violating a building code or failing to obtain required permits. This duty is independent of any other available ground for a remedy.

Courts have carved out additional exceptions, which we call idiosyncratic, also summarized in table 4.1. These are exceptions peculiar to a few states or not uniformly recognized even within the same state. The label "idiosyncratic" does not refer to innovations as such (as in chapter 3); it merely denotes exceptions rejected by other courts. For each case that we classify as decided on the basis of an idiosyncratic exception, there is a factually similar case in which the ELR was applied.

Most of the idiosyncratic exceptions are independent duties created by courts. A few courts subject builders or architects to a tort duty to property owners or subcontractors. For example, the courts in Colorado have consistently held that builders owe property owners a tort duty independent of the ELR. Most courts, however, have rejected this view, including courts in neighboring Utah.[13] Likewise Virginia does not impose duties on builders toward property owners, while neighboring West Virginia and Maryland do.[14] Sometimes cases recognizing an idiosyncratic exception are inconsistent with other cases in the same state. In an early Illinois case, an architect was held to owe an independent duty to purchasers of residential property, but most Illinois cases apply the ELR in such cases.[15] Similarly, Florida imposed duties to property owners on architects, overturning cases that had held that no such duties existed.[16]

Some courts recognize an exception for cases in which the plaintiff has no contractual remedy, or confine the ELR to commercial but not to residential property owners. These exceptions, which seem motivated by sympathy for harmed plaintiffs seemingly barred by the ELR, are rejected by other courts. It is difficult to reconcile idiosyncratic exceptions with the view that different legal rules are efficient in different states at the same time, or in the same state at different times, since construction is a stable industry, similar across states, with no significant technological change during the period covered by our sample.

Table 4.2 summarizes how we use the exceptions to test our hypotheses. Under the strict view of efficiency, decisions by appellate courts over time should eliminate exceptions. Under the middle view of efficiency, they should eliminate idiosyncratic exceptions but not generally recognized ones.[17] Under the broad view of efficiency, as well as under the hypothesis that the law does not converge to efficiency over time, we should not expect to see systematic diminution in the employment of exceptions.

2.3 Summary of the Data

Cases are not distributed uniformly across the years covered by the dataset, 1970–2005. In some years we have no observations, while the maximum number of cases in one year is 28. Figure 4.1, which plots the number of cases each year, reveals a clear upward trend in appeals cases in which ELR is mentioned. The growth in the number of cases is affected by our search strategy in constructing the dataset. Many construction cases from the 1970s and 1980s do not refer to the ELR explicitly and hence are not included in our sample. The result is to bias the plaintiffs' success rate downward in the early years, since a plaintiff is more likely to have recovered economic

Table 4.2
How We Use the Incidence of Exceptions to Test Our Hypotheses.

Candidate view of efficient rule	Which exceptions are contradictory to this view of efficiency?	What does convergence to the candidate efficient rule look like?
Strict view (Bright-line ELR with no exceptions)	All exceptions	The use of *all exceptions* should be declining over time
Middle view (ELR with generally recognized exceptions)	Idiosyncratic exceptions	The use of *idiosyncratic exceptions* should be declining over time

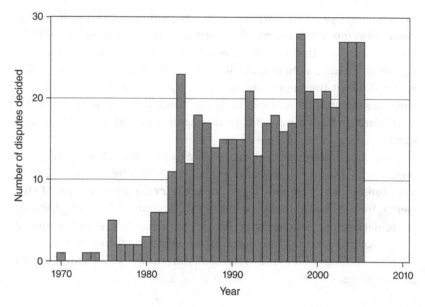

Figure 4.1
Number of cases in each year of our dataset.

damages in a case in which the ELR is not mentioned than in one in which it was.

In the majority of cases, a plaintiff property owner is suing a builder, architect, engineer, inspector, or manufacturer. In 328 cases (71.15 percent), the plaintiff is a property owner. Builders are the only other significant plaintiff category (involved in 25.81 percent of the cases). The most frequent defendants are builders (involved in 34.71 percent of all cases), followed by manufacturers (27.33 percent), architects, engineers, and inspectors (21.04 percent), and property owners (14.32 percent). Table 4.3 summarizes these data.

Table 4.4 summarizes the application of exceptions to the ELR in our 461 cases. Exceptions were applied in 171 cases (37.09 percent). Courts applied generally recognized exceptions to the ELR in 114 of the 171 cases in which an exception was applied (66.67 percent) and idiosyncratic exceptions in the other 57 cases (33.33 percent). The most frequent exceptions are other property (26.31 percent of all cases where an exception was applied by the court), idiosyncratic independent duties (22.81 percent), and independent torts (21.64 percent).

The data on means begin to tell the story of how the ELR has been applied. About 63 percent of the cases apply the ELR and thus bar the

Table 4.3
Breakdown of the Parties to the 461 Disputes.

PLAINTIFF	DEFENDANT				
	Property owner	Builder	Architect, engineer, inspector	Manufacturer	Other	Total
Property owner	46	131	44	98	9	328 (71.15%)
Builder	18	20	53	25	3	119 (25.81%)
Architect, engineer, inspector	1	7	0	1	0	9 (1.95%)
Manufacturer	1	1	0	2	0	4 (0.87%)
Other	0	1	0	0	0	1 (0.22%)
Total	66 (14.32%)	160 (34.71%)	97 (21.04%)	126 (27.33%)	12 (2.60%)	461

Table 4.4
Outcomes of Cases and Frequency of Exceptions.

	Observations
Generally recognized exceptions	
Other property	45
Independent torts	37
Generally recognized independent duties	32
Total generally recognized exceptions	*114*
Idiosyncratic exceptions	
Idiosyncratic independent duties	39
Other reasons	18
Total idiosyncratic exceptions	*57*
Total cases where exceptions used	**171**

plaintiff's tort claims, while in nearly 25 percent a generally recognized exception is applied instead. In the other 12 percent of cases, an idiosyncratic exception is applied. On average, then, the ELR plus its generally recognized exceptions are widely but not universally accepted by state appellate courts. The question arises whether this acceptance has grown over time, which would suggest convergence. If it has grown, what exceptions have declined? If it has not grown, what exceptions are responsible? We address these questions next.

3 Aggregate Outcomes

3.1 Convergence to the "Strict View"
We measure convergence to the strict view by asking: are courts increasingly applying the ELR without exceptions? If the strict view represents the efficient rule and the law converges to efficiency, the application of exceptions should decline over time. Figure 4.2 presents the fraction of cases each year in which exceptions were applied. It reveals a U-shaped pattern: the resort to exceptions declines steadily over the first 20 years of the data but rises in the last decade. The frequency with which claims are rejected based on the ELR rises in the 1970s and 1980s, but falls after the mid-1990s.

There are various ways in which to establish the U shape more formally. A simple quadratic model fitting case outcomes with *time* and *time²* yields statistically significant results. The coefficient on *time* is −3.9453 with a *t*-statistic of −2.80. The coefficient on *time²* is 0.0009 with a *t*-statistic of 2.80. Both are significant at the 1 percent level.

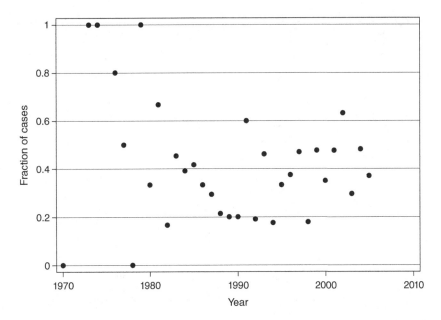

Figure 4.2
Fraction of cases that apply exceptions in each year.

Figure 4.3 shows the trend over time of all 461 observations using Locally Weighted Least Squares (lowess) to fit the curve.[18] The lowess curve suggests that outcomes indeed follow a U-shaped curve over time, with the minimum use of exceptions reached in the early 1990s. We also estimate linear regressions, dividing the sample at various points in the late-1980s or early-1990s. These specifications yield a negative and statistically significant trend in the use of exceptions in the earlier subsample and a positive and statistically significant trend in the later one. These trends show that the law is not converging to the strict view of the ELR—the view that the law should always bar recovery of economic loss in tort. In section 4, we show that the upward trend in the use of exceptions is partially explained by changes in plaintiffs' claims.

3.2   Convergence to the "Middle View"

To examine convergence to the middle view, we ask whether courts are applying exceptions to the ELR that are only generally recognized or whether they are also applying idiosyncratic exceptions. Judges might experiment with many different exceptions to the rule in the early years of our sample. But under the middle view of efficiency, the application

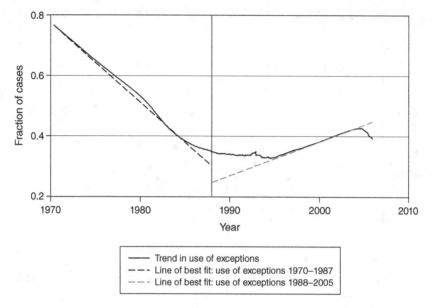

Figure 4.3
Graph illustrating the significance of the downward trend in the use of exceptions from 1970 to 1985 ($t = 1.97$) and the upward trend from 1988 to 2005 ($t = 2.28$). The solid black line is a lowess curve illustrating the trend over time for all 461 observations.

of inefficient idiosyncratic exceptions should decline over time as the efficient ones become generally recognized and the inefficient ones discarded, as the law converges to the efficient rule.

As shown in figure 4.4, the application of both generally recognized and idiosyncratic exceptions trends down in the 1970s and 1980s, except that the number of cases decided on the basis of generally recognized exceptions bottoms out earlier, in the mid-1980s, at about 20 percent of all cases, and then begins rising gently (and not statistically significantly) in the mid-1990s to about 30 percent of all cases, with a decline at the end of the sample period back to 20 percent. Idiosyncratic exceptions fall until the mid-1990s, to about 10 percent of all cases—a testament to apparent convergence to the ELR with generally recognized exceptions—except that they then rise toward the end of the sample period. Both the downward trend before the mid-1990s and the subsequent upward trend in idiosyncratic exceptions are significant.[19]

The real story told by these data is the growth of idiosyncratic exceptions both as a percentage of all cases and as a percentage of all excep-

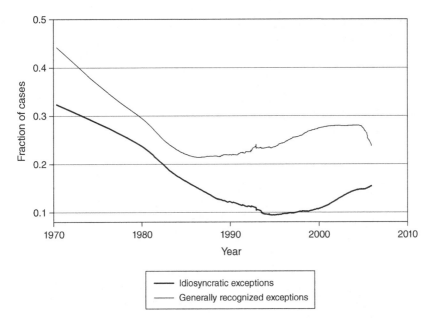

Figure 4.4
Fraction of all cases applying generally recognized exceptions (light gray) and idiosyncratic exceptions (black).

tions in the last decade of the sample. We do not see convergence to ELR with generally recognized exceptions, and we thus reject the middle version of the ELR's efficiency as well as the strict one. Yet, had this chapter been written a decade ago, we would have concluded that the legal rule had converged to nearly universal acceptance of the ELR with generally recognized exceptions. The substantial and statistically significant growth in cases decided in plaintiffs' favor by application of idiosyncratic exceptions in the last decade of the sample precludes such a conclusion today.

We also track instances in which an idiosyncratic exception is recognized and approved by the court but nonetheless is not applied because the plaintiff failed to bring his claim within its scope. There are 61 such cases in our dataset. Including the 57 cases in which idiosyncratic exceptions are applied to defeat the ELR, we have 118 cases (25.60 percent of cases in our dataset) in which idiosyncratic exceptions are recognized as valid. Figure 4.5 shows the trend in recognizing idiosyncratic exceptions, whether or not that exception applied in the case. We find a U-shaped curve in these data as well. The upward trend in

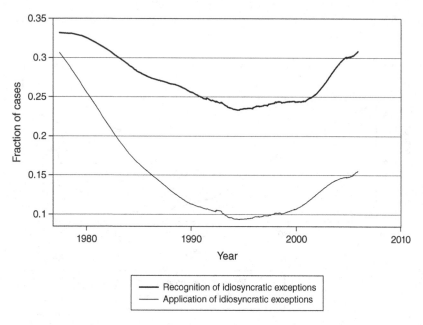

Recognition of idiosyncratic exceptions
Application of idiosyncratic exceptions

Figure 4.5
The fraction of cases where idiosyncratic exceptions were applied (light gray) as well as those cases where idiosyncratic exceptions were recognized as existing in the state, but not applied in the case (black). The light gray line is the same lowess curve as in figure 4.4.

recognition of idiosyncratic exceptions over the period 1995 to 2005 is significant at the 5 percent level ($t = 2.01$). This significant upward trend confirms our conclusion that we have not seen convergence toward the "middle view" of efficiency. The downward trend in the recognition of idiosyncratic exceptions until the mid-1990s is no longer significant. These results are further evidence against convergence to efficiency.

Another way to look at the patterns is by focusing on dissents in judicial opinions; 55 of our 461 cases include at least one dissenting opinion. Overall there is no difference between the frequency of dissents in cases in which the ELR is upheld and cases in which an exception is applied. But in cases in which the court relies on an idiosyncratic exception, the incidence of dissent is, as one would expect, significantly higher, as "idiosyncratic" implies that the law is unsettled. Only ten of the 114 cases in which generally recognized exceptions were applied (8.77 percent) had a dissent, while 11 of the 57 cases in which idiosyncratic exceptions were applied (19.29 percent) had a dissent. This difference is significant at the 5 percent level ($t = 1.99$).

3.3 Summary of Aggregate Outcomes

The evolution of the law reveals some fascinating patterns. The first twenty years after the *Seely* decision—the case that set the law on its modern path—are best described as years of growing acceptance of the ELR, with declining application of either generally recognized or idiosyncratic exceptions. In the final decade of the sample, however, courts moved away from strict application of the doctrine by more frequently applying some of the generally recognized exceptions, such as the independent-tort and other-property exceptions, and some of the idiosyncratic exceptions as well. Courts also increasingly recognized idiosyncratic exceptions in cases in which they nevertheless concluded that the facts do not bring the plaintiff within the scope of one of them. The data reveal no convergence to any rule, let alone an efficient rule under either of our candidate definitions of efficiency.

As noted in the introduction, we cannot reject the hypothesis that judicial decisions are efficient if we adopt a sufficiently broad definition of efficiency, one that allows for the possibility that the law and the facts are more complicated that one can learn from reducing a judicial opinion to a handful of variables. At one level, therefore, what we call the "broad" view of efficiency eludes falsifiability. Suppose there are two cases in two different jurisdictions, and one case applies the ELR, explicitly rejecting an idiosyncratic exception, and the other case rejects it, explicitly endorsing and applying that very exception. Both cannot be efficient at the level of doctrine, though a more searching investigation of each case might show that both outcomes were efficient because of factual differences that the opinions had not used to qualify the scope of the doctrine being applied. However, the fact that dissents are more frequent when idiosyncratic exceptions are applied casts doubt on the hypothesis that those decisions would be seen as efficient if only enough details were known about them.

So what is behind the time patterns we observe: both the convergence toward the ELR in the first 20 years of the sample and the movement away from it afterwards? In the next section we address this question from different perspectives.

4   Behind the Patterns

We try to deepen our understanding of the patterns uncovered in section 3 by examining five aspects of the evolution of the ELR in the construction industry. First, we examine the claims that plaintiffs make and ask whether changes in those claims can explain the patterns of court decisions. We can expect plaintiffs to try new strategies when they encounter barriers to recovery with old ones. Perhaps the movement away from the ELR in later years reflects such adaptation, as plaintiffs discover or invent claims to which courts are more receptive. Second, we examine whether the application of the ELR is influenced by the presence of an explicit contract between the parties, implying that they considered the various risks of their relationship. Third, we investigate the relative economic power of plaintiff and defendant. Judges' sympathy for weaker parties may help explain deviations from the ELR in cases in which plaintiffs have less economic power than defendants. Fourth, we examine judicial leadership. In 1986 the U.S. Supreme Court issued a decision in an admiralty case, *East River*,[20] which broadly endorsed the ELR. Although *East River* did not involve construction and was not binding on state courts applying state law, we can ask whether the decision influenced those courts. Fifth, we examine state variation in decisions. We ask whether the lack of convergence to the ELR is explained by the fact that in many states there are very few appellate cases involving ELR in construction. Perhaps it is those states that account for lack of convergence in the aggregate while the states with the highest caseloads exhibit a greater tendency to convergence.

4.1 Claims

Figure 4.6 graphs the evolution of tort theories advanced by plaintiffs. The proportion of cases in which the plaintiff alleges negligence has been falling (statistically significantly) since the mid-1980s. While claims of strict liability have also trended downward since the beginning of our sample, the trend is significant only in some periods. As the ELR becomes increasingly accepted, plaintiffs are using types of claim less likely to be barred by it. The increase in claims of fraud is marginally significant since the early 1980s, while the increase in claims of negligent misrepresentation over the same period is strongly significant.[21] The increase in claims for "other torts" is significant over the course of our entire sample.[22] We get very similar trends if we look at the claims made in cases in which exceptions were applied, rather than simply looking at all cases.

The change in tort theories can explain some of the increase in the use of generally recognized exceptions—for example, plaintiffs claim fraud and courts are receptive. But the changes do not explain the rise

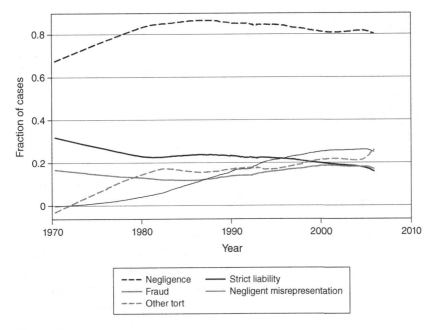

Figure 4.6
Trends in tort theories claimed by plaintiffs.

in idiosyncratic exceptions. It might seem that the increase in applications of idiosyncratic exceptions would stem from plaintiffs basing their claims on new, innovative theories that might persuade the courts to limit the scope of the ELR. This would imply, however, that new and different idiosyncratic exceptions would be applied by courts in the last ten years of our sample. This is not what we observe. Rather, the increase in applications of idiosyncratic exceptions is due to courts embracing exceptions previously considered and rejected by other courts.

4.2   ELR and the Contractual Relationship between Parties
We consider whether judicial application of the ELR depends on whether the parties have an express written contract—thus excluding oral contracts, implied warranties, and contractual rights as a third-party beneficiary of someone else's contract. If the courts want to promote efficiency, they may be more willing to apply the ELR when the parties have defined their relationship in a contract, since the parties presumably have a better idea of the optimal terms of their relationship than a judge would have.

Table 4.5
Breakdown of Incidence of All Exceptions and Incidence of Idiosyncratic Exceptions
Depending On Whether Parties Had an Express Written Contract.

	Cases	Exceptions %	Idiosyncratic %
Parties did not have an express written contract	288	39.27%	14.58%
Parties did have an express written contract	173	33.53%	8.67%

We see in table 4.5 that the percentage of cases that apply exceptions is indeed greater when plaintiffs do not have an express written contract. But the difference is not significant ($t = 1.42$). Courts are, however, significantly more likely to apply idiosyncratic exceptions when the parties do not have a contract ($t = 1.87$). These courts in effect "make" a contract for the plaintiff rather than penalizing him for having failed to negotiate a contract that would have protected him from the loss that he is suing to recover. The reason that some courts are more likely to use idiosyncratic than generally recognized exceptions may be that those courts are not committed to the position that when transaction costs are low, parties should be forced to define their mutual duties in a contract rather than requiring the courts to do so in the name of tort law.

If courts are moving toward efficiency, the incidence of exceptions in those cases where parties have an express written contract should fall over time. The data in figure 4.7 do not support this hypothesis. Both the use of exceptions and the use of idiosyncratic exceptions rise significantly after 1997 when parties have an express contract.

4.3   Relative Economic Power of the Parties

Table 4.6 divides parties into two groups on the basis of rough proxies for economic power. Table 4.7 shows the rate of plaintiff recovery and application of idiosyncratic exceptions for the four types of plaintiff-defendant combinations.

There is no statistically significant difference between the groups in the courts' use of exceptions overall. Courts, however, are more likely to apply an idiosyncratic exception when facing a weak plaintiff and strong defendant (17.64 percent of cases) compared to cases in which both parties are strong (7.43 percent of cases). This difference is highly significant ($t = 2.97$). But the application of idiosyncratic exceptions is

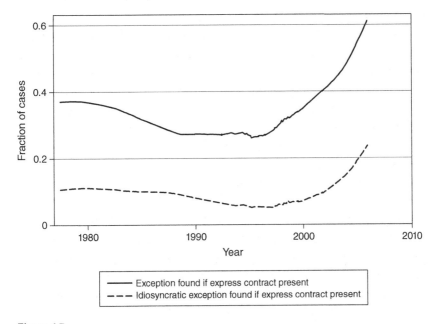

Figure 4.7
Use of exceptions and use of idiosyncratic exceptions when parties have an express contract.

Table 4.6
Broad Division of Parties into "Weak" and "Strong."

Weak parties	Strong parties
• Individual property owners and tenants	• Commercial property owners
• Associations of residents	• Public property owners
• Subcontractors and small builders	• General contractors
	• Developers
	• Architects and engineers
	• Inspectors
	• Manufacturers
	• Suppliers
	• Other parties (banks, insurance companies, real estate agents)

Table 4.7
Breakdown of the Incidence of All Exceptions and the Incidence of Idiosyncratic Exceptions by Relative Economic Power of the Parties.

Relationship	Cases (%)	Exceptions %	Idiosyncratic %
Weak plaintiff–weak defendant	73 (15.84%)	43.86%	12.33%
Weak plaintiff–strong defendant	152 (32.97%)	38.15%	17.64%
Strong plaintiff–weak defendant	34 (7.38%)	35.29%	17.64%
Strong plaintiff–strong defendant	202 (43.82%)	33.66%	7.43%

also higher when courts face a strong plaintiff and a weak defendant (17.64 percent) than when both parties are strong ($t = 1.89$). No other differences are significant. This evidence mildly supports the hypothesis that sympathy moves courts to use idiosyncratic exceptions to help weak plaintiffs.

Multivariate regression analysis confirms the above results, controlling for state- and time-fixed effects. Table 4.8 illustrates that the relative strength of the parties does not significantly affect the application of exceptions overall (specifications (1) through (4)), but it does affect the application of idiosyncratic exceptions. Specifications (5) through (8) indicate that courts are more likely to introduce an idiosyncratic exception when parties do not have an express contract and when the plaintiff is weak.

4.4 The U.S. Supreme Court's Decision in East River

In *East River* (1986), the Supreme Court strongly endorsed the ELR. A plaintiff shipbuilder had a contract with the defendant to design, manufacture, and install turbines for four supertankers. The ships malfunctioned and were damaged, and the plaintiff sought to recover the costs of repair plus income lost while the ships were out of service. The plaintiff initially made claims in both contract and tort; but the contract claims turned out to be barred by the statute of limitations. The negligence claims were rejected by the Supreme Court, which held that customer dissatisfaction with product quality is not a cognizable claim in admiralty tort law. Following the reasoning in *Seely*, the Court held that such claims can be brought only as claims for breach of warranty.

Table 4.8
Multivariate Regression (OIS) Illustrating the Effects of Contractual Relationships Between the Parties and Their Relative Economic Power on the Incidence of All Exceptions and the Incidence of Idiosyncratic Exceptions.

Dependent variable	(1) exception	(2) exception	(3) exception	(4) exception	(5) idiosyn	(6) idiosyn	(7) idiosyn	(8) idiosyn
Express contract	-0.0621	-0.0683	-0.0625	-0.0659	-0.0542*	-0.0660**	-0.0517	-0.0601*
	(0.0475)	(0.0490)	(0.0477)	(0.0492)	(0.0322)	(0.0330)	(0.0323)	(0.0330)
Strong plaintiff	-0.0376	-0.0509	-0.0374	-0.0511	-0.0621**	-0.0788**	-0.0633**	-0.0794**
	(0.0465)	(0.0500)	(0.0466)	(0.0500)	(0.0316)	(0.0337)	(0.0316)	(0.0335)
Strong defendant	-0.0711	-0.0798	-0.0708	-0.0814	-0.0172	-0.0244	-0.0194	-0.0285
	(0.0556)	(0.0563)	(0.0557)	(0.0564)	(0.0377)	(0.0379)	(0.0378)	(0.0378)
State controls	No	Yes	No	Yes	No	Yes	No	Yes
Time controls	No	No	Yes	Yes	No	No	Yes	Yes
Observations	461	461	461	461	461	461	461	461
R^2	0.0096	0.1392	0.0096	0.14	0.0178	0.1587	0.0201	0.1682
F	1.477	1.456*	1.108	1.430*	2.755**	1.698***	2.340**	1.777***

Standard errors in parentheses *** $p < 0.01$, ** $p < 0.05$, * $p < 0.1$

Although the *East River* decision was not binding on state courts, we examine whether it had a significant influence on them in construction cases. Influence is difficult to ascertain here, since, as we showed in section 3, the use of exceptions had been trending down for at least a decade before *East River* and bottomed out later, in the early 1990s. We find no effect of *East River* on the speed of convergence.

Another way to assess influence is by number of citations. Since *East River* denies recovery, we expect that state court decisions that cite *East River* are likely to deny liability. Indeed, 52 of the 68 cases (76.47 percent) in our sample that cite *East River* deny the plaintiff recovery while only 196 of the 310 cases since *East River* that do not cite the case deny recovery (63.22 percent). This difference is significant ($t = 2.17$). Still, one needs to be cautious: cases that cite *East River* may do so as cover, trading on the prestige of the Supreme Court, whereas cases that do not cite *East River* can justify not citing it on the ground that an admiralty case is irrelevant to construction disputes. If this explanation is correct, the citation evidence yields some support for the "legal realist" hypothesis that state courts do what they want and use citations to provide rhetorical support for their conclusions.

While *East River* may have had some influence in consolidating support for the ELR, the proportion of cases citing the decision has fallen since the early 1990s. This trend is significant ($t = -2.24$ for years 1990–2005). We cannot conclude from our data that the U.S. Supreme Court has had a major influence on the state courts' treatment of ELR, at least in the construction industry.

4.5   Variation across States

There is tremendous variation in the application of exceptions across states. Kentucky has *only* cases that apply exceptions to the ELR, while Wyoming, Kansas, Virginia, and Maine have no cases that apply exceptions. We ask whether the use of exceptions can be explained by geographical or economic differences; the answer appears to be no.[23] We ask whether the differences in the use of exceptions can be explained by the methods by which judges are selected and retained that different states employ, and again the answer is no.[24] Nor can the differences in the use of exceptions be explained by differences among judges in political ideology.[25]

Might state courts that have the most experience with the ELR have greater respect for the doctrine? To examine this hypothesis, we focus on the five states with the highest ELR caseloads. The incidence of

Table 4.9
Incidence of All Exceptions and Incidence of Idiosyncratic Exceptions in Five States With Highest Caseloads.

State	Total cases	Exceptions	Exception %	Idiosyncratic	Idiosyncratic %
CA	34	18	52.94	3	8.82
FL	47	19	40.43	3	6.38
OH	32	12	37.50	2	6.25
IL	56	18	32.14	4	7.14
NY	44	7	15.91	2	4.55
Total	213	74	34.74	14	6.57

exceptions turns out to vary greatly in these states (see table 4.9). New York is very strict on plaintiffs, applying exceptions to the ELR in a mere 15.91 percent of cases, while California is far more lenient (52.94 percent).[26]

Not only do the averages differ greatly across the five busiest states, but so do the trends among the five states (figure 4.8). The application of exceptions in California is high on average but significantly decreasing over time ($t = -2.62$), while the application of exceptions in New York and Illinois is considerably less frequent but becoming more so. In Florida there has been a highly significant increase in the application of exceptions since the early 1980s ($t = 3.49$).

Across all states in our sample, the incidence of exceptions is not significantly correlated with the number of cases decided in a state. The proportion of cases that apply *idiosyncratic* exceptions is, however, correlated with caseload. A simple linear regression indicates that states with higher caseloads use idiosyncratic exceptions less frequently ($t = -2.85$). This negative relationship is even stronger in the cases that recognize, without necessarily applying, idiosyncratic exceptions ($t = -3.41$). The implication is that idiosyncratic exceptions are more likely to be applied when courts have less experience with the ELR in construction cases. This hypothesis is further supported by a comparison of the first ten decisions heard in each state with the subsequent decisions in those states (restricting the sample to those states that hear more than ten cases). The early cases are significantly more likely both to apply idiosyncratic exceptions ($t = 2.56$) and to recognize them ($t = 2.53$) than the later cases.

The punch line of this analysis is that light ELR caseloads in some states might explain why we have not seen stronger national

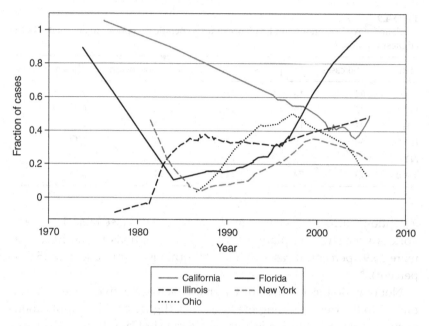

Figure 4.8
Use of exceptions over time in the five states with the highest caseloads.

convergence to the ELR, and more specifically why we have seen an increase in the application of idiosyncratic exceptions in the past decade. Although the ELR is widely accepted, the law has not come to a rest and courts in different states continue experimenting, often in ways inconsistent with the ELR and its generally recognized exceptions. Experience slows this experimentation, but does not stop it.

The increase in the application of idiosyncratic exceptions is not limited to states with low caseloads. In fact, 76 percent of the cases that apply idiosyncratic exceptions since 1997 have come from states with ten or more cases. Wisconsin (the state with the sixth highest caseload) has seen a sharp rise in cases decided by the application of idiosyncratic exceptions. Four of the five largest states have applied an idiosyncratic exception in the last six years of our sample. Thus, even in busy states we see an increasing tendency of courts to apply idiosyncratic exceptions to the ELR.

5   Conclusion

Over the 35 years covered by our study, the ELR has evolved in a way that cannot be easily described as convergence to efficiency. While over the first quarter century the law moved significantly toward adopting the ELR with generally recognized exceptions, over the last decade it has moved away from this equilibrium. Had we written this paper ten years ago, we would have found the law converging to ELR with generally recognized exceptions, but the law moved away from that rule afterward with no changes in the economic environment to explain the movement. Moreover, the law has evolved very differently in different states, which is inconsistent with efficiency in the absence of evidence of relevant economic differences in construction disputes across states.

The lack of convergence does not mean that judicial behavior is random or that the law is entirely unpredictable. The lack of *nationwide* convergence is consistent with settled law in individual states. And on average in our sample, courts applied the ELR with generally recognized exceptions about 88 percent of the time, although in about 15 percent of these cases the courts accepted the validity of idiosyncratic exceptions but did not think the facts warranted their application. Overall, idiosyncratic exceptions were recognized by appellate courts in about 25 percent of cases. But many states are increasingly applying idiosyncratic exceptions to limit the ELR, and the amount of appellate litigation involving the ELR in construction disputes is growing. These are not signs of the law settling down.

Some additional evidence developed in this study sheds light on how legal evolution works. Plaintiffs' claims respond to what courts are receptive to, such as claims of fraud. But that is not the whole story. The key reason for nonconvergence is that courts distinguish earlier cases and create idiosyncratic exceptions to the prevailing legal doctrine that other courts reject. In the last decade covered by our study, courts increasingly applied such exceptions even when the parties had express contracts and so might have been thought unsympathetic tort claimants.

Idiosyncratic exceptions differ across states, with many states going in their own direction. State courts at first responded to a nonbinding 1986 U.S. Supreme Court ruling embracing the bright-line ELR in an admiralty case, but its influence declined over time. There is evidence that state courts with heavier caseloads in this area of litigation are more likely to converge to the adoption of the ELR with generally recognized exceptions, but even in those states there is residual uncertainty.

We conclude that appellate courts exercise a significant amount of discretion in deciding cases, leaving the law far from certain even after three and a half decades of evolution. The deviations from efficiency do not disappear over time. There may be evolutionary benefits of such legal flexibility, but the hypothesis that, in commercial fields, the common law is predictable and efficient, or at least is moving there, is not supported by our study. It would be illuminating, in this regard, to examine legal evolution in other areas of law; we would expect the pressures for efficiency outside the purely economic environments such as construction to be weaker.

Appendix: Construction of the Database

All data were obtained from the LexisNexis "Construction" library. To find the cases, we searched the library for state appeals court cases decided prior to December 31, 2005, that satisfy the following criteria: (1) the phrase "economic loss" is found in either the Overview or the Core Terms; and (2) any of the following terms—"contract," "agree," or "warrant"—are found in the Overview or the Core Terms. The Overview is a summary of the case of approximately 150 to 200 words. The Core Terms is a list of 30 to 50 key terms that appear in the decision. This search strategy captures all state appeals cases from the construction industry where the ELR defense is raised by defense lawyers. No issue of different coverage periods for different states arises in our sample period.

This search yielded 1,171 cases. Of these, 209 were not appellate cases and so were dropped, and another four were not from state courts. Another 496 cases were excluded as irrelevant because the *LexisNexis* Construction library turns out to include cases that do not pertain to construction. In 50 cases, more than one dispute is addressed on appeal. For example, a plaintiff may bring claims against the general contractor and subcontractors in one case. When the plaintiff brings different claims against the two defendants and both claims are being heard on appeal, we divide the case into two distinct observations. When the plaintiff brings claims against multiple defendants but the appeal addresses only one of them, it is left as one observation. We have 46 cases that give rise to two observations and four cases that give rise to three observations; the other 412 cases involve single claims decided on appeal. Of the 516 individual disputes thus coded, 39 do not involve tort claims and another 16 involve tort claims that were not appealed. After removing these 55 disputes, we have our sample of 461 observations.

5   Courts

with Simeon Djankov, Rafael La Porta, and
Florencio Lopez-de-Silanes

1   Introduction

A fundamental proposition in economics holds that the security of
property and the enforcement of contracts are essential for investment,
trade, and ultimately economic growth to come about (Montesquieu
1748; Smith 1776). Many institutions serve to secure property and
enforce contracts. Some of them are entirely private, such as reputations and informal discussions among neighbors, and do not rely on
the government (Macaulay 1963; Galanter 1981; Ellickson 1991). Other
institutions securing property and enforcing contracts, such as regulators and courts, are governmental. Regulatory agencies restrict private
conduct that might adversely influence others, and courts resolve property and contractual disputes.

Economic theory does not tell us which of these mechanisms of
securing property and enforcing contracts is the best, and in reality they
are all far from perfect. Private security and enforcement, while working
well in some environments, often degenerate into violence. Indeed,
Smith (1776) saw "a tolerable administration of justice" as one of the
few proper functions of government, enabling an ordinary citizen to
seek justice against richer and more powerful offenders who control
private enforcement. Public regulation, likewise, while sometimes
effective, is often corrupted and "captured" by the very violators, such
as monopolists and pollutants, it needs to restrain (Stigler 1971). Economists have been generally most optimistic about courts as the institution securing property and enforcing contracts (Coase 1960), and with
few exceptions (e.g., Johnson, McMillan, and Woodruff 2002; Bianco,
Japelli, and Pagano 2001) have devoted little attention to analyzing
their limitations. From the point of view of evaluating alternative institutional arrangements, however, it is crucial to understand the factors
that make courts function more or less effectively.

In this paper, we present an empirical study of the effectiveness of courts as mechanisms of resolving simple disputes in 109 countries. We examine how a plaintiff can use an official court to evict a non-paying tenant and to collect a bounced check. We find that even these simple disputes are resolved extremely slowly by courts in most countries, taking an average of over 200 days. We also find huge variation among countries in the speed and quality of courts.

We try to explain this variation from the perspective of three broad theories. The "development" theory holds that courts, like many other institutions, work better in countries that have richer and more educated populations (Demsetz 1967; North 1981). According to this theory, there are fixed costs of setting up institutions, which only become socially worth paying once the demand for them—largely driven by the level of economic development—becomes high enough. A poor society may rely on informal dispute resolution; a richer one relies on more complex contracts and needs courts to resolve disputes. Similarly, a better educated population both raises the efficiency of courts (if human capital is an input) and the demand for them.

The "incentive" theory holds that the efficiency of courts is shaped by the incentives of the participants in dispute resolution, including the judges, the lawyers, and the litigants (Messick 1999; Buscaglia and Dakolias 1999). According to this theory, courts work poorly when the participants have weak or wrong incentives: judges do not care about delays, lawyers are paid to prolong proceedings, and defendants seek to avoid judgment. The implication is that factors such as mandatory deadlines for judges, contingency fees for attorneys, and "loser pays" rules improve court performance.

The third theory—which is more novel and central to this paper—is that performance of courts is determined by how the law regulates their operation, what we call procedural formalism or formalism for short. The main contribution of this paper is to explain theoretically and to measure empirically the determinants of procedural formalism, as well as to assess its consequences for the quality of dispute resolution in courts.

In a theoretical model of an ideal court, a dispute between two neighbors can be resolved by a third on fairness grounds, with little knowledge or use of law, no lawyers, no written submissions, no procedural constraints on how evidence, witnesses, and arguments are presented, and no appeal (Shapiro 1981). Yet in reality, all legal systems heavily regulate dispute resolution: they rely on lawyers and professional judges, regiment the steps that the disputants must follow, regulate the collection and presentation of the evidence, insist on legal justification of claims and judges' decisions, give predominance to written submissions, and so on. We examine the reasons for procedural formalism, as well as its consequences for the performance of courts.

To this end, in cooperation with Lex Mundi, the largest international association of law firms, we describe the exact procedures used to resolve two specific disputes in 109 countries. These are the eviction of a residential tenant for non-payment of rent and the collection of a check returned for non-payment. We describe the cases to a law firm in each country in great detail, and ask for a complete write-up of the legal procedures necessary to dispute these cases in court and the exact articles of the law governing these procedures. We use the responses to construct measures of formalism, defined as the extent to which regulation causes dispute resolution to deviate from the neighbor model.

Research in comparative law and legal history suggests that formalism varies systematically among legal origins (Berman 1983; Merryman 2007; Damaska 1986; Schlesinger et al. 1988). In particular, civil law countries generally regulate dispute resolution, including the conduct of the adjudicators, more heavily than do common law countries. Our data provide a striking empirical confirmation of this proposition. Legal origins alone explain around 40 percent of the variation in our measures of formalism among 109 countries. We also find that adjudication is more formalized in the less developed than in the rich countries.

We next turn to the three hypotheses on the determinants of judicial quality. From the participating law firms, we obtain estimates of the expected duration of our two disputes in calendar days, from the original filing of a complaint to the ultimate enforcement of judgment. In addition, we use assessments of judicial quality from other data sources, covering such areas as enforceability of contracts, access to justice, and corruption, as well as data from the World Business Environment Survey of small firms on the fairness, consistency, honesty, and other aspects of the legal system. We also collect data on per capita income and educational level in each country, as well as several measures of incentives facing judges, attorneys, and litigants.

We find that *ceteris paribus* higher procedural formalism is a strong predictor of longer duration of dispute resolution. Higher formalism also predicts lower enforceability of contracts, higher corruption, as well as lower honesty, consistency, and fairness of the system. The results hold for both eviction and check collection. In our data, there is no evidence that formalism secures justice.

We also find some evidence consistent with the development hypothesis, namely that countries with richer populations have higher quality courts. On the other hand, we find almost no evidence that the incentives of the participants in the legal system influence its quality. Our findings advance the previous research in three distinct ways. First, the paper takes the research on the quantitative measurement of institutions in a new direction: the study of courts. Finding objective measures of institutional structure is sometimes more useful than just focusing on survey assessments of quality, as is often done, because it may point to the specific directions of efficiency-improving reform. Second, with respect to the study of courts, the paper is novel in attributing both their efficiency and their ability to deliver justice to the characteristics of the legal procedure, rather than to general underdevelopment of the country or to poor incentives. Third, the paper links both the lack of efficiency of courts and their inability to deliver justice to the transplantation of legal systems. As such, it supports the hypothesis that transplantation is in part responsible for the structure and quality of the existing institutions.

2 Theories of Procedural Formalism

According to Shapiro (1981), the essence of an idealized universal court is the resolution of a dispute among two neighbors by a third, guided by common sense and custom. Such resolution does not rely on formal law and does not circumscribe the procedures that the neighbors employ to address their differences. Yet courts everywhere deviate from this ideal. They employ professional judges and lawyers to resolve disputes. They heavily regiment procedures, restricting how claims and counter-claims are presented, how evidence is interpreted, and how various parties communicate with each other. Rather than holding an informal meeting, many courts assemble written records of the proceedings, and allow disputants to appeal the decisions of a judge. Most jurisdictions, in short, heavily regulate their civil procedures.

The reasons for regulating dispute resolution are similar to those for regulation in general: the sovereign may wish to control the outcome. He may wish to punish some conduct to a greater extent than a judge-neighbor would, to establish precedents, or to reduce errors relative to informal adjudication. He may also wish that disputes be resolved in a consistent way across his domains, so as to promote trade or political uniformity. Finally, he may wish disputes to be resolved so as to favor himself and his political supporters, or to punish his enemies and opponents. To achieve these goals, sovereigns regulate the judicial procedure so that "judges are no more than the mouth that pronounces the words of the law, mere passive beings, incapable of moderating either its force or rigour" (Montesquieu [1748] 1984, p. 194).

A further reason to regulate dispute resolution is that informal triad justice is vulnerable to subversion by the powerful. If one of the two disputants is economically or politically more powerful than the other, he can encourage the supposedly impartial judge to favor him, using either bribes or threats. The other side of this coin is access to justice: the less advantaged members of a society must expect justice rather than abuse from the state or powerful opponents. As the great German jurist Rudolf von Jhering exclaimed, "form is the sworn enemy of arbitrary rule, the twin sister of liberty" (1898, p. 471).

For these, and possibly other reasons, most jurisdictions in the world heavily formalize legal procedures. Moreover, as legal historians clearly recognize, patterns of such regulation are intimately related to the civil versus common law origin of the country's laws. These legal families originate in Roman and English law respectively, and were transplanted to many countries through conquest and colonization (by France, Germany, and Spain in the case of civil law and England in the case of common law). Although legal systems of most countries have evolved since colonial times, key features of legal origin are often preserved through the centuries (La Porta et al. 1998, 1999).

There are different theories of how legal origin has shaped legal procedure in general and formalism in particular. Hayek (1960) and Merryman (2007) attribute the differences to the ideas of the Enlightenment and the French Revolution. In France, the revolutionaries and Napoleon did not trust the judges, and codified judicial procedures in order to control judicial discretion. According to Schlesinger et al. (1988), in civil law countries "the procedural codes are meant to be essentially all-inclusive statements of judicial powers, remedies, and procedural devices." Consistent with von Jhering's logic, procedural formalism was seen as a guarantee of freedom. In England and the United States, in contrast, lawyers and judges were on the "right" side of the revolutions, and hence the political process accommodated a great deal more judicial independence. In the common law tradition, "a code is supplemental to the unwritten law, and in construing its provisions and filling its gaps, resort must be had to the common law" (Schlesinger et al. 1988). As a consequence, less formalism is required in the judicial procedure.

Dawson (1960), Berman (1983), Damaska (1986), and chapter 8 argue that the procedural differences between common and civil law actually go back to the twelfth and thirteenth centuries. Chapter 8 attributes greater formalism to the need to protect law enforcers from coercion by disputing parties through violence and bribes. This risk of coercion was greater in the less peaceful France than in the more peaceful England, where neighborly dispute resolution by juries (coming closer to Shapiro's ideal) was more feasible. The different approaches to legal procedure—motivated by the different law and order environments of England and France—were then transplanted through conquest and colonization to most of the rest of the world (Watson 1974; La Porta et al. 1998; Berkowitz et al. 2003).

The fact that most countries inherited significant parts of their legal procedures—often involuntarily—is important for our analysis. The nature of transplantation enables us to distinguish two hypotheses. If countries select their legal procedures voluntarily, then one can argue that greater formalism is an efficient adaptation to a weaker law and order environment. If, however, legal procedures are transplanted through conquest or colonization, the efficient adaptation model does not apply. Rather, we can attribute the consequences of legal formalism to the exogenously determined features of the legal procedure, and in this way consider the efficiency of alternative rules.

3   Data

3.1   Collection Procedures
Our data are derived from questionnaires answered by attorneys at Lex Mundi and Lex Africa member firms. Lex Mundi and Lex Africa are international associations of law firms, which include as their members law firms with offices in 115 countries. Of these 115 countries, Lex Mundi members in six did not accept our invitation to join the project, and these six jurisdictions (Burkina Faso, Cambodia, Nicaragua, Northern Ireland, Scotland, St. Kitts, and Nevis) were removed

from the sample. We have received and codified data from all the others.

The 109 cooperating law firms received a questionnaire designed by the authors with the advice of practicing attorneys from Argentina, Belgium, Botswana, Colombia, Mexico, and the United States. The questionnaire covered the step-by-step evolution of an eviction and a check collection procedure before local courts in the country's largest city. The focus on these two specific disputes has a number of advantages. First, they represent typical situations of default on an everyday contract in virtually every country. The adjudication of such cases illustrates the enforcement of property rights and private contracts in a given legal environment. Second, the case facts and procedural assumptions could be tailored to make the cases comparable across countries. Third, the resolution of these cases involves lower level civil trial courts in all countries (unless Alternative Dispute Resolution is used). Because these are the courts whose functioning is most relevant to many of a country's citizens, the focus on the quality of such courts is appropriate in a development context. For more complex disputes, additional issues arise, and it may not be appropriate to generalize our findings. For example, commercial arbitration is available in many countries to large companies, though not to ordinary citizens. Perhaps even more importantly, formalism may be essential for justice in complex disputes even when informality is adequate for the simple cases we consider.

In presenting the cases, we provided the respondent firm with significant detail, including the amount of the claim, the location and main characteristics of the litigants, the presence of city regulations, the nature of the remedy requested by the plaintiff, the merit of the plaintiff's and the defendant's claims, and the social implications of the judicial outcomes. Furthermore, to understand how courts work, we specified that there is no settlement. These standardized details enabled the respondent law firms to describe the procedures explicitly and in full detail, and allowed us to get around the problem that different procedures arise in different circumstances.[1]

The questionnaires provided to law firms were divided into two parts: (1) description of the procedure of the hypothetical case step by step, and (2) multiple choice questions. The following aspects of the procedure were covered: (1) step-by-step description of the procedure, (2) estimates of the actual duration at each stage, (3) indication of whether written submissions were required at each stage, (4) indication of specific laws applicable at each stage, (5) indication of mandatory time limits at each stage, (6) indication of the form of the appeal, and (7) the existence of alternative administrative procedures. Multiple-choice questions were used both to collect additional information and to check the answers at the initial stage. In addition, we asked questions about the incentives of judges, attorneys, and the litigants.

At each firm, the answers were prepared by a member of the Litigation Department, and reviewed by a member of the General Corporate and Commercial Department. Two lawyers in each law firm, from different departments, were required to read, approve, and sign the questionnaire. As an additional check, the law firms were required to indicate when a particular law governed the relevant stage of the procedure, and to provide a copy of that law. The answers provided by member law firms were coded using the descriptions of the procedures and answers to multiple-choice questions. In most cases, coding was followed by an additional round of questions to the completing attorneys aimed to clarify the inconsistencies in their answers.

3.2 Measuring Formalism
Comparative law textbooks and manuals of civil procedure point to several areas where the laws of different countries regulate dispute resolution differently. In our choice of the areas of such regulation, we were guided by the 1994 *International Encyclopaedia of Laws: Civil Procedure* published by Kluwer Law International. The *Encyclopaedia* covers 17 countries from different legal origins, and discusses such broad areas of civil procedure as judicial organization, jurisdiction, actions and claims, nature of proceedings, legal costs, evidence, enforcement of judgments, and arbitration. Some of the areas covered in the *Encyclopaedia* were not relevant to the simple disputes we considered. Others, such as Alternative Dispute Resolution, are covered briefly in our survey, although we focus on courts.

We focus on seven areas of formalism, and codify the answers provided by Lex Mundi firms from the perspective of the neighbor model. Below, we briefly describe our approach to organizing these data. The exact definitions of the variables are contained in table 5.1.

The first area covers the required degree of professionalism of the main actors in the judicial process, namely judges and lawyers. This covers three specific areas. First, a basic jurisdictional distinction is between general and specialized courts. For the simple cases we consider, access to specialized courts generally entails procedural simplification aimed at "mass production" (similar to traffic courts in the U.S.). We therefore take the resolution of disputes in specialized courts to be closer to the neighbor model than that in a general jurisdiction court.

Second, we distinguish between judges who have undergone complete professional training, and arbitrators, administrative officers, practicing attorneys, merchants, or any other lay persons who may be authorized to hear or decide the case. In some countries (e.g., New Zealand, United Arab Emirates) all disputes between landlords and tenants are resolved by housing tribunals composed of neighbors or by representatives of associations of landlords and tenants. Such nonprofessional judges are closer to the neighbor model.

Third, in some countries it is mandatory to have an attorney to appear before the judge, while in others it is entirely voluntary or even prohibited. Evidently, the absence of legal representation is closer to the neighbor model. Indeed, in the absence of such representation, the judge frequently assumes the position of a mediator guiding the parties to an agreement.

Using the data provided by law firms, we combine these three pieces of information to construct the "professional versus laymen" index for each of the two disputes for each country.

The second area we consider is the preeminence of written versus oral presentation at each stage of the procedure, including filing, service of process, defendant's opposition, evidence, final arguments, judgment, notification of judgment, and enforcement of judgment. We take oral presentation to be closer to the neighbor model, and aggregate this information for each country and each case into the index of "written versus oral" elements.

The third area is the need for legal justification (meaning reference to the legal reasons and articles of the law) in the complaint and in the judgment, as well as the necessity of basing the judgment in the law as opposed to equity. In many countries, a judgment must be justified by statutory law or settled precedents. In other countries, judgment must still be justified, but in equity rather than in law. In still other countries, judicial decisions require no justification whatsoever. Since the neighbor model presumably does not call for such legal justifications, we aggregate this information into an index of "legal justification."

Table 5.1
Description of the Variables.
This table describes the variables in the paper. Unless otherwise specified, the source for the variables is the survey to law firms and the laws of each country.

Variable	Description
Professionals vs. laymen	
General jurisdiction court	The variable measures whether a court of general jurisdiction or a court of limited jurisdiction would be chosen or assigned to hear and decide the case under normal circumstances. For the purposes of this study, we define a court of general jurisdiction as a state institution, recognized by the law as part of the regular court system, generally competent to hear and decide regular civil or criminal cases. A limited jurisdiction court is defined as a court that would hear and decide only some type of civil cases, which encompasses specialized debt-collection or housing courts, small-claims courts, and arbitrators or justices of the peace. The variable equals 1 for a court of general jurisdiction, and 0 for a court of limited jurisdiction.
Professional vs. non-professional judge	The variable measures whether the judge, or the members of the court or tribunal, could be considered as professional judges or not. A professional judge would be a judge who has undergone a complete professional training to this effect as required by law, and whose primary activity is to act as judge or member of a court. A non-professional judge would be an arbitrator, administrative officer, practicing attorney or merchant, or any other layperson that may be authorized to hear and decide the case. The variable equals 1 for a professional judge and 0 for a non-professional judge.
Legal representation is mandatory	The variable measures whether for the case provided the law requires the intervention of a licensed attorney. The variable equals 1 when legal representation is mandatory, and 0 when legal representation is not mandatory.
Index: Professionals vs. laymen	The index measures whether the resolution of the case provided would rely mostly in the intervention of professional judges and attorneys, as opposed to the intervention of other types of adjudicators and lay people. The index is formed by the normalized sum of the following variables: (i) general jurisdiction court, (ii) professional vs. non-professional judge, and (iii) legal representation is mandatory. The index ranges from 0 to 1, where higher values mean a higher intervention of professionals.

Table 5.1
(continued)

Variable	Description
Written vs. oral elements	
Filing	The variable equals 1 if the complaint normally has to be submitted in written form to court, and 0 if it can be presented orally.
Service of process	The variable equals 1 if the defendant's first official notice on the complaint content is most likely received in writing, and 0 otherwise.
Opposition	The variable equals 1 if under normal circumstances the defendant's answer to the complaint should be submitted in writing, and 0 if it may be presented orally to court.
Evidence	The variable equals 1 if evidence is mostly submitted to the court in written form, in form of attachments, affidavits, or otherwise, and equals 0 if most of the evidence, included documentary evidence, is presented at oral hearings before the judge.
Final arguments	The variable equals 1 if final arguments on the case would normally be submitted in writing, and 0 if on the contrary they would likely be presented orally at court before the judge.
Judgment	The variable equals 1 if the final decision for the case is adopted and issued by the judge in written form, and 0 if, on the contrary, it is adopted and issued by the judge in open court at an audience attended by the parties. The defining factor is whether the judge normally decides the case at the hearing or not. Therefore, if the judge at the hearing simply reads out the content of a previously adopted written decision, the variable equals 1, and conversely, an orally adopted judgment that is later transposed into writing for enforcement purposes would still be considered as orally issued and score 0.
Notification of judgment	The variable equals 1 if normally the parties receive their first notice of the content of the final decision in written form, either by notice mailed to them, publication in a court board or gazette, or through any other written means. The variable equals 0 if they receive their first notice in an open court hearing attended by them.
Enforcement of judgment	The variable equals 1 if the enforcement procedure is mostly carried out through the compliance of written court orders or written acts by the enforcement authority, and 0 otherwise.

Table 5.1
(continued)

Variable	Description
Index: Written vs. oral elements	The index measures the written or oral nature of the actions involved in the procedure, from the filing of the complaint, until the actual enforcement. The index is calculated as the number of stages carried out mostly in a written form over the total number of applicable stages, and it ranges from 0 to 1, where higher values mean higher prevalence of written elements.
Legal justification	
Complaint must be legally justified	The variable measures whether the complaint is required, by law or court regulation, to include references to the applicable laws, legal reasoning, or formalities that would normally call for legal training. The variable equals 1 for a legally justified complaint, and 0 when the complaint does not require legal justification (specific articles of the law or case-law).
Judgment must be legally justified	The variable measures whether the judgment must expressly state the legal justification (articles of the law or case-law) for the decision. The variable equals 1 for a legally justified judgment, and 0 otherwise.
Judgment must be on law (not on equity)	The variable measures whether the judgment may be motivated on general equitable arguments, or if it must be founded on the law. The variable equals 1 when judgment must be on law only, and 0 when judgment may be based on equity grounds.
Index: Legal justification	The index measures the level of legal justification required in the process. The index is formed by the normalized sum of the following variables: (i) complaint must be legally justified, (ii) judgment must be legally justified, and (iii) judgment must be on law (not on equity). The index ranges from 0 to 1, where higher values mean a higher use of legal language or justification.
Statutory regulation of evidence	
Judge cannot introduce evidence	The variable equals 1 if, by law, the judge cannot freely request or take evidence that has not been requested, offered, or introduced by the parties, and 0 otherwise.
Judge cannot reject irrelevant evidence	The variable equals 1 if, by law, the judge cannot refuse to collect or admit evidence requested by the parties, even if she deems it irrelevant to the case, and 0 otherwise.
Out-of-court statements are inadmissible	The variable equals 1 if statements of fact that were not directly known or perceived by the witness, but only heard from a third person, may not be admitted as evidence. The variable equals 0 otherwise.

Table 5.1
(continued)

Variable	Description
Mandatory pre-qualification of questions	The variable equals 1 if, by law, the judge must prequalify the questions before they are asked to the witnesses, and 0 otherwise.
Oral interrogation only by judge	The variable equals 1 if parties and witnesses can only be orally interrogated by the judge, and 0 if they can be orally interrogated by the judge and the opposing party.
Only original documents and certified copies are admissible	The variable equals 1 if only original documents and "authentic"or "certified"copies are admissible documentary evidence, and 0 if simple or uncertified copies are admissible evidence as well.
Authenticity and weight of evidence defined by law	The variable equals 1 if the authenticity and probative value of documentary evidence is specifically defined by the law. The variable equals 0 if all admissible documentary evidence is freely weighted by the judge.
Mandatory recording of evidence	The variable equals 1 if, by law, there must be a written or magnetic record of all evidence introduced at trial, and 0 otherwise.
Index: Statutory regulation of evidence	The index measures the level of statutory control or intervention of the administration, admissibility, evaluation and recording of evidence. The index is formed by the normalized sum of the following variables: (i) judge cannot introduce evidence, (ii) judge cannot reject irrelevant evidence, (iii) out-of-court statements are inadmissible, (iv) mandatory prequalification of questions, (v) oral interrogation only by judge, (vi) only original documents and certified copies are admissible, (vii) authenticity and weight of evidence defined by law, and (viii) mandatory recording of evidence. The index ranges from 0 to 1, where higher values mean a higher statutory control or intervention.
Control of superior review	
Enforcement of judgment is automatically suspended until resolution of appeal	The variable equals 1 if the enforcement of judgment is automatically suspended until resolution of the appeal, when a request for appeal is granted. The variable equals 0 if the suspension of the enforcement of judgment is not automatic, or if the judgment cannot be appealed at all.
Comprehensive review in appeal	The variable equals 1 if both issues of law and issues of fact (evidence) can be reviewed by the appellate court. The variable equals 0 if only new evidence, or only issues of law can be reviewed in appeal, or if judgment cannot be appealed.

Table 5.1
(continued)

Variable	Description
Interlocutory appeals are allowed	The variable equals 1 if interlocutory appeals are allowed, and 0 if they are always prohibited. Interlocutory appeals are defined as appeals against interlocutory or interim judicial decisions made during the course of a judicial proceeding in first instance and before final ruling on the entire case.
Index: Control of superior review	The index measures the level of control or intervention of the appellate court's review of the first-instance judgment. The index is formed by the normalized sum of the following variables: (i) enforcement of judgment is automatically suspended until resolution of appeal, (ii) comprehensive review in appeal, and (iii) interlocutory appeals are allowed. The index ranges from 0 to 1, where higher values mean a higher control or intervention.

Engagement formalities

Mandatory pretrial conciliation	The variable equals 1 if the law requires plaintiff to attempt a pretrial conciliation or mediation before filing the lawsuit, and 0 otherwise.
Service of process by judicial officer required	The variable equals 1 if the law requires the complaint to be served to the defendant through the intervention of a judicial officer, and 0 if service of process may be accomplished by other means.
Notification of judgment by judicial officer required	The variable equals 1 if the law requires the judgment to be notified to the defendant through the intervention of a judicial officer, and 0 if notification of judgment may be accomplished by other means.
Index: Engagement formalities	The index measures the formalities required to engage someone into the procedure or to hold him/her accountable of the judgment. The index is formed by the normalized sum of the following variables: (i) mandatory pretrial conciliation, (ii) service of process by judicial officer required, and (iii) notification of judgment by judicial officer required. The index ranges from 0 to 1, where higher values mean a higher statutory control or intervention in the judicial process.

Independent procedural actions

Filing and service	The variable equals the total minimum number of independent procedural actions required to complete the following stages of the process: filing, admission, attachment, and service.

Table 5.1
(continued)

Variable	Description
Trial and judgment	The variable equals the total minimum number of independent procedural actions required to complete the following stages of the process: opposition to the complaint, hearing or trial, evidence, final arguments, and judgment.
Enforcement	The variable equals the total minimum number of independent procedural actions required to complete the following stages of the process: notification of judgment and enforcement of judgment.
Index: Independent procedural actions	An independent procedural action is defined as a step of the procedure, mandated by law or court regulation, that demands interaction between the parties or between them and the judge or court officer (e.g., filing a motion, attending a hearing, mailing a letter, or seizing some goods). We also count as an independent procedural action every judicial or administrative writ or resolution (e.g., issuing judgment or entering a writ of execution) which is legally required to advance the proceedings until the enforcement of judgment. Actions are always assumed to be simultaneous if possible, so procedural events that may be fulfilled in the same day and place are only counted as one action. To form the index, we: (1) add the minimum number of independent procedural actions required to complete all the stages of the process (from filing of lawsuit to enforcement of judgment); and (2) normalize this number to fall between 0 and 1 using the minimum and the maximum number of independent procedural actions across the countries in the sample. The index takes a value of 0 for the country with the minimum number of independent procedural actions, and a value of 1 for the country with the maximum number of independent procedural actions.

Formalism index	
Formalism index	*The index measures substantive and procedural statutory intervention in judicial cases at lower-level civil trial courts, and is formed by adding up the following indices: (i) professionals vs. laymen, (ii) written vs. oral elements, (iii) legal justification, (iv) statutory regulation of evidence, (v) control of superior review, (vi) engagement formalities, and (vii) independent procedural actions. The index ranges from 0 to 7, where 7 means a higher level of control or intervention in the judicial process.*

Table 5.1
(continued)

Variable	Description
Incentives of parties	
Mandatory time limit for admission	The variable equals 1 if the judge is required by law to admit or reject the lawsuit within a certain period of time, and 0 otherwise.
Mandatory time limit to present evidence	The variable equals 1 if the period in which the parties may collect or present evidence is fixed by law to a certain number of days after service or number of days before hearing, and 0 otherwise.
Mandatory time limit to present defense	The variable equals 1 if the defendant is required by law to file the opposition within a certain time limit, either in terms of number of days from service or number of days before the hearing. The variable equals 0 otherwise.
Mandatory time limit for judgment	The variable equals 1 if the judge is required by law to enter judgment within a specified period of time after the conclusion of the hearing or the final pleadings, and 0 otherwise.
Mandatory time limit for notification of judgment	The variable equals 1 if the court is required by law to notify the parties within a specified period of time after judgment is entered, and 0 otherwise.
Index: Mandatory time limits	The index measures the presence of mandatory time limits in the procedure. The index is calculated as the average of the following variables: (i) term for admission, (ii) term to present evidence, (iii) term to present defense, (iv) term for judgment, (v) term for compliance, (vi) term for notification of judgment. The index ranges from 0 to 1, where higher values mean more mandatory deadlines.
Quota litis prohibited	The variable equals 1 if quota litis or contingent fee agreements are prohibited by law in all cases, and 0 otherwise.
Loser pays rule	The variable equals 1 if the loser is required to pay all the costs, and 0 otherwise.
Duration in practice	
Duration until completion of service of process	The variable measures the average duration in calendar days, between the filing of the complaint and the moment of service of process to the defendant.
Duration of trial	The variable measures the average duration, in calendar days, between the service of process and the moment the judgment is issued.

Courts 121

Table 5.1
(continued)

Variable	Description
Duration of enforcement	The variable measures the average duration, in calendar days, between the judgment and the moment the landlord repossesses the property (for the eviction case) or the creditor obtains payment (for the check collection case).
Total duration	The variable measures the total estimated duration in calendar days of the procedure under the factual and procedural assumptions provided. It results from the sum of: (i) duration until completion of service of process, (ii) duration of trial, and (iii) duration of enforcement.

Other judicial quality measures

Enforceability of contracts	"The relative degree to which contractual agreements are honored and complications presented by language and mentality differences." Scale for 0 to 10, with higher scores indicating higher enforceability. *Source: Business Environmental Risk Intelligence.* Exact definition in *Knack, Stephen and Philip Keefer, 1995.*
Legal system is fair and impartial	"In resolving business disputes, do you believe your country's court system to be fair and impartial?" The scale ranges from 1 to 6, where higher scores mean a fairer and more impartial legal system. *Source: World Business Environment Survey.*
Legal system is honest or uncorrupt	"In resolving business disputes, do you believe your country's court system to be honest/uncorrupt?" The scale ranges from 1 to 6, where a higher score signals a more honest and uncorrupt system. *Source: World Business Environment Survey.*
Legal system is affordable	"In resolving business disputes, do you believe your country's court system to be affordable?" The scale ranges from 1 to 6, where a higher score means a more affordable legal system. *Source: World Business Environment Survey.*
Legal system is consistent	"In resolving business disputes, do you believe your country's court system to be consistent?" The scale ranges from 1 to 6, where a higher score means a more consistent legal system. *Source: World Business Environment Survey.*
Confidence in legal system	The questionnaire asks the managers the degree to which they believed the system will uphold contracts and property rights in a business dispute. The scale ranges from 1 to 6, where a higher score means a higher degree of confidence in the system. *Source: World Business Environment Survey.*

Table 5.1
(continued)

Variable	Description
Corruption	A composite index for the year 2000 that draws on fourteen data sources from seven institutions: the World Economic Forum, the World Business Environment Survey of the World Bank, the Institute of Management Development (in Lausanne), PricewaterhouseCoopers, the Political and Economic Risk Consultancy (in Hong Kong), the Economic Intelligence Unit, and Freedom House's Nations in Transit. The score ranges between 10 (highly clean) and 0 (highly corrupt). *Source: Transparency International* (www.transparency.org).
Law and order	Integrity of legal system in 2000. This component is based on the Political Risk Component 1 (Law and Order) from the PRS Group's International Country Risk Guide (various issues). Rankings are modified to a ten-point scale. *Source: Economic Freedom of the World* (Gwartney, Lawson, and Block 2001).

Other variables	
Log of GNP per capita	Logarithm of GNP per capita in 1999, Atlas method, expressed in current U.S. dollars. *Source: World Development Indicators.*
Legal origin	Identifies the legal origin of the company law or commercial code of each country (English, French, Socialist, German, Scandinavian). *Source: La Porta et al. (1999).*
Latitude	The absolute value of the latitude of the capital of the country, scaled to take values between 0 and 1. *Source: CIA Factbook.*
Average years of schooling	Average number of years of schooling received per person aged 25 and over in 1992 (last available). *Source: Human Development Report (1994).*
Ethnic fractionalization	Ethnic fractionalization is computed as one minus the Herfindahl index of ethnic group shares. This calculation considers the probability that two persons randomly chosen from a population belong to different groups. *Source: Alesina et al. (2003).*

The fourth area is statutory regulation of evidence. The rules of evidence are sometimes considered to be a key factor in differentiating the overall efficiency of legal procedures among countries (Langbein 1985). First, in some countries, the judge cannot request evidence not requested by the parties, a restriction on the neighbor model. Second, the judge in some countries cannot refuse to collect or admit evidence requested by the parties, even if the judge feels this evidence is irrelevant to the case. This, too, presents a restriction on the discretion of the judge in the neighbor model. Third, hearsay evidence is not admissible in some countries while in others the judge can weigh it. Presumably, the inadmissibility of out-of-court statements is a restriction on judicial freedom in the neighbor model. Fourth, in some jurisdictions, the judge must prequalify a question before it is posed to the witness while in others parties may ask witnesses questions without such prequalification. We take the latter scenario as more compatible with the neighbor model. Fifth, in some jurisdictions, only original documents and certified copies are admissible, a restriction not present in other jurisdictions. Presumably, the neighbor model would not have these restrictions. Sixth, in some countries, authenticity and the weight of evidence are defined by law; in others, they are not. In the neighbor model, we would not expect the evidence to be subjected to rigid rules on admissibility and weight. Seventh, in some countries, but not others, there is mandatory recording of evidence, designed to facilitate the superior authority's control over the judge. We do not take such recording to be consistent with the neighbor model. As before, we aggregate these seven dimensions into the index of "statutory regulation of evidence."

The fifth area of regulation of formalism is the control of the superior review of the first instance judgment. The scope of appellate review determines the level of sovereign control over the trial court proceedings (Damaska 1986). In general, we take the control of a judge by a superior court as inconsistent with the neighbor model, and consider a variety of mechanisms of superior review. First, in some countries, the enforcement of judgment is automatically suspended until the resolution of the appeal, which substantially reduces the importance of the first instance judgment. In others, the suspension of enforcement is either non-automatic, or even not allowed. We take the automatic suspension as being inconsistent with the neighbor model. Second, in some countries, the review and appeal of judicial decisions are comprehensive. In others, more compatibly with the neighbor model, only new evidence or issues of law can be reviewed on appeal, or the judgment cannot be appealed at all. Third, some countries, but not others, allow interlocutory appeals (those of interim judicial decisions), which we take to be incompatible with the neighbor model. We aggregate these three aspects of review into an "index of control of superior review."

The sixth area is engagement formalities that must be observed before a party is legally bound by the court proceedings. In some countries a lawsuit cannot be initiated unless a formal pretrial conciliation is attempted between the parties. The notification procedures also vary markedly among countries. In some places, the complaint can be notified to the defendant by the plaintiff himself or by his attorney, or simply by mailing a letter. In others, the defendant cannot be held accountable unless he is served the claim by an appointed court officer. Finally, in some countries the judgment is deemed notified to the parties when pronounced in open court; in others it must be personally notified to the parties by a duly appointed court employee. We submit that entirely voluntary pretrial conciliation and flexible rules of notification of process and judgment are more compatible with the neighbor model. These three dimensions are aggregated into the index of "engagement formalities."

The seventh area is the count of independent procedural actions involved in pursuing a claim through a court, covering the filing and service of a complaint, trial and judgment, and enforcement. An independent procedural action is defined as every step in the procedure, mandated by the law or by court regulation, which demands interaction between the parties or between them and the judge or court officer, such as filing a motion or attending a hearing. We also count as an independent procedural action every judicial or administrative writ or resolution, such as issuing judgment or entering a writ of execution, which is legally required to advance the proceedings until the enforcement of judgment. Actions are always assumed to be simultaneous if possible, so procedural events that may be fulfilled in the same day and place are only counted as one action.[2] In the idealized neighbor model, there would be only three procedural actions: (1) a claimant would request the judge's intervention, (2) the judge and the claimant would together meet the defendant and the judge would issue a decision following a discussion, and (3) the judgment would be enforced. As the evidence below shows, in some countries, checks can be collected and tenants evicted in just eight or nine steps, while in others it takes 40 to 45 steps—a far cry from the neighbor model. We aggregate these counts into an index of "independent procedural actions" and normalize the index to fall between zero and one based on the minimum and the maximum number of actions among countries.

Having assembled the data, we combine the seven sub-indices into the index of formalism. We scale each sub-index to fall between 0 and 1, so the formalism index falls between 0 and 7, with 7 representing, according to our conception, the greatest distance from the neighbor model. The exact method of the construction of the formalism index is not crucial, since the various sub-indices generally point in the same direction as to which countries regulate adjudication more heavily.

3.3   Other Variables

Our data contain information on the quality of dispute resolution. One measure of quality is an estimate—in calendar days—of duration of dispute resolution by the lawyers who completed the questionnaires. Duration is measured as the number of calendar days counted from the moment the plaintiff files the lawsuit in court until the moment of actual repossession (eviction) or payment (check). This measure includes both the days when actions take place and waiting periods between actions. The participating firms make separate estimates of the average duration until the completion of service of process, the issuance of judgment (duration of trial), and the moment of payment or repossession (duration of enforcement).[3] To the extent that we are interested in the ability of ordinary persons to use the legal system, these estimates of duration are highly relevant for efficiency.

In addition to the data from the questionnaires, we use data from surveys of business people on the quality of the legal system. These include measures of the enforceability of contracts, corruption, and "law and order." In addition, we use information from small firm assessments of various aspects of the quality of the legal system, including consistency, honesty, and fairness, contained in the World Business Environment Survey. These data will be used to shed light on the crucial question: does formalism secure justice?

Finally, we assemble some data to examine alternative hypotheses concerning the determinants of judicial quality. From Lex Mundi member firms, we get data on whether judges face mandatory time deadlines, whether lawyers are allowed to charge contingency fees, and whether losers in civil disputes must pay the winners' legal fees. We also obtain data on per capita income in each country, the average years of schooling, and ethno-linguistic and religious fractionalization. Fractionalization measures are used as controls because studies find that fractionalization has adverse consequences for institutional performance (La Porta et al. 1999; Alesina et al. 2003b).

4 Formalism and Its Determinants

Table 5.2 presents the sub-indices and the overall index on procedural formalism, arranged by legal origin. Table 5.2a focuses on eviction, and table 5.2b on check collection. Countries are arranged by legal origin, and we report the means for each legal origin and the tests of the differences in these means. For both check collection and eviction, common law countries have least formalized, and French civil law countries most formalized, dispute resolution, with other legal origins in the middle. For eviction, the differences hold for all sub-indices, but are stronger in some areas (legal justification, number of independent procedural actions) than in others (evidence, superior review). The differences in formalism among civil law countries (French, German, Socialist, and Scandinavian) are less pronounced, and typically not as statistically significant (except that German and Scandinavian origin countries regulate less heavily than Socialist and French ones). For check collection, the pattern of results is similar, except that one of the sub-indices is lower in French civil law countries than in common law countries. The rankings of legal origins hold also within per capita income quartiles. These findings are broadly consistent with the thrust of the comparative law literature.

Table 5.3 examines the consistency of this evidence across the various sub-indices measuring alternative aspects of procedural formalism, as well as across the two cases. The evidence shows a clear picture of consistency. The various sub-indices are positively correlated with the overall index within each case. Moreover, across the two types of cases, the same sub-indices are strongly positively correlated with each other. The correlation of the formalism index between check collection and eviction is 0.83. In contrast to the general pattern, the evidence and superior review sub-indices are uncorrelated with the others. For most aspects of formalism, however, it appears that some countries regulate dispute resolution more heavily than others.

In table 5.4, we examine the determinants of formalism looking at the sub-indices and the overall index. Panel A deals with eviction, and panel B with check collection. The omitted dummy is common law

Table 5.2A

Eviction of a Tenant.

This table classifies countries by legal origin and shows the professional *vs.* laymen, written *vs.* oral elements, legal justification, statutory regulation of evidence, control of superior review, engagement formalities indices, and the normalized number of independent procedural actions for the case of eviction of a tenant. All variables are described in table 5.1.

	Professional vs. laymen	Written vs. oral elements	Legal justification	Statutory regulation of evidence	Control of superior review	Engagement formalities	Independent procedural actions	Formalism index
Legal origin (mean)								
English	0.48	0.63	0.52	0.30	0.67	0.17	0.25	3.02
Socialist	0.67	0.67	0.79	0.35	0.96	0.06	0.32	3.83
French	0.72	0.81	0.83	0.42	0.69	0.53	0.38	4.38
German	0.61	0.79	0.83	0.27	0.72	0.11	0.24	3.57
Scandinavian	0.60	0.63	0.67	0.23	0.87	0.13	0.21	3.32
Mean for all countries	**0.58**	**0.71**	**0.68**	**0.33**	**0.71**	**0.27**	**0.30**	**3.58**
Tests of means (*t-stats*)								
Common vs. Socialist	-3.08[a]	-1.13	-2.89[a]	-1.31	-4.57[a]	1.87[c]	-1.98[c]	-3.87[a]
Common vs. French	-4.34[a]	-5.61[a]	-5.20[a]	-3.21[a]	-0.41	-7.07[a]	-3.38[a]	-7.77[a]
Common vs. German	-1.31	-2.53[b]	-2.29[b]	0.50	-0.54	0.7	0.22	-1.74[c]
Common vs. Scandinavian	-1.10	0.01	-0.98	1.20	-1.77[c]	0.42	0.72	-0.86
Socialist vs. French	-0.78	-3.14[a]	-0.57	-1.27	3.38[a]	-7.00[a]	-0.94	-2.49[b]
Socialist vs. German	1.71	-1.68	-0.28	1.31	4.12[a]	-0.57	1.29	1.10
Socialist vs. Scandinavian	1.90[c]	0.65	0.80	2.07[c]	1.36	-0.76	1.57	1.93[c]
French vs. German	0.98	0.35	0.00	1.81[c]	-0.24	4.09[a]	1.56	2.37[b]
French vs. Scandinavian	0.99	2.44[b]	1.63	2.23[b]	-1.25	3.55[a]	1.72[c]	2.82[a]
German vs. Scandinavian	0.13	1.48	1.06	0.59	-1.51	-0.21	0.39	1.04

a = significant at 1% level; b= significant at 5% level; c = significant at 10% level.

Table 5.2B

Collection of a Check.

This table classifies countries by legal origin and shows the professional vs. laymen, written vs. oral elements, legal justification, statutory regulation of evidence, control of superior review, engagement formalities indices, and the normalized number of independent procedural actions for the case of collection of a check. All variables are described in table 5.1.

	Professional vs. laymen	Written vs. oral elements	Legal justification	Statutory regulation of evidence	Control of superior review	Engagement formalities	Independent procedural actions	Formalism index
Legal origin (mean)								
English	0.43	0.58	0.42	0.31	0.68	0.13	0.20	2.76
Socialist	0.67	0.72	0.79	0.38	0.96	0.06	0.35	3.93
French	0.68	0.85	0.80	0.42	0.63	0.49	0.41	4.29
German	0.50	0.77	0.72	0.33	0.50	0.11	0.21	3.15
Scandinavian	0.53	0.68	0.53	0.23	0.87	0.13	0.18	3.15
Mean for all countries	**0.57**	**0.71**	**0.64**	**0.36**	**0.70**	**0.25**	**0.30**	**3.53**
Tests of means (t-stats)								
Common vs. Socialist	-3.29[a]	-3.38[a]	-4.19[a]	-1.55	-4.53[a]	1.45	-3.38[a]	-5.24[a]
Common vs. French	-3.85[a]	-7.97[a]	-6.29[a]	-2.71[a]	0.82	-7.42[a]	-4.63[a]	-7.52[a]
Common vs. German	-0.59	-2.73[a]	-2.25[b]	-0.37	1.84[c]	0.30	-0.11	-1.12
Common vs. Scandinavian	-0.79	-1.35	-0.75	1.22	-1.70[c]	0.02	0.33	-1.03
Socialist vs. French	-0.21	-3.05[a]	-0.12	-0.74	4.07[a]	-6.47[a]	-0.92	-1.36
Socialist vs. German	3.81[a]	-0.73	0.55	0.67	7.13[a]	-0.70	1.78[c]	3.23[a]
Socialist vs. Scandinavian	3.11[a]	0.93	1.71	2.35[b]	1.36	-0.95	1.95[c]	2.81[b]
French vs. German	1.40	1.24	0.78	0.96	1.02	3.58[a]	1.88[c]	2.72[a]
French vs. Scandinavian	1.05	2.55[b]	2.32[b]	2.05[b]	-1.64	3.09[a]	1.94[c]	2.45[b]
German vs. Scandinavian	-0.30	1.17	0.99	1.51	-3.32[a]	-0.21	0.44	-0.02

a = significant at 1% level; b = significant at 5% level; c = significant at 10% level.

Table 5.3
Correlations of Formalism Index and Its Components.

Indices	Formalism index	Professionals vs. laymen	Written vs. oral elements	Legal justification	Statutory regulation of evidence	Control of superior review	Engagement formalities	Independent procedural actions
Panel A: Eviction								
Professionals vs. laymen	0.6420[a]	1.0000						
Written vs. oral elements	0.6614[a]	0.3073[c]	1.0000					
Legal justification	0.6840[a]	0.2598	0.3976[a]	1.0000				
Statutory regulation of evidence	0.4161[a]	0.1471	0.2390	0.2049	1.0000			
Control of superior review	0.4573[a]	0.2342	0.1009	0.2121	0.0090	1.0000		
Engagement formalities	0.5988[a]	0.2349	0.4041[a]	0.2795	0.1995	0.0037	1.0000	
Independent procedural actions	0.5353[a]	0.3952[b]	0.3858[b]	0.1799	0.1546	0.1110	0.1713	1.0000
Panel B: Check collection								
Professionals vs. laymen	0.7625[a]	1.0000						
Written vs. oral elements	0.7305[a]	0.5090[a]	1.0000					
Legal justification	0.7573[a]	0.4921[a]	0.6083[a]	1.0000				
Statutory regulation of evidence	0.4800[a]	0.1845	0.3052[c]	0.3184[b]	1.0000			
Control of superior review	0.3264[b]	0.1255	−0.0439	0.1051	0.0316	1.0000		
Engagement formalities	0.6125[a]	0.4082[a]	0.4391[a]	0.2977[c]	0.2296	−0.0296	1.0000	
Independent procedural actions	0.6517[a]	0.4836[a]	0.4538[a]	0.3406[b]	0.2869	0.0957	0.2909[c]	1.0000

Table 5.3
(continued)

Panel C: Correlations between eviction and check collection indices

Indices	Formalism index	Professionals vs. laymen	Written vs. oral elements	Legal justification	Statutory regulation of evidence	Control of superior review	Engagement formalities	Independent procedural actions
Formalism index	0.8257[a]							
Professionals vs. laymen		0.5229[a]						
Written vs. oral elements			0.7054[a]					
Legal justification				0.7502[a]				
Statutory regulation of evidence					0.9086[a]			
Control of superior review						0.7866[a]		
Engagement formalities							0.8126[a]	
Independent procedural actions								0.8575[a]

a = significant at 1% level; b = significant at 5% level; c = significant at 10% level.

Table 5.4
Indices Regressions.
Ordinary least squares regressions of the cross-section of countries. The dependent variables are the indices of formalism and its component indices. Robust standard errors are shown in parentheses. All variables are described in table 5.1.

Dependent variables	Independent variables					Constant	N [R^2]
	Log GNP per capita	Socialist legal origin	French legal origin	German legal origin	Scandinavian legal origin		
Panel A: Eviction of a tenant							
Formalism index	-0.1254[b]	0.7437[a]	1.3681[a]	0.7842[a]	0.5729[b]	4.0386[a]	109
	(0.0489)	(0.1791)	(0.1712)	(0.2257)	(0.2677)	(0.3789)	[0.44]
Professionals vs. laymen	-0.0115	0.1843[a]	0.2410[a]	0.1556[b]	0.1482[c]	0.5697[a]	109
	(0.0180)	(0.0387)	(0.0562)	(0.0744)	(0.0851)	(0.1469)	[0.20]
Written vs. oral elements	-0.0047	0.0435	0.1887[a]	0.1714[b]	0.0092	0.6644[a]	109
	(0.0102)	(0.0395)	(0.0342)	(0.0774)	(0.0790)	(0.0865)	[0.26]
Legal justification	0.0057	0.2710[a]	0.3092[a]	0.2991[b]	0.1306	0.4769[a]	109
	(0.0216)	(0.0902)	(0.0602)	(0.1273)	(0.1203)	(0.1776)	[0.22]
Statutory regulation of evidence	-0.0435[a]	0.0274	0.1171[a]	0.0489	0.0169	0.6557[a]	109
	(0.0102)	(0.0357)	(0.0333)	(0.0660)	(0.0524)	(0.0808)	[0.26]
Control of superior review	-0.0276	0.2768[a]	0.0263	0.1053	0.2585[a]	0.8914[a]	109
	(0.0171)	(0.0464)	(0.0617)	(0.0736)	(0.0931)	(0.1409)	[0.17]
Engagement formalities	-0.0218	-0.1239[b]	0.3514[a]	-0.0242	0.0049	0.3520[a]	109
	(0.0141)	(0.0571)	(0.0497)	(0.0772)	(0.0876)	(0.1190)	[0.46]
Independent procedural actions	-0.0221[b]	0.0647	0.1343[a]	0.0281	0.0045	0.4285[a]	109
	(0.0107)	(0.0424)	(0.0398)	(0.0520)	(0.0640)	(0.0909)	[0.17]

Table 5.4
(continued)

Dependent variables	Independent variables						
	Log GNP per capita	Socialist legal origin	French legal origin	German legal origin	Scandinavian legal origin	Constant	N [R²]
Panel B: Check collection							
Formalism index	-0.2072[a]	1.0579[a]	1.5422[a]	0.7622[a]	0.8339[a]	4.4465[a]	109
	(0.0501)	(0.1915)	(0.1922)	(0.2464)	(0.2977)	(0.4042)	[0.48]
Professionals vs. laymen	-0.0420[b]	0.2154[a]	0.2568[a]	0.1473	0.1939[b]	0.7712[a]	109
	(0.0185)	(0.0462)	(0.0656)	(0.0899)	(0.0952)	(0.1555)	[0.21]
Written vs. oral elements	-0.0162	0.1386[a]	0.2751[a]	0.2207[a]	0.1330[a]	0.7090[a]	109
	(0.0099)	(0.0373)	(0.0343)	(0.0726)	(0.0467)	(0.0767)	[0.42]
Legal justification	-0.0328[c]	0.3533[a]	0.3809[a]	0.3609[a]	0.1824	0.6884[a]	109
	(0.0193)	(0.0852)	(0.0586)	(0.1191)	(0.1684)	(0.1615)	[0.32]
Statutory regulation of evidence	-0.0402[a]	0.0437	0.1080[a]	0.0965	0.0009[c]	0.6376[a]	109
	(0.0115)	(0.0398)	(0.0372)	(0.0656)	(0.0557)	(0.0915)	[0.20]
Control of superior review	-0.0131	0.2687[a]	-0.0486	-0.1589[c]	0.2119[b]	0.7893[a]	109
	(0.0169)	(0.0456)	(0.0615)	(0.0864)	(0.0940)	(0.1357)	[0.21]
Engagement formalities	-0.0262[b]	-0.0866[c]	0.3580[a]	0.0235	0.0540	0.3485[a]	109
	(0.0138)	(0.0446)	(0.0482)	(0.0745)	(0.0852)	(0.1175)	[0.47]
Independent procedural actions	-0.0366[a]	0.1247[b]	0.2120[a]	0.0723[c]	0.0576	0.5025[a]	109
	(0.0120)	(0.0478)	(0.0453)	(0.0429)	(0.0495)	(0.1039)	[0.26]

a = significant at 1% level; b = significant at 5% level; c = significant at 10% level.

(English) legal origin. Richer countries exhibit lower levels of procedural formalism than poorer ones. The data for most sub-indices and the overall index also show that dispute resolution in socialist and French civil law countries is more formalized than in common law countries, even holding per capita income constant. The point estimates in the regressions are consistent with the means in table 5.2, yielding roughly the same order of legal origins, and in most cases the coefficients are statistically significant. Dispute resolution in German and Scandinavian origin countries also appears to be more formalized than in common law countries, although the results for sub-indices are generally statistically insignificant. The incremental R^2 in explaining the formalism index from the legal origin dummies is 40 percent: nearly half of the residual variation in formalism (holding per capita income constant) is explained by the legal tradition. These results are robust to inclusion of other controls, such as latitude, average years of schooling, and ethno-linguistic and religious fractionalization.[4]

These results provide striking support of the comparative law hypothesis that there are systematic differences in legal procedure across legal families. Specifically, civil law countries have more formal dispute resolution than do common law countries.

5 Determinants of the Quality of Courts

In this section, we evaluate the alternative theories of the determinants of the quality of courts. Table 5.5 presents the means by legal origin of the estimated duration of dispute resolution, with countries arranged by legal origin. A striking finding is the extraordinary length of time it takes, on average, to pursue either claim in court. The worldwide average time for accomplishing an eviction is 254 (median of 202) calendar days, and for collecting a check 234 (median of 197) calendar days. With all the other costs, this number suggests why individuals in most countries choose not to use the formal legal system to resolve their disputes.

There is tremendous variation in the estimated duration of each procedure among countries. Eviction is estimated to take 49 days in the U.S., 547 in Austria, and 660 in Bulgaria. Check collection is estimated to take 60 days in New Zealand, 527 in Colombia, and 645 in Italy. The comparison by legal origin for eviction puts common law and Scandinavian legal origin countries on top (shortest duration) and socialist and French legal origin countries at the bottom. Interestingly,

Table 5.5
Duration in Practice.
This table classifies countries by legal origin and shows the duration in practice for the eviction and the check case. All variables are described in table 5.1.

By legal origin	Eviction of a tenant				Check collection			
	Duration until completion of service of process	Duration of trial	Duration of enforcement	Total duration	Duration until completion of service of process	Duration of trial	Duration of enforcement	Total duration
Legal origin (mean)								
English	26	112	61	199	26	88	62	176
Socialist	47	187	113	347	42	169	116	327
French	27	167	72	266	34	147	90	272
German	19	230	107	357	26	92	75	193
Scandinavian	14	139	33	187	27	101	42	170
Mean for all countries	29	151	74	254	31	122	80	234
Tests of means (t-stats)								
Common vs. Socialist	-2.05^b	-1.84^c	-2.46^b	-2.42^b	-1.74^c	-2.37^b	-2.91^a	-2.85^a
Common vs. French	-0.16	-1.66	-0.77	-1.64	-0.93	-2.66^a	-2.16^b	-2.94^a
Common vs. German	0.47	-2.49^b	-1.65	-2.36^b	0.03	-0.13	-0.52	-0.30
Common vs. Scandinavian	0.76	-0.52	0.95	0.17	-0.05	-0.39	0.76	0.10
Socialist vs. French	2.23^b	0.37	1.80^c	1.14	0.71	0.51	1.33	0.91
Socialist vs. German	1.90^c	-0.51	0.15	-0.07	1.06	0.94	1.18	1.12
Socialist vs. Scandinavian	2.08^c	0.51	1.91^c	1.14	0.88	0.78	2.05^c	1.23
French vs. German	0.68	-0.83	-1.14	-1.03	0.45	1.04	0.57	1.10
French vs. Scandinavian	1.03	0.33	1.23	0.83	0.35	0.82	1.72^c	1.33
German vs. Scandinavian	0.82	1.43	2.44^b	2.63^b	-0.08	-0.19	1.19	0.32

a = significant at 1% level; b = significant at 5% level; c = significant at 10% level.

and consistent with earlier work on creditor rights in Germany (La Porta et al. 1997a), German legal origin countries are comparatively more efficient at check collection than at eviction. But the bottom line of table 5.5 is the higher expected duration in civil law countries. In the words of an Indonesian legal scholar, "in connection with the nature of judicial process itself and considering the formal, punctual, and rather complicated manners and usages upheld by courts according to the Law of Procedure (especially for the laymen), it could be said that correct judgment cannot be performed in a short time" (Gandasurbrata 1980, p.7).

Table 5.6 presents the regression results of the determinants of judicial quality, including the log of per capita income, average years of schooling, latitude, ethnic fractionalization, and the formalism index (we consider incentives later). Panel A focuses on eviction, and panel B on check collection. For both procedures, expected duration is not related to either the level of per capita income or the years of schooling in a statistically significant way. (The two controls—fractionalization and latitude—are also insignificant.) These results are inconsistent with the development hypothesis.

In contrast, expected duration is highly correlated with procedural formalism. Countries with higher formalism, not surprisingly, have longer expected times of using the judicial system to evict a non-paying tenant or to collect a check. This result has important implications: it suggests that legal structure, rather than the level of development, shapes this crucial dimension of judicial efficiency.

Some examples illustrate the findings of table 5.6. Malawi is a low-income common law country, with per capita income of $180. It has a formalism index of 3.14 for eviction, and expected duration of only 35 days. It also has a formalism index of 2.95 for check collection, and expected duration of 108 days. By comparison, Mozambique is a low-income French legal origin country, with per capita income of $220. It has one of the highest formalism indices of 5.15 for eviction, and expected duration of 540 days. For check collection, its formalism index is 4.49, and expected duration is 540 days. The same pattern emerges if we compare middle-income countries (e.g., New Zealand versus Portugal), as well as rich countries (e.g., United Kingdom versus Austria).

The results on expected duration raise the crucial question: does procedural formalism, at the cost of longer proceedings, secure better justice? The answer suggested by table 5.6 is No.

Table 5.6
Outcomes and the Formalism Index.
Ordinary least squares regressions of the cross section of countries. Robust standard errors are in parentheses. All variables are described in table 5.1.

	Independent variables						
Dependent variables	Log GNP per capita	Formalism index	Ethnic fractionalization	Average years of schooling	Latitude	Constant	N [R²]
Panel A: Eviction of a tenant							
Log of duration	-0.0736	0.3012[a]	-0.2202	0.0305	0.1635	4.5593[a]	91
	(0.0937)	(0.0812)	(0.4766)	(0.0556)	(0.5432)	(0.7183)	[0.15]
Enforceability of contracts	0.7728[a]	0.5648[a]	1.7036[a]	0.0755	0.7046	0.1959	50
	(0.1237)	(0.0863)	(0.4907)	(0.0612)	(0.5646)	(0.9043)	[0.85]
Legal system is fair and impartial	0.3501[a]	-0.5032[a]	-0.8773[c]	-0.1729[a]	0.0481	4.0479[a]	60
	(0.1094)	(0.0827)	(0.5192)	(0.0514)	(0.6593)	(0.9578)	[0.49]
Legal system is honest or uncorrupt	0.5087[a]	-0.4637[a]	-0.9113[c]	-0.1938[a]	0.2377	2.6552[a]	60
	(0.1050)	(0.0703)	(0.4679)	(0.0491)	(0.5956)	(0.8661)	[0.54]
Legal system is affordable	-0.0344	-0.1374[b]	-0.7111[b]	-0.0953[b]	0.3681	4.6225[a]	60
	(0.0918)	(0.0663)	(0.3528)	(0.0377)	(0.4174)	(0.6865)	[0.26]
Legal system is consistent	0.3379[a]	-0.2847[a]	-0.6666	-0.1621[a]	0.3352	2.7261[a]	60
	(0.1060)	(0.0774)	(0.4376)	(0.0466)	(0.5306)	(0.8494)	[0.41]
Confidence in legal system	0.3250[a]	-0.1289[c]	-0.4663	-0.0781[c]	-0.7303	2.6542[a]	60
	(0.0999)	(0.0758)	(0.4223)	(0.0411)	(0.4862)	(0.8153)	[0.29]
Corruption	1.5238[a]	-0.6393[a]	-0.2640	-0.0998	0.5314	-4.5186[a]	76
	(0.1365)	(0.1189)	(0.5182)	(0.0632)	(0.7226)	(0.9537)	[0.87]
Law and order	0.9416[a]	-0.3594[c]	-0.0867	-0.1632	4.4505[a]	0.1644	82
	(0.2245)	(0.2107)	(0.7624)	(0.1048)	(1.2861)	(1.9529)	[0.57]

Table 5.6
(continued)

Dependent variables	Independent variables						
	Log GNP per capita	Formalism index	Ethnic fractionalization	Average years of schooling	Latitude	Constant	N [R²]
Panel B: Check collection							
Log of duration	-0.0377 (0.0826)	0.3038a (0.0598)	0.7677 (0.4969)	0.0693 (0.0599)	0.0866 (0.4612)	3.6403a (0.6473)	91 [0.20]
Enforceability of contracts	0.6013a (0.1310)	-0.5041a (0.0684)	1.6713a (0.4586)	0.1304b (0.0618)	0.8437 (0.5685)	0.8848 (0.8835)	50 [0.86]
Legal system is fair and impartial	0.2567b (0.1080)	-0.4415a (0.0582)	-1.0089b (0.4777)	-0.1522a (0.0524)	0.0171 (0.5951)	4.4417a (0.8833)	60 [0.52]
Legal system is honest or uncorrupt	0.4258a (0.1076)	-0.3950a (0.0568)	-1.0105b (0.4347)	-0.1756a (0.0522)	0.2284 (0.5504)	2.9389a (0.8239)	60 [0.55]
Legal system is affordable	-0.0564 (0.0940)	-0.1074b (0.0497)	-0.7225b (0.3493)	-0.0906b (0.0388)	0.3811 (0.4141)	4.6416a (0.6895)	60 [0.25]
Legal system is consistent	0.2814b (0.1071)	-0.2637a (0.0539)	-0.7670c (0.4261)	-0.1493a (0.0485)	0.2951 (0.4998)	3.0424a (0.8246)	60 [0.44]
Confidence in legal system	0.2943a (0.0996)	-0.1393b (0.0530)	-0.5487 (0.4193)	-0.0707c (0.0411)	-0.7808 (0.4766)	2.9304a (0.8039)	60 [0.31]
Corruption	1.4255a (0.1494)	-0.4528a (0.1077)	-0.2994 (0.5308)	-0.0761 (0.0707)	0.7321 (0.7556)	-4.6737a (1.0804)	76 [0.85]
Law and order	0.9261a (0.2160)	-0.2647 (0.1915)	-0.0359 (0.7375)	-0.1615 (0.1063)	4.5262a (1.2763)	-0.1441 (1.7720)	82 [0.57]

a = significant at 1% level; b = significant at 5% level; c = significant at 10% level.

Note first that countries with richer populations generally have higher quality justice as indicated by nearly all survey measures, consistent with the development hypothesis. However, our measure of human capital, the average years of schooling, often enters with the "wrong" (negative) sign and is statistically significant. The latter result is not just a consequence of education and per capita income being highly correlated; education comes in negative about half the time even without the inclusion of per capita income. Latitude is generally unimportant, but ethnic fractionalization exerts a negative, though usually insignificant, influence on judicial quality. The evidence on the development hypothesis is thus mixed: our measure of income, but not our measure of education, yields results consistent with this hypothesis.

Nearly all survey measures suggest that higher formalism is associated with inferior justice, holding other things constant. This result holds, with minor differences, for both eviction and check collection. It holds for enforceability of contracts, law and order, and corruption, but also for World Business Environment Survey measures. Higher formalism is associated with less fairness and impartiality, less honesty, less consistency, and less confidence in the legal system.[5] Table 5.6 contains the basic bottom line of this paper: at least for simple disputes, higher formalism is associated not only with the expected higher duration of dispute resolution, but also with lower quality justice as perceived by participants.

We repeated the analysis of table 5.6 using legal origin dummies as instruments for formalism (results are reported in Djankov et al. (2003)). With no exceptions, the results remain statistically significant, and confirm that formalism has adverse effects on both the expected duration of proceedings and other aspects of quality of the legal system. The exogeneity of legal origin for most countries suggests that it is unlikely to be the case that countries with a worse law and order environment *choose* heavier formalism. The instrumental variable results suggest the opposite direction of causality: countries that have inherited legal systems with heavily formalized dispute resolution end up with lower quality legal systems, at least for simple disputes.[6]

Finally, we consider the hypothesis that the quality of adjudication is shaped by the incentives facing the participants (Messick 1999; Buscaglia and Dakolias 1999). In table 5.7, we present the results for three frequently mentioned measures of incentives: mandatory time limits for judges, loser pays rules, and prohibition of contingency fees for attorneys. Mandatory deadlines are sometimes seen as effective

Table 5.7
Outcomes and Incentives.
Ordinary least squares regressions of the cross section of countries. The regressions also include log of GNP per capita, ethnic fractionalization, average years of schooling, latitude, and a constant term. Robust standard errors are in parentheses. All variables are described in table 5.1.

Dependent variables	Selected independent variables				
	Formalism index	Index of mandatory time limits	Quota litis prohibited	Loser pays rule	N[R^2]
Panel A: Eviction of a tenant					
Log of duration	0.4303[a]	−0.6335	0.3162[c]	0.0383	91
	(0.1030)	(0.3931)	(0.1768)	(0.1722)	[0.21]
Enforceability of contracts	−0.5465[a]	−0.4260	−0.0642	0.1393	50
	(0.0965)	(0.4977)	(0.2147)	(0.2278)	[0.86]
Legal system is fair and impartial	−0.4019[a]	−0.4282	0.0520	−0.2147	60
	(0.1135)	(0.3504)	(0.1550)	(0.1574)	[0.52]
Legal system is honest or uncorrupt	−0.3557[a]	−0.5440	−0.0751	−0.2704	60
	(0.1024)	(0.3527)	(0.1650)	(0.1694)	[0.58]
Legal system is affordable	−0.2077[b]	0.2588	−0.2991[c]	−0.1124	60
	(0.1019)	(0.3326)	(0.1652)	(0.1432)	[0.33]
Legal system is consistent	−0.1820[c]	−0.4575	−0.0045	−0.2557[c]	60
	(0.0951)	(0.2974)	(0.1423)	(0.1404)	[0.47]
Confidence in legal system	−0.0234	−0.4047	−0.0717	−0.4249[a]	60
	(0.0882)	(0.3114)	(0.1365)	(0.1386)	[0.43]
Corruption	−0.5351[a]	−0.4128	0.0527	−0.1617	76
	(0.1670)	(0.6082)	(0.2273)	(0.2230)	[0.87]
Law and order	−0.0543	−1.2233	1.1384[a]	0.3560	82
	(0.2562)	(0.7414)	(0.3702)	(0.3745)	[0.64]
Panel B: Check collection					
Log of duration	0.3239[a]	−0.1918	0.1040	0.1054	91
	(0.0850)	(0.3328)	(0.1930)	(0.1544)	[0.20]
Enforceability of contracts	−0.4557[a]	−0.2515	−0.0242	−0.0785	50
	(0.0967)	(0.4798)	(0.2259)	(0.2032)	[0.86]
Legal system is fair and impartial	−0.2930[a]	−0.8371[a]	0.0897	−0.3587[b]	60
	(0.0735)	(0.2968)	(0.1440)	(0.1490)	[0.61]
Legal system is honest or uncorrupt	0.2870[a]	−0.5676	−0.0619	−0.4496[a]	60
	(0.0799)	(0.3458)	(0.1654)	(0.1666)	[0.62]
Legal system is affordable	−0.1394[c]	0.1677	−0.2870[c]	−0.1541	60
	(0.0755)	(0.3198)	(0.1649)	(0.1392)	[0.31]

Table 5.7
(continued)

Dependent variables	Selected independent variables				
	Formalism index	Index of mandatory time limits	Quota litis prohibited	Loser pays rule	N[R²]
Legal system is consistent	−0.1683[b] (0.0714)	−0.5283[c] (0.2909)	−0.0081 (0.1535)	−0.3085[b] (0.1384)	60 [0.51]
Confidence in legal system	−0.0866 (0.0710)	−0.1780 (0.3231)	−0.1018 (0.1502)	−0.4514[a] (0.1277)	60 [0.43]
Corruption	−0.2762[b] (0.1243)	−0.6330 (0.4452)	0.1550 (0.2436)	−0.5330[b] (0.2175)	76 [0.86]
Law and order	0.1890 (0.2369)	−2.3986[a] (0.7659)	1.3469[a] (0.3783)	0.1304 (0.3639)	82 [0.67]

a = significant at 1% level; b = significant at 5% level; c = significant at 10% level.

mechanisms for speeding up proceedings, and loser pays rules may make justice quicker and fairer because they discourage delays by defendants who are at fault, while prohibitions of contingency fees may dis-incentivize lawyers and thus delay proceedings. There is no convincing evidence, however, that these measures of incentives systematically influence either the duration of proceedings, or the subjective measures of the quality of the legal system. Moreover, despite the inclusion of the three new variables, the formalism index retains its effect and statistical significance in nearly all specifications.

This analysis concludes our presentation of the evidence on the three theories of what determines court performance. The results on the incentive theory are negative but must be interpreted with caution, since we might not have the most appropriate measures of incentives facing the participants in a dispute. The results on the development theory are mixed: countries with richer populations have better (in some respects) courts, though this is not true for countries with more educated populations. Finally, consistent with our analysis of regulation of dispute resolution, countries with heavier procedural formalism have both slower and lower quality systems of dispute resolution, at least when one focuses on the simple disputes examined here.

6 Conclusion

We present an analysis of legal procedures triggered by resolving two specific disputes—the eviction of a non-paying tenant and the collection of a bounced check—in 109 countries. The data come from detailed descriptions of these procedures by Lex Mundi member law firms. For each country, the analysis leads to an index of formalism—a measure of the extent to which its legal procedure differs from the hypothetical benchmark of a neighbor informally resolving a dispute between two other neighbors. We then ask whether formalism varies systematically across countries, and whether it shapes the quality of the legal system.

Consistent with the literature on comparative law, we find that judicial formalism is systematically greater in civil law countries, and especially French civil law countries, than in common law countries. Formalism is also lower in the richest countries. The expected duration of dispute resolution is often extraordinarily high, suggesting significant inefficiencies. The expected duration is higher in countries with more formalized proceedings, but is independent of the level of development. Perhaps more surprisingly, formalism is nearly universally associated with lower survey measures of the quality of the legal system. These measures of quality are also higher in countries with richer populations. We find no evidence that incentives facing the participants in litigation influence the performance of courts.

There are two broad views of this evidence. According to the first, greater formalism is efficient in some countries: it can reduce error, advance benign political goals, or protect the judicial process from subversion by powerful interests. On this view, the various regulatory steps, such as reliance on professional judges and collection of written evidence, are there to secure a fair judicial process. Put differently, while heavily formalized adjudication appears problematic on some measures, it would be even more problematic without the regulation.

According to the second view, many developing countries accepted the formalism in adjudication they now have as part of the transplantation of their legal system by their colonizers. On this view, there is no presumption that the transplanted system is efficient. Although heavy procedural formalism has theoretically plausible reasons for its existence, the reality it brings is extreme costs and delays, unwillingness by potential participants to use courts, and ultimately injustice. At least some of the burdens of formalism may therefore be unnecessary, and could be relieved through reform, especially for simple disputes.

The evidence in this paper supports the second theory. Specifically, the evidence points to extremely long expected duration of dispute resolution, suggesting that courts are not an attractive venue for resolving disputes. Furthermore, we find no offsetting benefits of formalism, even when looking at a variety of measures of the perception of fairness and justice by the users of the legal system. Moreover, legal origin itself appears to determine judicial quality, other things equal, suggesting that formalism is unlikely to be part of an efficient design.

The evidence suggests that the systems of dispute resolution in many countries may be inefficient—at least as far as simple disputes are concerned. In particular, one cannot presume in economic analysis, especially as applied to developing countries, that property and contract are secured by courts. This conclusion has two implications. First, it may explain why alternative strategies of securing property and contract, including private dispute resolution, are so widespread in developing countries. Second, our results suggest a practical strategy of judicial reform, at least with respect to simple disputes, namely the reduction of procedural formalism.

6 The Rise of the Regulatory State

with Edward L. Glaeser

1 Introduction

Before 1900, significant commercial disputes in the United States were generally resolved through private litigation. Courts ruled on corporate liability in industrial accidents, on anti-competitive practices such as railroad rebates, on safety of foods and medicines, and even on the constitutionality of the income tax.[1] In the three decades between 1887, when Congress passed the Interstate Commerce Act, and 1917, when "participation in the war put an end to the progressive movement" (Hofstadter 1955), this situation changed radically. Over thirty years, reformers eroded the nineteenth-century belief that private litigation was the sole appropriate response to social wrongs. During the Progressive Era, regulatory agencies at both the state and the federal level took over the social control of competition, anti-trust policy, railroad pricing, food and drug safety, and many other areas. At the same time, U.S. politics experienced other important changes, such as reform of the civil service, use of voter referendums to decide local issues, direct election of senators, recall of judges, and the growth of government more generally.

In this paper, we attempt to understand why these changes occurred in the United States between 1887 and 1917. To this end, we develop a theory of law enforcement in which private litigation, government regulation, a combination of the two, and doing nothing are considered as alternative institutional arrangements to secure property rights. In our theory, whatever law enforcement strategy the society chooses, private individuals will seek to subvert its workings to benefit themselves. The efficiency of alternative institutional arrangements depends in part on their vulnerability to such subversion. The theory leads to predictions as to what institutions are appropriate under what circumstances. We use this theory to explain at least some of the changes in law enforcement strategies in the Progressive Era but also to examine appropriate law enforcement institutions for transition economies and emerging markets.

Traditional economic theories of regulation do not explain the Progressive movement. The standard public interest theory holds that regulation deals with market failures and externalities (Pigou 1938; Stiglitz 1989), but does not explain why either contract or tort law could not successfully address these problems in the first place (Coase 1960). Posner (2003) and Shavell (1984a) discuss this choice between litigation over damages and regulation from the efficiency perspective. Posner (2003) emphasizes the fixed cost of lawsuits as a potential argument for regulation, whereas Shavell (1984a) points to the limits on the violator's ability to pay as a drawback of litigation. These theories predict that as cases became larger and the defendants' pockets deeper during the Gilded Age, efficiency calls for more litigation and less regulation. The reality, of course, was the opposite.

The most successful recent attempt to shed light on progressivism emerged from the "capture" or "special interest" theories of regulation. Stigler (1971), Posner (1974), Peltzman (1976), and McChesney (1987) rejuvenated the theory of regulation by questioning the motives and the capabilities of regulators. Applied to the Progressive Era, these theories hold that government regulation was sought by firms in order to restrain competition, usually coming from technologically superior rivals. We compare the two approaches after presenting our ideas.

To discuss Progressive reforms, we present a model of design of a law enforcement regime, which can include liability for accidents, regulation of precautions, a combination of the two, or doing nothing. In our model, the crucial difference between liability and regulation as alternative mechanisms of controlling market behavior is their vulnerability to subversion by the potential violator. By subversion we mean a number of both legal and illegal strategies. The legal ones include acquiring favorable legislation and regulation (even after an accident), lobbying for an appointment of friendly law enforcers (including both judges and regulators), hiring top lawyers, or using delay tactics in case of a suit. Illegal subversion strategies include intimidating and bribing judges, regulators, or juries. By expending sufficient resources on subversion of justice, the potential violator can avoid regulatory fines and liability payments.

Because pure liability regimes entail large payments with a small probability, such regimes are more vulnerable to ex post subversion than the regulation of inputs, especially in environments lacking law and order in the first place. In such circumstances, the regulation of inputs, or a combination of regulation and liability, is more efficient than a pure liability regime. This reason for the growth of regulation complements others relevant to Progressive reform, such as the stronger incentives and greater specialization of regulators compared to judges (Landis 1938; chapter 7).

The theoretical analysis points to a fundamental change that made it efficient for American society to increasingly rely on regulation. Commercialization and industrialization of the economy in the second half of the nineteenth century created firms with vast resources. As the scale of enterprise increased, the damage from industrial accidents rose proportionately, as did the incentives to avoid paying damages. However, the cost of influencing justice did not rise as fast. As a consequence, individuals and small companies were unlikely to prevail against "robber barons" in accident, restraint of trade, or discriminatory tactics disputes. From this perspective, the regulation of markets was a response to the dissatisfaction with litigation as a mechanism of social control of business. Other political changes of this period, such as the Civil Service reform, increasing importance of direct elections, and judicial recalls, can also be understood from the perspective of controlling subversion.

Woodrow Wilson repeatedly complained about the failure of courts to stand up to large corporations because, he said, "the laws of this country do not prevent the strong from crushing the weak" (1913, p. 15). He articulated his vision of government regulation in his *New Freedom* program.

It was no business of the law in the time of Jefferson to come into my house and to see how I kept house. But when my house, when my so-called private property, became a great mine, and men went along dark corridors amidst every kind of danger in order to dig out of the bowels of the earth things necessary for the industries of a whole nation, and when it came about that no individual owned these mines, that they were owned by great stock companies, then all the old analogies absolutely collapsed and it became the right of the government to go down into these mines to see whether human beings were properly treated in them or not; to see whether accidents were properly safeguarded against; to see whether modern economical methods of using these inestimable riches of the earth were followed or were not followed. If somebody puts a derrick improperly secured on top of a building or overtopping the street, then the government of the city has the right to see that that derrick is so secured that you and I can walk under it and not be afraid that heavens are going to fall on us. Likewise, in these great beehives where in every corridor swarm men of flesh and blood, it is the privilege of the government, whether of the State or of the United States, as the case may be, to see that human life is protected, that human lungs have something to breathe (1913, pp. 23–24).

Writing during the New Deal, Landis (1938) likewise saw regulation as a political response to the failure of private litigation to keep up with community ideas of justice. He thought that the advocacy of "leaving the problems of railroad charges and management to work themselves out in the courts as questions arise from time to time . . . indicates a singular unawareness of the fact that the chief drive for the resort to the administrative process in the field of railroad regulation arose from a recognition that the remedies that the courts could provide were insufficient to make effective the policies that were being demanded." In effect, our model provides an efficiency rationale for this rise of regulation.

In addition to interpreting a crucial period of U.S. economic history, the model sheds light on the general problem of securing private property. Economists since Coase (1960) have been interested in the question of whether regulation or litigation is a better way to deal with tort problems. Coase argued generally that "transaction costs" should determine the answer, and the successive literature has identified a range of such costs (e.g., Shavell 1984a, b). But the literature has not focused on a central problem raised by Coase, namely the efficiency of alternative strategies of law enforcement. By focusing on subversion, we present a comparative analysis of such strategies. This approach helps us understand why Becker's (1968) "boil them in oil" enforcement strategies, which entail very high penalties with a very small probability and hence minimize investigation costs, are rarely workable: they will be subverted ex post.

More generally, our framework provides one way of understanding which institutions are appropriate to secure property rights in different circumstances—a question that gained new pertinence as transition economies struggled to secure law and order. Although economists have generally agreed on the importance of securing property rights, the analysis of alternative institutional arrangements is still in its infancy. Some scholars prefer private, non-governmental enforcement of good conduct (Galanter 1981; Ellickson 1991; Greif 1989). Private enforcement sometimes works effectively when parties experience

repeated interactions or can post large bonds. In the context of developing and transition economies, however, private enforcement often
degenerates into a Hobbesian state of violence and disorder (Hay and
Shleifer 1998; Hay, Shleifer, and Vishny 1996). Indeed, Smith (1776) saw
"a tolerable administration of justice" as one of the few proper functions of government, precisely because he felt that private justice is
subverted to benefit the rich and the strong.

But what is the optimal form of *public* enforcement? Economists in
the Coasian tradition typically focus on courts as enforcers of good
conduct, but recent research demonstrates empirically that courts in
developing countries are often unreliable and inefficient (Johnson,
McMillan, and Woodruff 2002; chapter 5). Economists of the left argue,
in contrast, that government regulation is needed to prevent harmful
conduct, especially in developing countries (Stiglitz 1989). The evidence shows, however, that such regulation more often than not
leads to corruption and insecurity of private property (De Soto 1989;
chapter 10).

The focus on subversion of justice allows for a tentative comparison
of alternative institutional arrangements. In situations of extreme vulnerability to influence, corruption, or intimidation, appropriate institutions might involve no legal or regulatory restrictions at all, as the
alternative is a socially costly regime in which law enforcement is
simply subverted. This prediction contrasts with the standard "public
interest" view, in which the less developed countries, exhibiting relatively greater market failures, require the heaviest government intervention (Stiglitz 1989). Indeed, this prediction might account for the
evidence of pervasive failure of regulation in emerging markets and
transition economies.

In the regimes of intermediate "law and order," some regulation, or
a combination of regulation and litigation, may be efficient. Although
not as efficient as private litigation *absent subversion*, regulation may be
less vulnerable to subversion than litigation, and might be part of an
efficient law enforcement regime. Finally, in the regimes where the
system of justice is least vulnerable to subversion, a regulation-free litigation regime, with either a strict liability or a negligence standard,
becomes optimal. In broad terms, the paper suggests that the appropriate institutions of law enforcement depend on how much order the
country has in the first place.

In the next section, we sketch the U.S. regulatory situation in the
second half of the nineteenth century, and the changes it underwent

during the Progressive Era. In section 3, we present a model of the choice of a law enforcement strategy. In section 4, we apply the model to the U.S. experience with progressivism. In section 5, we compare our approach with the interest group analysis of the Progressive Era. In section 6, we examine the implications of our approach for appropriate institutions for social control of business in transition and developing economies.

2   Enforcement by Courts in the Nineteenth Century

We start with three claims about the United States during the "Gilded Age" between the Civil War and the Progressive Era. First, until the end of the nineteenth century, the U.S., especially at the federal level, followed the laissez-faire ideal in which private litigation was the principal way of dealing with socially harmful acts. Second, after the Civil War, wealth and power regularly subverted the workings of this mechanism. Third, this subversion of private litigation entailed outcomes radically different from those suggested by Coase's (1960) benign vision of common law. Traditional arguments for the failure of the Coase theorem, such as transaction costs (Shavell 1987), do not explain the limits of late nineteenth-century American justice. Instead, late nineteenth-century private litigation failed because money and power influenced the path of justice.

By the late nineteenth century, the development of tort law was greatly accelerated by the Industrial Revolution, especially the railroads. "Trains were also wild beasts; they roared through the countryside, killing livestock, setting fires on houses and crops, smashing wagons at grade crossings, mangling passengers and freight. Boilers exploded; trains hurtled off tracks; bridges collapsed; locomotives collided in a grinding scream of steel. Railroad law and tort law grew up, then, together. In a sense, the two were the same (Friedman 1985, p. 468)." In cases of both personal and social harm, individuals sought damages primarily in common law courts. Horwitz (1992) describes how the maxim *sic utere*, "use your own so as not to injure others," was invoked by many common law judges. This maxim justified court action against a variety of perceived nuisances (saloons, gunpowder storage facilities, slaughterhouses) "which could be abated without any justification of the defendant."

In the development of tort law, the nineteenth century saw the great debate between strict liability (plaintiff just needs to show cause) and negligence (plaintiff needs to show fault or negligence) standards (Horwitz 1992). In the English case of *Rylands v. Fletcher* (1868), a court held a landowner strictly liable when a reservoir he built on his own property accidentally flooded the plaintiff's coal mine. In contrast, American jurists such as Holmes (1881) sought to make negligence a more common rule. "The contribution of nineteenth century law was the creation of independent law of torts, freed from common law procedural constraints and dominated by the negligence principle" (Kaufman 2000).[2]

During this period, tort law developed significantly to accommodate the changing economy. A greater reliance on the negligence standard was one such accommodation. Still, tort law was not developing fast enough, at least for the demands of popular politics. Courts regularly struck down nascent attempts at regulation by appeals to freedom of contract. In *Lochner v. New York* (1905), the New York and U.S. supreme courts ruled that maximum hours legislation was unconstitutional for bakeries because "there is no reasonable ground for interfering with the liberty of person or the right of free contract, by determining the hours of labor, in the occupation of a baker." In the Gilded Age, private litigation remained the dominant form of dealing with torts, and courts kept down the growth of regulation.

Despite the dominance of private litigation, many observers of the Gilded Age saw it as ineffective in achieving justice. Skocpol (1992) complains about the pro-business attitudes of the courts. Horwitz (1992) argues that this era is replete with pro-business jurists, and associates the negligence principle with attempts by pro-business jurists to protect firms from lawsuits. Lockard and Murphy (1992) claim that judges supported corporations because of "a campaign to 'educate' judges about the sacredness of private property." According to Friedman (1985), "What they [the leading concepts of tort law] added up to was also crystal-clear. Enterprise was favored over workers, slightly less so over passengers and members of the public. . . . The thrust of the rules, taken as a whole, approached the position that corporate enterprise should be flatly immune from actions for personal injury (p. 475)."

Judicial ideology was itself shaped by the selection of judges, and through their influence on the political machines, industrialists participated in choosing who sat on the bench. According to Woodrow Wilson (1913, p. 242), "The disease lies in the region where these men [judges] get their nominations; and if you can recover for the people the *selecting* of judges, you will not have to trouble about their recall. Selection is of more radical consequence than election." Callow (1966, p. 135) writes that "the appointment of the right men to key posts is the third step in making the law as much a matter of politics as of justice."

In addition to influencing the selection of judges and prosecutors, nineteenth-century corporations projected substantial political influence, superior lawyers, and ready access to large legal war chests. Their lawyers produced briefs that exonerated their clients and slowed down the wheels of justice for years. They used the threat of being overruled on appeal to bring judges to their positions.

Nor were these perfectly legal forms of subversion the whole story. In the Gilded Age, corporations appear to have routinely bribed legislators, judges, and juries. Lloyd (1894) describes how Standard Oil subverted the attempts of its opponents to secure damages in courts by intimidation and bribery of witnesses, payments and political pressures on judges and legislators, and theft and destruction of evidence. Tarbell (1903) corroborates the outline of Lloyd's account. In "Robber Barons," Josephson (1934) relates the story of the battle for the Erie railroad between Commodore Vanderbilt and Jay Gould. The battling barons acquired a number of judges and legislators who issued laws, rules, and injunctions preventing each party from exercising their powers over the railroad on request. The battle culminated in an open auction of policies by the New York legislature, which Gould won by paying higher bribes to more legislators.

Illegal subversion of justice is a pervasive theme of the muckrakers. In "Tweed Days in St. Louis," Lincoln Steffens tells the story of a young circuit attorney, Mr. Folk, who was put on the Democratic ticket by mistake, and upon election began putting both Democratic and Republican officials behind bars for corruption. Having failed to persuade Mr. Folk to cease and desist, the local political machine decided to get rid of him. "At the meeting of corruptionists three courses were decided upon. Political leaders were to work on the Circuit Attorney by promise of future reward, or by threats. Detectives were to ferret out of the young lawyer's past anything that could be used against him. Witnesses would be sent out of town and provided with money to remain away until the adjournment of the grand jury." In Minneapolis, Steffens describes the coercion of the jury in the trial of the corrupt Mayor Ames. He points to the foreman of the jury, "to whom $28,000 was offered to quit, and for whose slaughter a slugger was hired to come from Chicago" (Steffens, 1906).

Albert Cardozo—the father of Benjamin Cardozo—exemplifies a judge in league with a political machine. Appointed by William Marcy Tweed to the New York State Supreme Court, Albert Cardozo served Tweed ably. "He became a kind of escape hatch for criminals; through his good offices he pardoned or dismissed several hundred known criminals who were or might be useful to the [Tweed] Ring" (Callow 1966). At his own impeachment hearings, Cardozo was accused of crimes ranging from standard nepotism, to releasing convicted clients, to helping Fisk and Gould reduce the losses from their Gold Conspiracy through the legal system.

It is often argued that the distortion of justice through legal and illegal forms of influence decided many cases and had a broad influence on the nineteenth-century economy. Courts often failed to address the grievances of the parties damaged in the new economy, such as workers suffering from accidents, producers suffering from abusive tactics by the railroads, or consumers poisoned by bad food, and ruled in favor of large corporations. Tort claims against railroads, following large scale accidents that often killed third parties, proved to be slow and often unsuccessful. In *Ryan v. New York Central Railroad* (1866), the New York court of appeals argued that even if a railroad caused a fire, its liability extended only to the immediately adjacent house and not to other homes destroyed by the fire. The court held that "to sustain such a claim . . . would subject [the railroad] to a liability against which no prudence could guard, and to meet which no private fortune could be adequate" (Friedman 1985, p. 469). More generally, the courts' view of such accidents was "nobody to blame" (Friedman 1985, p. 470).

Fishback and Kantor (2000) describe the extreme inequality between firms and employees in industrial accident claims. The legal strength of corporations meant that many injured families settled for relatively small amounts of money. Summarizing a number of studies, Fishback and Kantor estimate that families of workers killed in industrial accidents received an average of eight months' pay, and nothing in about 40 percent of the cases (p.34). Under political (and perhaps more direct) pressure from manufacturers, courts adopted the position that the estate of an injured worker must prove negligence by the company, and that evidence of negligence by the worker himself, or by one of his coworkers, absolved the company of liability. According to Woodrow Wilson, "it was practically impossible for workingmen in New Jersey to get justice from courts" (1913, p. 248).

Although both the historical accounts and the contemporary political rhetoric may be biased, the image of social control of business during the Gilded Age is consistent across a spectrum of sources. The system of private litigation, which emerged in agrarian America in the eighteenth and early nineteenth centuries, was not suited for the conditions of the late nineteenth century. One reason for this failure is that large corporations possessed economic resources far in excess of those at the disposal of their opponents—whether individuals or small firms—and used these resources to subvert justice. The problem of "inequality of weapons" became too extreme. The mechanisms of subversion ranged from superior legal talent to political pressure to outright bribery. For our purposes, the exact mechanism does not matter. What matters is that courts did not make the perpetrators pay for the social harm of their actions, at least to the satisfaction of the public. As a consequence, the system broke down.

2.1 The Regulatory Response

In response to the public dissatisfaction with the status quo, political actors sought a range of remedies against social harm. These remedies were not just to make courts less friendly to corporations, but rather to also change *the form* of social control of business. Starting with Charles Francis Adams and the Massachusetts Railroad Commission, regulatory agencies became a complement to judicial action. The reforms started with states and municipalities, but eventually moved to the federal level, in part because the increase in the scale of firms made state regulation too difficult. In 1887, the Interstate Commerce Act created the Interstate Commerce Commission, which—combined with subsequent legislation—had the power to stop railroad rebates and ultimately, under the Hepburn Act of 1906, to set rates. In 1890, Congress passed the Sherman Act, restricting the formation of trusts.

The real growth of regulatory activity occurred after the turn of the century, during the presidencies of Roosevelt and Wilson. In 1906, under muckraking pressures, Congress passed Pure Foods and Drugs to control the distribution of medicines, as well as a federal meat-inspection law. Under Wilson, the regulation of both banking under the Federal Reserve Act of 1913 and competition under the Clayton Act in 1914 intensified. Fishback and Kantor (2000) see the adoption of workers' compensation laws by several U.S. states around the turn of the century as a response to the failure of courts to address the problems of workers injured or killed in industrial accidents. The new laws replaced a negligence standard in courts with a combination of regulation and strict liability.

Although the growth of regulation slowed down, and arguably retreated, under the Republican presidencies of the 1920s, it revived and accelerated under Franklin Roosevelt in the 1930s. Among the most notable measures of this period were the Securities Acts of 1933 and 1934, written in part by Landis, which brought securities markets under federal regulation. When Landis wrote in 1938, he could confidently conclude that "the administrative" has replaced "the judiciary" as the principal form of social control of business.

There are three broad efficiency reasons why regulation might supplement or replace private litigation. First, as many champions of Progressive reforms believed, regulators may have stronger incentives than do judges to pursue costly investigations necessary to establish—either to themselves or to a court—that a violation of a rule has occurred. Such stronger incentives might come from career concerns if regulators are rewarded for finding violations, or from the better specialization of regulators (Landis 1938; chapter 7). A specialized regulator, for example, is in a better position to establish a manufacturer's negligence than a generalist judge.

Second, regulation may be more efficient than pure litigation because the regulator can either simplify private litigation or solve the free rider problem among the private plaintiffs by representing their mutual interest. For example, a regulator can issue rules that lower the cost of private action by making it easier to prove damages, or even bring suit himself. (In the latter case, the effects of regulation are similar to those of class action lawsuits.) La Porta et al. (2006) examine securities regulation around the world from this perspective, and find that regulatory sanctions and rules organizing private litigation are beneficial for securities market development. This is not, however, what we focus on here.

Third, a crucial difference between litigation and regulation is that the former deals with damages after the harm is done, whereas the latter deals with ex ante precautions. Because of this difference, regulation can be designed to make the identification of violations cheaper and more certain, especially when third parties can be involved—it is easier to ascertain whether a piece of safety equipment has been installed than whether the producer is negligent. Glaeser and Shleifer (2001) argue that this logic of cheap verification of violations explains the prevalence of quantity regulations. Here, we take this point further, and argue that the higher probability of detection of violations in the case of regulation assures compliance at lower levels of fines. As a consequence, regulation is less vulnerable to subversion than litigation. For this argument to hold, it does not matter that the regulator must ultimately litigate the matter in court: the point that justice involving lower fines is less likely to be subverted holds regardless of whether or not a court is ultimately involved. Moreover, this argument does not preclude the possibility that regulation supplements rather than replaces private litigation, as we show in the next section.

3 The Model

We present a model in the spirit of Posner (1972) in which the ultimate goal of social control of torts is to elicit the optimal level of precaution. Becker's (1968) and Posner's work initiated a large literature, recently surveyed by Polinsky and Shavell (2000). An important contribution to this literature that addresses the problem of corruption but does not focus on alternative law enforcement strategies is one by Polinsky and Shavell (2001).

A firm can take a level of precaution, equal to Q_1 or Q_2, in order to avoid an accident. The high level of precaution, Q_2, requires a cost of $S \times C$, while the low level of precaution, Q_1, is free. The parameter C represents the cost of precaution per unit of production; the level of S represents the scale of the firm. There are two types of firms that might be responsible for the accident: α's and β's. For α types the probability of an accident is unaffected by precaution and equals P_α. This implies, importantly, that it is not efficient for type α firms to invest in a high level of precaution. Let π_α be a proportion of firms that are of type α. For type β firms the probability of an accident equals P_1 or P_2, with $P_1 > P_2$, depending on whether the level of precaution is Q_1 or Q_2, and we assume that $P_\alpha < P_1$.[3] The accident imposes a social cost of $S \times D$, where D refers to the social cost per unit of economic activity and S refers again to the scale of the firm. The assumption that damages scale up with the size of the firm corresponds most closely to massive calamities, such as train wrecks or factory fires. However, legal precedents raise the stakes for large firms even in accidents affecting individual workers.

For our purposes, it is not important whether D is concentrated (as in the case of a workplace accident) or widely shared (as in the case of pollution). When the damage is concentrated, simple ex ante contracts can sometimes deal with possible damages, even without a liability regime. For example, an employee working in a dangerous occupation would receive a higher wage, which compensates him for the risk of an accident. Even in such situations, however, it is generally efficient for the firm to provide the risk-averse employee with some accident insurance (Shavell 1987). As a consequence, the firm has an incentive to avoid paying after an accident occurs. To the extent that the dispute needs to be settled in court, as such issues often are (Fishback and Kantor 2000), our analysis remains pertinent. We make:

Assumption 1 $(P_1 - P_2)D > C$, so that for the β types, unlike for the α types, the high level of precaution is socially valuable.

Finally, we assume that the regulator learns that the firm chose a low level of precaution with exogenous probability p.[4] To allow regulation to be a potentially efficient scheme in the presence of subversion we make:

Assumption 2 $p > P_1$.

The idea behind this assumption is that some regulations can be designed so that detection of the failure to invest in precaution is relatively inexpensive and certain. This could involve mandating well-specified "bright line" rules, such as the installation of safety equipment in factories or on trains, use of fire-proof materials and fire exits in buildings, the disclosure of potential conflicts of interest, or the use of warning labels. In addition, some regulations are designed to encourage third party enforcement. For example, employees or customers themselves can occasionally cheaply identify violations and complain, as in the case of blue laws prohibiting liquor sales on Sundays (Glaeser and Shleifer 2001).

We initially consider a menu of three possible law enforcement schemes: (1) strict liability, (2) negligence, and (3) regulation of inputs:

(1) Strict liability requires that, in case of an accident, the firm must pay a fine any time that damages occur.

(2) Negligence means that a fine is charged whenever damages occur and when the firm undertakes the low level of precaution.

(3) Regulation requires that the high level of precaution be taken and imposes a fine, F, whenever the firm is caught failing to do so. We

assume that the regulator cannot distinguish between the two types of firms.

We assume that the firm produces a fixed output and its objective is to minimize costs, given by the sum of the costs of precaution and the expected fine. We first compare the three pure regimes, and then consider the possibility of combining regulation with litigation.

3.1   The Three Pure Law Enforcement Regimes
With no problems of enforcement, strict liability can achieve the first best as long as the fine (denoted by F) is greater than

$$\frac{SC}{P_1 - P_2}.$$

Negligence can also achieve the first best whenever

$$\frac{SC}{P_1} < F < \frac{SC}{P_\alpha}.$$

Note that

$$\frac{SC}{P_1} < \frac{SC}{P_1 - P_2}.$$

Because strict liability uses less information, it requires a larger fine. At the same time, strict liability provides no incentives for the type α firms to invest in the useless-for-them high level of precaution, and therefore eliminates this source of inefficiency. Finally, regulation assures that both types of firms invest in precaution as long as $F > SC/p$. In the absence of subversion, pure regulation is never efficient in this model because it inefficiently forces α types to invest.

We turn next to optimal law enforcement in the presence of subversion. The firm still minimizes its costs, but we assume that it subverts justice when doing so is cheaper than paying fines. To model subversion, we assume that the firm can escape either the regulatory fine or the liability payment if it invests X in protection from the law, where X can include acquiring a legal team, a lobbying team, or political protection. X is interpreted as the maximum fine that can be enforced by either regulators or courts without subversion. We assume that X is paid after the firm is caught but before a fine is levied.[5] In our model, we do not distinguish between a judge and a regulator: it costs the same to subvert either. A reduction in X can be interpreted as an improvement in the technology to subvert justice available to the firm, so we think of regimes with a higher X—a higher maximum fine—as possessing higher levels of "law and order."

In this formulation, if X is lower than the fine, the firm would rather subvert justice than submit to the law. Recall that we have assumed (assumption 2) that $\dfrac{C}{p} < \dfrac{C}{P_1} < \dfrac{C}{P_1 - P_2}$, where $\dfrac{C}{p}$, $\dfrac{C}{P_1}$, and $\dfrac{C}{P_1 - P_2}$ are minimal fines per unit of output that incentivize the firm to take precautions in regulation, contributory negligence, and strict liability schemes respectively. We can now formulate

Proposition 1 If $P_\alpha < P_1$, then:

(a) for $\dfrac{X}{S} < \dfrac{C}{p}$ the only feasible option is laissez-faire;

(b) for $\dfrac{C}{p} < \dfrac{X}{S} < \dfrac{C}{P_1}$ regulation dominates laissez-faire if

$$D > \frac{C}{(1 - \pi_\alpha)(P_1 - P_2)},$$ and vice versa if this condition does not hold;

(c) for $\dfrac{C}{P_1} < \dfrac{X}{S} < \dfrac{C}{P_1 - P_2}$ negligence achieves first best; and

(d) for $\dfrac{X}{S} > \dfrac{C}{P_1 - P_2}$ both negligence and strict liability achieve first best.

If $P_\alpha > P_1$, then:

(a) for $\dfrac{X}{S} < \dfrac{C}{p}$ the only feasible option is laissez-faire;

(b) for $\dfrac{C}{p} < \dfrac{X}{S} < \dfrac{C}{P_1 - P_2}$ regulation dominates laissez-faire if

$$D > \frac{C}{(1 - \pi_\alpha)(P_1 - P_2)}$$ (negligence achieves the same social outcomes but requires larger fines), and vice versa if this condition does not hold.

(c) for $\dfrac{X}{S} > \dfrac{C}{P_1 - P_2}$ strict liability achieves the first best.

For $P_\alpha < P_1$, figure 6.1 illustrates the proposition graphically.

In sum, among the three pure law enforcement schemes, only negligence or strict liability can in principle achieve the first best. Strict liability, to be feasible, requires strong barriers to the subversion of

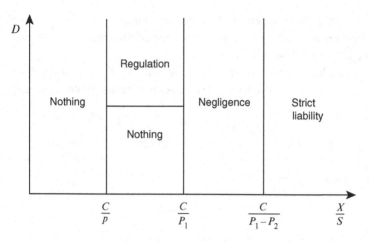

Figure 6.1

justice (a high X), but has the advantage that it does not incentivize firms that do not benefit from precaution to invest in it. The negligence standard is less vulnerable to subversion, but can distort the incentives of the firms that do not benefit from it. Pure regulation works best at high levels of subversion, but is never fully efficient. Doing nothing is best when subversion is the highest.

3.2   Combining Regulation and Litigation

We have assumed so far that a firm never faces a double risk of both paying a fine if it does not invest in precaution and is caught by the regulator *and* being sued if an accident occurs. But of course, one can easily imagine a firm that does not invest in precaution facing double jeopardy: from a regulator who discovers the violation and from the victim should an accident occur. We show in this subsection that such enforcement strategies often work better.

Assume for simplicity that the probabilities of being caught by a regulator and the victim of an accident are independent. Assume also that the regulator simply collects a fine, denoted by R, when a firm is discovered with a low level of precaution. We denote the payment in litigation by F, and again consider strict liability and negligence, each combined with regulation, separately.

To fix ideas, consider the case of no subversion first. In this case, we can obtain first best from a combination of regulation and strict liability provided that:

$$pR + (P_1 - P_2)F > SC > pR .$$ (1)

Indeed, as we showed above, with no subversion we can get the first best even with $R = 0$, that is, no regulation. Similarly, we can obtain first best from a combination of regulation and negligence provided that:

$$pR + P_1F > SC > pR + P_\alpha F .$$ (2)

Again, with no subversion, we can get first best with no regulation, as we saw before.

Consider now what happens when courts or regulators can be subverted, so we must have both R and F less than or equal to X for law enforcement to work. We then have:

Proposition 2 If $P_\alpha < P_1$, then:

(a) A combination of negligence and regulation can achieve first best provided that

$$X(p + P_1) > SC .$$

(b) A combination of strict liability and regulation can achieve the first best provided that

$$X(p + (P_1 - P_2)) > SC .$$

Proposition 2 establishes that a combination of regulation and litigation can generally do better than regulation alone (it achieves first best). Moreover, the combination expands the set of circumstances where some law enforcement can work to all $X > SC/(p + P_1)$. This result is not surprising: since subversion puts an upper bound on feasible fines, having two instruments applied in moderation must do better than one. Importantly, proposition 2 establishes that the introduction of regulation does not lead to abandonment of litigation: the two strategies of law enforcement are rather complementary. Proposition 2 also confirms the finding of proposition 1 that, for high enough levels of subversion, law enforcement cannot achieve the first best. Indeed for high enough levels of subversion the optimal policy remains to do nothing.

So what is the bottom line of this analysis? Perhaps the principal message of our model is the tight relationship between the "law and order" already prevailing in a society and the optimality of alternative law enforcement schemes. As figure 6.1 illustrates (and the analysis of proposition 2 confirms), in the environment of weak law and order, doing nothing is superior to imposing legal and regulatory rules that are only going to be subverted at some social cost. In either case, harmful conduct is not punished, but with laissez-faire, corruption and other forms of subversion are avoided. In the regime of intermediate law and order, regulation—alone or more likely in combination with litigation—is efficient precisely because the fines it entails to achieve compliance are modest, and therefore will not be resisted. The efficiency of regulation comes precisely from the fact that the penalties associated with a pure liability regime are too high, and therefore in such a regime justice is subverted. Finally, after high levels of law and order are already achieved, society can attempt to resolve disputes purely through private litigation, using either a negligence or a strict liability standard. These schemes call for the imposition of high fines ex post, and are therefore only feasible when the liable parties can be compelled to pay these fines without subverting justice.

A subtler message of the model is that economic inequality—which here is driven by the growth in the scale of enterprise—can undermine the functioning of institutions of law enforcement through subversion. Economic inequality exacerbates the problem of "inequality of weapons," which has been central to the discussions of legal design for several centuries (Glaeser, Scheinkman, and Shleifer 2003). Inequality can make institutions that would function well in a more equal environment—such as private litigation in nineteenth-century U.S.—fail to deal with new problems. Growth in inequality—of the sort seen in the U.S. after the Civil War or in Russia during the 1990s—would be accompanied by deterioration of existing institutions and the political demand for the creation of new ones that restore law and order.

In chapter 8, we also consider the problem of subversion of justice, but focus on the historical development of common and civil law. We argue that the civil law institutions of state-employed professional judges following clear legal rules under constant superior review developed in France as a response to high levels of disorder prevailing in the society. These institutions were a mechanism of protecting law enforcers from subversion by powerful litigants. In contrast, the common law institutions of adjudication by lay juries following broad principles of community justice with only perfunctory appeal were more appropriate for the relatively more orderly England, where subversion of justice by the powerful magnates was a less pervasive problem.

There are two important conceptual differences between this chapter and chapter 8. First, this chapter highlights the use of the regulation of inputs—the expanding scope of government—as a tool for fighting the subversion of justice. Chapter 8, in contrast, focuses on the use of royal judges—the expanding centralization of government—as a tool against the subversion of justice. Second, in chapter 8, the cost of fighting private subversion of institutions is that the state extracts more surplus for itself. Here, in contrast, the cost of fighting subversion is somewhat inefficient regulation. In reality, regulation itself can become a tool of the state, so its true cost is regulatory abuse of citizenry by the government, as well as by private individuals influencing the government. This is the essence of the regulatory capture theories, to which we return below.

4   Implications of the Model for the Progressive Era

We can use the model of the previous section to understand the rise of regulation in the United States at the end of the nineteenth and the beginning of the twentieth centuries. Our interpretation is that S—the scale of economic activity—rose dramatically over the nineteenth century. During the Industrial Revolution, firms grew sharply in size. The social costs of harm grew roughly proportionately, but the costs of subverting justice did not. As a result, a legal system that may have operated well during the agrarian period failed when faced with entities that had huge incentives to subvert it both legally and illegally. Because higher levels of S lead to subversion of both strict liability and negligence, adding regulation was the efficient response.

During the first half of the nineteenth century, the bulk of the economy was agricultural; 64 percent of workers in 1850 were in farm occupations. The manufacturing that did exist was concentrated in small firms. The McLane report, a large but incomplete survey of the economy, found only 106 manufacturing firms in 1832 with assets above $100,000. Chandler (1977) saw production in the mid-nineteenth century as "being carried out by a large number of small units employing less than fifty workers. . . ."

When a firm caused social harm in 1830, the judicial system could usually deal with it. Assessed damages would generally be small and the firm did not have a strong incentive to subvert justice. Moreover, the firm itself was small and did not have the resources to subvert the system. We take this to mean that many sectors in the U.S. in 1830 are best described by the right part of figure 6.1, where

$$X > \frac{SC}{P_1 - P_2}$$

and strict liability yields the first best outcome.

This situation changed after the Civil War. The building of railroads, the growth of industrial enterprises and mines, and the creation of large financial firms introduced into the American economy disputes between parties of highly differentiated economic and political resources. America became far less agricultural; by 1900, only 37 percent of workers were in farm occupations. The manufacturing industry grew more than tenfold (measured by number of employees) over this time period. The new technologies often proved to be deadly. Thousands of passengers and third parties died in railroad accidents. By 1900, there were approximately 35,000 deaths and two million injuries annually in industrial accidents (Friedman 1985).

New technologies also raised the scale of both railroads and manufacturing firms, as national markets developed. Innovations in organizational form made larger firm size feasible. Chandler (1977) identifies 278 firms with more than $20 million in assets in 1917. "The Morgan interests at the peak of the financial system held 341 directorships in 112 corporations . . . with aggregate resources or capitalization of $22,245,000,000" (Hofstadter 1955). This vast expansion in firm size in many sectors corresponds to an increase in the parameter S in the model.

The model corresponds most closely to situations where the Industrial Revolution raised both the precaution costs and the size of single accidents, for example, train wrecks or factory fires (such as the Triangle Shirtwaist Fire, where 146 workers died). In other instances, such as industrial accidents involving individual workers, the cost of precaution and the number of accidents rise with enterprise size, but the size of each individual case remains small. If such cases are isolated, it might not benefit a firm to subvert justice. In practice, however, the stakes in such cases are large for large firms, because of the power of legal precedents. When a steel mill or a railroad concedes liability in an industrial accident, it becomes vulnerable to claims in all the future similar accidents. As a consequence, even in such situations, the assumption of the model that the willingness to subvert justice rises with the scale of the firm is appropriate. We must be clear, however, that we are not arguing that S rose in all sectors; and indeed the model predicts that those in which it did not should not have seen the rise of regulation.

The model treats S as exogenous, but also points to an incentive for firms to increase it. In the regimes of either strict liability or negligence, rising values of S make no difference to corporate profits when corporations actually pay the fines, as long as fines scale with S. However, when X is independent of S, when firms subvert justice, higher values of S lead to lower payments for social harm. The payment per unit of economic activity is X/S, so larger firms pay less.[6] Indeed, the advantage of scale in subverting the legal system is a competitive edge of nineteenth-century corporations. Woodrow Wilson and the muckraking literature see the largest firms as particularly effective in shaping legal outcomes.

The economic creations of the late nineteenth century, such as national railroad systems and trusts, may have been designed to gain political and not just economic power. The entrepreneurs could use the economic and political resources that such combinations brought to buy both politics and justice. In a similar vein, and for similar reasons, financial-industrial groups were created in Russia in the 1990s with the basic goal of attaining political rather than economic influence (Nagel 1999).[7]

The Progressives cited the rise in the scale of enterprise as a primary reason for new government action. In 1888, Charles Eliot noted that a modestly sized Boston railroad had three times as many employees as the Commonwealth of Massachusetts. The first chapter of Wilson's manifesto *The New Freedom* states that "the employer is now generally a corporation or a huge company of some kind," and as a result "new rules must be devised. . . ." Wilson's Progressive rival Theodore Roosevelt viewed Herbert Croly's *The Promise of American Life* as his intellectual sourcebook. Because of "the existing concentration of wealth and financial power in the hands of few irresponsible men," Croly believes "efficient regulation there must be." Progressives saw the scale of industrial enterprise as the root of the republic's problems.

The model helps us understand Croly's call for regulation. As S rises, the society moves leftward across figure 6.1. First, negligence becomes optimal and should replace strict liability. We have already noted that, in the 1870s, negligence replaced strict liability as the standard in tort law. As S continues to rise, negligence itself fails to produce desirable results. When S is sufficiently high, and when D is also high, regulation with or without litigation provides the only reliable recourse against social harms. This is ultimately our explanation of why the Progressives saw the need for regulation. Because input regulation is more consistently applied and involves smaller penalties, it provides a weaker incentive for the subversion of justice. If government action is at all responsive to efficiency, the model predicts exactly the course of the Progressive Era: increased government regulation of business following the increase in its scale.

The Progressives themselves saw the problems of the judiciary and advocated regulation. In *The New Freedom*, Wilson bitterly complains about the performance of courts:

There have been courts in the United States which were controlled by the private interests. There have been supreme courts in our states before which plain men could not get justice. There have been corrupt judges; there have been controlled judges; there have been judges who acted as other men's servants and not as servants of the public. Ah, there are some shameful chapters in the story. The judicial process is the ultimate safeguard of the things that we must hold stable in this country. But suppose that that safeguard is corrupted; suppose that it does not guard my interests and yours, but guards merely the interests of a very small group of individuals; and whenever your interest clashes with theirs, yours will have to give way, though you represent ninety percent of the citizens, and they only ten percent. Then where is your safeguard? (1913, p. 240).

Wilson answers his own question by making the case for regulation: "We must see to it that there is no overcrowding, that there is no bad sanitation, that there is no unnecessary spread of avoidable diseases, that the purity of food is safeguarded, that there is every precaution against accident, that women are not driven to impossible tasks, nor children permitted to spend their energy before it is fit to be spent" (p. 275, see also the quote in the introduction). Croly also casts aspersions on judges and calls them "creatures of the political machine," and advocates his own more ambitious plan of government ownership. As Hofstadter (1955) writes: "the average American tended more and more to rely on government regulation, to seek in governmental actions a counterpoise to the power of private business."

4.1 Understanding the Progressive Program

The Progressive program was not merely a revolution in regulation. The law saw a switch from strict liability to negligence, which according to the model should follow an increase in scale. More generally, the model suggests that efficient reforms should aim to raise X or reduce S. Many Progressive reforms can indeed be understood from this perspective.

One Progressive innovation was the introduction of regulatory agencies to oversee specific areas of the economy and to punish socially harmful conduct. In part, the logic of such reforms was to raise the incentives of law enforcers to punish violations (since regulators are easier to politicize than judges), and thereby to increase X. In a similar vein, many Progressives supported the "recall" of government officials, especially judges, who were corrupt or failed to perform as the public wanted. Because the fear of recall makes judges more resistant to subversion, we see this reform as another attempt to raise X.

Equally important to the Progressives was the professionalization of bureaucracies, or civil service reform. Croly advocates a more widespread use of life tenure for judges, which would have a similar effect of reducing the political influence on them. The Progressives' simultaneous support of increased democracy in the form of judicial recall and of reduced democracy in the form of civil service reform may seem puzzling. Both reforms, however, can be understood as attempts to increase X. While the recalls aimed to punish bad judges, civil service reform attempted to decrease the influence of the political machines in the administrative process. Since political machines were used by business to select and coopt judges, eliminating their influence raised the cost of subverting justice, X.

An alternative to using regulation or raising X was to reduce S directly. In his platform of *The New Freedom*, Woodrow Wilson opposed "the [Roosevelt] doctrine that monopoly is inevitable and that the only course open to the people of the United States is to submit to and regulate it." Instead, he advocated reducing firm size "to prevent private monopoly by law, to see to it that the methods by which monopolies have been built up are legally made impossible."

Indeed, the whole trust-busting program aimed at eliminating the power of trusts to coerce politics and justice as much as reducing prices. Hofstadter (1955, p. 227) writes:

The progressive case against business organization was not confined to economic considerations, nor even to the more intangible sphere of economic morals. Still more widely felt was a fear founded in political realities—the fear that the great business combinations, being the only centers of wealth and power, would be able to lord it over all other interests and thus put an end to traditional democracy.

Our model sheds light on such comments. Competitive prices may prevail in a duopoly with two very large firms, but the scale of these enterprises may enable them to subvert justice. Progressive trust-busting should be seen as a response to the subversion of justice, as well as a means of addressing standard problems of monopoly pricing.

Along similar lines, our model also helps explain the support for labor unions among many Progressives. Traditionally, economists understand labor unions as a means of restricting labor supply and raising wages. Unions, however, can also become a political "countervailing power" to large firms by projecting comparable economic resources (Galbraith 1952). When large firms meet large unions in a political and economic marketplace, the efforts to subvert justice by one meet countervailing efforts by the other. The formation of labor unions parallels the creation of trusts and large industrial firms as a competitive reaction to subversion. Galbraith was not the first to appreciate this point. In *Veghelan v. Gunther*, Justice Holmes wrote: "Combination on the one side is potent and powerful. Combination on the other is the necessary and desirable counterpart, if the battle is to be carried out in a fair and equal way" (1896, p.108).

A final reform proposed by many Progressives is the complete control of industry by the government. If large firms subvert justice, or corrupt politicians to extract rents, then government ownership may appear attractive. Because the nature of ownership changes a firm's objective function (as in Hart et al. 1997), government-owned firms may be less likely to corrupt the system to extract rents (Glaeser 2004). Croly in particular favored this response to subversion of justice: "if the interest of a corporation is so essentially hostile to the public interest . . . the logical inference is not a system of semi-official and semi-private management, but a system of exclusively public management." This type of reform was unpopular in the U.S., perhaps because the many problems of public ownership were appreciated, but European countries moved in that direction. In those countries weaker rule of law meant that less extreme measures could not be relied on to discipline large firms.

5   Comparison with Interest Group Theory

The traditional view of the Progressive Era, associated with the great historians such as Goldman (1947) and Hofstadter (1955), saw the reformers as selflessly serving the public interest, and focused entirely

on the benefits of reforms to consumers. In our analysis, we have generally followed this "public interest" approach, except we recognized the
centrality of enforcement to the design of reform. This analysis is not
intended as a suggestion that regulation is always, or even usually,
efficient—some of our own empirical work indeed suggests the opposite. Even for the case of the Progressive Era, however, the economic
analysis of regulation since the 1970s has been dominated by the
"capture" or "interest group" theories, which see regulation as shaped
primarily by producer or bureaucratic interests (Stigler 1971; Posner
1974; McChesney 1987). According to this view, producers either water
down regulation to render it irrelevant, or else subvert it for their own
benefit, such as raising prices. Bureaucrats, in turn, use regulation to
enhance their budgets or bribes. Any discussion of the Progressive Era
requires at least a brief overview of this research.[8]

The most dramatic evidence bearing on the capture theory deals
with the lobbying efforts around the passage of Progressive Era legislation. For example, established firms often supported the passage of the
Pure Food Act in 1906 as a way to raise the costs of new entrants and
rivals (Okun 1986; Wood 1986; Young 1989; High 1991; Coppin and
High 1988; High and Coppin 1999). Coppin and High (1988) show that
Harvey Wiley, the Chief Chemist of the Agriculture Department and
perhaps the most influential advocate of the 1906 Act, was significantly
influenced by traditional whiskey producers attempting to stop new
technologies, as well as by a desire to grow his department. Libecap
(1992) sees the Meat Inspection Act of 1891 as an attempt by traditional
slaughterhouses to stop the more efficient Chicago meatpackers through
legislation. Troesken (2003) studies the letters of Senator Sherman, and
argues that he "intended to protect small and inefficient firms (especially oil refiners) from their larger competitors, regardless of the effect
on consumer welfare." The list goes on, but the basic point remains:
Progressive Era regulation was captured by the industry, leaving consumer interests in the dustbin.

We do not regard this lobbying evidence as dispositive. Even in our
model, firms themselves may prefer regulation to strict liability because
they bear the costs of subverting justice and regulation might lower
these costs. In more general models, it is easy to have some firms benefiting, and others losing, from *socially efficient* regulation as compared
to litigation, with the winners lobbying ex ante for reform. Put differently, neither the fact that Harvey Wiley was supported by the traditional whiskey producers nor the fact that his bureau expanded

following the 1906 Act is convincing evidence that the Act did not serve the public interest.[9]

As we have already indicated, other evidence is consistent with the importance of consumer interest for Progressive reforms. We have discussed statements of presidential candidates and others, as well as the muckraking literature. Moreover, "clean government" reforms, such as reforms of the civil service, direct election of senators, recall of judges, and so on, are difficult to reconcile with the pure industrial capture perspective.

Occupational trends are also consistent with the importance of consumer interest. By the end of the nineteenth century, a growing number of voters became involved in the commercial and industrial economy, and thus were affected by the subversion of justice. More and more people working for corporations and railroads were exposed to industrial accidents. Increasing numbers of people lived in cities and suffered from the subversion of city administration. More and more farmers and small businessmen were expropriated by railroads with market power, or by larger competitors who made special deals with the railroads. "Politically, the rage of the victims counted for very little in 1840, not much in 1860; by 1890, it was a roaring force" (Friedman 1985, p. 476).

While this rage was the dominant factor behind the success of the Progressives, at least three other forces mattered. First, in the middle of the nineteenth century, relations between the North and the South dominated politics. For years after the Civil War, venal Republican candidates could whip up public support by "waving the bloody shirt," and reminding voters of the North–South issue. The reforming Horace Greeley was soundly beaten at the polls by Ulysses S. Grant, whose corrupt administration symbolized Northern dominance. Second, changing technology in publishing facilitated the rise of popular muckraking journals. Free entry into this national industry made it possible for journals such as McClure's to thrive without the support of the local business community, and indeed to flourish by attacking industry. Finally, a crucial development in U.S. politics was the ascent of Theodore Roosevelt, who ran both his first term and the election of 1904 on the platform of subversion of the judiciary and of restoration of justice through regulation.

Ultimately, however, we must look at the consequences of regulation to shed light on its reasons, and here the picture is muddy, even for the Progressive Era. Unquestionably, many outcomes were getting better during the relevant period. The use of child labor declined significantly, paralleling the introduction of child labor laws (Moehling 1999). Between 1900 and 1915, railroad passenger fatalities per million passenger miles declined from 0.0155 to 0.006, and employee fatalities from 0.159 to 0.066 (Lerner 1975). This happened precisely in the period of railroad safety regulation. One can also look at energy prices as one indication of the effectiveness of the Sherman Act, one of whose main targets was the Standard Oil Company. Between 1900 and 1915, prices of fuel and lighting rose 12 percent, compared to 22 percent for the BLS price index. This is not merely an impact of progress: over the 1890s, the BLS index fell by 7.4 percent while fuel and lighting prices rose by 21.5 percent (Lerner 1975). Wermiel (2000) describes the dramatic decline in catastrophic city fires in the U.S. around the turn of the century, which she attributes to technological progress and municipal regulation. Temin (1980), whose analysis is significantly influenced by the capture theory, nonetheless recognizes some benefits of the 1906 Pure Food Act—such as elimination of some false claims on medicine bottles, and the reduction in alcohol content of patent medicines.

Such evidence of progress is not uncontroversial. Some studies argue that progress would have occurred anyway, under the pressure of market forces, so regulation was irrelevant. Moehling (1999), for example, argues that industrial firms were reducing the use of child labor even without the constraint of the laws. Gilligan, Marshall, and Weingast (1989) is a particularly balanced study of the consequences of the Interstate Commerce Act of 1887. The authors recognize that many parties, including farmers, different kinds of railroads, and consumers, were influenced by and therefore tried to shape the Act. They show that the shipping rates on short hauls, where monopoly power was particularly pronounced, were reduced by the Act, but those on more competitive long hauls were increased. They argue that, at least to some extent, the Act helped sustain railroad cartels.

In the end, the evidence appears to point to significant social progress happening at least coincidentally with the Progressive Era reforms, as well as significant instances of regulatory capture by industry. Conceptually, we do not see our theory of institutional subversion and capture theory as hostile to each other. Capture theory easily allows a role for efficiency and consumer interest (Peltzman 1976; Grossman and Helpman 2001). And other versions of our institutional subversion theory allow, indeed emphasize, the abuse of law enforcement by the state, and the greater vulnerability of regulation than private litigation to such subversion (chapters 7 and 8). With respect to the Progressive Era, however, we find it difficult to deny that American capitalism of the 1920s was less corrupt and less abusive of workers and consumers than it was in 1900. In this episode, efficiency as a criterion for institutional choice goes a long way toward explaining the data.

6 Appropriate Institutions

As we argued in the introduction, the key goal of economic institutions is the same across times and places, namely to secure property rights and to make perpetrators of harmful acts accountable. But even though the goals are constant, which institutions are appropriate for achieving them varies. We argued in the introduction that empirical analysis reveals significant flaws in private dispute resolution, litigation, and regulation. Our model allows us to begin an analysis of appropriate institutions that recognizes their imperfections.

Figure 6.1 sheds light on the desirability of alternative modes of law enforcement in different countries and for different activities. We can think of X—the cost of subverting justice—as varying across countries and across activities. Some countries might have highly independent, disciplined, and efficient judges and regulators, who are invulnerable to political pressure and bribes; this is the situation of a very high X. Other countries might have poor, politically vulnerable, and easily corruptible officials, who cannot stand up to the pressure from private parties they are supposed to regulate; this is a situation of low X. We can also think of X varying across activities: a country might have enough bureaucratic prowess to control violence, but not enough to administer securities or anti-trust laws. Our framework allows us to consider the consequences of such variations. In this discussion, we take X to be exogenous, even though many Progressive and other reforms aimed to increase X.

The first, and arguably most important, message of the model is that in situations of extremely low X, the optimal government policy is *to do nothing*. When the administrative capacity of the government is severely limited, and both its judges and regulators are vulnerable to pressure and corruption, it might be better to accept the existing market failures and externalities than to deal with them through either the administrative or the judicial process. For if a county does attempt to correct market failures, justice will be subverted, and resources will be wasted on subversion without successfully controlling market failures.

This implication of the model is of great significance. Some economists (e.g., Stiglitz 1989) see market failures as pervasive in the emerging and transition economies, and recommend heavier regulation of economic activity in such economies than in advanced welfare states. Our model, in contrast, implies that countries operating at low levels of law and order in the first place should institute fewer regulations of economic activity, because their officials cannot administer more without being subverted. In these countries, if the policy of laissez-faire is followed, significant torts and monopoly abuses will be common. But such evidence of market failure does not imply an error of the regulatory stance. Rather, the law and order resources necessary to secure private property may be so limited that a regime of heavier regulation would perform even worse. A number of examples illustrate this point.

In 1992, under pressure from Western donors, the government of the Russian Federation established an anti-monopoly commission to address the problems of industrial consolidation. It became immediately apparent that the new commission could not stand up to the political power of large enterprises, and it did not even try to regulate their activities. Instead, the commission started to compile lists of small firms, such as bakeries, taking the position that such firms had the potential of abusing their local market power. Small entrepreneurs had to register with the commission, and often to pay bribes just to get off the lists of potential monopolies. The commission did nothing about the real problems of market power, added a level of regulation of small firms, and provided lucrative opportunities for its own employees (Boycko et al. 1995).

This phenomenon is more general. Most countries in the world, including the poorest ones, require many procedures for new firms to begin operating legally. Most of these procedures on paper have market failure justifications: officials check that the new entrepreneurs do not have criminal records, have professional qualifications and bank accounts, obey sanitary restrictions, and so on. These regulations, however, are often subverted through bribes or operations in the unofficial economy (De Soto 1989). In a cross-section, countries with more regulations of entry exhibit higher corruption and larger unofficial economies, but not superior social outcomes that regulation allegedly aims for (chapter 10).

The model, then, helps us reconcile the apparent greater extent of market failures in emerging economies stressed by Stiglitz (1989), with the equally apparent failure of regulation. The problem is not that these countries do not have a need for dealing with social harm. Rather, the problem is that their governments cannot administer the solutions. When neither courts nor regulators can resist subversion, the optimal policy is to leave even imperfect markets alone and to count on private arrangements to support trade (Johnson, McMillan, and Woodruff 2002).

The second message of the model is that, with intermediate enforcement capacity, especially in cases of high social damage from market activities, regulation is desirable. When externalities cause large damages, fines necessary to ensure desirable conduct are very high, and therefore pure liability regimes are especially vulnerable to subversion. In such circumstances, court enforcement might fail to achieve efficiency, but regulation of inputs stands a better chance. This case is even stronger if, as Landis (1938) maintains, it is more expensive to subvert career regulators than judges. The United States in the early twentieth century may in fact have exhibited the conditions under which, for efficiency reasons, regulation was preferred to tort.

This analysis also sheds light on a well-known recommendation of Becker (1968) that an optimal penalty system in the world of costly law enforcement should exhibit low probabilities of detection and conviction with very high penalties or fines. Such a strategy combines desirable deterrence effects with cost-savings on enforcement. A large literature explains why we do not see such law enforcement schemes in reality (Kaplow and Shavell 2002). Leading explanations of limited penalties include risk aversion or bankruptcy constraints of the violators (Polinsky and Shavell 1979) and considerations of fairness. We argue, alternatively, that the defendants are likely to spend enormous resources subverting a Beckerian scheme of high penalties, and may well succeed. Becker's solution of raising fines may have precisely the reverse effect: it only increases the incentives to subvert justice and diminishes the likelihood of good conduct.

Finally, the model implies that societies with the highest levels of law and order should rely on private litigation rather than regulation. The reason for this is that the liability system—as long as it is not subverted—can achieve first best efficiency, whereas regulation alone never can. Is this prediction realistic? Advanced economies appear to have both more litigation and more regulation, consistent with the logic of proposition 2. At the same time, it is striking that, since the 1970s, the United States has followed the path of significant deregulation of many industries, such as gas transmission, trucking, financial services, and airlines. One interpretation of such deregulation is that many issues can now be effectively addressed through private litigation, and therefore regulation is relatively less efficient.

In concluding this section, we return to its general point. The law and order conditions in a country are in themselves a crucial determinant of its optimal strategies for social control of business. Institutions cannot be built without recognizing where the country is in the first place. The finesse with which courts resolve disputes is appropriate for a country that has high levels of law and order. In the extreme contrast, a country beginning with low levels of law and order should tread gingerly in giving officials more power to shape economic life.

7 Conclusion

In 1960, Ronald Coase posed a crucial problem for economics: what is the optimal strategy of securing property rights—also known as establishing law and order? Many of Coase's followers have interpreted his article as supporting the "free market" idea that a well-functioning market economy, with well-defined property rights, only requires the common law to deal with the problem of social harm. In such a world, regulation is unnecessary. But Coase's reasoning does not necessarily imply the superiority of pure private litigation. Efficiency depends on whether private litigation, regulation, both, or neither, work better to address the problems raised by Coase. Different institutions might be most efficient—and most attractive to a libertarian—under different circumstances.

We have presented a model in which the optimal choice of a law enforcement strategy depends crucially on the vulnerability of law enforcement to subversion by powerful interests that might be affected. We argued that, in line the model, regulation became the increasingly efficient strategy of law enforcement in the United States between 1887 and 1917. The rise of the regulatory state may have been an efficient response to changing conditions.

None of this is to say, of course, that regulation is generally or even usually efficient as a solution to the problem of market failure. We often see regulation being subverted by special interests, or by the very bureaucrats supposed to enforce it. The empirical record of regulation around the world is mediocre at best—and we have argued that in many times and circumstances, doing nothing is the most efficient response to market failure. Indeed, a more general view of social control of business emphasizes the tradeoff between the vulnerability of alternative institutional arrangements to private and public abuse (Djankov et al. 2003).

At the most general level, this chapter argues that establishing law and order is itself an economic problem. Different countries at different times attempt to solve this problem differently—sometimes successfully, sometimes not. We have presented one approach to the efficiency of alternative institutional arrangements—based on the idea of subversion of justice. We believe that this approach provides a constructive strategy for comparing the efficiency of many basic institutions of a market economy.

Appendix: Proofs

Proof of Proposition 1   We consider four different cases with respect to the level of the cost of the subversion of justice, X/S, relative to the minimum fines necessary to implement alternative enforcement schemes (see figure 6.A1).

(1) $\dfrac{X}{S} < \dfrac{C}{p}$. In this case, the firm has access to cheap intimidation technology, so no regulatory scheme can force the firm to invest in precaution. Any fine—from regulation or social loss if there is no regulation—equals $L_N = \pi_\alpha P_\alpha SD + (1 - \pi_\alpha)P_1 SD$.

(2) In this case, neither strict liability nor negligence schemes can implement efficient levels of precaution for the type β firms. The two relevant options are to regulate or to do nothing. Regulation forces firms to maintain the high level of precaution if the fine, F, is set in the interval $\dfrac{SC}{p} \le F < X$. Under our assumptions, both types of the firms choose the high level of precaution, which is excessive for type α firms. The expected social loss under regulation equals $L_R = \pi_\alpha P_\alpha SD + (1 - \pi_\alpha)P_2 SD + SC$. When C is small, that is, $(1 - \pi_\alpha)(P_1 - P_2)D > C$, then excessive precaution is less wasteful than the expected damage from

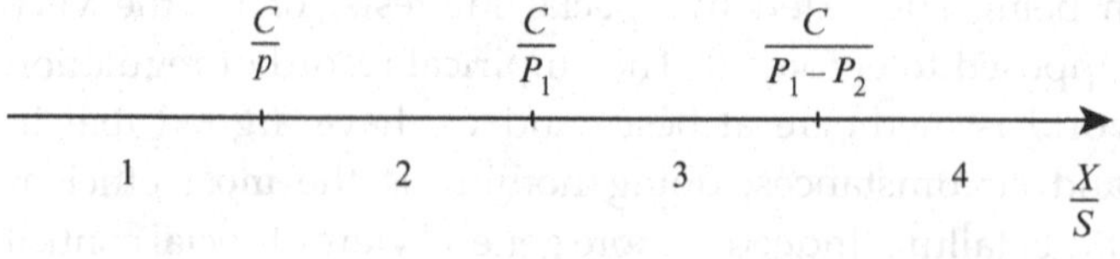

Figure 6.A1

its absence, and regulation dominates laissez-faire regime. When $C > (1 - \pi_\alpha)(P_1 - P_2)D$, then doing nothing is more efficient.

(3) For X/S in the interval $\dfrac{C}{P_1} < \dfrac{X}{S} < \dfrac{C}{P_1 - P_2}$ negligence becomes a subversion-of-justice-proof option. If $P_\alpha < P_1$ then negligence achieves the first best outcome when F is set in the interval $\dfrac{SC}{P_1} < F < \min\{X, \dfrac{SC}{P_\alpha}\}$. The expected loss in this case is equal to $L_{CN} = \pi_\alpha P_\alpha SD + (1 - \pi_\alpha)(P_2 SD + SC) = L_{FB}$.

If $P_\alpha > P_1$ then negligence cannot achieve both the efficiently low level of precaution for the type α firms and the efficiently high level of precaution for the type β firms. The social loss coincides with that under regulation, and the choice between laissez-faire and regulation is the same as in case 2.

(4) If $\dfrac{X}{S} > \dfrac{C}{P_1 - P_2}$, then the subversion of justice is not an acute problem, and high fines necessary for strict liability scheme cannot be avoided. Any fine larger than $\dfrac{SC}{P_1 - P_2}$ and smaller than X leads to the first best outcome in the strict liability scheme.

Proof of Proposition 2 For both parts of the proof, we propose a penalty scheme (F, R), and then show that the proposed values of F and R are weakly less than X, and that with these values of F and R, inequality (2) (in the case of claim (a)) and inequality (1) (in the case of claim (b)) hold.

For claim (a) (negligence), if $X > SC/P_\alpha$, then set $F = SC/P_\alpha - (P_1 - P_\alpha)SC/2(P_1 \bullet P_\alpha)$ and $R=0$. Condition (1) must hold as $P_1 \bullet F = \dfrac{SC(P_1 + P_\alpha)}{2P_\alpha}$ which is greater than SC and $P_\alpha \bullet F = SC - \dfrac{(P_1 - P_\alpha)SC}{2P_1}$ which is less than SC. When $SC/P_\alpha > X > SC/P_1$, then set $F = X$ and $R = 0$ and condition (2) holds as $P_1 X > SC > P_\alpha X$. When $X < SC/P_\alpha$, then set $F = X$ and $R = X - \varepsilon/p$, where $(P_1 + p)X - SC > \varepsilon > (P_\alpha + p)X - SC$ and again condition (2) holds.

For claim (b) (strict liability), always set $F = X$. If $(P_1 - P_2)X > SC$, set $R = 0$ and condition (1) holds. If $SC > (P_1 - P_2)X$, but $X > SC/p$, set $R = (SC - \varepsilon)/p$ where $(P_1 - P_2)X > \varepsilon$, and again condition (1) holds. If $SC > (P_1 - P_2)X$ and $SC/p > X$, set $R = X$, and the condition must hold.

7   Coase versus the Coasians

with Edward L. Glaeser and Simon Johnson

1   Introduction

At the heart of economists' traditional skepticism about government regulation is the Coase theorem (Coase 1960). The theorem states that when property rights are well defined and "transaction costs" are zero, market participants will organize their transactions in ways that achieve efficient outcomes. When they can do so, it is not necessary for the government to engage in "corrective" actions through taxes, regulations, or even legal rules. Financial markets are often used to demonstrate the Coase theorem's case against regulation. Advocates of the regulation of these markets point to a variety of potential failures, such as the ability of security issuers to "expropriate" both potential and existing investors through misrepresentation or profit diversion. Investors' fear of such expropriation prevents firms from raising external funds, and keeps efficient projects from being undertaken.

Not so, reply the Coasians. They point out that most securities transactions take place between sophisticated adults, and that both the buyers and the issuers of securities have available to them a vast range of private arrangements to achieve efficiency, including contracts such as corporate charters, certification by intermediaries, and various forms of bonding. Such contracts render most laws and regulations unnecessary (Stigler 1964; Easterbrook and Fischel 1991).

On the face of it, the Coasians' argument is powerful. Yet it crucially relies on, among other assumptions, the possibility of effective judicial enforcement of complicated contracts. Judges must be able, and more importantly willing, to read complicated contracts, verify whether the events triggering particular clauses have actually occurred, and interpret broad and ambiguous language. These requirements on the judges apply as strongly to the judicial enforcement of laws, where the interpretation and application of particular statutes require significant investment. In reality, as discussed in chapter 1, courts in many countries are underfinanced, unmotivated, unclear as to how the law applies, unfamiliar with economic issues, or even corrupt. Such courts cannot be expected to engage in costly verification of the facts of difficult cases or contingencies of complicated contracts. Indeed, even when contracts are restricted by statutes, the courts may not have the resources or incentives to verify whether or how particular statutes apply.

Financial contracting illustrates these problems. When is the information that a firm's manager fails to disclose to shareholders "material," and hence has to be disclosed because of a statute or a contract? When does a corporation "abuse" minority shareholders, as opposed to just following the managers' best "business judgment"? When does a broker fail to engage in "honest trading" in executing customer orders? When does a manager trade on "inside information" rather than simply happen to be lucky? The interpretation of the contracts or statutes involving such terms is expensive, and requires powerful incentives to motivate an adjudicator to invest in understanding the case. Absent such incentives, courts often postpone decisions or simply let go the potential violators of rules and contracts.

An alternative strategy is the enforcement of legal rules by regulators as opposed to judges. One critical distinction between judges and regulators is that the latter can be more easily provided with incentives to punish violations of particular statutes.[1] Judges, in contrast, are by design more independent and therefore harder to motivate. The stronger incentives of the regulators have the benefit of bringing about more aggressive enforcement than can be achieved through courts. Yet these incentives also have the potential cost of excessively aggressive enforcement when regulators motivated to find violations penalize innocent suspects. There is thus a tradeoff between enforcement by judges facing relatively weak but unbiased incentives and enforcement by regulators facing stronger but possibly biased incentives.[2]

We present a theoretical model that sheds light on this tradeoff, and identifies the circumstances under which enforcement by judges or regulators is preferred. The model shows that, relative to judges, regulators may be better motivated to invest in understanding the laws and circumstances of a case, but also more likely—if over motivated—to reach politically desirable decisions at the expense of doing justice. The model also shows how reducing the costs of the investment in information by law enforcers can improve enforcement efficiency.

We then illustrate the model by comparing the regulation of securities markets through corporate and securities laws in Poland and the Czech Republic. In these transition economies, financial regulation was designed essentially from scratch, and hence we can compare both the design of laws and regulations and their consequences. The model bears in particular on the design of securities laws, since these laws shape the incentives of market regulators as well as the costs of information acquisition by the enforcers.

We show that, in its securities law, Poland adopted a more stringent regulatory stance than the Czech Republic. This difference was reflected not just in the general philosophies of regulation, but in the statutes and the mechanisms of law enforcement. In contrast to the Czech Republic, Poland adopted legal rules highly protective of investors, mandated extensive information disclosure by securities issuers and intermediaries, and created an independent and highly motivated regulator to enforce the rules. We find that this approach to regulation in Poland has stimulated rapid development of securities markets, and enabled a number of firms to raise external funds. The expropriation of investors has been relatively modest. In contrast, the lax regulations in the Czech Republic, enforced by an unmotivated office in the finance ministry, have been associated with security delistings and a notable absence of equity finance through a public market by either new or existing firms. Expropriation of investors has been rampant, and has acquired a new Czech-specific name, tunneling (Coffee 1996; Pistor 2001; Johnson et al. 2000b). Starting in 1996, the Czech government tightened its regulations.

2   A Model of Enforcement Incentives

2.1   Basic Model
We consider a situation in which the government wishes to punish particular conduct creating negative externalities, such as non-disclosure of material information by a manager or "market manipulation" by a broker. This task is assigned to an enforcement official (an adjudicator). The question we address is whether the government wants this adjudicator to be a judge or a regulator. In the case of a judge, we focus on the inquisitorial legal system of civil law countries, where the judge must himself undertake an investigation into the facts of the situation and the law. The model we present focuses on the case where there is a legal rule or law that restricts certain conduct. The question

of who should adjudicate, however, equally well applies to a situation in which two private parties such as an investor and a broker contractually agree on their conduct and have a dispute on whether this contract was followed.

Our general assumption is that society does not have full control over the incentives facing law enforcement officials. Its ability to reward them for "enforcing the law" is limited because "doing justice" is largely unverifiable. Many of the rewards that these officials receive for doing justice are intangible, including self-esteem and the respect of one's peers. On the other hand, the government does have the ability to politicize the enforcement of particular legal rules by rewarding the enforcers for certain outcomes such as finding violations. We are interested in the conditions under which the government would choose such politicization.

We consider an adjudicator (who can be a judge or a regulator) examining a possible violation of a legal rule. For a cost $c > 0$, this adjudicator can undertake an investigation—which for simplicity we call search—and find out for sure whether a violation has taken place. We think of c as a personal cost to the adjudicator, which includes the time he might otherwise spend working on other matters. The adjudicator has complete discretion as to whether to penalize the potential violator, and can decide to do so without searching and incurring the cost c.

The adjudicator derives a payoff of b from following the law, or doing justice, which here means punishing a violator of the rule and letting go an innocent person. We can think of b as self-esteem or long-run respect of peers, which evidently matters to judges (Posner 1995). We assume that, in the short run, the government cannot increase b since it cannot verify whether the adjudicator actually searches and/or makes correct decisions. Training judges and building up their prestige presumably raises b, but such policies may take decades to pay off.

In addition, the adjudicator derives the payoff a from each suspect he punishes whether or not this suspect actually violated the rules. If $a = 0$, this adjudicator is only interested in justice, and is not motivated by "politics" or short-run career concerns. If $a > 0$, this adjudicator has a personal interest in finding violations. This can be so for a number of reasons. The state may be concerned with finding violators of particular rules to achieve its broader political goals, such as fighting drugs or persecuting particular ethnic minorities. More narrowly, only successful punishments of violators may be recorded by the superiors of an enforcer, and hence his future career or budget may be determined by the number of penalties he metes out. Still another important reason why adjudicators may wish to achieve certain outcomes is that these improve their career opportunities following government service. In principle, law enforcement can be heavily politicized and a could be a lot higher than b. We can also imagine the case where $a < 0$, which might describe regulators "captured" by the industry which they are supposed to regulate (Stigler 1971). In this case, the analysis becomes very simple: the adjudicator will generally not find any violations. Note that, as we have set up the model, a, b, and c capture the private rather than social payoffs and costs to the adjudicator.

To complete the model, we assume that the fraction p of suspected violators of the legal rule are actually guilty, and the fraction $(1 - p)$ are innocent. The payoffs to the adjudicator and the associated probabilities are shown in table 7.1.

The adjudicator makes the ex ante decision of whether to search. We refer to the strategy of letting everyone go regardless of violation as "leniency" and the strategy of punishing everyone regardless of violation as "abuse." With $b>0$, it never pays the adjudicator to sink the cost c and then ignore the information he obtains and be either lenient or abusive. If he searches, he always punishes the violators and lets go the innocent. But before search, it may benefit the adjudicator to be either lenient or abusive, depending on the magnitudes of a, b, c, and p.

To analyze the adjudicator's incentives for enforcement, we first consider his payoffs to the three strategies he can pursue: leniency, abuse, and search. These payoffs are given by:

(1) Leniency: $(1 - p)b$;

(2) Abuse: $a + pb$;

(3) Search: $b + pa - c$.

These payoffs define the optimal strategies of the enforcer, as summarized in:

Proposition 1 Fix b and p. The following strategies are followed for respective parameter values:

Leniency: $a \leq (1-2\,p)b$ and $c \geq (a + b)p$;

Abuse: $a \geq (1-2p)b$ and $c \geq (b-a)(1 - p)$;

Search: $c \leq (a + b)p$ and $c \leq (b-a)(1 - p)$.

Table 7.1

	Not punish	Punish	Probability
Innocent	b	a	$1 - p$
Guilty	0	$a + b$	p

These conditions divide the space of parameter values into three regions, as shown in figure 7.1.[3]

The interpretation of these conditions is straightforward. For low-powered punishment incentives and high cost of search, the adjudicator chooses leniency. For high-powered punishment incentives and high cost of search, the adjudicator turns to abuse. He only searches for the truth as long as the cost of investigation is low enough that, for low a's, he prefers search to leniency and, for high a's, he prefers search to abuse.

Even this simple analysis in figure 7.1 has several implications. First, we can think of c as a measure of the efficiency of the judicial system, the cost to the adjudicator of obtaining information. In principle, c can

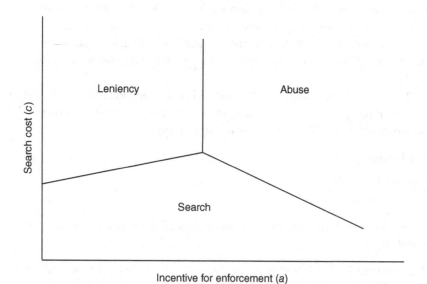

Figure 7.1
A simple model of incentives for enforcement. The adjudicator's incentive for enforcement divides the space of parameter values into three regions: leniency, abuse, and search.

be reduced through legal and regulatory reform. In the context of financial markets, for example, c can be reduced by improving accounting systems and disclosure by issuers and intermediaries. The model implies that reductions in the level of c always lead to increases in search. For high levels of c, search may not be achievable. Increasing career or financial incentives of the enforcers only moves the system from leniency to abuse—a risk that a society may not wish to take if it prefers the former to the latter. Put differently, a relatively efficient legal system—which could potentially be designed using appropriate legal rules—is necessary for achieving just outcomes; without it, it may be better to settle for leniency.

Second, for moderate and low levels of c, increasing incentives for punishment may indeed have the effect of moving the adjudicator from leniency to search. Even here, however, significant increases in a move the adjudicator out of search and into abuse. This analysis cautions against the Becker-Stigler (1974) enthusiasm for the high-powered enforcement incentives as it shows the risk for abuse, particularly in inefficient legal systems.

We can use this model to provide further comparative statics results, summarized in:

Proposition 2 Assume that $b > a$ and that $p < 1/2$. An increase in adjudicator professionalism, b, always 1) strictly reduces the region of abuse, 2) strictly increases the region of search, and 3) diminishes leniency for low a's—to favor search—and expands leniency for high a's—at the expense of abuse (figure 7.2). An increase in the fraction of suspects who are guilty, p, always 1) reduces the region of leniency, 2) expands the region of abuse, and 3) expands search for low a's—at the expense of leniency and reduces it for high a's—to favor abuse.

The intuition behind these results is straightforward. An increase in the adjudicator's concern for justice raises his aversion to both letting the guilty go (resulting from leniency) and punishing the innocent (resulting from abuse). As a consequence, for a broader range of parameter values, he conducts a search. Since with $p < 1/2$ most suspects are innocent, a higher b makes leniency more attractive relative to abuse, further shrinking the latter region.

An increase in the guilty share of the population, p, obviously expands the range of abuse and contracts the range of search. For low incentives, the attractiveness of search rises relative to that of leniency and hence the scope of search expands. For high incentives, the

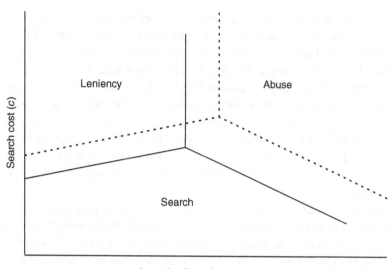

Figure 7.2
Comparative statics: adjudicator professionalism (*b*). The adjudicator's incentive for enforcement divides the space of parameter values into three regions: leniency, abuse, and search. Increasing adjudicator professionalism (*b*) reduces the region of abuse.

attractiveness of search falls relative to that of abuse, and hence the scope of search contracts.

2.2 Implications

What does this analysis imply for the choice of optimal enforcement incentives? To begin, we can think of $a = 0$ as the case of "true justice," which is perhaps provided by judges truly independent of the government. We can alternatively think of high a's as regulators or prosecutors whose careers and budgets depend not only on doing justice, but also on finding violations. One further difference between judges and regulators might be the greater specialization of the latter, leading to lower search cost c, but one can of course imagine specialized judges, as in the cases of bankruptcy or family law. The intermediate a's may perhaps correspond to civil law judges, who are part of the civil service and hence may be dependent on the government, but who at the same time have less of an incentive to find violations than regulators do (Ramseyer and Rasmusen 1997). Using this interpretation, the question becomes: Who should enforce a particular legal rule?

The model illustrates the costs and benefits of enforcement by judges and regulators. The government must choose the incentives of an enforcer, namely a (as long as career concerns are not dominated by outside opportunities), to achieve two objectives. The first is to stimulate search, as opposed to leniency, and thereby to punish the violators (this is the problem that Coasians largely ignore). The second objective is to achieve justice by not punishing the innocent (this is the problem that the advocates of government regulation usually ignore). Increasing a has the benefit of stimulating search relative to leniency, and thereby making it more likely that the violators are punished, but also the cost of increasing the likelihood of abuse—the punishment of the innocent as well as the violators without search. Put differently, turning the enforcement of a legal rule over to an apolitical judge has the benefit that the innocent would be rarely punished, but a judge—especially a judge with a low b—would also tend toward leniency. In contrast, politicizing the system and turning the enforcement to a regulator moves it away from leniency (provided that this regulator is not captured, i.e., $a > 0$), but risks abuse.

In principle, the government would wish to have judges with very high b's—a very professional and motivated judiciary which has both sufficient incentives to investigate and a strong interest in justice. But this may not be possible. In this event, the model suggests that the best enforcement strategy—particularly when investigations are personally expensive (though not prohibitively expensive)—may be to have a regulator with a high enough a to get some search but not so high as to risk abuse. How high an a the government chooses would depend on how much it cares about punishing the violators relative to avoiding punishing the innocent. Presumably, in the cases where punishing the innocent is particularly expensive to the society, such as criminal law, the costs of abuse are sufficiently high that most governments would still set a low and allocate adjudication to judges. In civil situations, however, the case for regulation is stronger, at least when c is moderately high. The other way of looking at this is that enforcement reforms which lower c are likely to stimulate search and lead to more efficient outcomes, regardless of whether a judge or a regulator handles the enforcement.

These predictions of the model relate to the case for securities markets regulation made by James Landis (1938), the architect of such regulation in the United States and one of the first SEC commissioners.

Landis was skeptical that the courts were motivated enough to punish dishonesty in security issuance and trading in a world where the opportunities for promoters and insiders to expropriate investors were extensive. He thought that an independent and highly motivated SEC, whose only objective would be to assure the integrity of financial markets, could do this better. He also argued that using regulators as adjudicators is a better strategy because they face lower costs of investigation. Lower costs encourage search and make abuse less likely for a given level of incentives. The model can thus account for some basic intuitions for when regulation might be preferred to judicial enforcement.

In the following sections, we examine the implications of the model for financial regulation in Poland and the Czech Republic. We examine the reform in two crucial areas governing financial markets: corporate law and securities law. Corporate law deals in particular with the relationship between corporate insiders and shareholders, and is typically enforced through private litigation. Securities law regulates financial markets. As such it also deals with some aspects of shareholder protection. In addition, securities law specifies the status and the powers of the securities regulator and deals with disclosure of information by securities issuers and intermediaries. Variation in the securities laws, therefore, can be interpreted as variation in a and c in the model: a more motivated regulator would have a higher a, and greater disclosure would correspond to a lower c. We show that Poland and the Czech Republic have adopted very different strategies toward shareholder protection, especially in their securities laws, and that these strategies can be interpreted in light of the model. Our evidence suggests that the greater success of financial development in Poland than in the Czech Republic might be related to the more appropriate regulatory stance in Poland, in line with the predictions of the theoretical analysis.

3 Background on Poland and the Czech Republic

In broad terms, Poland and Czechoslovakia share similar histories over the past 50 years. Both countries turned communist and became Soviet satellites shortly after World War II, and spent the next 40 years building socialism. In 1989, the two countries spearheaded the anti-communist revolution. In Poland, Solidarity won overwhelming support in the June 1989 elections, and by September 1989 was able to form a government. In Czechoslovakia, the communists gave up their "leading role" in the country in the face of massive protests in November 1989, and the communist President resigned in December. Free elections in June 1990 completed a sequence of events that came to be known as "the Velvet Revolution."

At the beginning of reforms, Poland had a larger population of 38 million people, compared to 10.3 million in the Czech Republic. The Czech Republic in 1989 had per capita income of $5,727 in constant 1995 U.S. dollars compared to Poland's $3,045. Both countries were fully industrialized, with an industrial structure largely shaped by decades of Soviet-style central planning. Both countries border on Western Europe and in particular Germany, although Warsaw is 569 miles from Frankfurt while Prague is only 261 miles away.

Both countries initiated economic reforms immediately after shedding communism. In Poland, critical legislation on liberalization was passed in the fall of 1989, and the key measures came into effect on January 1, 1990. Small-scale privatization began in May 1990, although large scale privatization started with a whisper in 1991, ran into political obstacles, and spread over most of the 1990s. In Czechoslovakia, reforms were also initiated in early 1990, with the devaluation of the currency, budget cuts, and banking reform. The formal reform package, including price increases, started on January 1, 1991. The law on large scale privatization was adopted on February 1, 1991. Privatization through vouchers took place in two waves: in 1992 (completed in mid-1993) and 1993 (completed in 1994). Most rules of privatization, including those on Investment Privatization Funds, were developed in 1991 (Coffee 1996).

Moreover, both countries were virtually finished with these basic reforms by 1994. They received virtually identical scores on every World Bank indicator of the pace of transition (de Melo et al. 1996). The European Bank for Reconstruction and Development also ranked them very closely (see table 7.2). Although the Czech Republic moved more rapidly on large scale privatization and so had a somewhat higher share of its GDP generated in the private sector, in matters such as small-scale privatization, governance and restructuring, price and trade liberalization, competition policy, banking reform, and financial institutions, the countries were neck in neck and very far advanced.[4] In short, both countries were rapid and thorough reformers in their emergence from communism, especially in comparison with other transition economies.

Table 7.2
Comparison of Economic Reform Policies by the EBRD.

	Poland	Czech Republic	Poland	Czech Republic	Poland	Czech Republic
	Transition indicators 1997		*Transition indicators 1996*		*Transition indicators 1995*	
Private sector share of GDP	65	75	60	75	60	70
Large-scale privatization	3+	4	3	4	3	4
Small-scale privatization	4+	4+	4	4	4	4
Governance and restructuring	3	3	3	3	3	3
Price liberalization	3	3	3	3	3	3
Trade and foreign exchange system	4+	4+	4	4	4	4
Competition policy	3	3	3	3	3	3
Banking reform and interest rate liberalization	3	3	3	3	3	3
Securities market and nonbank financial institutions	3+	3	3	3	3	3

Scale is from 1 (no reform) to 4+ (full reform).
Source: European Bank for Reconstruction and Development (1997, 1996, 1995).

There are, however, two differences which we come back to below. First, the Czech large-scale voucher privatization was faster and more extensive than privatization in Poland, which over time utilized a variety of methods from direct sales to share transfers to mutual funds. As a consequence, the number of publicly held companies in the early 1990s was significantly higher in the Czech Republic than in Poland. Second, during this period, Poland grew faster but also had higher inflation than the Czech Republic. The assessments of growth rates depend on exactly how they are calculated. The level of GDP in Poland in 1997 stood at 110 relative to 100 in 1989, whereas in the Czech Republic it stood only at 90. Using constant 1995 dollars, however, Poland's advantage is smaller. During 1992–1997, the Czech inflation averaged 13.9 percent per annum, while Polish inflation was significantly higher at 26.5 percent.

In legal development, the two countries again appear similar. In the universe of transition economies, both get perfect or nearly perfect scores, although these scores have only been kept after 1995. The European Bank for Reconstruction and Development evaluates transition economies on the extensiveness of laws (since 1996), effectiveness of laws (since 1996), and overall legal development (since 1995). Table 7.3, panel A, presents the scores for Poland and the Czech Republic, which again are close to each other and as high as those of any transition economy. The legal systems of the two countries, however, lagged behind those of rich market economies. Gwartney and Lawson (1997) present an index of "equality of citizens under the law and access of citizens to a non-discriminatory judiciary." In 1995–1996, both Poland and the Czech Republic received scores of 5 out of 10, compared to between 7.5 and 10 for the rich industrial countries. The 1997 World Competitiveness Yearbook (IMD 1997) in its question on the legal framework gave Poland 4.16 out of 9 and the Czech Republic 4.66. This compares to 8.46 for the world leader, Singapore (and over 8 generally for rich industrial countries) and the low of 2.35 for Venezuela. Finally, the 1996 World Competitiveness Report (World Economic Forum 1996), in its question on confidence in the fair administration of justice, gives 2.93 out of 6 to the Czech Republic and 2.92 to Poland. This compares to the high of 5.78 for New Zealand, and the low of 1.77 for Russia. All the surveys, then, treat the judicial systems of the two countries as about equally advanced, ahead of world laggards yet far behind the rich industrial countries.

Table 7.3
Legal Environment.

	1997		1996		1995	
	Poland	Czech Republic	Poland	Czech Republic	Poland	Czech Republic
Panel A						
EBRD						
Extensiveness of laws	4	4	4	4	n.a.	n.a.
Effectiveness of laws	4+	4	3	4	n.a.	n.a.
Overall	4	4	4	4	4	4

Panel B				
Wall Street Journal CEER survey	December 1997– January 1998	December 1996– January 1997	December 1995– January 1996	February 1995
Rule of law / legal safeguards	8.7	9	8.8	9.1	9.1
Legal framework				9.8	9.8

Scale for legal extensiveness and legal effectiveness is from 1 (no reform) to 5 (full reform).
Scale for rule for law/legal safeguards, and legal framework is from 1 to 10 (the highest/best score).
Source: European Bank for Reconstruction and Development (1997, 1996, 1995), and *Central EuropeanEconomic Review*, a supplement of the *Wall Street Journal Europe* (issues indicated in table).

In summary, the economies and the economic policies of Poland and the Czech Republic share some remarkable similarities during the 1990s. The two countries emerged from socialism with a need to massively reorganize their economies and proceeded to do so both rapidly and effectively. In many crucial respects, they followed similar policies toward this goal, and achieved similar results, especially compared to other, less successful, transition economies.

4 Company Law and Securities Law and Regulation

Empirical research shows that investor protection through company laws and commercial codes is an important deterrent of expropriation of outside investors, and as such a key determinant of the development of securities markets across countries (La Porta et al. 1997a, 1998). Using the index of anti-director rights from La Porta et al. (1998), Polands's score is 3 out of 6, and the Czech Republic's score is 2 out of 6. These differences do not seem sufficient to account for the differences in financial development documented below.

The two countries followed different approaches to reform in terms of the government's interest in regulatory intervention. This difference did not escape the early observers of the two countries, who viewed Czech economic policy as more laissez-faire than Polish economic policy. For example, in each of the three years 1994–1996, the conservative Heritage Foundation gave the Czech Republic a perfect (from its perspective) score of 1 and Poland a mediocre score of 3 on its measure of "regulation"—the extent to which government restricts economic activity. Along similar lines, Euromoney considered Poland to be riskier for foreign investment and lending than the Czech Republic, in part because property rights were less secure from government intervention.

These observers had every right to form such opinions based on the pronouncements about markets and market reform coming from economic officials in the two countries. Vaclav Klaus, the Czech Finance Minister and later Prime Minister, was both tremendously articulate and unabashedly anti-government in his vision of reforms: "We knew that we had to liberalize, deregulate, privatize at a very early stage of the transformation process, even if we might be confronted with rather weak and, therefore, not fully efficient markets. . . . Conceptually it was—at least for me—rather simple: all you had to do was to apply the economic philosophy of the University of Chicago" (Klaus 1997, from a 1995 speech). Leszek Balcerowicz, the champion of Polish reforms, was more cautious: "The capacity of the state to deal with various problems varies, mainly because of varying informational requirements. On this basis, one can distinguish on the one hand, the sphere of the state's natural competence (legislating and enforcing the law, dealing with other states, for example) and on the other hand, its sphere of natural incompetence (a massive and detailed industrial policy, for example)" (1995, p. 176).

These differences revealed themselves most clearly in the regulation of capital markets. The Polish Law of Public Trading in Securities and Trust Fundswas adopted on March 22, 1991 and became effective in early April 1991. The Czech Securities Act was adopted in 1992, and became effective on January 1, 1993. Although this Act was passed after privatization had started, financial institutions, such as Investment Privatization Funds (IPFs), apparently did not lobby for or against it. In fact, the Czech rules were established before privatization started and before the IPFs existed, and only codified later (Coffee 1996). They were a product of the government's economic philosophy, not lobbying.

In our analysis of securities laws, we focus especially on two issues. First, we show that there were significant differences in the institutions of securities regulation in the two countries, particularly with respect to the independence and the power of securities regulators. We interpret the greater independence and power of the regulator as an increase in the parameter a in the model: the incentives of the adjudicator. Second, we show that the issuers and the intermediaries in the two countries faced radically different disclosure requirements, so that the regulators had very different access to information. We interpret the greater mandatory disclosure, and the use of intermediaries to enforce it as reductions in the parameter c in the model: the cost of search.

From this perspective on regulation, an examination of securities laws in Poland and the Czech Republic reveals profound differences. To begin, the two laws differed in the identity of the government body supervising securities markets. In Poland, it was an independent Securities Commission. In the Czech Republic, such a commission was not established initially, and markets were supervised by the Capital Markets Supervisors Office of the Ministry of Finance. The Ministry of Finance during this period was first under Klaus, and later, when he became Prime Minister, remained indifferent to regulating securities markets. Both supervisory bodies received the power to generate regulations, to issue and revoke licenses, and to impose fines for violations of security laws and regulations, but had to refer criminal cases to the public prosecutor. The criminal channel was scarcely used in either country. The fact that the Polish Securities Commission was independent, and charged solely with supervision of securities markets, is likely to have provided it with greater incentives to find violations than those faced by the Czech Ministry of finance, with its much broader agenda.

A key difference in the structure of securities laws in the two countries is in the emphasis on the regulation of intermediaries. The idea of focusing the regulation of securities markets on intermediaries is sometimes credited to James Landis (Landis 1938; McCraw 1984), who reasoned that the U.S. SEC could monitor neither the compliance with disclosure, reporting and other rules by all listed firms, nor the trading practices of all market participants. Rather, the SEC would regulate intermediaries, such as brokers, accounting firms, investment advisors, etc., placing on them the burden of assuring compliance with regulatory requirements by issuers and traders. By maintaining substantial administrative power over the intermediaries, including the power to issue and revoke licenses, the Commission could force them to monitor market participants. Moreover, the intermediaries would be relatively few in number, and more concerned with their own reputations with the SEC compared to most of the issuers. By privatizing part of the enforcement of disclosure to the intermediaries, the regulator could reduce the share of the enforcement costs he had to bear himself—a reduction in c in our model.

Table 7.4 compares the two laws from the perspective of the regulation of financial intermediaries. In the regulation of individual brokers, Poland instituted relatively elaborate licensing requirements, accompanied by tests. Brokers were supposed to engage in "honest trading" as interpreted by the Commission, and could lose their license. The Czech Republic had much more pro forma licensing of brokers, with easy exams, no warning concerning "honest trading," and evidently no real power of the Commission to revoke licenses. The Polish Commission used the broad "honest trading" requirement, and its own power to interpret it, to discourage brokers' practices that might not have served the interests of clients.

Brokerage firms were also licensed in both countries but faced considerably stiffer regulations in Poland. For example, the regulator

Table 7.4
Regulation of Intermediaries.

	Poland		Czech Republic	
Individual brokers				
Licensed by securities market regulator	Yes	Articles 18.2 and 14.1	Yes	Section 49
Must pass exam administered by securities market regulator	Yes	Article 14.1(4)	No	Section 49
Required to engage in "honest trading" and act in the interest of clients	Yes	Article 17.1	No	Section 49
License can be suspended or revoked by Securities Commission	Yes	Articles 16.2 and 16.3	Yes	Section 49
Brokerage enterprises				
Licensed by securities market regulator	Yes	Article 18.2	Yes	Section 45
Securities market regulator has right of access and inspection	Yes	Article 26	No	Sections 45–48
License can be suspended or revoked by securities market regulator	Yes	Article 25.3	Yes	Section 48(2)
Required to engage in "honest trading" and act in the interest of clients	Yes	Article 25.2(3)	No	Sections 45–48
Must not conduct other business with the same name	Yes	Article 18.6	No	Sections 45–48
Must report who has more than 5 percent of voting rights at general meeting of shareholders	Yes	Article 23.2	No	Sections 45–48
Must report any change of voting rights for one person above 2 percent	Yes	Article 23.3	No	Sections 45–48
Bank engaged in brokerage operations must have organizational and financial separateness of department for public trading in securities	Yes	Article 24	No	Sections 45–48
Must not trade securities issued by parent or subsidiary company	Yes	Article 31	No	Sections 45–48
Investment advisers (firms engaged in advisory activity in the field of public trading)				
Licensed by securities market regulator	Yes	Article 33	No	Not mentioned in the Czech law

Table 7.4
(continued)

	Poland		Czech Republic	
Must pass exam set by securities market regulator	Yes	Article 33.3	No	Not mentioned in the Czech law
Securities market regulator has right of access and inspection	Yes	Article 33	No	Not mentioned in the Czech law
License can be suspended or revoked by securities market regulator	Yes	Article 33	No	Not mentioned in the Czech law
Required to engage in "honest trading" and act in the interest of clients	Yes	Article 33	No	Not mentioned in the Czech law
Must not conduct other business with the same name	Yes	Article 33	No	Not mentioned in the Czech law
Must report who has more than 5 percent of voting rights at general meeting of shareholders	Yes	Article 33	No	Not mentioned in the Czech law
Must report any change of voting rights for one person above 2 percent	Yes	Article 33	No	Not mentioned in the Czech law
Bank engaged in investment advisory operations must have organizational and financial separateness of department for public trading in securities	Yes	Article 33	No	Not mentioned in the Czech law
Must not trade securities issued by parent or subsidiary company	Yes	Article 33	No	Not mentioned in the Czech law

Sources: Poland: Act of Trading in Securities and Trust Funds, 1991; Czech: Securities Act 1992.

Stock markets

	Poland		Czech Republic	
Trading must take place on a stock exchange	Yes	Article 54.1	No	Section 50 of the Securities Law
Securities regulator controls stock exchange rules	Yes		No	Not mentioned in the Czech law
Securities exchange should ensure a uniform market	Yes	Article 57(1)	No	Not mentioned in the Czech law

Table 7.4
(continued)

	Poland		Czech Republic	
Securities exchange should ensure dissemination of uniform information on the value of securities	Yes	Article 57(3)	No	Not mentioned in the Czech law
Agreements among any groups to artificially raise or lower the price of securities are prohibited	Yes	Article 64.3	No	Not mentioned in the Czech law
Mutual funds				
Mutual funds may be administered solely by mutual fund companies	Yes	Article 89.2	No	Not mentioned in the Czech law
Mutual fund companies are licensed by securities regulator	Yes	Article 89	Yes	Section 8
Mutual fund company can be dissolved by securities regulator	Yes	Article 98	Yes	Section 37
Mutual fund companies must be joint stock companies	Yes	Article 90.1	No	Section 2
Only registered shares are allowed in mutual fund companies (no bearer shares)	Yes	Article 92.2	No	Not mentioned in the Czech law
Closed-end funds are allowed	No	Article 104	Yes	
Founder limited to 10 percent of share capital	Yes	Article 93(1)	No	Not mentioned in the Czech law
Founder not allowed to be on Management Board	Yes	Article 93(1)	No	Not mentioned in the Czech law
Publicly traded securities or government obligations	Yes	Article 107	No	Section 17
No more than 5 percent of the assets can be in securities issued by one issuer	Yes	Article 108	No	Section 17
Custodian banks (for mutual funds)				
All fund assets must be entrusted to a trustee bank	Yes	Article 112.1	Yes	Section 31
Trustee bank must make sure that sale and retirement of participation units in the fund are consonant with the law and house rules of the fund	Yes	Article 112.2(2)	No	Not mentioned in the Czech law

Table 7.4
(continued)

	Poland		Czech Republic	
Trustee bank must compute the net worth of the fund's assets	Yes	Article 112.2(3)	No	Not mentioned in the Czech law
Trustee bank must not execute instructions that are in conflict with the law or house rules of the fund	Yes	Article 112.2(4)	No	Not mentioned in the Czech law
Trustee bank must make sure income of the fund is made public	Yes	Article 112.2(6)	No	Not mentioned in the Czech law
Trustee bank may not be a founder of the mutual fund company, or a buyer of its securities, or the administrator of the company	Yes	Article 113.1	No	Not mentioned in the Czech law
Mutual fund company may not buy securities issued by the trustee bank or a related company	Yes	Article 113.2	No	Not mentioned in the Czech law

Source: Polish Act of Trading in Securities and Trust Funds, 1991; Czech Investment Companies and Investment Funds Act April 1992 and Stock Exchange Act 1992.

received the right to access and inspect the books of brokerage firms, and these firms had to disclose their ownership structure, stay away from trading in the securities issued by a parent or a subsidiary company, and retain organizational and financial separateness from banks which owned some of them. These regulations did not exist in the Czech Republic. It is clear that the Czech Republic adopted a very hands-off stance toward brokers and brokerage firms, in contrast to Poland.

The Czech securities law contained no regulation of investment advisors; the Polish law contained substantial regulations, including licensing. The Polish law restricted trading to take place on a stock exchange, and regulated these exchanges to ensure some transparency in trading. The Czech law did not include such regulations. The Polish law contained detailed regulations of mutual funds, and in fact for several years the entry into this activity was severely limited. The Czech law took a much more lenient approach again. Finally, the Polish law contained stringent regulations of custodian banks, which are an important checkpoint for changes in ownership that might facilitate tunneling. The Czech law again was less restrictive.

Finally, the Polish securities law, to a much greater extent than the Czech law, established administrative procedures enabling the securities market regulator to discipline the intermediaries without recourse to the judicial system. The intermediaries could then appeal the decisions of the regulator to administrative courts, but then they, rather than the regulator, had to face the delays and the inefficiency of the judicial system. Because the judiciary in neither country is corrupt, the regulators had little fear of their lawful decisions being overturned.

Table 7.5 compares the two original laws from the perspective of the regulation of security issuers, especially in the area of disclosure. Recall that greater disclosure of financial information can serve to reduce the cost of information acquisition by a regulator or a judge. In Poland the introduction of securities to public trading required both a permission of the regulator and a prospectus. The Czech law required neither. The Polish law required monthly, quarterly, semi-annual, and annual reporting of financial information; the Czech law only the annual results. The Polish law required disclosure of all material information; the Czech law only that of significant adverse developments.

Financial results are one area where disclosure may be important; ownership structure is another. The Polish law required disclosure of substantial minority shareholdings; the Czech law did not. Indeed, under the original Polish law, a shareholder crossing 10, 20, 33, 50, 66, and 75 percent ownership stakes had to publicly disclose his ownership. The lack of disclosure of minority shareholdings has been seen as a problem in several West European countries, since it enables anonymous large shareholders to collude with management and expropriate small shareholders (European Corporate Governance Network 1997). Finally, the original Polish law also required a mandatory bid for the remaining shares when a 50 percent ownership threshold was reached; the Czech law did not. Such mandatory bids, combined with disclosure of ownership, are intended to prevent the expropriation of minority shareholders in tender offers, since they force an acquirer to buy out minority shareholders when he gains control.

This evidence shows that Poland chose to regulate its securities markets more stringently than the Czech Republic. In line with the model, its law provided for extensive disclosure of financial and ownership information, a way to reduce c and thus to facilitate regulation (as well as private governance). The Polish reliance on financial intermediaries to ensure financial disclosure can also be seen as a reduction in c. Also in line with the model, Poland relied on administrative control over markets by a motivated securities regulator, an increase in a relative to judicial enforcement. This could, in principle, motivate the regulators to become informed and reduce the likelihood of leniency. We next consider whether this approach worked.

5   Outcomes

5.1   Qualitative Assessments

Stable prices, rapid privatization, and openness to the West combined to generate favorable initial assessments of the Czech economic reforms. By 1996, however, there was mounting evidence of systematic expropriation of minority shareholders by Investment Privatization Funds and company insiders colluding with them. Coffee (1996), who first presented his paper in 1994, drew attention to such expropriation—which came to be known as tunneling. In a typical scheme, the managers of an IPF holding a large stake in a privatized company would agree with the managers of this company to create a new (possibly off-shore) entity, which they would jointly control. The IPF might then sell its shares in the company to this entity at below market price, thereby expropriating the shareholders of the IPF. The company could also sell some of its assets or its output to the new entity, again at below fair value, thereby expropriating its own minority shareholders. These arrangements between corporate managers and their large shareholders (IPFs) enriched them at the expense of minority investors in both the firms and the IPFs.

The laxity of the securities law accommodated tunneling. First, since transactions did not need to take place on an exchange, large blocks of shares could change hands off the exchange at less than the prevailing market price. Even on an exchange, there was no guarantee of price uniformity. Moreover, brokers and brokerage firms had no restrictions on facilitating such transactions, nor did the custodian banks have any regulatory duty to stop them. Second, since there was no requirement of ownership disclosure, the acquirers of large blocks could remain secret. Third, without a mandatory bid, these acquirers had no obligation to buy out the remaining minority shareholders. Fourth, the IPFs appear to have been under no restrictions in pursuing such transactions, since their management did not owe any clearly regulated duty to their investors, let alone to the minority shareholders of the

Table 7.5
Regulation of Listed Companies.

	Poland		Czech Republic	
Regulation of listed companies				
Introduction of securities into public trading requires permission of the securities regulator	Yes	Article 49	No	Not mentioned in Czech law
Introduction of securities into public trading requires a prospectus	Yes	Article 50.2	No	Not mentioned in Czech law
False statement in prospectus is forbidden	Yes	Article 118	Yes	Section 79
Monthly reporting of financial information	Yes	Reg. of Sec. Comm. and Stock Exchange	No	Not mentioned in Czech law
Quarterly reporting of financial information	Yes	Reg. of Sec. Comm. and Stock Exchange	No	Not mentioned in Czech law
Semiannual reporting of financial information	Yes	Reg. of Sec. Comm. and Stock Exchange	No	Not mentioned in Czech law
Annual reporting of financial information	Yes	Reg. of Sec. Comm. and Stock Exchange	Yes	Section 80
Obligation to publish all material information	Yes	Reg. of Sec. Comm. and Stock Exchange	No	Section 80 just significant adverse developments
Constraints on purchasers/potential controlling shareholders				
Transparency of ownership requirement	Yes		No	Centre for Securities can change ownership without disclosure
Threshold at which must declare stake (percent)				None
10	Yes	Article 72	No	Not mentioned in Czech law
20	Yes		No	Not mentioned in Czech law

Table 7.5
(continued)

	Poland		Czech Republic	
33	Yes		No	Not mentioned in Czech law
50	Yes		No	Not mentioned in Czech law
66	Yes		No	Not mentioned in Czech law
75	Yes		No	Not mentioned in Czech law
Form of disclosure required to Securities Commission	Yes		No	Not mentioned in Czech law
Form of disclosure required to Anti-Monopoly Office	Yes		No	Not mentioned in Czech law
Form of disclosure required to company	Yes		No	Not mentioned in Czech law
Company must announce who owns more than 10 percent	Yes	In 2 national Polish newspapers	No	Not mentioned in Czech law
Threshold at which must make general offer				
Must make offer if intend to pass specified threshold for ownership stake	Yes	Article 73	No	Not mentioned in Czech law
Must make offer if actual ownership stake passes specified threshold	Yes	Article 87	No	Not mentioned in Czech law
Tender offer rules				
Not allowed to hide behind a related company	Yes	Cannot hide behind "dependent subject" (Article 72(2), Article 73(2))	No	Not mentioned in Czech law
Transactions in share on the stock exchange should be suspended	Yes	All transactions in this share on the stock exchange should be suspended	No	Not mentioned in Czech law
Time limit for subscribing	Yes	25 days	No	Not mentioned in Czech law

Table 7.5
(continued)

	Poland			Czech Republic
Must buy all the shares offered	Yes		No	Not mentioned in Czech law
Specified price for purchase	Yes	Article 74	No	Not mentioned in Czech Law
Conditions under which can "go private"	Yes	The price offered ... cannot be lower than the highest price paid thereby for the shares in the last 12 months	No	Not mentioned in Czech law
Securities Commission must approve	Yes			Not specified

Sources: Polish and Czech Securities Laws.

companies they tunneled. Fifth, there was no reason to disclose any financial transactions between the new owner of shares and the company, since such transactions were generally allowed and did not need to be disclosed except perhaps in the annual report several months later. Finally, the minority shareholders had virtually no legal recourse in stopping such expropriation except in a very few cases when the oppressed minority mechanism came into play, and even substantial minority shareholders could not elect their own directors to represent their interests.

During the mid-1990s, the heyday of tunneling in the Czech Republic, the regulators did very little to stop it. Part of the problem was the weakness of the laws. But equally important was probably the lack of interest of securities regulators combined with judicial ineffectiveness.

By 1996, it became widely believed that something had gone wrong with the regulation of the Czech financial markets. In March 1996 the Central European Economic Review, a publication of the Wall Street Journal, surveyed assorted brokerages and fund managers on corporate governance in four transition economies. The survey asked respondents to comment on the disclosure of large shareholdings, transparency of markets, quality of reporting, protection of small shareholders, and insider trading. The Polish market came out as the best of the four, followed by the Hungarian market. The Czech market came third, ahead of the Russian market, which received the lowest score on every dimension. The Polish market outscored the Czech market on every dimension, with large spreads on the disclosure of ownership and transparency.

The Polish regulators relied on the actual legal rules to protect investors; it was not just their ideology that made a difference. In a few cases we examined, they relied on specific rules to promote disclosure that did not exist in the Czech law, consistent with the view that reductions in c matter. The Polish regulator was also evidently motivated to police the market aggressively, consistent with the view that a level of a above that of the judges may be beneficial. Importantly (and in line with the model), the Polish regulators also had the power, and not just the motivation, to punish the violations of rules.

5.2 Quantitative Assessments

Table 7.6 presents basic indicators of stock market development in Poland and the Czech Republic. In terms of capitalization, the Czech market in 1994 was twice as large as the Polish market, thanks to the more than 1,500 firms listed on the Prague stock exchange as a result of privatization. As a share of GDP, the Czech market in 1994 was five times larger than the Polish market. By 1998, the valuation of the Polish market increased almost sevenfold. The valuation of the Czech market increased until 1996, but then fell and the market ended up at roughly double its 1994 value. Over this period, the Polish market rose to 14.1 percent of GDP, although the Czech market capitalization remained a larger share of GDP, at 24.2 percent.

Table 7.6 also presents the number of listed companies in Poland and the Czech Republic. It separates the Czech companies into those trading on the main market (most liquid), those trading on the secondary market (with more limited disclosure and occasional trading), and those listed on the free market (with hardly any disclosure and infrequent trading). The listed Polish companies are separated into those trading on the main market and those trading on the parallel (again, less liquid) market. The vast majority of Czech companies barely traded, and most of the firms trading on the free market were delisted by the late 1990s. The number of firms on the main market, having risen to 62 in 1995, fell all the way down to ten by 1998, with most of the firms being transferred to the less liquid secondary market. By 1998, most listed Czech firms had been either delisted or transferred to an exchange with only limited liquidity. In contrast, despite a much lower

Table 7.6
Stock Market Size in Poland and the Czech Republic.

	Market capitalization (U.S. $m, end of year)		Market cap./GDP		Number of issues listed						
					Poland (End of year)			Czech Republic (End of year)			
	Poland	Czech Republic	Poland	Czech Republic	Main market	Parallel market	Total	Main market	Second market	Fee market	Total
1991	144		0.19%		9	0	9				
1992	222		0.26%		16	0	16				
1993	2706		3.15%		22	0	22	3	0	966	969
1994	3057	5938	3.30%	14.9%	44	0	44	34	0	990	1024
1995	4564	15664	3.84%	30.8%	65	0	65	62	6	1630	1698
1996	8390	18077	6.23%	32.0%	83	0	83	42	51	1535	1628
1997	12135	12786	8.95%	24.6%	143	0	143	45	58	217	320
1998	20461	12045	14.10%	24.2%	198	20	218	10	94	179	283

Sources: Polish numbers are from the International Finance Corporation 1998 and 1999 and include National Investment Funds; Czech numbers are from the Prague Stock Exchange webpage and the International Finance Corporation 1997 and 1999.

initial level, the number of listed Polish firms rose steadily over time, and hardly any firms were transferred to the parallel market.

Figure 7.3 reports the number of Czech and Polish stocks over time included in the IFC Investable Index compiled by World Bank's International Finance Corporation, the maker of standard emerging market indices. The IFC Investable Index generally includes only the stocks liquid enough that foreign investors can "practically" take positions in them. This index for Poland started out with nine stocks in 1992 and rose to 34 stocks in 1998. In the Czech Republic, the Index included five stocks in 1993 and only 13 in 1998. Almost all of these 13 stocks were either government or foreign controlled. The value of the IFC Investable Index in Poland, having started below that in the Czech Republic, has by the end of 1998 far surpassed it (figure 7.4).

Perhaps the most significant indicator of success of a financial market is how effectively it enables firms to raise capital. Table 7.7 presents data on the number of initial public offerings (for cash as opposed to vouchers) in the Czech Republic and Poland. It also distinguishes between offerings of shares in privatizing companies coming into public ownership through flotation and offerings by new private companies—the latter being perhaps a more potent indicator of a

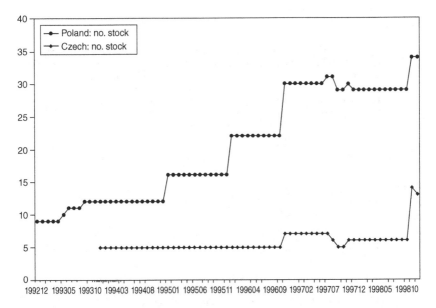

Figure 7.3
Number of stocks in IFC Investable Index in Poland and the Czech Republic.

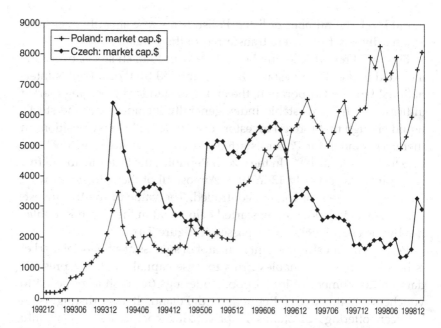

Figure 7.4
Market capitalization of stocks in IFC Investable Index in Poland and the Czech Republic.

Table 7.7
Initial Public Offering (for Cash).

	Czech Republic initial public offerings		Poland initial public offerings	
	Issued as part of privatization	Issued by private companies	Issued as part of privatization	Issued by private companies
1991	0	0	9	–
1992	0	0	5	2
1993	0	0	4	2
1994	0	0	8	14
1995	0	0	6	15
1996	0	0	3	15
1997	0	0	10	36
1998	0	0	5	52
Total	0	0	50	136

Figures do not include the National Investment Funds that were listed on the Warsaw Stock Exchange, or public issues for vouchers in the Czech Republic.
Source: Polish data are from the Warsaw Stock Exchange; Czech data are from Pioneer Investment Fund.

market's effectiveness. Between 1991 and 1998, no Czech company sold equity for cash as part of initial privatization, whereas 50 Polish companies did.[5] This is not surprising, since the Czech Republic has followed a noncash privatization strategy. At the same time, the data show that no private Czech company had done an IPO on the Prague exchange. By comparison, 136 non-privatizing companies had gone public on the Warsaw exchange. This is perhaps the strongest evidence of the differential effectiveness of the two markets.

The evidence is consistent with both the reading of the laws and the qualitative assessments. The regulated Polish stock market grew faster, maintained greater liquidity, and has been a better source of capital for firms than the less regulated Czech market.

After a period of hostility toward any criticism of its policies toward the stock market, the Czech government introduced a number of reforms starting in 1996. These included disclosure of blockholdings, greater regulation (through disclosure and otherwise) of investment funds, restrictions on trading off the exchange, some separation of investment and commercial banking, and finally, in April 1998, the creation of an independent Securities Commission.

6   Conclusion

Our analysis leads to three conclusions. First, the evidence corroborates recent research arguing that financial markets are helped by the legal protection of outside investors—both shareholders and creditors—from expropriation by issuers and financial intermediaries. This indeed has been the focus of the Polish financial regulations in their emphasis on disclosure and the administrative oversight of the intermediaries.

Second, the evidence is consistent with the prediction of the model that an important element of investor protection is the disclosure of information by issuers and intermediaries. Such disclosure is often mandated by securities laws, which thus play a key role in investor protection. The benefits of disclosure are both to reduce the cost to the regulators (and judges) of getting informed, and to enable private corporate governance mechanisms to function more effectively.

Third, and most generally, the analysis bears on a crucial question in law and economics: who should enforce laws or contracts? We establish the conditions under which regulatory enforcement presents an attractive alternative to judicial enforcement. In emerging markets, where the costs of verifying the circumstances of specific cases and interpreting statutes are high, judges may not be sufficiently motivated to enforce legal rules. Enforcement by regulators, with more lopsided but powerful incentives, may then be a more efficient way to protect property rights. The Polish regulation of securities markets presents one example of such evidently beneficial regulation taking place in precisely the circumstances suggested by our model.

8 Legal Origins

with Edward L. Glaeser

1 Introduction

The laws of many countries are heavily influenced by either the English common law or the French civil law.[1] The common law tradition originates in the laws of England, and has been transplanted through conquest and colonization to England's colonies, including the United States, Australia, Canada, and many countries in Africa and Asia. The civil law tradition has its roots in Roman law, was lost during the Dark Ages, but was rediscovered by the Catholic Church in the eleventh century and adopted by several continental states, including France. Napoleon exported French civil law to much of Europe, including Spain, by conquest. French civil law was later transplanted through conquest and colonization to Latin America and parts of Africa and Asia.

Structurally, the two legal systems operate in very different ways: civil law relies on professional judges, legal codes, and written records, while common law relies on lay judges, broader legal principles, and oral arguments. In addition, recent research reveals significant differences between common law and (French) civil law countries in a variety of political and economic conditions. At the same level of development, French civil law countries exhibit heavier regulation, less secure property rights, more corrupt and less efficient governments, and even less political freedom than do the common law countries (La Porta et al. 1999; chapter 5; chapter 10).

These observations raise two crucial questions. First, why did such very different legal systems evolve in France and in England? Second, why are these differences in the organization of legal systems associated with such different social and economic outcomes? In this paper we argue that the historical evolution of legal systems in

France and England starting in the twelfth and thirteenth centuries has shaped how these systems operate. Legal historians such as Dawson (1960), Berman (1983), and Damaska (1986) show that the two countries chose very different strategies for law enforcement and adjudication. Specifically, they opted for different levels of control that the sovereign exercised over judges. France went in the direction of adjudication by royally controlled professional judges, while England moved toward adjudication by relatively independent juries. Over the subsequent millennium, the conditions in England and France reinforced the initial divergence in the legal systems. Moreover, the transplantation of the two legal systems through conquest and colonization may account for some crucial differences in social and economic outcomes among countries that are reported in the empirical studies.

The different choices made in England and France in the twelfth and thirteenth centuries are especially puzzling in light of the widely recognized observation that, at that time, the English king commanded greater power over his subjects than did the French king (Dawson 1960; Reynolds 1994). By that time, the English kings had clearly prevailed over the nobles. In contrast, the French king was at best the first among equals with various dukes, and did not even have full military control over the Ile-de-France. It would seem natural, then, for the more powerful English kings to create a legal system that extended royal control more deeply into the life of the country, while for the weaker French king to accept more decentralized adjudication of disputes. Yet the opposite happened.

What explains the different choices in legal design? A central goal of a national legal system is to protect law enforcers from being bullied with either physical force or bribes by powerful local interests. In the Middle Ages, judges and juries faced both physical and financial incentives to cater to the preferences of local feudal lords. "A celebrated statement in the Yorkshire eyre roll of 1294 stated that 'Justice and Truth are completely choked,' as a result of the way in which influential men manipulated legal proceedings" (Prestwich 1997, p. 283). In another instance, "A conspiracy in 1287 on the part of some sailors at Dunwich was a serious matter. They had prevented the local court from sitting, had appropriated fines imposed by royal justices, and prevented the execution of royal writs and judgments" (Prestwich 1997, p. 281). More recently, in Russia's transition economy in the 1990s, businessmen occasionally bribed judges to excuse breaking the law. In one instance, when a judge jailed a powerful executive, the judge's husband was assassinated. A rapid release of the executive followed.

For a legal system to protect property, the effects of coercion and corruption must be limited. When bullying is moderate, it is more efficient to leave the adjudication of disputes to independent local decision makers, such as juries, than to delegate it to possibly biased state-employed judges who are better insulated from bullying. In contrast, when bullying is extreme, it is better to accept the distortions inherent in more biased but better insulated adjudication by state-employed judges than to leave decisions in the hands of the vulnerable locals. The politicization of justice may be necessary when the state is the only institution with enough military power to fight local bullies. Consistent with the historical evidence, we argue that France chose to rely on state-employed judges precisely because local feudal lords were too powerful: there was no possibility of effective local justice when these lords' interests were involved. England, in contrast, had weaker local magnates, and so its juries were less vulnerable to subversion and could be trusted with adjudication. Moreover, these differences in basic conditions persisted for centuries, mainly because of persistently greater power of local magnates in France than in England. As a result, different legal systems persisted as well.

There is another, perhaps more general, way to make this point. Feudal lords in France were so powerful that they were more afraid of each other than of the king, and as a consequence it was more efficient to delegate dispute resolution to the sovereign, even if he had his own stake in the matter. People demand a dictatorship when they fear a dictator less than they fear each other (Olson 1993; Grossman 2002). Feudal lords in England, in contrast, were less powerful, and more afraid of the king than of their neighbors. As a consequence, they were willing to pay the king to allow them to resolve disputes locally. This could occur because in England, but not in France, the royal power was sufficient to protect local law enforcers. Both France and England thus opted for a system that was more efficient for each country at the time. In fact, we argue that the English Magna Carta was a Coasian bargain supporting the efficient outcome.

This analysis of the structure of common and civil law—with its emphasis on protecting law enforcers—helps understand many of the structural differences in the organization of the two systems. Many writers see the nineteenth-century codification, which involves greater reliance on specific "bright line" rules rather than broad principles for adjudication, as a defining element of a civil law system (Mehren 1957; Merryman 1969). Codification emerges in our model as an efficient attempt by the sovereign to control judges as his knowledge of individual disputes deteriorates (as it did when the states and the economies developed). The simplicity of bright line rules, and the possibility of verifying their violation, enables the king to use them to structure incentive contracts for judges. Codification thus naturally follows from the original choice of royal judges over juries. Our model also sheds light on such differences between the two systems as the reliance on written records versus oral argument, importance of trials, role of appeal, combining versus separating prosecution from judging, and the importance of precedent. In all these dimensions, common and civil law systems differ, and the difference can be plausibly traced to the fundamental choice of state-controlled versus independent justice.

Our approach also sheds light on legal convergence and transplantation. We show that as the accuracy of codes improves and the local pressure on the judges declines, common and civil law systems tend to produce similar resolutions of specific disputes. In contrast, the transplantation of rules designed for a system with a relatively benign government into a system with a more autocratic regime can lead to poor outcomes. In our model, civil law works very badly in dictatorships, where it becomes a method of control by a sovereign unresponsive to public preferences. These results may explain the evidence of the comparative effectiveness of common and civil law in securing property rights in different countries and markets.

We note three alternative explanations of why such different legal systems, with different procedures and social outcomes, developed in England and France. According to the first theory, the choice of law was shaped by a country's predisposition to Catholicism, and the institutions of the Catholic Church, rather than by its law and order environment. This explanation ignores the fact that at the time all states in Europe were Catholic yet trying to establish secular law. France nonetheless adopted the institutions of the Church, while England did not. According to the second theory, distance from Rome was critical to legal adoption. This theory is contradicted by the fact that Scotland adopted civil law. Finally, some scholars argue that only the much later developments of the eighteenth and nineteenth centuries, such as codification, really distinguished the two legal systems. Codification was indeed crucial, but we agree with legal historians like Dawson (1960) and Berman (1983) that the systems diverged much earlier, when the choice of royal judges versus independent juries was made in France and England.

2 Royal Judges versus Independent Juries

A central choice in the design of a legal system is that between judges controlled by the sovereign (royal judges) and judges who are not (juries). In this section we formally consider this choice. Historians of legal systems, such as Berman (1983) and Dawson (1960), agree that this choice is central for the divergence between the French and English legal systems in the twelfth and thirteenth centuries, and explains many persistent differences between civil and common law.

We focus on the twelfth and thirteenth centuries because the legal systems of the two countries until then were similar and governed primarily by religious and customary law. In the eleventh century the Gregorian revolution delineated the scope of secular and ecclesiastical authority, opening up the need for secular legal systems (Berman 1983). We focus on what Berman calls royal law, which in the early years covered major crimes and civil disputes. Our analysis does not apply to many other areas of law, such as manorial, feudal, and urban law, where adjudication was entirely local and governed by custom, and where the issues we discuss were not central. On the other hand, it is the royal law that eventually came to dominate. We present a theoretical account of the development of royal law.

In the twelfth century, England under Henry II develops the jury system. Pollock and Maitland (1898) define the jury as "a body of neighbors summoned by some public officer to give upon oath a true answer to some question" (Vol. 1, p. 138). Despite a long-standing debate on the true novelty of juries (e.g., to what extent were they just a slight modernization of the Frankish inquest), there is no question that the jury became a primary tool of English law around that time. In its original formulation (dated roughly to the various royal assizes in the 1150s and 1160s), the jury was an assembled body of local notables who would inform itinerant royal judges of local facts. The jury of novel disseisin, for example, had to inform a royal judge of who was seized (roughly meaning "in possession") of the land at some past date. In its initial incarnation, the jury was responsible for providing vere dicta (true statements) and not actually given control over the outcome of the case. While the public nature of the juries' verdicts surely made it difficult for judges to completely ignore them, initially juries were an efficient means of gathering information, not a check on the royal prerogative.

In fact, in the twelfth and early thirteenth centuries, English kings did not surrender ultimate control to juries. "Behind the keen interest of Henry II and John in the operations of the courts of justice there lay a ready instinct to ensure that judgments inclined favourably towards the king's friends and ministers and away from those who were out of favour or distrusted. On occasion John's writs assumed that customary procedure should give way, if necessary, to royal prohibition" (Holt 1992, p. 84). "It is noteworthy that the one novelty with which the king (John) can reasonably be linked was designed to investigate, and if needed quash, the verdicts of local jurors. Its purpose was supervisory. And it is fitting that it should appear on the Fine roll, for it is in this roll that the king's control of government is seen at its most immediate and unremitting" (Holt 1992, p. 182).

In subsequent years there was a gradual movement to ensure that judges could not convict without the consent of a jury. The critical statement of this veto power is the Magna Carta. At Runnymede, in exchange for cash and peace, King John agreed that he and his subjects were to be governed by rule of law and that "no person may be amerced (i.e., fined) without the judgment of his peers" (Cap. 39). At this point, there is little doubt that the king accepted juries as a check on royal judges and royal power.

After 1215, the influence of the juries generally increased. In the fourteenth century Parliament "interpreted the phrase 'lawful judgment of peers' to include trial by peers and therefore trial by jury, a process which existed only in embryo in 1215. Secondly, 'the law of the land' was defined in terms of yet another potent and durable phrase—'due process of law,' which meant procedure by original writ or by an indicting jury" (Holt 1992, p. 10). In fact, an important phenomenon in English legal history is jury nullification, whereby juries systematically refused to convict suspects of crimes when the penalties were seen as excessive (such as a hanging for theft of value above one shilling).[2]

During the ensuing centuries, despite the fact that English judges continued to serve the king, juries remained a check on royal discretion. "The presence of the jury as fact-finder and the absence of any effective modes of controlling the juries, meant during the earlier centuries that the judge's role was limited to maintaining courtroom order, framing the questions that the juries must answer, and ensuring compliance with the ground rules of the various forms of action" (Dawson 1960, p. 136). In addition, even the judges in England have been traditionally more independent than those in France. Throughout history, common law judges insisted that the principal source of English law was historical precedent rather than the will of the sovereign, with Coke emerging as the leading advocate of this view. The Tudors responded to the increasing independence of judges and juries by creating new courts more subordinate to the monarchy, such as the Star Chamber, and by punishing juries whose decisions they disliked. Only the Revolution of the seventeenth century conclusively removed royal control over the legal system. The Star Chamber was abolished in 1641, and the Act of Settlement in 1701 confirmed judicial independence from both king and Parliament. Starting in the eighteenth century, judicial independence was an undisputed element of the English legal system, in contrast to the sovereign control of judges in France.

Indeed, the French path was radically different. The Frankish inquest existed in France as well, and institutions like juries—such as enquête par turbe—continued to show up throughout the ancien régime. However, the critical step in France was the decision under Philip Augustus and Louis IX (who organized the Parlements de Paris in 1256) to move toward a judge-inquisitor model governed by Romano-Canon law. This model became widely available in the twelfth and especially thirteenth centuries, after the Justinian code was rediscovered in 1080, and the scholars of Bologna modernized it for use by the Catholic Church in its own courts.[3] In this system, judges would question witnesses privately and separately, prepare written records, and themselves determine the outcome of the case. These judges were directly beholden to the king, and there is no question that the king had the ability to strongly influence their actions through appointments, reappointments, and bribes.

As in England, royal control over judges in France was not absolute. Sale of judicial offices afforded judges at least some independence. Indeed, through the centuries, French kings made efforts to redesign the system of courts, and to create new courts of law whose judges would be more responsive to the king's will (Ford 1953). Some, like Louis XIV, succeeded better than others, like Louis XV. Yet despite this ongoing tug-of-war between the king and the judges, sovereign control over the judiciary remained greater in France than in England, and culminated in an effort at a complete subordination of the judiciary by Napoleon.

To explain the different choices in England and France, we rely on the generally accepted historical fact that the power of local magnates in the twelfth and thirteenth centuries, including influence over lower level local notables such as knights, was greater in France than in England. "In practice relations between kings and counts (in France) were still in many cases more like those between independent powers than Suger would have admitted" (Reynolds 1994, p. 272). In contrast, "The power of the English government meant that all English fees in the twelfth and the thirteenth centuries were to some extent precarious, but the same power also protected free property from anyone except the government" (p. 394).

In this environment, a jury of notables in France would not have been able to deliver justice when the interests of the local magnates were involved. It was more efficient to surrender adjudicatory powers to royal judges even when the preferences of the king did not reflect community justice. In England, in contrast, local magnates were weaker relative to the knights, in large part because William the Conqueror prevented the creation of vast contiguous land holdings. As a consequence, local pressure on the juries was weaker, and the decisions they could reach were probably closer to the community standards of justice. It was more efficient, then, to delegate the adjudicatory powers to the juries, and the magnates were willing to pay the king for that privilege. "The French kings could not make effective use of local village and county institutions, as English kings could, because the tradition of local self-government was less developed in the Frankish than in the Anglo-Saxon kingdom and was therefore more vulnerable to a take-over by the feudal barons" (Berman 1983, p. 465).

We examine the choice of the legal system from the viewpoint of social welfare, including that of the king and the nobles. In this model, the king always prefers adjudication by a royal judge beholden to him. However, if the nobles want a jury system strongly enough, they are willing to fight and to pay for it. As long as there is some way of enforcing a bargain whereby the king agrees to decentralized adjudication in exchange for taxes, there might be efficiency pressures toward such a bargain, including efforts to secure peace. The Magna Carta, as a document in which the king gave up some control over adjudication in exchange for peace and taxes, might reflect such a bargain. To consider this possibility more closely, we examine the conditions under which either of the two systems sits on the Pareto frontier.

We focus on the adjudication of cases involving local magnates or their interests. The key advantage of juries is that they reflect the preferences of the community, not those of the king. By assumption, juries, unlike judges, cannot be incentivized or controlled by the king, or at least there are significant limits of such control. The disadvantage of juries is that they are vulnerable to influence by local magnates, which can take the form of either physical bullying or corruption intended to influence the verdict. A royal judge is less vulnerable to bullying by a powerful local lord than a jury both because of the king's own military resources and because the king's payments offset the influence of local magnates. On the other hand, a royal judge caters to the king's rather than the subjects' preferences. In our model, the trade-off is between a judge incentivized by the king and therefore less vulnerable to local magnate pressure and a jury whose preferences are closer to those of the community but which faces no incentives and can be more easily coerced.

2.1 The Setup

We think of a king and the community of his subjects, including knights and nobles (the peasants were not important for the administration of justice at that time). Some of the members of the community, whom we call the magnates, are especially powerful and have the ability to subvert justice when their interests are infringed upon. We examine the vulnerability of alternative mechanisms of law enforcement to subversion by the magnates.

We focus on violations, like the takings of land, which involve the interests of local magnates, or of parties close to them. We think of these violations as crimes, as they would be today, but in the twelfth century there was no clear distinction between civil and criminal justice. For concreteness, we suppose that one magnate has taken the land of another, and that the offender is powerful enough to threaten or corrupt the adjudicator. In a more general model, both sides would bully adjudicators.

Violations differ on two dimensions, denoted by D and R. D captures the severity of the violation. The utility of the community from punishing a violation of type D is normalized to equal D. These gains combine deterrence, incapacitation, and taste-for-vengeance and subtract social costs of punishment. The community wants to punish all violations for which $D > 0$.

The variable R captures the extent to which the king wants to punish a violator. R might be positive in the case of political violations that are dangerous to the king. Alternatively, if the violator is a royal ally, R might be negative. The king's utility from conviction is given by $D + \theta R$, where $\theta > 0$. The term θ captures the degree to which the preferences of the king do not match those of the community. In a perfect democracy, θ is presumably close to zero, but it rises as the sovereign becomes less constrained by his subjects. In this section we assume that D and R are common knowledge, and that the two attributes are independently distributed with smooth cumulative distribution functions $F(D)$ and $G(R)$ and finite variances. The expected value of D is positive, and the expected value of R is zero.

To compare the efficiency of alternative systems of adjudication, we define "social welfare" as a weighted average of the preferences of the king and the community, with the king's weight in the social welfare function given by λ and the community's by $1-\lambda$. The total social payoff from each conviction therefore equals $D + \lambda\theta R$. For most of history, the king's resources were relatively meager relative to those of the community, and hence we concentrate on the case of λ close to zero. In fact, $\lambda = 0$ is an important special case, for which all of our results hold. Our model can also deal with the case of λ close to 1, in which an outcome close to the king's preferences materializes. This may be a useful case to describe the developments of the nineteenth and especially twentieth centuries, but not for most of history.

With these assumptions, social welfare is given by

$$\iint (D + \lambda\theta R)f(D)g(R)dDdR. \tag{1}$$

We consider two possible modes of adjudication: the jury, which is a group of members of the community, and the royal judge. The jury and the royal judge have two features in common, and one crucial difference. Both the jury and the royal judge have some preferences over punishing particular violations (although these preferences may differ). Both the jury and the royal judge are also subject to pressure from the magnate—through bullying and bribes—to rule in his favor. We assume that the amount of pressure brought on the jury and on the royal judge is exactly the same, although one could argue that, especially with a unanimity rule for juries, it might be cheaper to bribe one juror. Jury unanimity, however, is neither a universal nor a fundamental element of the jury system. "From the reign of Edward I onwards the function of the jury was slowly being judicially defined; questions of law became separated from questions of fact, and gradually unanimity was required—although for some time whether a verdict by eleven jurors was not sufficient, in which case the twelfth might be committed to prison" (Plucknett 1956, p. 129).

The fundamental difference between juries and royal judges in our model is that the latter, but not the former, can be put on an incentive scheme ("protected") by the king, so as to either counter the pressure from the magnate or follow the king's own preferences. The defining feature of juries in our model is their independence—in fact, that was the whole point of juries in the Magna Carta. There are many reasons why juries are much harder than judges for the sovereign to control: there are many more of them, they rotate from case to case, and the sovereign usually does not even know who the jurors are to "incentivize" them. Sometimes, of course, kings try. In the sixteenth and seventeenth centuries, the Tudors and the Stuarts engaged in jury intimidation, possibly contributing to the English Revolution. After the Revolution, acts of Parliament specifically reaffirmed the independence of the juries, and prohibited various forms of bullying them.

We assume that the tastes of the jury mirror those of the community, in part because the jurors come from among them. The jurors do not care about R, but want to see the violators of community rules punished. They also—to some extent—internalize the social costs of punishment because one day a juror might himself be accused. The jury's utility from conviction is taken to be $\beta D - A$. The shift parameter β reflects the extent to which the jury cares about doing justice relative to being bullied or bribed. The term A captures the pressure put on the jury by the local magnate, whose interests are jeopardized. These could be direct physical reprisals for conviction, but also bribes that the juror receives if he acquits the magnate.

In some well-functioning societies A is small and jurors are well protected from physically or financially powerful interested parties. But elsewhere A may be higher. In the twelfth and thirteenth centuries, a central problem of government was the division of control over local affairs (including adjudication) between local feudal lords and the king. In a more recent context of the developing world, unpaid or low-paid judges and jurors are subject to local political pressures and corruption from oligarchs, landowners, and local officials. In Russia today, influence by the oligarchs and regional governments over courts is the central problem of rule of law. Even in the United States, local juries and judges have been routinely intimidated or bribed (as in various acquittals of Al Capone or civil rights cases in Southern courts). The susceptibility of law enforcers to bullying, A, is the central parameter of the model.

Under these assumptions, the jury convicts if $\beta D > A$, which always leads to fewer convictions than the society wants. Obviously, in cases where local magnates wish to convict a rival, magnate pressure might also lead to over conviction.

Because the unconditional expectation of R is zero and the juries ignore R, social welfare under the jury system equals $\int_{D>A/\beta} Df(D)dD$. Figure 8.1 illustrates the social welfare loss from jury coercion relative to the first best when $\lambda = 0$. The area to the right of $D = 0$ is the social optimum, the area to the right of $D = A/\beta$ is where the bullied jury still convicts, and the shaded area, in which the community wants to convict but the jury does not, is the social loss. This social loss is increasing in A and decreasing in β. Juries perform worse when local magnates are more powerful, and better when they are more committed to their own independent preferences.

The royal judge, like the jury, has some set of innate preferences and is also subject to local pressure. However, unlike the jury, the judge can be punished and rewarded by the king who perfectly observes all aspects of the case. The judge's utility from convicting is $\beta_j(D + \theta_j R) - A$

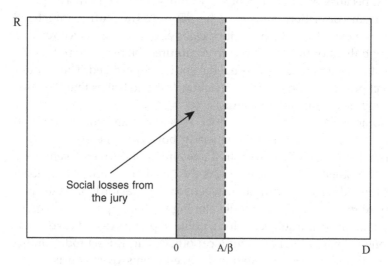

Figure 8.1
Social losses from jury coercion relative to the first best when $\lambda = 0$.

plus whatever the king chooses in his incentive scheme. The parameters β_J and θ_J are meant to keep the judge's preferences flexible.[4] However, as the king observes R and knows the preferences of the judge, a simple incentive scheme can easily induce the judge to exactly follow the king's preferences. The king simply pays the judge $A + \beta_J(\theta-\theta_J)R$ if the judge convicts. This payment compensates for both the coercion by the magnate and the deviation in the judge's preferences from those of the king. After the judge has been incentivized, he convicts whenever the king would; that is, if and only if $R > -D/\theta$. For any given D, then, a fraction of cases equal to $1 - G(-D/\theta)$ reach conviction.

For $\lambda = 0$, total social welfare in this case equals

$$\int_D D\left(1 - G\left(-\frac{D}{\theta}\right)\right) f(D) dD,$$

and the total social losses are shown in the two triangles in figure 8.2. The top triangle covers the king's enemies whose crimes are mild by the standards of the community but who are nonetheless convicted by the king's judge. The bottom triangle covers the king's friends whose crimes are major but who are nonetheless acquitted by the king's judge. Unsurprisingly, the social losses from the royal judge system increase when the preferences of the king and the community fail to overlap. More generally, the following proposition holds (all proofs are in the appendix):

Proposition 1   When λ is sufficiently close to zero, there exists a value of $A^* > 0$ at which "social welfare" is the same under royal judges and independent juries. For $A > A^*$, royal judges yield higher social welfare. For $A < A^*$, juries yield higher welfare. The value of A^* rises with β and falls with λ. When λ is sufficiently close to zero, A^* rises with θ.

The crucial parameter in proposition 1 is A, which represents the ability of local notables to bully, coerce, or corrupt the arbiters of the king's justice. Across societies, A is generally higher when there is significant local inequality—powerful local lords have the resources to bribe or bully. A is also a function of the general level of violence in the society. When the supply of armed warriors is high, it is cheaper to coerce the king's justice. A is also higher when the crown is weak and cannot punish violators. The crown may be weak either because it has access to few tax revenues or because transport costs prevent its forces from enforcing justice.

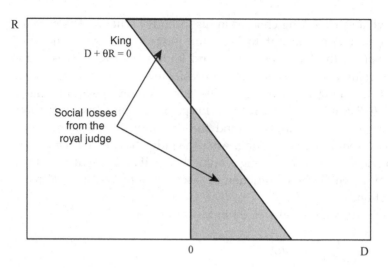

Figure 8.2
Social losses from the royal judge system when $\lambda = 0$.

Throughout the past millennium, the ability of local bullies to control their environment was higher in France than in England. During the earlier period, the nobles such as the Duke of Burgundy or the Constable Bourbon essentially ran independent principalities within the technical borders of France.[5] In the nineteenth century, France saw major regional fights over the Revolution (the Chouans resisting the forces of the Directory; the merchants of Bordeaux acquiescing only nominally to the revolution of 1848). Even during the apotheosis of the centralized French power under Louis XIV and Napoleon Bonaparte, the ability of local authorities to undermine central control was much greater in France than in the age of Parliamentary control in England (Woloch 1994).

Why were the local magnates so much weaker in England than in France? We see two key differences. First, in 1066 William the Conqueror gave out to his followers dispersed holdings of land, precisely to minimize the ability of any general to create a local power base. As a consequence, while the French nobles held sway over vast, contiguous areas of land, the English nobles had parcels that were dispersed over the country. This initial allocation of land holdings limited the creation of concentrated local authority.

Second, during the last millennium, England experienced much more limited warfare on its territory than did France. Without recounting the full history of hostilities, we estimate that between 1100 and 1800, France had a war on its soil during 22 percent of the years, and England only 6 percent of that time (one can also argue that the wars on English soil were relatively bloodless). The constant war on French soil meant that weapons and warriors were readily available to anyone who wanted to subvert justice.

Interestingly, the two periods of lengthy battle on English soil were the War of the Roses in the second half of the fifteenth century and the English Civil War. As our model suggests, the ability of local nobles to subvert justice increased during the War of the Roses, and after the war Henry Tudor brought English justice closer to the French model through the courts of Star Chamber. The English Civil War was fought in part to secure the independence of the legal system from royal control, and in fact succeeded in doing so.

Our theory, then, suggests that England and France went their different ways in adopting judicial systems for reasons of efficiency. The relatively higher ability of the magnates to subvert justice in France led to the adoption of the civil law system controlled by the crown. The relatively lower ability of such magnates in England to subvert justice led to the adoption of the jury-controlled common law system. Both outcomes were efficient at the time for their environments. In fact, one can view the Magna Carta as a remarkable example of an early Coasian bargain, in which the community and the crown agree on a cash transfer needed to support the efficient outcome. It is perhaps too far-fetched to think of the Magna Carta literally as an enforceable Coasian contract. A broader view of the Coase theorem is to identify the incentives and pressure to move toward efficiency. To the extent that decentralized jury-controlled adjudication was more efficient in England, the Magna Carta might reflect such pressure.

This analysis is broadly consistent with the available historical accounts of the divergence in approaches to adjudication, and in particular with the classic work of Dawson (1960).

So we return to the question why France, which started with institutions so similar (to the English), followed in the end such a different course. The answer that has been given centers on weakness—weakness at the critical times. The marks of weakness had appeared very early. The community courts, analogous to the English county and hundred courts, had been captured by local feudal lords during the breakdown of government in the tenth and eleventh centuries. When the rebuilding of monarchy began, the French crown lacked an important resource that the Norman kings of England had already put to very good use. But it was much more than this. Over large parts of France that owed a nominal fealty to the king, great territorial lords had effective control; in them, for long, the king's writ did not run. Even within the king's own domain there could be no massive enlistment of free subjects whose allegiance was to the crown as a symbol of national government transcending and displacing the bonds of feudal tenure (p. 299).

In Dawson's view, the adoption of canonist inquest by royal judges was a sign of the crown's weakness in France, not of strength.

In broader terms, this analysis reveals how the royal judge versus independent jury decision hinges upon the extent to which the magnates fear the crown more or less than they fear each other. This point has much broader implications. It suggests in part that the connection between English legal origin and rule of law, emphasized by Hayek (1960), may flow as much from rule of law to the common law system as vice versa. Juries are better systems when local magnates are not freely able to terrorize them; that is, when peace prevails. Without peace, state inquisitors may be the only means of enforcing the law. It is not entirely surprising in this regard that tight state control of adjudication has often been introduced as part of national liberation or unification, often in the aftermath of civil war and other disorder. Without internal peace to begin with, a system of juries may simply not work.

Proposition 1 has several other implications for the optimal choice of a legal system. When juries care more about community justice and are less vulnerable to the influence of the local magnate (β is higher), jury systems work better. This may explain why juries in England were often made up of twelve local knights. Presumably a body of twelve fighting men was not as easy to bully as that of unarmed but otherwise respected citizens. When the sovereign has greater political power in bargaining with the community, or alternatively, when the social welfare function puts a higher weight on his preferences (λ is higher), the system of royal judges is more likely to emerge. It is not surprising, in this regard, that centralized civil law systems were often championed by the great autocrats, like Napoleon.

Finally, the value of θ captures the extent to which the preferences of the king differ from those of the society. Proposition 1 holds that so long as the social welfare function does not put too much weight on the preferences of the king, the further these preferences are from those of the community, the less efficient is the system of royal judges. Put differently, civil law works better when the government is more constrained by its subjects or more democratic.

This result has significant implications for the effectiveness of alternative legal arrangements in different political regimes. On the one hand, this argument suggests that the problems with centralized justice are less severe in democratic societies. As democracy replaces royal government and the community trusts the democratically elected leaders who control the judicial system, then juries may become less essential. This analysis might account for the expansion of public law and regulation in the twentieth century, even in common law countries such as the United States and England. Such growth of parliamentary control over lay justice is broadly consistent with our analysis, yet, as Hayek (1960) so clearly emphasized, is likely to undermine the freedoms inherent in the Magna Carta. On the other hand, the argument suggests that in autocratic societies the power that the sovereign obtains by controlling judges will lead to politicization of justice and socially inefficient outcomes. As we argue in section 4, this result has profound implications for legal transplantation, and for the consequences of centralized justice for the security of property rights and other aspects of governance.

3 The Adoption of Bright Line Rules

In the eighteenth and nineteenth centuries, civil law systems in France and Germany experienced an important change, namely codification. Codification aims to provide adjudicators with clear bright line rules, as opposed to broad legal principles or standards, for making decisions. Compared with a legal principle, a bright line rule describes which specific actions are prohibited. Some modern examples clarify the difference. The law can prohibit dangerous driving (a standard) or it can impose a speed limit (a BLR). The law can prohibit stock trading by insiders on nonpublic information (a standard) or all trading by insiders within N days of a public announcement by a firm (a BLR). The law can prohibit self-dealing by corporate officers (a standard) or require that all financial transactions by such officers be approved by a vote of the majority of disinterested directors of the firm (a BLR). The law can prohibit all "sham transactions designed to evade taxes" (a standard) or very specific trades in the capital market (a BLR).

No system is made up entirely of bright line rules, but civil codes are basically collections of rules intended to restrict the actions of the participants in the legal system. We maintain that the purpose of such rules is to enable sovereigns—whether kings or parliaments—to control judges; they are a natural consequence of the reliance on state-controlled judiciaries. Merryman (1969) describes the role of the judge and the code as seen by the writers of Code Napoleon as follows:

> If the legislature alone could make laws and the judiciary could only apply them (or, at a later time, interpret and apply them), such legislation had to be complete, coherent, and clear. If a judge were required to decide a case for which there was no legislative provision, he would in effect make law and thus violate the principle of rigid separation of powers. Hence it was necessary that the legislature draft a code without gaps. Similarly, if there were conflicting provisions in the code, the judge would make law by choosing one rather than another as more applicable to the situation. Hence there could be no conflicting provisions. Finally, if a judge were allowed to decide what meaning to give to an ambiguous provision or an obscure statement, he would again be making law. Hence the code had to be clear (p. 30).

Common law countries also have codes of laws, such as the Uniform Commercial Code in the United States, and the many codes of the State of California. Some of these codes have even more statutes than civil codes do. However, as Merryman (1969) explains, the codes in common law countries often summarize prior judicial decisions. Moreover, a common law judge, to the extent that he can focus on the differences between the case under review and specific provisions of the code, has some flexibility to disregard these provisions when they conflict with the basic principles of common law. In civil law countries, in contrast, judges are not even supposed to interpret the codes very much, and in principle must seek not to differentiate a specific situation, but to fit it into the existing provisions of the code. As a restraint on the judge, codes are much more powerful in civil than in common law countries.

Historically, codification has often been associated with efforts to control judges. Although there is some dispute of whether the Code of Justinian has the character of modern codes as opposed to the summary of cases, there is little doubt that Justinian himself was interested in the control of justice. Similarly, the work of the Glossators and their successors for the Roman Church and the continental kings was centrally focused on developing centralized control over adjudication through a system of clear rules. The early Stuarts tried to introduce codification in seventeenth-century England out of their frustration with the failure of common law judges to cater to royal preferences. Absent the rebellion against the king, they might have succeeded. Elsewhere, codification was promulgated by Philip II in Spain, Frederick the Great in

Prussia, and Napoleon Bonaparte in France. These men saw their codes as a means of controlling their judges. Napoleon wrote that he wanted to turn French judges into automata simply enforcing his code. We believe that this perspective explains the history of codification better than the view that bright line rules make adjudication "less complex," which focuses more on the control of individual conduct than on the control of the judges (Kaplow 1992, 1995).

We keep the basic structure of the previous model, and again compare the efficiency of royally controlled judges and juries. Violations have attributes D and R. We assume that the king no longer observes the values of D and R. Instead, he observes only a bright line, namely whether $D > \bar{D}$. The value $\bar{D}$ represents some fixed threshold of severity. We assume that $\bar{D}$ does not equal zero (which would yield the first best). Increases in the absolute value of $\bar{D}$ correspond to higher imprecision of BLRs.

The assumption that the king can observe (or verify) less than all the attributes of the violation may indeed accurately reflect the fundamental changes in law enforcement in the eighteenth and nineteenth centuries. In the twelfth and thirteenth centuries, the range of violations subject to royal justice was extremely limited. Judges were often members of the king's household, and the king himself got involved in many decisions. The assumption that D and R were known to the king is appropriate for this period. Over the centuries, both the states and their economies grew tremendously, and royal justice became more anonymous. This necessarily led to the loss of information at the center, and therefore eliminated the possibility of incentivizing every royal judge to do what the king wants in every case. The assumption that only limited information trickles up to the king or the top judges becomes more suitable. Below we describe the circumstances under which codification is an efficient response to such information loss.

We also make the following assumption.

Assumption 1 $\quad E(D|D > \bar{D}) > 0 > E(D|D < \bar{D})$

This assumption ensures that if the only thing known about an act is its relation to the BLR, the king would want to convict violators and acquit non-violators. We think of this signal as exogenously given by nature rather than a choice by the king as to where "to draw the line."

What is the optimal policy for the king when he can verify whether a bright line has been crossed? We take the view that the community and the king can strike a Coasian bargain over the type of system, but that the king cannot credibly commit to not influencing his judges. The incentive contract for the judge is then the one the king chooses.

After each case, the king receives two pieces of information: (1) was the bright line rule violated and (2) did the judge convict. Any incentive scheme must be based exclusively on these two pieces of information. Since both of these items are binary, it must be the case that any optimal incentive system contains at most four different payouts. Furthermore, since we are not concerned with the absolute level of payment to the judge but only with the quality of the judge's decisions, we can normalize the payouts in the case of non-conviction to zero regardless of whether the BLR has been violated. The judge's decision is affected only by the incremental payment for conviction, which would depend on whether the BLR has been violated or not.

Denote this increment by P_i for $i = V,NV$ (i.e., the BLR has been violated or not violated).

The judge convicts if

$$\beta_j(D + \theta_j R) + P_i > A.$$

The king chooses incremental payments for conviction, P_V and P_{NV}, for the cases when the BLR has been violated $(D > \bar{D})$ and when it has not $(D < \bar{D})$, to maximize his welfare. For example, when $D > \bar{D}$ the king chooses P_V to maximize

$$\int_{D>\bar{D}}\int_{R>(A-P_v)/\beta_j\theta_j-(D/\theta_j)}(D+\theta R)f(D)g(R)dDdR \text{ when } \theta_j > 0,$$

and

$$\int_{D>\bar{D}}\int_{R<(A-P_v)/\beta_j\theta_j-(D/\theta_j)}(D+\theta R)f(D)g(R)dDdR \text{ when } \theta_j < 0.$$

The value of P_{NV} is chosen in a similar manner.

We define a pure bright line rule system as one where the king commands a royal judge to punish an act if and only if the bright line has been crossed. The question is under what circumstances would the king choose to use this pure bright line rule system as the incentive contract for the judge that maximizes the king's welfare. We can show the following.

Proposition 2   If the density g is sufficiently close to uniform, then the king's optimal strategy is a pure bright line rule system if and only if $\theta_j < 0$.

When $\theta_j < 0$, as the king raises P, the marginal violator (holding D constant) has an increasingly higher value of R, and the king wants to pay even more for convictions. This makes the king's problem convex, so it is optimal for the king to get either universal conviction or universal acquittal within a given region of D's. Since assumption 1 guarantees that convictions dominate when the bright line rule is violated, and acquittals dominate when it is not, the king just orders the judge to follow the bright line rule to the letter.

The condition that the density function of R—of how much the king dislikes a violator—is near uniform has an interesting interpretation. By adopting a pure bright line rule system, the king accepts the impartiality of law and gives up on using the justice system to discriminate between his friends and enemies. If the density function g places a lot of weight on either high R's—the king's enemies—or low R's—the king's friends—he would choose a more elaborate incentive system for his judges, which discriminates between friends and enemies. Such a system would use the information in bright line rules, but not rely on it exclusively.

Proposition 2 illustrates the importance of judicial tastes in pushing the king toward bright line rules. Bright line rules are particularly attractive to a sovereign when the tastes of the judges are far from his own (e.g., when $\theta_j < 0$). Napoleon's judiciary was made up of men trained in prerevolutionary times and sometimes holding monarchist views. These judges did not share Napoleon's preferences, and he could not count on their unconstrained choices to reflect his views. Napoleon's Code was his attempt to control such disagreeable judges.

As in the previous section, the next question we address is that of comparative efficiency of the two alternatives of juries and royal judges, the latter now incentivized through bright line rules. We continue to assume that the fundamental difference between juries and royal judges is that juries cannot be put on any incentive system. Even bright line rules are subject to jury nullification. A good example of this is the response of English juries to the Tudor innovation of mandatory hangings for theft of value above one shilling. In response to this bright line rule, English juries refused to declare the value of stolen property as exceeding one shilling when they did not want to hang the offender, even when the stolen goods were much more valuable.

With a pure bright line rule system, social welfare is $\int_{D > \bar{D}} Df(D)dD$, assumed to be strictly positive by assumption 1. The key parameter shaping the relative attractiveness of juries and BLRs is again A.

Proposition 3   There exists a value of A, denoted A^{**}, at which social welfare is the same under independent juries and a pure bright line rule system. For $A > A^{**}$, bright line rules dominate, and for $A < A^{**}$, independent juries dominate. The value of A^{**} rises with the absolute value of $\bar{D}$.

Proposition 3 shows that pure bright line rules are socially desirable when A is high (jurors are susceptible to pressure) and when $\bar{D}$ is close to zero (bright line rules are accurate). This proposition, we believe, goes to the heart of von Mehren's observation of complementarity between civil law and codification. The common law regime is efficient when juries are capable of making roughly efficient and independent decisions, and therefore bright line rules are unnecessary to control adjudication. In contrast, when pressures on adjudicators are high, the king chooses to employ his judges and to restrict their discretion through codes. Through bright line rules inherent in the codes, the king uses the information he can verify to monitor and shape the decisions of the judges, and thus to protect them—and justice—from subversion. Bright line rules are the optimal instrument of control as long as they can be made sufficiently precise. Bright line rules thus emerge as a central element of a civil law regime because, in the absence of full verifiability of information by the sovereign, they allow state control over adjudication.

The use of bright line rules, the violations of which can be verified by higher level authorities, as an instrument of control is more general than our application to legal design. For example, bright line rules can be used to control agents in a bureaucracy. In his classic study of the United States Forest Service, Kaufman (1960) describes how forest rangers in the United States were obligated to follow extremely detailed operating manuals regulating their behavior in a large number of foreseeable circumstances. The focus of forest rangers is especially interesting because they operate nearly alone in remote locations, and are subject to significant pressures from the logging interests to make favorable decisions on harvesting trees. In this instance, as well, precise instructions are used as an antidote to local bullying.

To conclude, this section has focused on our central theme: a key goal in the design of a legal system is to control law enforcers. Starting with Becker (1968), the law and economics literature has focused on the regulation of the behavior of individuals as the principal goal of legal design (Polinsky and Shavell 2000). Becker and Stigler (1974) consider the compensation of law enforcers as a way of preventing corruption, but the focus on the design of law enforcement has remained peripheral. In our view, the control of law enforcers has historically been as or more important to the design of legal systems as the control of individual behavior. Not just the compensation of enforcers, but legal rules themselves are shaped with the purpose of verification of the decisions of law enforcers, such as judges. Codification, which many have seen as one of the defining elements of a civil law system, is best understood from this perspective. In the next section we argue that other differences between common and civil law systems are also best understood from the perspective of efficient design of enforcement.

4 Consequences of Alternative Systems

4.1 Legal Procedure

In the previous sections we described the difference between legal systems of France and England as the outcome of an efficient choice. This is the choice between a regime that favors incentivized decision makers to protect against local pressure and corruption, and a regime that favors un-incentivized decision makers to protect against the state. Once we focus on this choice, we can understand many of the aspects of the two legal traditions, both in terms of the procedures used by the legal system and in terms of the implications for social outcomes.[6] We begin with legal procedure. In our comparison, we rely on the standard comparisons of the two approaches to adjudication presented in comparative law textbooks, such as von Mehren (1957), Merryman (1969), and Schlesinger et al. (1988).

Comparative law textbooks emphasize the following procedural differences between civil and common law systems. The common law system greatly relies on oral argument and evidence, while in civil law systems much of the evidence is recorded in writing. Trials play a much larger role in a common law than in a civil law system. Civil law systems rely on regular and comprehensive superior review of both facts and law in a case; in common law systems, in contrast, the appeal is much less frequent, and is generally restricted to law rather than facts.

Common law systems, at least in the last century, have generally relied on heavily incentivized state prosecutors, who are separate from judges, especially in criminal cases. In civil law systems, in contrast, judging and prosecution are generally combined in the person of the same judge. Finally, although this distinction is less clear-cut, common law systems generally rely to a greater extent on the precedents from previous judicial decisions than do civil law systems. We argue below that these differences can be understood from the perspective of our model.

First, compare the English tradition of oral argument and evidence with the French reliance on written evidence. The key feature of written evidence is that it facilitates oversight of the court by higher level officials. For the central authorities to monitor judges, it is much easier to verify whether the decisions adhere to the rules and to the preferences of the sovereign when there are written records. A higher authority would find it difficult to punish and reward judges in the hinterland if the judges do not produce any written records and decisions are made based on oral evidence provided to the jury. Furthermore, written evidence in a jury-type system would have been hard in any modern period because of high rates of illiteracy among the general population. In fact, insofar as in the twelfth- and thirteenth-century kings wanted to control their judges, they needed written records, and because of the need for such records they needed to use literate clerics as judges.

Second, the more central role of trials in the common law system is obviously linked with adjudication by generally illiterate juries. Evidence can only be collected from and presented to such juries in a public trial. In civil law systems, in contrast, most evidence is collected prior to the trial by a judge-inquisitor, and hence the trial plays only a secondary role of rehashing this evidence publicly. The surprises and revelations of a common law courtroom play no role in this process. Moreover, the reliance on trials makes it harder to review judicial decisions than does the written report of the findings, which is inconsistent with the centrality of such review in civil law. This difference, then, is also linked to the choice of the method of adjudication.

Third, review by higher level courts is automatic in a civil law system and reconsiders both law and evidence. Review by higher level courts in a common law system restricts itself largely to law. Again, this appears to be closely linked to the problem of monitoring judges. As we argued, the defining element of the civil law system is the reliance on state-employed judges, who need to be incentivized to follow the preferences of the sovereign. Appellate review is how this incentive scheme works; it is one of the main ways that judicial incompetence and corruption are detected. In a system based on incentivizing judges, this type of review creates crucial data for providing these incentives. In a common law system, in contrast, it is the un-incentivized juries rather than the state-employed judges that render verdicts. The need to monitor the decisions of such juries is less pronounced, except to the extent that the judges must be properly informing the juries about the basic outline of the law.

The extensive superior review in the civil law systems leads to very different manpower requirements. Dawson (1960) reports that "The total number of royal judges (in France) at this stage (sixteenth century) must certainly have exceeded 5000. These estimates from France should be compared with figures from England: from 1300 to 1800 the judges of the English central courts of common law and Chancery rarely exceeded fifteen. These judges, furthermore, conducted most of the trials and all the appellate review that English courts undertook" (p. 71).

Fourth, with independent and weakly incentivized judges and juries, a common law system needs to rely on state prosecutors to develop cases. Judges and juries do not care strongly enough about convictions to invest resources in collecting information and otherwise developing cases. In the instances of private litigation, private parties bringing suit have strong enough incentives to do the work. In criminal cases (which were brought privately in England until well into the nineteenth century for obvious incentive reasons), in contrast, it may be necessary to have motivated prosecutors who are paid for convictions, even if they end up being advocates of the state's position rather than seekers of justice.[7] In a civil law system, to the extent that a judge is already motivated to do the state's bidding, a state prosecutor is less necessary to pursue the goals of the state. Thus, the difference in approaches to advocacy and prosecution in the two systems emerges as a consequence of the difference in incentives faced by the judges.

Our model also suggests why precedents play a larger role in a common law system, as exemplified by the doctrine of stare decisis. Absent bright line rules and other guides for adjudicators, precedents may serve to remind judges and juries where the law has drawn lines previously. Despite precedents, it is common for advocates in common law systems to draw subtle distinctions between cases, unlike in the civil law systems, where similarities are sought by a judge (Damaska

1986; chapter 3). Nonetheless, precedents may serve to eliminate excessive unpredictability, which may be a natural consequence of the importance of individual trials and of particular sentiments of the juries. "Certainty is achieved in the common law by giving the force of law to judicial decisions, something theoretically forbidden in civil law" (Merryman 1969, p. 51). Precedents have the further advantage that, unlike bright line rules, they have been established by independent judges rather than by the sovereign. As such, they again may provide protection from the ability of the state to change the rules through dictate. It is for this reason that writers like Coke and Hayek have celebrated the reliance on precedents as a key guarantee of freedom in the English legal system.

4.2 Social Outcomes

Recent research identifies some systematic differences between French civil law and common law countries in a variety of social outcomes. Holding the level of economic development constant, French civil law countries have less secure property rights, greater government regulation and intervention, greater government ownership of banks and industry, and higher levels of corruption and red tape than do common law countries (La Porta et al. 1999, 2002; chapter 10). There is also evidence that, at the same level of development, common law countries are more financially developed than their civil law counterparts (La Porta et al. 1997a, 1998). Can our model help explain such findings?

In thinking about this question, it is important to distinguish between countries that have chosen their legal rules and regulations and countries into which such rules were transplanted, sometimes involuntarily. For the countries that choose their legal rules, our model suggests that the reliance on more extensive regulation is an efficient response to lack of law and order, since regulation facilitates the enforcement of laws. For such countries, the insecurity of property rights causes heavier regulation, rather than regulation making property rights less secure.

However, as we argued in the introduction, most countries have not developed their legal systems on their own but rather have inherited them from their colonizers. Indeed, the empirical results described above are driven almost entirely by former colonies rather than by England and France. For such countries, it is incorrect to think about the choice of a legal regime as an efficient response to the law and order environment. Instead, we need to think about the transplantation of rules developed in one environment into another.

From this perspective, our results suggest that the transplantation of a civil law system into a new environment may raise significant problems for the security of property rights. Proposition 1 shows that civil law systems work relatively better when the preferences of the sovereign are close to those of the community; that is, when θ is low. If a civil law system is introduced into a community with a high θ, the sovereign will use his control over judges and legal rules to politicize dispute resolution. He will punish his enemies rather than violators of community justice. The transplantation of common law does not suffer from this problem to the same extent, since law enforcement is relatively depoliticized—juries (and judges) are independent. A sovereign whose tastes do not reflect those of the community cannot use the common law system as extensively to promote his goals as he can a civil law system. As a consequence, when a civil law system is transplanted into a country with a "bad" government, it will lead to less secure property rights, heavier intervention and regulation, and more corruption and red tape than does a common law system transplanted into a similar environment. Put simply, regulations and controls are much more vulnerable to misuse by the sovereign than is community justice. This, of course, is exactly what the evidence shows.

Our approach might also explain why civil law works better in some areas of law than in others. Suppose that the choice of the form of adjudication is system wide, rather than specific to a given area of law. The analysis implies that, for a given level of pressure on adjudicators, A, civil law systems work better when bright line rules accurately capture community justice (i.e., $\bar{D}$ is close to zero), while common law systems work better when BLRs are inaccurate (i.e., $\bar{D}$ is far from zero). One area in which BLRs notoriously fail to catch undesirable conduct is the expropriation of investors by corporate insiders, generally governed by company and security laws. BLRs do not work well in this area because a broad range of creative behavior designed to expropriate investors "falls between the cracks" in the rules (Johnson et al. 2000b). When the resources at stake are enormous, the creativity in such conduct rises accordingly. As a result, the model predicts that common law regimes would do better than civil law in the areas of law governing investor protection, just as the evidence indicates (La Porta et al. 1997a, 1998).

In summary, this section has argued that many of the key features of a civil law system—as seen both in the legal procedures and in the social outcomes—"come with" its reliance on state-employed judges to adjudicate disputes. Many of these features do not have a role in a system that relies heavily on adjudication by local un-incentivized juries.

5 Convergence

In this section we ask under what circumstances do common and civil law systems converge, that is, lead to similar decisions, and alternatively, when do they yield different outcomes?

Some writers argue that, judging by substantive outcomes, there has been a great deal of convergence in wealthy economies between common and civil law systems in the twentieth century (Coffee 2002). To understand this phenomenon, we consider the degree of overlap in the decisions between the BLR and the independent jury systems. Assume that $A / \beta > 0 > \bar{D}$. In this scenario, the range of cases in which the two regimes lead to different decisions is given by $A / \beta \geq D \geq \bar{D}$. When bright line rules are inaccurate ($\bar{D}$ is far from zero) and there is no rule of law (A is high), the two systems deliver very different outcomes. Which one does better depends on whether the lack of rule of law or the inaccuracy of the BLRs is a bigger problem.

The degree of divergence of the two systems is (1) rising with A, (2) falling with β, and (3) falling with $\bar{D}$. Unsurprisingly, we expect to see convergence in outcomes as juries become more immune to pressure and corruption (i.e., as either A falls or as β rises). The tendency of juries to be swayed by local influence would have fallen as the ability to protect them rose over the twentieth century. This may be one reason for the tendency of systems to converge.

A second reason is that codifications may have been brought more into line with the tastes of the public at large; that is, $\bar{D}$ has gotten closer to zero. As societies became more democratic, parliaments wrote laws and codes that better reflected the views of the entire community. As a result, the tendency of codes to reflect the preferences of the elite rather than the will of the people must have declined. Bright line rules may also have become better as the information systems in the society have improved, and hence it became possible to draw sharper "lines" between different forms of conduct. As $\bar{D}$ goes to zero, when A is low, civil codes will resemble jury systems more and more. In that case, the two systems are both more or less accurately reflecting the will of the public. In fact, as we take the limit as both A and $\bar{D}$ converge to zero, the two systems converge to efficiency in terms of the outcomes they deliver.

6   Conclusion: The Practice of Justice

Economists generally agree that the state's main role in the economy is to protect property rights. But efficient solutions to the problem of the design of legal systems to protect property rights may lead to very different answers in different environments. When the law and order environment is benign to begin with, a system of law enforcement relying on decentralized adjudication by peers may be the most efficient. In such a system, we would see greater security of property rights and relatively little state intervention in the economy and society. In contrast, when law and order is weak to begin with, a system of law enforcement relying on more centralized adjudication of disputes by government employees may be the most efficient. In such a system, we would see less security of property rights, more regulation, and more state intervention in the economy. Indeed, we might see some institutions that can be viewed as unfriendly to a free market economy, even though—from a broader perspective—they might be efficient for the environment. Put differently, people might demand some level of "dictatorship" and "state control" because the alternative is lawlessness.

Unfortunately, however, this assessment of government control and regulation as an antidote to lawlessness is too optimistic. As our propositions show, the civil law approach to law enforcement, with its reliance on enforcers beholden to the sovereign and on bright line rules, is especially vulnerable to abuse by a bad government. Such a government can use the controls inherent in civil law to politicize justice to its own end rather than to pursue community standards of justice. As a consequence, civil law, if used to direct justice to political ends, will lead to heavy government intervention, insecure property rights, and poor governance in general. Common law, with its decentralization of adjudication, is less vulnerable to politicization.

Appendix: Proofs

Proof of Proposition 1   Because the unconditional expectation of R is zero, social welfare under the jury system equals $\int_{D>A/\beta} Df(D)dD$. This expression both is monotonically declining in A and converges to zero as A increases to infinity. The social welfare under the royal judge equals

$$\int_D D\left(1-G\left(-\frac{D}{\theta}\right)\right)f(D)dD + \lambda\theta \int_D \int_{R>-D/\theta} Rf(D)g(R)dDdR \qquad (A1)$$

The first term is positive because $E(D) > 0$ and the weighting function puts a higher weight on higher D's. The second term is positive because $E(R \mid R > -D/\theta)$ is positive for every D. Because social welfare under royal judges is strictly positive, and social welfare under juries converge to zero as A increases, for sufficiently high levels of A judges must dominate juries.

When $A = 0$ and $\lambda = 0$, social welfare under juries reaches the first best and therefore strictly dominates social welfare under judges of $\int_D D(1 - G(-D/\theta))f(D)dD$, which does not reach the first best. Because social welfare under judges is continuous in λ, for values of λ close to zero judges still dominate juries at $A = 0$. Using the mean value theorem, for these values of λ, there must exist a value of A (denoted by A^*) at which social welfare under judges and that under juries are equal. By monotonicity of social welfare under judges with respect to A, for values of A above A^* juries dominate judges and for values of A below A^*, judges dominate juries.

Note next that the value of A^* is defined through

$$\int_{D>A^*/\beta} Df(D)dD = \int_D \int_{R>-D/\theta} (D + \lambda\theta R)f(D)g(R)dDdR. \tag{A2}$$

For (A2) to hold, A^*/β must remain constant as β rises. Differentiation then shows that

$$\frac{\partial A^*}{\partial \beta} = \frac{A}{\beta} > 0.$$

Differentiating both sides of (A2) and inverting gives us that

$$\frac{\partial A^*}{\partial \lambda} = \frac{-\beta^2 \int_D \int_{R>-D/\theta} \theta R f(D)g(R)dDdR}{A^* f(A^*/\beta)}, \tag{A3}$$

which is always negative since $E(R \mid R > -D/\theta) > 0$.

Differentiating both sides of (A2) and inverting gives us that

$$\frac{\partial A^*}{\partial \theta} = \frac{\beta^2 \left[\int_D ((1-\lambda)D^2/\theta^2)f(D)g(-D/\theta)dD - \int_D \int_{R>-D/\theta} \lambda R f(D)g(R)dDdR \right]}{A^* f(A^*/\beta)}, \tag{A4}$$

which is positive if and only if

$$\frac{1-\lambda}{\lambda\theta^2} \int_D D^2 f(D)g\left(-\frac{D}{\theta}\right)dD > \int_D \int_{R>-D/\theta} Rf(D)g(R)dDdR, \tag{A5}$$

which always holds when λ is sufficiently small.

Proof of Proposition 2   For any subset of D's (denoted Ω_i) captured by any bright line, the problem is to choose P_i, the subsidy toward conviction, to maximize

$$\int_{D\in\Omega_i}\int_{R>(A-P_i)/\beta_j\theta_j-(D/\theta_j)}(D+\theta R)f(D)g(R)dDdR$$

when $\theta_j > 0$ and

$$\int_{D\in\Omega_i}\int_{R<(A-P_i)/\beta_j\theta_j-(D/\theta_j)}(D+\theta R)f(D)g(R)dDdR$$

when $\theta_j < 0$. This problem yields the first-order condition:

$$\frac{1}{\beta_j\theta_j}\int_{D\in\Omega_i}\left(\frac{\theta_j-\theta}{\theta_j}D+\frac{\theta(A-P_i)}{\beta_j\theta_j}\right)g\left(\frac{A-P_i}{\beta_j\theta_j}-\frac{D}{\theta_j}\right)f(D)dD=0 \qquad (A6)$$

P_i is defined as the solution to (A6), and when second-order conditions hold, this will represent the optimal incentive scheme (from the king's perspective). The second derivative of the maximand is

$$\int_{D\in\Omega_i}\left(\frac{-\theta}{\beta_j^2\theta_j^2}\right)g\left(\frac{A-P_i}{\beta_j\theta_j}-\frac{D}{\theta_j}\right)f(D)dD-\left(\frac{1}{\beta_j\theta_j}\right)^2 \qquad (A7)$$

$$\times\int_{D\in\Omega_i}\left(\frac{\theta_j-\theta}{\theta_j}D+\frac{\theta(A-P_i)}{\beta_j\theta_j}-\frac{D}{\theta_j}\right)g'\left(\frac{A-P_i}{\beta_j\theta_j}-\frac{D}{\theta_j}\right)f(D)dD,$$

when $\theta_j > 0$ and -1 times this quantity when $\theta_j < 0$. Thus, if terms involving $g'(.)$ are small, that is, $g(.)$ is close to uniform, (A7) is positive if and only if $\theta_j < 0$. When (A7) is positive for any finite value of P_i, then no system with finite payoffs can be an optimum. Thus, we need only consider schemes where the judge is given infinite positive or infinite negative incentives to convict. In the case of high levels of D, convicting is, on average, better than letting go. In the case of levels of D below the bright line rule, convicting is, on net, worse than letting go. Thus, when $\theta_j < 0$, it is optimal to pursue a pure bright line rule strategy.

When $\theta_j > 0$, second-order conditions hold, and (A6) determines the optimal subsidy for conviction. Since (A6) implies finite rewards and judicial discretion, a pure bright line rule system is not optimal for the king when $\theta_j > 0$.

Proof of Proposition 3   As before, social welfare under juries is a function of A and social welfare under bright line rules is not. At $A = 0$, juries produce the social optimum, and bright line rules do not, so juries are preferable. For sufficiently large values of A, social welfare under juries is arbitrarily close to zero, and social welfare under bright line rules is assumed to be strictly positive. Because the social welfare under juries is monotonically and continuously decreasing in A, there must exist a value of A for which the levels of social welfare under juries and bright line rules are identical. Above that value, bright line rules dominate, and below that value, juries dominate.

A^{**} is defined by

$$\int_{D>A^{**}/\beta} Df(D)dD = \int_{D>\bar{D}} Df(D)dD,$$

and taking derivatives yields

$$\frac{\partial A^{**}}{\partial \bar{D}} = \frac{\bar{D}f(\bar{D})\beta^2}{A^{**}f(A^{**}/\beta)}. \tag{A8}$$

Because (A8) takes on the sign of $\bar{D}$, this means that A^{**} rises with the absolute value of $\bar{D}$.

9 The Extent of the Market and the Supply of Regulation

with Casey B. Mulligan

1 Introduction

In a classic paper, Demsetz (1967) argues that the creation of institutions requires a fixed cost, and is therefore limited by the extent of the market. Introducing an institution becomes efficient only when the scale of an activity it supports becomes significant enough to cover the fixed costs of creating and running it. Using the example of Indians in the Quebec region circa 1700, Demsetz maintains that the aggregate value of fur trading explains the emergence of enforced land ownership rights. In this paper, we show that Demsetz's logic concerning the role of fixed costs in creating and enforcing additional rules and regulations is quite general theoretically but also valid empirically. We present a model in which the supply of regulation is limited by the extent of the market, and test its predictions for whether and how particular activities are regulated across communities.

The two main traditions of regulatory economics do not focus on the fixed costs of introducing and administering regulations. Neither the public interest theory (Pigou 1928) nor the special interest theory (Tullock 1967; Stigler 1971; Peltzman 1976; Becker 1983; McChesney 1987) deals with this issue. Yet, at least in principle, fixed costs are important. It takes some political and administrative resources to organize a community to draft and adopt each new regulation, especially when the government enters a new area. In many cases, a new bureau must be set up and staffed to administer the new regulation, including finding violators. At least for some communities, these costs might be significant.

Consider military conscription. As an addition to the volunteer army,[1] conscription is a common form of reliance on regulation rather than contract to meet social needs. Conscription has significant fixed adoption, administration, and enforcement costs. The adoption costs include reaching a political consensus on not only how many people should serve in the armed forces, but the fraction of the force to be drafted, the length of service, the population subject to the draft, occupation-specific terms of service, exemptions, deferrals, and possibilities for commutation fees, substitutes, and conscientious objection. The political costs may be especially significant for conscription because some of the issues involved are so controversial. Administrative and enforcement costs include deriving algorithms for enumerating the population subject to the draft, setting up and staffing offices throughout the country to administer the draft, verifying qualifications for exemptions, including medical ones, establishing institutions specializing in catching draft dodgers, and policing the system itself to assure fairness and avoid corruption.

Conscription transforms some of the marginal costs of the volunteer army into fixed costs, especially for the less selective conscription systems. For example, a small volunteer army might maintain just a few recruiting stations (or even just one located near the military headquarters), and plan for the training of a particular type of enthusiastic and able recruit. As the volunteer force grows, it would open additional recruiting stations and learn to train a more heterogeneous group of recruits. These costs would be marginal. But a universal or random conscription system pays these costs regardless of the number of troops to be recruited, because the system recruits a cross-section of the population.

We study how the extent of the market and regulatory costs shape the adoption of regulations such as conscription. In our model, communities choose from a range of possible modes of solving social problems, including private orderings, judicial enforcement, and regulation (Djankov et al. 2003). Regulation wins out—either from the efficiency perspective or in the political marketplace—when it is cheaper than the alternatives. We assume that regulation requires a fixed cost of adoption and administration and derive the equilibrium quantity of regulation in a community as a function of its population and the fixed and variable costs, as well as the benefits, of regulation.

Several predictions follow. First, the theory predicts that, other things equal, more populous communities should regulate more activities, and do so more intensively. This yields a novel prediction that population is a determinant of the quantity of regulation, which we test using data on U.S. states as well as a cross-section of countries.

Second, if we compare two communities with different levels of incremental fixed costs of introducing and administering new regulations, the community with lower fixed costs should have more extensive regulations. We test this prediction in two ways. We consider the diffusion of regulation across U.S. states and argue that regulation should diffuse from higher- to lower-population states, since the latter as imitators face lower fixed costs of regulation. In addition, we argue that legal origin can serve as a proxy for regulatory costs. Following the historical analysis of Woloch (1994), we suggest that the pervasive administrative state introduced in France by its Revolution lowered the fixed costs of administering incremental regulations. Such a state was never created in England. As legal and regulatory frameworks have spread through conquest and colonization, so did the cost structures of incremental regulations. The model then implies that legal origin predicts the extent of regulation in a cross-section of countries. This approach offers a test of the fixed cost theory quite separate from that using population.

2   A Simple Model of the Supply of, and Demand for, Regulation

Consider a jurisdiction, such as a U.S. state, where people interact with each other and may have a dispute. These disputes are sometimes resolved informally or in courts using community standards of fairness. But when such strategies do not work, communities introduce legislation and regulation, which delineate the rights and obligations of various members. Some legislation just describes the rules of the game, and leaves the enforcement of these rules to private parties. Its main function is to reduce the cost of settling disputes in court. In other instances, enforcement is also taken over by the state, as in the case of regulatory agencies.

Interactions, and hence the nature of disputes, are heterogeneous. For example, a day laborer's interaction and potential disputes with his employer are different from those between a salaried employee and his employer. We let $t \in [0, \infty)$ index the type of interaction that might occur in a community, or more literally the type of dispute that might occur. The index t is ordered so that the more frequent disputes have lower values of t. $f(t)$ is a monotone decreasing density function, describing the likelihood that a randomly chosen dispute is of type t. When population is of size N, the total number of disputes of type t is $Nf(t)$. Let b denote the political-market value of having legislation or regulation in place in order to help resolve any one dispute, so that $bNf(t)$ is the total value of having legislation or regulation pertaining to interactions of type t.

The value per regulation can be graphed versus the index t, and slopes down. In this sense, $bNf(t)$ is the "demand" for regulation. As in any market, demand does not necessarily coincide with social value: $bNf(t)$ is a political-market value, and not necessarily a social value, because some groups' interests might not be adequately represented in the political marketplace—perhaps because they do not vote or are otherwise politically inaudible. Nevertheless, we expect the extent of the market to be an important determinant of both social and political-market values.

Creating and enforcing regulations pertaining to a dispute of type t costs $s(t) = \rho + cNf(t)$. $s(t)$ is a political-market cost function, and does not necessarily coincide with social cost due to inefficiencies in the political market. $s(t)$ has a fixed component ρ and a variable component $cNf(t)$, which is proportional to the total number of disputes of type t. For simplicity, we treat ρ, b, and c as constants even though in principle they can vary with GDP per capita, education, and other characteristics of the community being regulated.

This specification assumes the same function f across all communities, and that the ordering of activities on the t axis is the same everywhere, which is clearly not true. Some communities specialize in particular economic activities or social groups. In this case, what determines the adoption of regulation is not the total population, but the number of people who would benefit from the activity being regulated. Moreover, communities might endogenously specialize in regulation, hoping to attract more of a given activity—as is the case with Delaware's specialization in corporate law. In empirical applications, we recognize that sometimes it is not the total population of a community, but the total affected population, that limits the adoption of regulations.

Legislation pertaining to disputes of type t is created *if and only if* demand exceeds supply:

$$Nf(t)b \geq s(t) = \rho + cNf(t) \tag{1}$$

If $b \leq c$ there will be no regulation regardless of the dispute frequency or the population size. In particular, if $b < 0$, there is no political-market value of regulating rather than relying on private orderings or common law, and regulation will not be adopted. Accordingly, we focus on the activities for which $b > c$.[2]

With $b > c$, we graph in figure 9.1 the supply of regulation in the same plane as the demand described above, with the supply sloping down less steeply than does demand. There is a critical value T such that regulation covers all disputes $t \leq T$, and no regulation pertains to disputes $t > T$. Hence, T is the total range of regulation, and is determined by the formula:

$$T = f^{-1}\left(\frac{\rho}{(b-c)N}\right) \tag{2}$$

The fraction of disputes that are subject to regulation is simply $F(T)$. Equation (2) yields comparative statics results that motivate our empirical work.

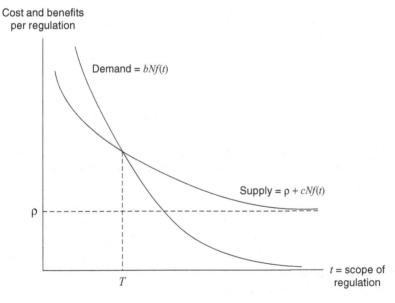

Cost and benefits
  per regulation

Demand = $bNf(t)$

Supply = $\rho + cNf(t)$

ρ

T

t = scope of
regulation

Figure 9.1
Supply of, and demand for, regulation. This figure shows the model's relationship between the scope of regulation t and either costs and benefits per regulation. The steeply sloped line graphs marginal benefit, while the flatter line graphs marginal cost. N denotes population. b (c) denotes marginal benefit (cost) per person affected by regulation. ρ is the fixed cost of supplying regulation. T is the critical scope of regulation at which marginal benefit equals marginal cost.

Proposition 1 An increase in population N increases the range of regulation T.

In the presence of fixed costs, jurisdictions with larger populations tend to regulate more activities. In addition, if we fix a particular activity, such as mining, jurisdictions may vary according to exactly where mining fits in their distribution f or what is the net value $(b - c)$ of regulating. For example, mining may be a common activity in West Virginia, but uncommon in Georgia, so a larger fraction f of West Virginia's population may stand to benefit from mining regulation. In this example, *total affected population Nf(t)* determines regulatory adoption, so that some states like West Virginia may regulate mining even though their overall population N is small. More generally, some states with small overall populations will regulate a particular activity because of their large desired intensity (as measured by f, $(b - c)$, or some combination).

In addition, equation (2) yields a prediction for the consequences of regulatory costs:

Proposition 2 A decrease in the fixed cost (ρ) or the variable cost (c) of regulation raises T.

Propositions 1 and 2 are readily proven by totally differentiating equation (2): $dT = \{d\rho/\rho + dc/(b - c) - dN/N\}\rho/[(b - c)Nf']$.

To test proposition 2 empirically, we use two approaches to measuring regulatory costs. First, creating and enforcing a new regulation in one jurisdiction is likely to be cheaper when there are precedents in similar jurisdictions. Given proposition 1, this means that new regulations first appear in larger jurisdictions—where the aggregate value of regulation exceeds the cost of creating and enforcing them—and then diffuse to smaller jurisdictions. Because the smaller jurisdictions benefit from the experience of the larger jurisdictions, they adopt the new regulation without having to wait to grow to the size of the larger jurisdictions that began the process.

Second, the fixed and variable costs of regulation (ρ and c, respectively) may not only spill across jurisdictions, but also across regulations. Legal origin is one proxy for the costs of regulation as inherited from long histories of state intervention, with civil law indicating lower costs than common law. Following the work of Djankov et al. (2003; chapter 10), we use legal origin as a measure of the cost of regulation in a cross-section of countries.

3   Regulation across States Measured in KB

3.1   Population and the Amount of Law

One aggregate measure of regulation is the number of pages of law, made famous by Ronald Reagan when he recalled the reduction during his administration in the number of *Federal Register* pages. To compute this indicator of regulation for states, we measure the number of kilobytes (KB) of unannotated *state* law in 37 states in 2001, 2002, or 2003. A kilobyte (KB) is 1024 bytes, and each byte represents a character. For example "Thou shalt not kill." is 20 bytes (including spaces and the period), or 0.0195 KB. We found that one page of law is roughly one kilobyte of law, and the typical state has tens of thousands of kilobytes.[3] Appendix 1 describes our algorithm for counting KB of law for the states, and explains why 13 states were excluded from the counting.

The empirical relation between statute KB and population is shown in figure 9.2. The correlation (of the logs) is 0.88 and the overall regression elasticity is 0.31. The comparison of Delaware and Wyoming, and of Texas and New York, illustrates the basic fact. Delaware and Wyoming have similar total populations, but different population

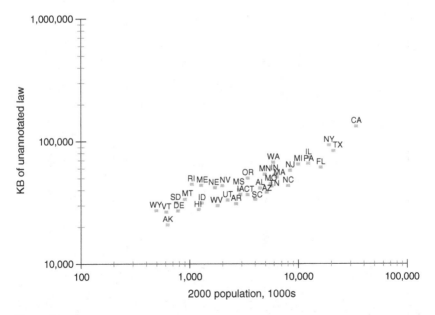

Figure 9.2
Statutes and population across states.

Table 9.1

Independent variables	(1)	(2)	(3)	(4)	(5)	Addendum: inclusion in sample
log(2000 population)	0.31 (0.06)	0.32 (0.07)	0.36 (0.09)	0.31 (0.02)	0.46 (0.06)	0.34 (0.24)
South	−0.21 (0.10)	−0.20 (0.09)	−0.22 (0.10)	−0.16 (0.06)	−0.17 (0.07)	−0.37 (0.23)
Lawyers per capita, log	0.20 (0.10)	0.21 (0.10)	0.23 (0.10)	0.16 (0.07)	0.11 (0.11)	−0.05 (0.24)
Land area, log	0.01 (0.04)	0.01 (0.04)	−0.01 (0.05)			−0.13 (0.12)
Income per capita, log	−0.28 (0.31)	−0.28 (0.31)	−0.23 (0.32)			−0.04 (0.73)
90–10 household income differential, log	0.13 (0.22)					
Fr. labor force coded with just 75 occ. codes		0.13 (1.53)				
Fr. population urban			−0.25 (0.44)			−1.45 (1.13)
Fr. of population white	0.19 (0.28)	0.17 (0.29)	0.18 (0.28)			−0.20 (0.81)
No. of state senators & representatives, log	−0.12 (0.11)	−0.12 (0.11)	−0.15 (0.12)			−0.41 (0.24)
Year of statehood/100	−0.08 (0.12)	−0.07 (0.12)	−0.05 (0.13)			0.03 (0.31)
log(1920 population)	0.03 (0.05)	0.03 (0.05)	0.01 (0.06)			−0.16 (0.15)
adj-R²	.82	.82	.82	.84	.85	.13
Sample	37	37	37	37	17	50

Each of the first five columns present results for a cross-state regression with log of number of kilobytes of law as the dependent variable. Columns differ in terms of independent variables, and states included. The last column reports marginal probabilities from a probit for inclusion in our 37 state sample.

(a) constant terms are estimated, but not displayed in the table. OLS standard errors displayed in parentheses.

(b) specification (5) limits sample to states with year 2000 population at least the median.

(c) see appendix 2 for variable definitions and sources.

densities (Wyoming is the second least densely populated state, while Delaware is seventh most). Since both states have a similar number of statute KB, and both fit near the regression line, population seems more important than density in determining regulation. Texas and New York offer a similar comparison since they have the same population and similar numbers of statute KB, but New York is about six times denser than Texas. Indeed, Delaware and New York have similar population densities (almost 400 persons per square mile), but pages of statutes that differ by almost an order of magnitude, as predicted by our model.

Table 9.1 examines the validity and the robustness of the relationship between population and regulation illustrated in figure 9.2. We include a southern state dummy, lawyers per capita, land area, income per capita, and several additional state characteristics as controls. The relationship between population and regulation remains strong, and the coefficient stays near 0.3. Southern states have fewer KB of law. More law and more lawyers go together.[4] The regressions in table 9.1 do not show any significant effect of income per capita on KB of law. This is a surprising result, especially in light of the fact that Demsetz (1967) and North (1981) generally think of the aggregate level of economic activity as a determinant of adoption of institutions. Indeed, our model's focus on population rather than aggregate activity distinguishes it from the earlier work. One reason that population rather than income may matter for regulation is that, as income rises, so do real wages and therefore the fixed labor cost of setting up and running a regulatory institution. If the fixed costs rise as fast as do the aggregate benefits per capita, population rather than income determines the adoption of a regulation.[5]

Alesina and Spolaore (2003a) present a model of the determinants of country size, in which the benefits of spreading the fixed costs of a particular policy among more people are traded off against the inefficiency of implementing uniform policies in a heterogeneous population. In their view, population is positively correlated with heterogeneity such as ethnic diversity. In our model, population is a proxy for a different kind of heterogeneity—namely the likelihood of having at least some minimum number of people engaged in esoteric activities—which could be found in a large jurisdiction even if it were very homogeneous in terms of race, geography, education, or income. Empirically for U.S. states, does population proxy for heterogeneity and, if so, which kind? Specifications (1)–(3) in table 9.1 suggest that population does not proxy for heterogeneity as measured by income inequality, occupational diversity, the importance of cities, or the prevalence of racial minorities, because these measures do not predict KB or affect the estimated population elasticity.[6]

Figure 9.2 also does not readily tell us whether the amount of law in a state today depends on its current population or, since statutes accumulate over time, the population it had in the distant past and/or the number of years the state has existed (as a state). As shown in table 9.1, these two variables (the former measured as 1920 population) have no power to predict statute KB conditional on current population. We also include log of the number of seats in each state's House and Senate, in case the amount of law depends on the number of lawmakers which just happens to be correlated with population.[7] This control does not matter either.

Our model calibrated with Zipf's law says that the population elasticity of regulation should be about 0.5. Although not included in our model, there may be a "necessary" range of activities such as murder, elections, or traffic that are regulated in some detail regardless of population. In this case, we expect the population elasticity to be less than 0.5 and then rise with population to approach 0.5 as the regulation moves significantly beyond the necessary range. A small state may also adopt a regulation more cheaply by imitating the earlier-adopting large states. Imitation induces a positive correlation between population and the cost of adopting regulations, which means that the cross-state population elasticity may be less than 0.5, especially among the smaller states, many of whose statutes are imitated. Figure 9.2 suggests, and specifications (4) and (5) confirm, that a larger elasticity in fact prevails among the larger states. Specification (4) is for the entire 37 state sample, and without the various controls other than southern, and displays an elasticity of 0.33. Specification (5) throws out the 20 of the 37 states with below median population (i.e., states with a smaller 2000 population than Kentucky's 4,041,000), and displays an elasticity of 0.46. The estimated population elasticity is similar if we cut the sample at three, five, or six million rather than 4,041,000.

3.2   What Do KB of Law Represent?

There are two reasons we believe that pages of statutes are correlated with the real amount of regulation. First, the aggregate time series of *Federal Register* pages (the *Federal Register* consists of new laws passed by Congress, executive orders, and federal government agency reports) deviates significantly from its trend during exactly those periods (since 1936) when it is commonly believed that federal regulation was accelerating the most—World War II and the 1970s. Second, as we show in section 4, the population gradient seen in figure 9.2 also appears in studies of the history of states' adoption of various laws, including occupational licensing, telegraph regulation, and workers' compensation. However, regulations like these diffuse quickly from large to small states and, at least in the case of occupational licensing, the cross-state regulation-population gradient falls over time as regulation diffuses. Hence the pages we measure in 2003 may not have much to do with the adoption of regulations such as occupational licensing and workers' compensation that began their diffusion decades ago, but rather with the adoption in more recent areas of regulation, with further elaboration of old regulations, or with the adoption of esoteric regulations by the big states that may never diffuse to the smaller ones.

Illinois and Indiana are an interesting comparison, as the states are similar in many ways, except that Illinois has twice the population. Both states are near the regression line; Illinois has 40 percent more bytes of law than Indiana. Part of this difference is that Illinois has almost twice the bytes of criminal law and corrections.[8] Can these byte counts be attributed to a number of activities that are legal in Indiana and illegal in Illinois? Or do both prohibit the same set of activities and Illinois is just more detailed in its regulation of them? Several examples suggest that both differences are present.

Relative to Indiana, Illinois has many acts devoted to pretty minor issues (such as the "Coin Slug Act" and the "Peephole Installation Act").[9] To our knowledge, Indiana has no statute covering peephole installation (apartment units must be built with peepholes for the occupants to see out). Among the issues covered in the criminal law of both states, Illinois seems to regulate them in more detail. For example, Illinois has 359 KB devoted to drug offenses while Indiana has only 124 KB.[10] Included among Illinois' 359 KB is an entire "Drug Asset Forfeiture Procedure Act" (22 KB) devoted to the forfeiture of assets by persons involved in drug offenses, where Indiana has only a civil law chapter "Forfeiture of Property Used in Violation of Certain Criminal Statutes" (21 KB) on the seizing of assets of criminals, and this chapter applies to all kinds of criminals, including thieves, (media) pirates, smugglers, and terrorists.

Consider offenses related to animal fighting. Indiana has only a few sections (totaling 2 KB) in a chapter on "Offenses Relating to Animals," while Illinois has a criminal section "Dog Fighting" plus two sections of the "Human Care for Animals Act" (with all three fighting sections totaling 11 KB). The Indiana statutes prohibit promotion, use of animals, or attendance with animal (or without) at animal fighting contests, and the possession of animal fighting paraphernalia. Conducting or attending a dog fight is also explicitly illegal in Illinois, but so is a whole range of other activities connected to dog fighting. Namely, Illinois explicitly prohibits a person to:

(a) "own, capture, breed, train, or lease a dog" for fighting,

(b) "promote, conduct, carry on, advertise, collect money for or in any other manner assist or aid in the presentation" of a dog fight,

(c) "sell or offer for sale, ship, transport, or otherwise move, or deliver or receive any dog which he or she knows has been captured, bred, or trained, or will be used, to fight another dog or human,"

(d) "manufacture for sale, shipment, transportation, or delivery any device or equipment which he or she knows or should know is intended for use in any [dog fight],"

(e) "possess, sell or offer for sale, ship, transport, or otherwise move any [dog fighting equipment],"

(f) "make available any site, structure, or facility, whether enclosed or not, that he or she knows is intended to be used for the purpose of conducting [a dog fight]."

Illinois law also details the procedures for sheltering animals found in connection with the enforcement of the animal fighting statutes.

The Indiana-Illinois comparison is likely to be representative of the population-animal regulation gradient for all 50 states. We have counted words of statute devoted to animal fighting for 37 states. Regressing log animal fighting words on log 2000 population and a dummy for south yields coefficients of 0.30 (s.e. = 0.14) and 0.02 (s.e. = 0.30), respectively. The population elasticity for animal laws is the same as that for all laws combined.

4   The Diffusion of Regulation across States

Proposition 2 implies that regulations are first introduced in the most populous states, and then diffuse to smaller ones. In this section, we test this prediction.

4.1   Patterns of Adoption: Occupation and Industry Regulation

Stigler (1971) looks at the licensing of 37 occupations in the 48 mainland U.S. states. He predicts the year a state licenses an occupation using the prevalence and urbanization of that occupation in the state, and occupation fixed effects. Our model suggests that total population, or the *absolute* size of the occupation, should be added to the licensing year regressions. Roughly speaking, the difference between Stigler's specification and that suggested by our model is the inclusion of log total population as a regressor in addition to, or instead of, occupational prevalence.[11] When we regress year of licensing on occupation dummies, the fraction of the population living in cities, and the log of 1910 population, the estimated population elasticity is –2.13 (standard error clustered by state = 0.55). Larger states tended to license occupations earlier.

The diffusion of regulation from large to small states is readily seen in our licensing data. The diffusion curve for, say, real estate broker licensing is a graph of year on the horizontal axis versus fraction of states licensing brokers by that year on the vertical axis. Stigler (1971) considered 36 other occupations as well, so we consider the cross-occupation average of the diffusion curves; our vertical axis measures the fraction of state-occupation cells licensed as of the year indicated on the horizontal axis. Figure 9.3 displays a separate diffusion curve for the ten largest states (solid line, classified on 1910 population) and the ten smallest states (dashed line).[12] The large state curve is to the left of the small state curve: licensing appears earlier in the large states. The difference is about five years in the middle of the sample period, which is a lot less time than it takes for the small states to grow to the size of the big ones (the former have average 1910 populations of 0.3 million, compared to 4.6 million for the latter). The result is what we would expect if the leading states lower the adoption costs for the followers.

Seven of the ten small states are western, and were not admitted to the Union until about 1900, so it may be possible that the dashed curve sits to the right merely because the represented states are young rather than small. The dotted line omits the seven western states, leaving DE, NH, and VT, which were among the first states of the United States. It still sits to the right of the solid line, despite the fact that the ten largest states average 20 years younger than DE, NH, and VT.

Other evidence is broadly consistent with our findings on Stigler's data. Nonnenmacher (2001) looks at the adoption of telegraph

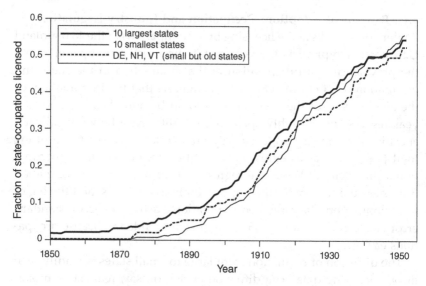

Figure 9.3
The diffusion of occupational licensing. The figure displays cross-occupation averages of the diffusion curves: the vertical axis measures the fraction of state-occupation cells licensed as of the year indicated on the horizontal axis. The figure displays a separate diffusion curve for the ten largest states (solid line, classified on 1910 population) and the ten smallest states (dashed line). The dotted line displays the diffusion curve for the three oldest of the ten smallest states.

regulation circa 1850. Figure 9.4 graphs total state population, measured in 1850 and on a log scale, versus the year of first telegraph regulation for each of the 32 U.S. states at the time. As expected, the populous states like NY, PA, MA, and VA were early adopters, and the last adopters (TX, FL, MN, IA, and AR) were relatively unpopulated. The correlation between year of first law and log population is –0.56 (t-stat = 3.73).

More populous states were also quicker to regulate working hours of women. Figure 9.5 graphs Landes' (1980, table 9.1) report of the year of first maximum female working hours legislation against (log-scaled) 1890 population. The correlation is –0.34 (t-stat = 2.3). Among the 23 states for which Landes reports there being a minimum wage law for women, the correlation between year of first minimum wage law and log population is –0.29 (t-stat = 1.0). TX, ND, DC, AR, and KS had an average 1890 population of 1.0 million and were the last of the 13 to legislate a minimum wage, while MA passed the first law and had an 1890 population of 2.2 million.

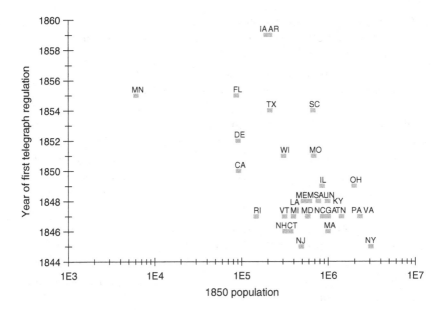

Figure 9.4
Telegraph regulation across states.

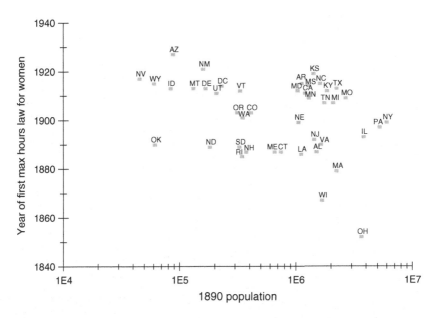

Figure 9.5
Female hours laws versus population.

4.2 Population or Affected Population?

In section 2, we noted that the exact specification of the model might be too narrow, and that what may matter is the size of the population (and the number of interactions and conflicts) affected by a given regulation. Some evidence indeed supports this view.

Workers' compensation provides an interesting application of our analysis, because the population relevant for determining whether there will be workers' comp regulation—namely, the individuals likely to be hurt in workplace accidents—can be quite different from the total state population, especially in the early twentieth century when states were first taking up these laws. For example, the 1910 Census shows Wyoming's ranking 47th out of 48 in terms of total population, but 29th out of 48 in terms of total number of persons working as miners (a group likely to experience serious work injury). Figure 9.6 graphs *total* state miners found in the 1910 Census PUMS, on a log scale, against the year of first workers' compensation law (from Fishback and Kantor (2000), table 4.3) for each of the 48 U.S. states at the time. The correlation is –0.27 (t-stat = 1.9). If we regress year of first law on log miners and miners per capita, log miners is the more important

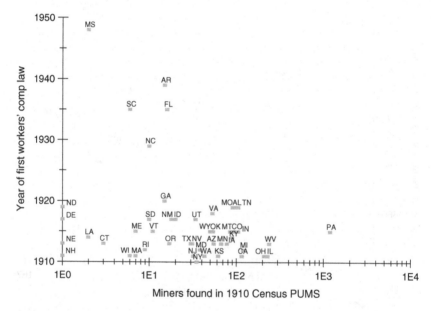

Figure 9.6
Total miner population and the adoption of workers' comp.

Table 9.2
Northern States, Classified by Their Employment Discrimination Laws.

	1968 employment discrimination law		
1950 black population	Enforceable	No enforcement commission	No law
Average	171,615	987	492
Percent of total	1.8	0.2	0.1

Enforceable states: AK, AZ, CA, CO, CT, HI, IL, IN, IA, KS, MA, MI, MN, MO, NE, NV, NH, NJ, NM, NY, OH, OR, PA, RI, UT, WA, WI, WY.
No commission states: ID, ME, MT, VT.
States w/o a law: ND, SD.

This table displays summary statistics for black populations of northern states, where the states are classified in columns by the type of Employment Discrimination Law they had in 1968. The last row of the table lists the states appearing in each column.
Source: Landes (1968), University of Virginia Geospatial and Statistical Data Center, and Texas A&M University (2002).

variable: the t-statistics on the regression coefficients are −1.5 and −0.5, respectively.

The size of the affected population also predicts which states were early to pass legislation "prohibiting discrimination in employment on the grounds of race, creed, color, or national origin" (Landes 1968, p. 507). When Landes wrote, 18 northern states had laws *and* agencies to enforce them. As table 9.2's "enforceable" column shows, the average 1950 black population in these states was 171,615. The four northern states with discrimination laws but no commission to enforce them (ID, ME, MT, VT) were much smaller—each had roughly 1,000 blacks. North Dakota and South Dakota were the only northern states without laws; their black populations were 257 and 727, respectively. Table 9.2 is consistent with our hypothesis that small states are late to adopt regulation. However, in this case total population is correlated with population frequency; the last row of the table shows that the regulating states were not only populous, but also had relatively large black population percentages.[13]

5   Regulation across Countries

In this section, we bring the predictions of our theory to the cross-country data. We check whether higher population countries are more likely to have several types of regulation for which we have data. In addition, we develop the argument that the origin of a country's laws is a proxy for the level of incremental fixed costs of adding new regulations. These origins include the laws of England (common law), and civil laws of France, Germany, Scandinavia, and the U.S.S.R. Legal traditions have spread throughout the world through conquest and colonization (La Porta et al. 1998, and chapter 5), and represent very different approaches to addressing social concerns. But transplantation did not just affect the legal systems available at the time; it influenced broader patterns of regulation in countries from different legal origins. Once a country used a particular way of meeting a social goal, the human capital of its administrators and the structure of its existing institutions made it cheaper to use a similar approach in the future.

Motivated by the work of Woloch (1994) on Napoleonic conscription in France, we suggest that the origin of a country's legal system is a proxy for the level of fixed regulatory costs. Woloch describes how, following the Revolution, France established a pervasive administrative state. The country was divided into 80 departments, which were further subdivided down to the village level, with each level administered through a vertical hierarchy and directly accountable to the center. The administration was involved in budgets, police, roads, courts, primary education, hospitals, and some social welfare. Given the level of penetration of the state administration into national life, Woloch argues, draft administration was only an extension of the existing structures. "By Napoleon's choice, conscription constituted the ultimate frontier of state building, of the articulation of the administrative state projected by the Revolution. . . . Conscription became the state's obsession, the preoccupation of officials up and down the government hierarchy . . ." (p. 433).

In our more prosaic view, conscription and other regulations were introduced successfully in France because the initial administrative innovations created sufficiently invasive governmental structures that could then regulate more without prohibitively expensive *incremental* mechanisms of assuring compliance. The French legal origin is, then, in part, a shorthand for this administrative or regulatory approach to addressing social problems (Djankov et al. 2003). Through Napoleonic conquest and colonization, it was then transplanted to much of continental Europe, all of Latin America, North and West Africa, and parts of Asia. Scandinavian, German, and Socialist civil law countries have developed similar approaches to social intervention. England and its colonies, in contrast, did not develop such an administrative state at the early stages, and therefore we take common law to be a shorthand for the more decentralized approach to solving social problems. If the transplantation of the administrative/regulatory approach to addressing social problems reduces the fixed (and perhaps also the variable) costs of dealing with incremental ones, then our theory predicts that common law countries should have fewer regulations than civil law countries.

A few studies have measured regulations for a broad cross-section of countries. Here we briefly analyze the business entry regulation index of from chapter 10, the employment laws index of Botero et al. (2004), the death penalty measures of Mulligan et al. (2004), and measures of military conscription of Mulligan and Shleifer (2005). Table 9.3 reports one cross-country regression in each column. The columns differ according to the regulation measure (one of the five referenced above), and to whether a broader set of political variables (namely "left power") are included. The broadest sample is the 127 country "MGX" sample of Mulligan et al. (2004), but includes only measures of death penalty, population, British legal origin, GDP per capita, democracy, whether a country belongs to Kornai's (1992) list of communist states, and some information about military activities. A narrower 71 country sample from chapter 10 includes both regulation measures and a political proxy for "left power."[14]

With the exception of the death penalty, all measures of regulation are lower in common law countries, and the effect is large and statistically significant. The death penalty results are puzzling, but other evidence is broadly consistent with our interpretation of the civil law tradition as lowering the fixed costs of introducing and administering new regulations.

What about the population effects? Specifications (1)–(2) suggest that, holding constant legal origin, GDP per capita, democracy, and communism, more populous countries have more business entry procedures and employment regulations. The impact of population on the number of procedures is statistically significant, while that on employment regulations is not. The result on business entry procedures is particularly supportive of our model since a higher index of regulations in this area reflects more "issues" that the government gets involved in. In contrast, the index of labor regulations is constructed to reflect higher costs, rather than more areas of government supervision.

Table 9.3
Four Regulations across Countries.

Dependent variable	Business entry procedures, log	Employment laws index	Death penalty		Have draft	
Independent variables	(1)	(2)	(3)	(4)	(5)	(6)
log(population)/10	**0.95** (0.32)	**0.11** (0.14)	**0.50** (0.20)	**0.71** (0.33)	**0.75** (0.24)	**0.17** (0.32)
British legal origin	−0.70 (0.10)	−0.24 (0.04)	0.30 (0.07)	0.40 (0.10)	−0.50 (0.08)	−0.66 (0.09)
Real GDP per capita, log	−0.32 (0.07)	0.01 (0.03)	0.09 (0.04)	0.06 (0.08)	−0.06 (0.05)	−0.06 (0.08)
Democracy index	−0.02 (0.18)	0.03 (0.08)	−0.56 (0.10)	−0.34 (0.19)	0.11 (0.12)	0.03 (0.17)
Communist dummy	−0.07 (0.15)	−0.06 (0.07)	0.09 (0.10)	0.39 (0.16)	0.15 (0.11)	0.01 (0.15)
Left power	−0.15 (0.13)	0.12 (0.06)		−0.28 (0.13)		0.08 (0.12)
Armed forces per male aged 15–24					1.62 (0.56)	1.69 (0.66)
Years at war since 1950					0.00 (0.02)	0.00 (0.01)
adj-R^2	.57	.34	.27	.32	.38	.50
Countries	71	71	127	71	127	70

Each column presents results for a cross-country regression with a measure of regulation as the dependent variable. Columns differ in the measure of regulation used, the independent variables, and countries included.
(a) Constant terms are estimated, but not displayed in the table. OLS standard errors displayed in parentheses.
(b) Democracy index is on 0–1 scale, and averaged 1975–1990.

In modern times, the death penalty administration is another example of a regulatory attempt to solve social problems using methods involving significant fixed costs. For example, modern polities with the death penalty prefer to set up a system of appeals in order to reduce the probability that an innocent person is executed by the state. It is said that each execution costs the state millions of dollars (http:// www.deathpenaltyinfo.org/costs-death-penalty). It appears that execution costs are less than proportional to population.[15] In line with our predictions, specifications (3) and (4) suggest that more populous countries are more likely to have the death penalty.

Conscription is relatively easy to measure for a large panel of countries—on both the intensive and extensive margins. We obtain data on the existence of the draft and on the number of draftees for 138 countries for the years 1985, 1990, and 1995 from *The Military Balance* published annually by the International Institute for Strategic Studies. Following Ross (1994), we use measures of the size of the Armed Forces, democracy, and economic development as predictors of a country's reliance on conscription.[16] Specifications (5) and (6) are like the previous four specifications, except that some military activity variables are added to the list of independent variables and the dependent variable is the fraction of the years 1985, 1990, and 1995 a country conscripts in its armed forces.

The population effect is large, significant, and consistent with our theory in the sample of 127 countries. However, once we restrict attention to the subsample of 71 countries for which we have measures of left power, the size of the effect falls and its significance disappears. This is a consequence of using the subsample of richer and more democratic countries: the correlation between left power and log population is −0.02 in the smaller sample, so omitting the left power variable has essentially no effect on the population coefficient. We also find that, when a country uses the draft, it uses it intensively, especially when the country is small (results not reported in the table). Among the countries with less than median population and having a draft, 75 percent have more conscripts than volunteers. This observation is consistent with fixed costs of having a draft system, and inconsistent with the hypothesis that small countries just happen to intend to use the draft lightly.

Overall, the cross-country evidence on both the effects of population and those of legal origins is broadly supportive of the fixed cost theory of regulation, and in particular with the predictions of propositions 1 and 2.

6 Summary and Conclusions

In this paper, we have presented a model of efficient regulation along the lines of Demsetz (1967). In this model, setting up and running regulatory institutions takes a fixed cost, and therefore jurisdictions with larger populations affected by a given regulation are more likely to have them. We then tested the model using data from both U.S. states and countries around the world. We found that higher-population U.S. states have more pages of legislation and adopt particular laws earlier in their history. We also found that specific types of regulation, including the regulation of entry, the regulation of labor, and the military draft are more extensive in countries with larger populations. Finally, we have found that civil law countries regulate various activities more heavily than common law countries, a result consistent with earlier work and with our interpretation of civil law as lowering the fixed costs of administering new regulations. Overall, the results are strongly supportive of the fixed cost theory of regulation.

Our results suggest that, because of increasing returns in regulation, we would expect to observe regulatory specialization, particularly in activities that can cheaply travel across jurisdictions. Delaware's specialization in corporate law is broadly consistent with the perspective of this model. Regardless of the exact model of fixed costs, the evidence is supportive of the view that overcoming such costs is an important determinant of regulatory choice.

Appendix 1: Algorithm for Counting KB of Law

A.1.1 Statute Types

There are two main formats for publishing state laws—"annotated" and "unannotated." The former are most commonly found in libraries—presumably because they are more useful to lawyers—and contain the text of each statute in effect at a point in time, *plus* some of the precedents that have affected interpretation of the statute and perhaps information about previous versions of the statute. The unannotated statutes contain only the text of the statute. Since we are interested in the relation between regulation and population, the distinction between annotated and unannotated statutes is important. A populous state is more likely to have had a court case that tested a particular statute, so we expect the quantity of annotations to increase with population.

A.1.2 Computer Algorithm for Counting KB of Law

Every state has unannotated statutes available for browsing on the Internet. The browsing is either in html, java, or pdf format, or in multiple formats. Our computer programs can only browse the Internet in html format, so we were unable to make counts for nine states which had laws online only in java format.[17] The byte counts of pdf files exceed the number of characters in the file (due to formatting), so we exclude the two states (Kentucky and North Dakota) for which online statutes are only in pdf format. The final two states, Georgia and New Hampshire, were excluded from the sample even though they had html statutes available because they were not in a format accessible by our programs. As we show below, the 13 states excluded from our data set are very similar to the 37 included in terms of population and many other characteristics.

Statutes online are usually presented in a tree format, where users first browse a list of titles, for each title a list of chapters, etc., with the final nodes in the tree being the actual texts of laws. The tree format can be used to categorized formats by their legal classification, for example, tax, criminal, schools, occupations, or estates. States differ in terms of the number of levels in the tree, the number of final nodes used to present a given set of statutes, and hence the number of statutes and KB of statutes per final node. For example, New York has less than 4,000 final nodes and South Dakota more than 40,000, even while the former has a lot more statutes than the latter. Since each html page usually includes headers and footers, this implies that the number of KB of html required to present a *given* set of statutes expands significantly with the number of html pages on which those statutes are presented. For example, SD has more bytes devoted to headers and footers than actual statutes, whereas NY has more than 80 bytes of actual statutes per byte of header or footer.[18] We therefore count statutes KB in four steps:

(1) A computer program automatically browses the entire html tree presenting a state's statutes and downloads each web page from the tree, stripped of html tags. The statutes browsed were those in effect in 2001, 2002, or 2003.[19]

(2) A sample of downloads are visually inspected for a number of bytes of headers and footers on a typical html page.

(3) The number of html pages is multiplied by the result from step (2) to give total KB of headers and footers, and then subtracted from the total KB downloaded in step (1).

(4) If applicable, the aggregate KB of annotations are estimated as in steps (2) and (3), and then subtracted from the total.

As a result, we interpret our KB counts as number of KB (and hence, roughly the number of pages) of unannotated statutes, exclusive of headers and footers, but inclusive of tables of contents used to organize those statutes.

Appendix 2: U.S. States Data Sources

1920 population by state. University of Virginia Geospatial and Statistical Data Center, plus AK & HI from Texas A&M University (2002).

1990 and 2000 population by state. Census Bureau (2001).

south. Alabama, Arkansas, Delaware, Florida, Georgia, Kentucky, Louisiana, Maryland, Mississippi, North Carolina, Oklahoma, South Carolina, Tennessee, Texas, Virginia, West Virginia.

lawyers per capita. 1990 Census PUMS weighted number of persons aged 25–54 and reporting working in 1989 and reporting occupation code 178.

land area. square miles from http://www.imagesoft.net/flags/usstate1.html.

90–10 family income differential. 10th and 90th percentiles of the within-state household income distribution from the March 2001 CPS (referring to year 2000 income). The 90th percentile is divided by the 10th percentile, and the ratio is used in log form in the regressions.

fraction of labor force coded with just 75 occupation codes. Labor force is 1990 Census PUMS persons aged 25–54, reporting work in 1989, and reporting an occupation. The fraction used is the ratio of total labor force persons in a state's 75 largest occupation codes to total labor force.

fraction of labor force employed in agriculture. Year 2000 from *Statistical Abstract of the United States* 2001, 2002; Census 2000 Summary File 1, 2 at http://factfinder.census.gov.

fraction of population urban, white. Year 2000, sources above.

income per capita. Year 2000, personal income, sources above.

number of state senators and representatives. Year 2002 from *Book of the States.*

year of statehood. http://cointown.com/htm/statehood_facts_2.htm.

Appendix 3

Table 9.A1
Summary Statistics for U.S. State Data (37 states with KB measures).

Variable name	mean	std dev	min	max
KB of law	47,723	21,963	20,922	132,862
2000 population (1000s)	5,970	6,975	493	33,871
1920 population (1000s)	2,165	2,321	55	10,385
South	.27	.45	0	1
Lawyers per 1000 people	2.25	0.80	0.70	3.93
Area (square miles)	75,632	97,895	1,054	570,833
Personal income per cap. (year 2000 $)	28,162	4,491	20,916	40,757
90–10 household inc. differential, log	2.07	0.16	1.79	2.42
Fraction of labor force coded with just 75 occupation codes	0.70	0.03	0.64	0.77
Fraction of population urban	0.72	0.16	0.38	0.94
Fraction of population white	0.78	0.14	0.24	0.97
No. of state senators & representatives	140	49	49	253
Year of statehood	1841	48	1787	1959

10 The Regulation of Entry

with Simeon Djankov, Rafael La Porta, and
Florencio Lopez-de-Silanes

1 Introduction

Countries differ significantly in the way in which they regulate the
entry of new businesses. To meet government requirements for starting
to operate a business in Mozambique, an entrepreneur must complete
19 procedures taking at least 149 business days and pay US$256 in fees.
To do the same, an entrepreneur in Italy needs to follow 16 different
procedures, pay US$3,946 in fees and wait at least 62 business days to
acquire the necessary permits. In contrast, an entrepreneur in Canada
can finish the process in two days by paying US$280 in fees and com-
pleting only two procedures.

In this paper, we describe the required procedures governing entry
regulation, as well as the time and the cost of following these procedures, in 85 countries. We focus on legal requirements that need to be
met before a business can officially open its doors, the official cost of
meeting these requirements, and the minimum time it takes to meet
them if the government does not delay the process. We then use these
data to evaluate economic theories of regulation. Our work owes a
great deal to de Soto's (1989) path-breaking study of entry regulation
in Peru. Unlike de Soto, we look at the official requirements, official
cost, and official time—and do not measure corruption and bureaucratic delays that further raise the cost of entry.

Pigou's (1920) public interest theory of regulation holds that unregu-
lated markets exhibit frequent failures, ranging from monopoly power
to externalities. A government that pursues social efficiency counters
these failures and protects the public through regulation. As applied to
entry, this view holds that the government screens new entrants to
make sure that consumers buy high quality products from "desirable"
sellers. Such regulation reduces market failures such as low quality

products from fly-by-night operators and externalities such as pollution. It is "done to ensure that new companies meet minimum standards to provide a good or service. By being registered, new companies
acquire a type of official approval, which makes them reputable enough
to engage in transactions with the general public and other businesses"
(SRI 1999, p. 14). The public interest theory predicts that stricter regulation of entry, as measured by a higher number of procedures in particular, should be associated with socially superior outcomes.

The public choice theory (Tullock 1967; Stigler 1971; Peltzman 1976)
sees the government as less benign and regulation as socially inefficient. It comes in two flavors. In Stigler's (1971) theory of regulatory
capture, "regulation is acquired by the industry and is designed and
operated primarily for its benefit." Industry incumbents are able to
acquire regulations that create rents for themselves, since they typically
face lower information and organization costs than do the dispersed
consumers. In this theory, the regulation of entry keeps out the competitors and raises incumbents' profits. Because stricter regulation
raises barriers to entry, it should lead to greater market power and
profits rather than benefits to consumers.   .

A second strand of the public choice theory, which we call the *tollbooth view*, holds that regulation is pursued for the benefit of politicians
and bureaucrats (McChesney 1987; de Soto 1989). Politicians use regulation both to create rents and to extract them through campaign contributions, votes, and bribes. "An important reason why many of these
permits and regulations exist is probably to give officials the power to
deny them and to collect bribes in return for providing the permits"
(Shleifer and Vishny 1993, p. 601). The capture and tollbooth theories
are closely related in that they both address rent creation and extraction
through the political process. The *capture theory* emphasizes the benefits
to the industry, while the tollbooth theory stresses those to the politicians even when the industry is left worse off by regulation.

In principle, the collection of bribes in exchange for release from
regulation can be efficient. In effect, the government can become an
equity holder in a regulated firm. In practice, however, the creation of
rents for the bureaucrats and politicians through regulation is often
inefficient, in part because the regulators are disorganized, and in part
because the policies they pursue to increase the rents from corruption
are distortionary. The analogy to tollbooths on a highway is useful.
Efficient regulation may call for one toll for the use of a road, or even
no tolls if the operation of the road is most efficiently financed through

general tax revenues. In a political equilibrium, however, each town through which the road passes might be able to erect its own tollbooth. Toll collectors may also block alternative routes so as to force the traffic onto the toll road. For both of these reasons, political toll collection is inefficient.

In the tollbooth theory, the regulation of entry enables the regulators to collect bribes from the potential entrants and serves no social purpose. "When someone has finally made the decision to invest, he then is subjected to some of the worst treatment imaginable. . . In a few cases this treatment consists of outright extortion: presenting the investor with insurmountable delays or repeated obstacles unless he makes a large payoff . . ." (World Bank 1999, p. 10). More extensive regulation should be associated with socially inferior outcomes, particularly corruption.

We assess the regulation of entry around the world from the perspective of these theories by addressing two broad sets of questions. First, what are the consequences of the regulation of entry, and in particular, who gets the rents? If the regulation of entry serves the public interest, it should be associated with higher quality of goods, fewer damaging externalities, and greater competition. Public choice theory, in contrast, predicts that stricter regulation is most clearly associated with less competition and higher corruption.

A second question we examine to distinguish the alternative theories of regulation is which governments regulate entry? The public interest model predicts that governments whose interests are more closely aligned with those of the consumers, which we think of as the more representative and more limited governments, should ceteris paribus regulate entry more strictly. In contrast, the public choice model predicts that the governments least subject to popular oversight should pursue the strictest regulations, to benefit themselves and possibly the incumbent firms. Knowing who regulates thus helps to discriminate among the theories.

Our analysis of exhaustive data on entry regulation in 85 countries leads to the following conclusions. The number of procedures required to start up a firm varies from the low of two in Canada to the high of 21 in the Dominican Republic, with the world average of around ten. The minimum official time for such a startup varies from the low of two business days in Australia and Canada to the high of 152 in Madagascar, assuming that there are no delays by either the applicant or the regulators, with the world average of 47 business days. The official cost of following these procedures for a simple firm ranges from under 0.5 percent of per capita GDP in the US to over 4.6 times per capita GDP in the Dominican Republic, with the worldwide average of 47 percent of annual per capita income. For an entrepreneur, legal entry is extremely cumbersome, time consuming, and expensive in most countries in the world.

In a cross-section of countries, we do not find that stricter regulation of entry is associated with higher quality products, better pollution records or health outcomes, or keener competition. But stricter regulation of entry *is* associated with sharply higher levels of corruption, and a greater relative size of the unofficial economy. This evidence favors public choice over the public interest theories of regulation.

In response, a public interest theorist could perhaps argue that heavy regulation in some countries is a reflection of both significant market failures and the unavailability of alternative mechanisms of addressing them, such as good courts or free press. In addition, corruption and a large unofficial economy may be inadvertent consequences of benevolent regulation, and hence cannot be used as evidence against the public interest view. Such inadvertent consequences might obtain as a side effect of screening out bad entrants (Banerjee 1997; Acemoglu and Verdier 2000), or simply as a result of a well-intended but misguided transplant of rich-country regulations into poor countries. Because of this logic, the question of which countries regulate entry more heavily may be better suited conceptually to distinguish the alternative theories.

We find that the countries with more open access to political power, greater constraints on the executive, and greater political rights have less burdensome regulation of entry—even controlling for per capita income—than do the countries with less representative, less limited, and less free governments. The per capita income control is crucial for this analysis because it could be argued that richer countries have both better governments and a lower need for the regulation of entry, perhaps because they have fewer market failures or better alternative ways of dealing with them. The fact that better governments regulate entry less, along with the straightforward interpretation of the evidence on corruption and the unofficial economy, point to the tollbooth theory: entry is regulated because doing so benefits the regulators.

The next section describes the sample. Section 3 presents our basic results on the extent of entry regulation around the world. Section 4 asks who gets the rents from regulation. Section 5 presents the main results on which governments regulate. Section 6 concludes.

2 Data

2.1 Construction of the Database

This paper is based on a new data set that describes the regulation of entry by start-up companies in 85 countries in 1999. We are interested in all the procedures that an entrepreneur needs to carry out to begin operating legally a firm involved in industrial or commercial activity. Specifically, we record all procedures that are officially required of an entrepreneur in order to obtain all necessary permits and to notify and file with all requisite authorities. We also calculate the official costs and time necessary for the completion of each procedure under normal circumstances. The study assumes that the information is readily available and that all governmental bodies function efficiently and without corruption.

We collect data on entry regulation using all available written information on start-up procedures from government publications, reports of development agencies such as the World Bank and USAID, and government web pages on the Internet. We then contact the relevant government agencies to check the accuracy of the data. Finally, for each country, we commission at least one independent report on entry regulation from a local law firm, and work with that firm and government officials to eliminate disagreements among them.

We use official sources for the number of procedures, time, and cost. If official sources are conflicting or the laws are ambiguous, we follow the most authoritative source. In the absence of express legal definitions, we take a governmental official's report as the source. If several official sources have different estimates of time and cost, we take the median. Absent official estimates of time and cost, we take the estimates of local incorporation lawyers. If several unofficial (e.g., a private lawyer) sources have different estimates, we again take the median.

Our countries span a wide range of income levels and political systems. The sample includes 14 African countries, nine East Asian countries including China and Vietnam, three South Asian countries (India, Pakistan, and Sri Lanka), all Central and Eastern European countries except for Albania and some of the former Yugoslav republics, eight former Soviet Union republics and Mongolia, ten Latin American countries, two Caribbean countries (Dominican Republic and Jamaica), six Middle Eastern countries (Egypt, Israel, Jordan, Lebanon, Morocco, and Tunisia), and all major developed countries.

We record the procedures related to obtaining all the necessary permits and licenses and completing all the required inscriptions, verifications, and notifications for the company to be legally in operation. When there are multiple ways to begin operating legally, we choose the fastest in terms of time. In some countries, entrepreneurs may not bother to follow official procedures or bypass them by paying bribes or hiring the services of "facilitators." An entrepreneur in Georgia can start up a company after going through 13 procedures in 69 business days and paying $375 in fees. Alternatively, he may hire a legal advisory firm that completes the start-up process for $610 in three business days. In the analysis, we use the first set of numbers. We do so because we are primarily interested in understanding the structure of official regulation.

Regulations of start-up companies vary across regions within a country, across industries, and across firm sizes. For concreteness, we focus on a "standardized" firm, which has the following characteristics: it performs general industrial or commercial activities, it operates in the largest city[1] (by population), it is exempt from industry-specific requirements (including environmental ones), it does not participate in foreign trade and does not trade in goods that are subject to excise taxes (e.g., liquor, tobacco, gas), it is a domestically owned limited liability company,[2] its capital is subscribed in cash (not in-kind contributions) and is the higher of (i) ten times GDP per capita in 1999 or (ii) the minimum capital requirement for the particular type of business entity, it rents (i.e., does not own) land and business premises, it has between five and 50 employees one month after the commencement of operations all of whom are nationals, it has turnover of up to ten times its start-up capital, and it does not qualify for investment incentives. Although different legal forms are used in different countries to set up the simplest firm, to make comparisons we need to look at the same form.

Our data almost surely underestimate the cost and complexity of entry.[3] Start-up procedures in the provinces are often slower than in the capital. Industry-specific requirements add procedures. Foreign ownership frequently involves additional verifications and procedures. Contributions in kind often require assessment of value, a complex procedure that depends on the quality of property registries. Finally, purchasing land can be quite difficult and even impossible in some of the countries of the sample (for example, in the Kyrgyz Republic).

2.2 Definitions of Variables

We use three measures of entry regulation: the number of procedures that firms must go through, the official time required to complete the process, and its official cost. In the public interest theory, a more thorough screening process requires more procedures and demands more time. In the public choice theory, more procedures and longer delays facilitate bribe extraction (tollbooth view) and/or make entry less attractive to potential competitors (capture view).

Theoretical predictions regarding our measure of cost are ambiguous. A benevolent social planner who wants to spend significant resources on screening new entrants may choose to finance such activity with broad taxes rather than with the direct fees that we measure, leading to low costs as we measure them. A corrupt regulator may also want to set fees low in order to raise his own bribe income if, for example, fees are verifiable and cannot be expropriated by the regulator.[4] In contrast, higher fees are unambiguously desirable as a tool to deter entry under the capture theory. Because of these ambiguities, we present statistics on cost mainly to describe an important attribute of regulation and not to discriminate among theories.

We keep track of all the procedures required by law to start a business. A separate activity in the start-up process is a "procedure" only if it requires the entrepreneur to interact with outside entities: state and local government offices, lawyers, auditors, company seal manufacturers, notaries, etc. For example, all limited liability companies need to hold an inaugural meeting of shareholders to formally adopt the Company Articles and Bylaws. Since this activity involves only the entrepreneurs, we do not count it as a procedure. Similarly, most companies hire a lawyer to draft their Articles of Association. However, we do not count that as a procedure unless the law requires that a lawyer be involved. In the same vein, we ignore procedures that the entrepreneur can avoid altogether (e.g., reserving exclusive rights over a proposed company name until registration is completed) or that can be performed after business commences.[5] Finally, when obtaining a document requires several separate procedures involving different officials, we count each as a procedure. For example, a Bulgarian entrepreneur receives her registration certificate from the Company Registry in Sofia, and then has to pay the associated fee at an officially designated bank. Even though both activities are related to "obtaining the registration certificate," they count as two separate procedures in the data.

To measure time, we collect information on the sequence in which procedures are to be completed and rely on official figures as to how many business days it takes to complete each procedure. We ignore the time spent to gather information, and assume that all procedures are known from the very beginning. We also assume that procedures are taken simultaneously whenever possible, for maximum efficiency. Since entrepreneurs may have trouble visiting several different institutions within the same day (especially if they come from out of town), we set the minimum time required to visit an institution to be one day.[6] Another justification for this approach is that the relevant offices sometimes open for business only briefly: both the Ministry of Economy and the Ministry of Justice in Cairo open for business only between 11am and 2pm.

We estimate the cost of entry regulation based on all identifiable official expenses: fees, costs of procedures and forms, photocopies, fiscal stamps, legal and notary charges, etc. All cost figures are official and do not include bribes, which de Soto (1989) has shown to be significant for registration. Setup fees often vary with the level of start-up capital. As indicated, we report the costs associated with starting to operate legally a firm with capital equivalent to the larger of (i) ten times per capita GDP in 1999 or (ii) the minimum capital requirement stipulated in the law. We have experimented with other capital levels and found our results to be robust.

Theoretical predictions for the cost of entry regulation are ambiguous. As an alternative measure, we consider only the component of the cost that goes to the government, which in the sample averages about half the total cost. The results for this cost variable are generally weaker than for the total out-of-pocket cost, but go in the same direction. Our basic cost estimates also ignore the opportunity cost of the entrepreneur's time and the foregone profits associated with bureaucratic delay. To address this concern, we calculate a "full cost" measure, which adds up the official expenses and an estimate of the value of the entrepreneur's time, valuing his time at the country's per capita income per working day. We report this number below, and have replicated the analysis using it as a measure of cost. The results obtained using this cost measure are very similar to those using the raw data on time and cost, and hence are not presented.

Table 10.1 lists typical procedures associated with setting up a firm in our sample. The procedures are further divided by their function: screening (a residual category, which generally aims to keep out "unattractive" projects or entrepreneurs), health and safety, labor, taxes, and environment. The basic procedure in starting up a business, present everywhere, is registering with the Companies' Registry. This can take more than one procedure; sometimes there is a "preliminary" license and a "final" license. Combined with that procedure, or as a separate procedure, is the check for uniqueness of the proposed company name. Add-on procedures comprise the requirements to notarize the Company Deeds, to open a bank account and deposit start-up capital, and to publish a notification of the company's establishment in an official or business paper. Additional screening procedures that include obtaining different certificates and filing with agencies other than the Registry may add up to 97 days in delays, as is the case in Madagascar. Another set of basic screening procedures, present in almost every country in the data set, covers certain mandatory municipal procedures, registrations with statistical offices and with Chambers of Commerce and Industry (or respective Ministries). In the Dominican Republic, these screenings take seven procedures and 14 days. There is large cross-country variation in terms of the number, time, and cost of screening procedures as the Company Registry performs many of these tasks automatically in the most efficient countries but the entrepreneur does much of the legwork in the less efficient ones.

Additional procedures appear in four areas. The first covers tax-related procedures, which require seven procedures and 20 days in Madagascar. The second is labor regulations, which require seven procedures and 21 days in Bolivia. The third area is health and safety regulations, which demand five procedures and 21 business days in Malawi. The final area covers compliance with environmental regulations, which takes two procedures and ten days in Malawi if all goes well.

Figures 10.1 and 10.2 describe the number, time, and cost of the procedures needed to begin operating legally in New Zealand and France, respectively. New Zealand's streamlined startup process takes only three procedures and three days. The entrepreneur must first obtain approval for the company name from the web site of the Registrar of Companies, and then apply online for registration with both the Registrar of Companies and the tax authorities.

In contrast, the process in France takes 15 procedures and 53 days. To begin, the founder needs to check the chosen company name for

Table 10.1
List of Procedures for Starting Up a Company.
This table provides a list of common procedures required to start-up a company in the eighty-five countries of the sample.

1. Safety and health requirements

   Notify the health and safety authorities and obtain authorization to operate from the Health Ministry

   Pass inspections and obtain certificates related to work safety, building, fire, sanitation, and hygiene

2. Environment-related requirements

   Issue environmental declaration

   Obtain environment certificate

   Obtain sewer approval

   Obtain zoning approval

   Pass inspections from environmental officials

   Register with the water management and water discharge authorities

3. Tax-related requirements

   Arrange automatic withdrawal of the employees' income tax from the company payroll funds

   Designate a bondsman for tax purposes

   File with the Ministry of Finance

   Issue notice of start of activity to the Tax Authorities

   Register for corporate income tax

   Register for VAT

   Register for state taxes

   Register the company bylaws with the Tax Authorities

   Seal, validate, rubricate accounting books

4. Labor/social security–related requirements

   File with the Ministry of Labor

   Issue employment declarations for all employees

   Notarize the labor contract

   Pass inspections by social security officials

   Register for accident and labor risk insurance

   Register for health and medical insurance

   Register with pension funds

   Register for Social Security

   Register for unemployment insurance

   Register with the housing fund

5. Screening procedures

   Certify business competence

   Certify a clean criminal record

   Certify marital status

Table 10.1
(continued)

Check the name for uniqueness

Notarize company deeds

Notarize registration certificate

File with the Statistical Bureau

File with the Ministry of Industry and Trade, Ministry of the Economy, or the respective ministries by line of business

Notify municipality of start-up date

Obtain certificate of compliance with the company law

Obtain business license (operations permit)

Obtain permit to play music to the public (irrespective of line of business)

Open a bank account and deposit start-up capital

Perform an official audit at start-up

Publish notice of company foundation

Register at the Companies Registry

Sign up for membership in the Chamber of Commerce or Industry or the Regional Trade Association

---

uniqueness at the Institut National de la Propriété Industrielle (INPI). He then needs the mayor's permit to use his home as an office. (If the office is to be rented, the founder must secure a notarized lease agreement.) The following documents must then be obtained, each from a different authority: proof of a clean criminal record, an original extract of the entrepreneur's certificate of marital status from the City Hall, and a power of attorney. The start-up capital is then deposited with a notary bank or Caisse des Dépôt, and is blocked there until proof of registration is provided. Notarization of the Articles of Association follows. A notice stating the location of the headquarters office is published in a journal approved for legal announcements and evidence of the publication is obtained. Next, the founder registers four copies of the articles of association at the local tax collection office. He then files a request for registration with the Centre de Formalités des Entreprises (CFE) which handles declarations of existence and other registration-related formalities. The CFE must process the documents or return them in case the request is incomplete. The CFE automatically enters the company information in the Registre Nationale des Entreprises (RNE) and obtains from the RNE identification numbers: numero SIRENE (Systéme Informatique pour le Répertoire des Entreprises), numero SIRET (Systéme Informatique pour le Répertoire des

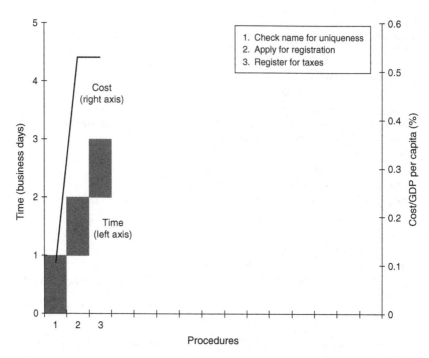

Figure 10.1
Start-up procedures in New Zealand. Procedures are lined up sequentially on the horizontal axis and described in the text box. The time required to complete each procedure is described by the height of the bar and measured against the left scale. Cumulative costs (as a percentage of per capita GDP) are plotted using a line and measured against the right scale.

Etablissements), and numero NAF (Nomenclature des Activités Fran-
caises). The SIRET is used by, among others, the tax authorities. The
RNE also publishes a notice of the company formation in the official
bulletin of civil and commercial announcements. The firm then obtains
proof of registration form "K-bis," which is effectively its identify card.
To start legal operations, the entrepreneur completes five additional
procedures: inform the post office of the new enterprise, designate a
bondsman or guarantee payment of taxes with a cash deposit, unblock
the company's capital by filing with the bank a proof of registration
(K-bis), have the firm's ledgers and registers initialed, and file for social
security. The magazine L'Entreprise comments: "To be sure that the file
for the Company Registry is complete, many promoters check it with
a counselor's service, which costs FF200 in Paris (about $30). But there's

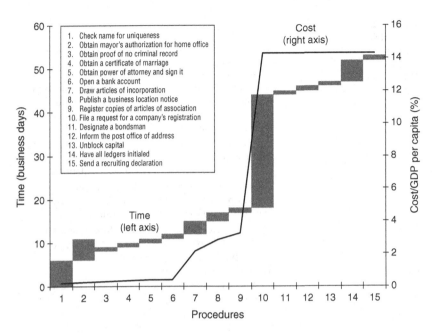

Figure 10.2
Start-up procedures in France. Procedures are lined up sequentially on the horizontal axis and described in the text box. The time required to complete each procedure is described by the height of the bar and measured against the left scale. Cumulative costs (as a percentage of per capita GDP) are plotted using a line and measured against the right scale.

always something missing, and most entrepreneurs end up using a lawyer to complete the procedure."

3 Basic Results

Table 10.2 describes all the variables used in this study and table 10.3 summarizes the data. We classify each procedure as one of five types: safety and health, environmental, tax, labor, and a residual category which we label "screening," whose purpose under the public interest theory is to weed out the undesirable entrepreneurs. We then compute and report the total number of procedures and their breakdown into our five categories for each country. We also compute the minimum number of business days that are officially required to comply with entry regulations, the costs arising from the official fees, and the total costs which impute the entrepreneur's time (as a fraction of GDP per

Table 10.2
The Variables.

Variable	Description
Number of procedures	The number of different procedures that a start-up has to comply with in order to obtain a legal status, that is, to start operating as a legal entity. *Source:* Authors' own calculations.
Safety & health	The number of different safety and health procedures that a start-up has to comply with to start operating as a legal entity. *Source:* Authors' own calculations.
Environment	The number of different environmental procedures that a start-up has to comply with to start operating as a legal entity. *Source:* Authors' own calculations.
Taxes	The number of different tax procedures that a start-up has to comply with to start operating as a legal entity. *Source:* Authors' own calculations.
Labor	The number of different labor procedures that a start-up has to comply with to start operating as a legal entity. *Source:* Authors' own calculations.
Screening	The number of different steps that a start-up has to comply with in order to obtain a registration certificate that are not associated with safety and health issues, the environment, taxes, or labor. *Source:* Authors' own calculations.
Time	The time it takes to obtain legal status to operate a firm, in business days. A week has five business days and a month has 22. *Source:* Authors' own calculations.
Cost	The cost of obtaining legal status to operate a firm as a share of per capita GDP in 1999. It includes all identifiable official expenses (fees, costs of procedures and forms, photocopies, fiscal stamps, legal and notary charges, etc.). The company is assumed to have a start-up capital of ten times per capita GDP in 1999. *Source:* Authors' own calculations.
Cost+time	The cost of obtaining legal status to operate a firm as a share of per capita GDP in 1999. It includes all identifiable official expenses (fees, costs of procedures and forms, photocopies, fiscal stamps, legal and notary charges, etc.) as well as the monetized value of the entrepreneur's time. The time of the entrepreneur is valued as the product of Time and per capita GDP in 1999 expressed in per business day terms. The company is assumed to have a start-up capital of ten times the GDP per capita level in 1999. *Source:* Authors' own calculations.

Table 10.2
(continued)

Variable	Description
GDP/POP1999	Gross domestic product per capita in current U.S. dollars in 1999. *Source:* World Bank (2001).
Quality standards	Number of ISO 9000 certifications per thousand inhabitants issued by the International Organization for Standardization as of 1999 to each country in the sample. "ISO standards represent an international consensus on the state of the art in the technology concerned ... " *Source:* International Organization for Standardization (www.iso.ch).
Water pollution	Emissions of organic water pollutants (kilograms per day per worker) for 1998. Measured in terms of biochemical oxygen demand, which refers to the amount of oxygen that bacteria in water will consume in breaking down waste. Emissions per worker are total emissions divided by the number of industrial workers. *Source:* World Bank (2001).
Deaths from accidental poisoning	Log of the number of deaths caused by accidental poisonings (including by drugs, medications, bio-products, solid and liquid substances, gases and vapors) per million inhabitants. Average of the years 1981 through 1994 (the most recent available figure). *Source:* World Health Organization (1998).
Deaths from intestinal infections	Log of the number of deaths caused by intestinal infections (including digestive disorders) per million inhabitants. Average of the years 1981 through 1994 (the most recent available figure). *Source:* World Health Organization (1998).
Size of the unofficial economy	Size of the shadow economy as a percentage of GDP (varying time periods). *Source:* Authors owns computations based on averaging over all estimates reported in Schneider and Enste (2000) for any given country as well as Sananikone (1996) for Burkina Faso, Chidzero (1996) for Senegal, Turnham and Schwartz (1990) for Indonesia and Pakistan, and Kasnakoglu and Yayla (2000) for Turkey.
Employment in the unofficial economy	Share of the labor force employed in the unofficial economy in the capital city of each country as a percent of the official labor. Figures are based on surveys and, for some countries, on econometric estimates. *Source:* Schneider (2000) and the Global Urban Indicators Database (2000) (www.urbanobservatory.org/indicators/database).

Table 10.2
(continued)

Variable	Description
Product market competition	Survey measure of the extent to which respondents agree with the following statement: "Competition in the local market is intense and market shares fluctuate constantly." Scale from 1 (strongly disagree) through 7 (strongly agree). *Source:* IMD (2001).
Corruption	Corruption perception index for 1999. Corruption is defined broadly as "the misuse of public power for private benefits, e.g., bribing of public officials, kickbacks in public procurement, or embezzlement of public funds." Descending score from 1 (most corrupt) to 10 (least corrupt). *Source:* Transparency International (www.transparency.de/).
Executive de facto independence	Index of "operation (de facto) independence of chief executive." Descending scale from 1 to 7 (1=pure individual; 2=intermediate category; 3=slight to moderate limitations; 4=intermediate category; 5=substantial limitations; 6=intermediate category; 7=executive parity or subordination). Average of the years 1945 through 1998. *Source:* Jaggers and Marshall (2000).
Constraints on executive power	Index of constraints on the executive power based on the number of effective veto points in a country. Average of the years 1945 through 1998. *Source:* Henisz (2000).
Effectiveness of legislature	Index of the effectiveness of the legislature. Ascending scale from 1 to 4. Average of the years 1945 through 1998. *Source:* The Cross-National Time-Series Data Archive (www.databanks.sitehosting.net/www/main .htm).
Competition in the legislature's nominating process	Index of the competitiveness of the nominating process for seats in the legislature. Ascending scale from 1 to 4. Average of the years 1945 through 1998. *Source:* The Cross-National Time-Series Data Archive (www .databanks.sitehosting.net/www/main.htm).
Autocracy	Indicates the "general closedness of political institutions." Scale from 0 to 10 with 0 being low in autocracy and 10 being high in autocracy. Average of the years 1945 through 1998. *Source:* Jaggers and Marshall (2000).
Political rights	Index of political rights. Average of the years 1972 through 1998. *Source:* Freedom House (2001).
Legal origin	Identifies the legal origin of each Company Law or Commercial Code of each country. *Source:* La Porta et al. (1998), Reynolds and Flores (1989), CIA World Factbook (2001).

Table 10.3.
The Data.

Panel A presents means of the variables by quartiles of GDP per capita in 1999. The variables are the total number of procedures and their breakup in the following five categories: (1) safety and health; (2) environment; (3) taxes; (4) labor; and (5) screening. The table also reports the time, direct cost (as a fraction of GDP per capita in 1999) associated with meeting government requirements, and direct cost plus the monetized value of the entrepreneur's time (as a fraction of GDP per capita in 1999) as well as the level of GDP per capita in dollars in 1999. Panel B presents t-statistics for differences in means across quartiles of per capita GDP in 1999. Table 10.2 describes the variables in detail.

	Number of procedures	Safety & health	Environment	Taxes	Labor	Screening	Time	Cost	Cost + time	GDP/ POP1999
Panel A: Means by quartiles of GDP per capita in 1999										
1st quartile	6.77	0.00	0.05	1.59	1.14	4.00	24.50	0.10	0.20	24,372
2nd quartile	11.10	0.24	0.14	2.14	2.38	6.19	49.29	0.33	0.53	5,847
3rd quartile	12.33	0.52	0.14	2.19	2.33	7.14	53.10	0.41	0.62	1,568
4th quartile	11.90	0.62	0.24	2.24	1.95	6.90	63.76	1.08	1.34	349
Sample average	10.48	0.34	0.14	2.04	1.94	6.04	47.40	0.4708	0.6598	8,226
Panel B: Test of means (t-statistics)										
1st vs. 2nd quartile	-4.20[a]	-2.07[b]	-0.87	-1.35	-3.64[a]	-3.34[a]	-3.71[a]	-3.03[a]	-3.97[a]	12.03[a]
1st vs. 3rd quartile	-4.58[a]	-3.02[a]	-0.87	-1.64[b]	-2.82[a]	-4.07[a]	-4.21[a]	-2.54[b]	-3.19[a]	16.35[a]
1st vs. 4th quartile	-4.04[a]	-2.08[a]	-1.55	-1.61	-2.43[b]	-3.18[a]	-4.09[a]	-3.53[a]	-4.06[a]	17.31[a]
2nd vs. 3rd quartile	-1.17	-1.34	0.00	-0.11	0.10	-1.51	-0.54	-0.52	-0.59	6.14[a]
2nd vs. 4th quartile	-0.72	-1.17	-0.61	-0.21	1.10	-0.89	-1.46	-2.54b	-2.73a	8.05[a]
3rd vs. 4th quartile	0.33	-0.27	-0.61	-0.11	0.82	0.26	-1.06	-2.17b	-2.27b	8.53[a]

Note: [a] Significant at 1%; [b] Significant at 5%; [c] Significant at 10%.

capita). We present averages by income level and report *t*-tests comparing the regulation of entry across income groups.

The data show enormous variation in entry regulation across countries. The total number of procedures ranges from two in Canada to 21 in the Dominican Republic and averages 10.48 for the whole sample. Very few entry regulations cover tax and labor issues. The worldwide average number of labor and tax procedures are 1.94 and 2.02, respectively. Procedures involving environmental issues and safety and health matters are even more rare (0.14 and 0.34 procedures on average, respectively). Instead, much of what governments do to regulate entry falls into the category of screening procedures. The worldwide average number of such procedures facing a new entrant is 6.04.

The number of procedures is highly correlated with both the time and cost variables. The correlation of the (log) number of procedures with (log) time is 0.83 and with (log) cost is 0.64. Translated into economic terms, this means that entrepreneurs pay a steep price in terms of fees and delays in countries that make intense use of ex ante screening. For example, completing 19 procedures demands 149 business days and 111.5 percent of GDP per capita in Mozambique. In Italy, the completion of 16 procedures takes up 62 business days and 20 percent of GDP per capita. The Dominican Republic is in a class of its own: completing its 21 procedures requires 80 business days and fees of at least 4.63 times per capita GDP. These figures are admittedly extreme within the sample, yet meeting the official entry requirements in the average sample country requires roughly 47 days and fees of 47 percent of GDP per capita.

When we aggregate time and out-of-pocket costs into an aggregate cost measure, the results for some countries become even more extreme. The world average full cost measure rises to 66 percent of per capita GDP, but varies from 1.7 percent of per capita GDP for New Zealand to 4.95 times per capita GDP in the Dominican Republic.

Panel A of table 10.3 reports averages of the total number of procedures and its components, time, and cost by quartiles of per capita GDP in 1999. Two patterns emerge. First, the cost-to-per-capita-GDP ratio decreases uniformly with GDP per capita. The average cost-to-per-capita-GDP ratio for countries in the top quartile of per capita GDP ("rich countries") is 10 percent and rises to 108 percent in countries in the bottom quartile of per capita GDP. This pattern merely reflects the fact that the income elasticity of fees (in log levels) is about 0.2. Second, countries in the top quartile of per capita GDP require fewer procedures and their entrepreneurs face shorter delays in starting a legal business than those in the remaining countries.[7] The total number of procedures in an average rich country is 6.8 which is significantly lower than the rest-of-sample average of 11.8 (t-stats are reported on panel B). Rich countries also have fewer safety and health, tax, and labor start-up procedures than the rest of the sample. Similarly, meeting government requirements takes approximately 24.5 business days in rich countries, statistically significantly lower than the rest-of-sample mean of 55.4 days. In contrast, countries in the other three quartiles of per capita income are not statistically different from each other in the number of procedures and the time it takes to complete them.

To summarize, the regulation of entry varies enormously across countries. It often takes the form of screening procedures. Rich countries (i.e., those in the top quartile of per capita GDP) regulate entry relatively less than do all the other countries. In principle, these findings are consistent with both the public choice and public interest theories. Market failures might be more pervasive in countries with incomes just below the first quartile of GDP per capita, generating a greater demand for benign regulation in these countries. Alternatively, income levels may proxy for characteristics of political systems that allow politicians and/or incumbent firms to capture the regulatory process for their own benefit. In the next two sections, we relate these patterns in the data to the theories of regulation.

4   Who Gets the Rents from Regulation?

Theories of regulation differ in their predictions as to who gets its benefits. The public interest theory predicts that stricter entry regulation is associated with higher measured consumer welfare. In contrast, the public choice theory sees regulation as a tool to create rents for bureaucrats and/or incumbent firms. Stricter regulation should then be associated with higher corruption and less competition.

Measuring rents is inherently extremely difficult, especially across countries. In this section, we present some measures that we have been able to find that bear—albeit quite imperfectly—on the relevant theories. To begin, consider some variables bearing on the public interest theory. These variables reflect the activities of all firms in the country, and not just the entrants. The first is a measure of a country's compliance with international quality standards. It is a natural variable to focus on if the goal of regulation is to screen out entrants who might sell output of inferior quality. Second, we consider the level of water pollution, which should fall if entry regulation aims to control externalities and does so successfully.[8] Third, we consider two measures of health outcomes that publicly interested entry regulation would guard against: the number of deaths from accidental poisoning and from intestinal infections.[9] In addition, we include two measures of the size of the unofficial economy based on estimates of unofficial output and employment, respectively. Since firms operating unofficially avoid nearly all regulations, a large size of the unofficial economy in countries with more regulations undermines the prediction of the public interest theory that regulation effectively protects consumers.[10] Finally, we use a survey measure of "product market competition." Stiffer entry regulation should be associated with greater competition in the public interest theory and lacking competition in the public choice theory, especially in its regulatory capture version.

Table 10.4 presents the results on these six measures of consequences of regulation using the number of procedures as dependent variables. For two reasons, we run each regression with and without the log of per capita GDP. First, the number of procedures is correlated with income per capita and we want to make sure that we are not picking up the general effects of good governance associated with higher income. Second, we use GDP per capita as a rough proxy of the prevalence of market failures in a country. Including per capita income as a control is a crude way to keep the need for socially desirable regulation constant, which allows us to focus on the consequences (and later causes) of regulation separately from the need.

The results in table 10.4 show that compliance with international quality standards declines as the number of procedures rises. Pollution levels do not fall with regulation levels. The two measures of accidental poisoning are not lower in countries with more regulations (if anything, the opposite seems to be true even controlling for per capita income). More regulation is associated with a larger unofficial economy, and statistically significantly so if we use the unofficial employment variable. Competition in countries with more regulation is perceived to be less intense, although this result is only statistically significant without the income control. We have also run all regressions using cost and time as independent variables, and obtained qualitatively similar results. While the data are noisy, none of the results support the predictions of the public interest theory.[11]

Table 10.4
Evidence on Regulation and Social Outcomes.
The table presents the results of OLS regressions using the following seven dependent variables: (1) quality standards as proxied by the number of ISO 9000 certifications; (2) water pollution; (3) deaths from accidental poisoning; (4) deaths from intestinal infection; (5) size of the unofficial economy as a fraction of GDP; (6) employment in the unofficial economy; and (7) product market competition. The independent variables are the log of the number of procedures and the log of per capita GDP in dollars in 1999. Table 10.2 describes all variables in detail. Robust standard errors are shown below the coefficients.

Dependent variable	Number of procedures	Ln GDP/ POP1999	Constant	R^2 N
Quality standards	−0.2781[a]		0.7649[a]	0.3311
(ISO Certifications)	(0.0496)		(0.1268)	85
	−0.1595[a]	0.0771[a]	−0.1140	0.5384
	(0.0443)	(0.0131)	(0.1484)	85
Water pollution	0.0127[b]		0.1557[a]	0.0247
	(0.0084)		(0.0174)	76
	−0.0037	−0.0131[a]	0.2984[a]	0.2310
	(0.0076)	(0.0027)	(0.0314)	76
Deaths from accidental	0.6588[a]		1.6357[a]	0.1179
poisoning	(0.2057)		(0.4381)	57
	0.0637	−0.4525[a]	6.8347[a]	0.4109
	(0.1958)	(0.0933)	(1.0929)	57
Deaths from intestinal	2.3049[a]		−2.2697[a]	0.3451
infection	(0.3081)		(0.6778)	61
	1.0501[a]	−0.8717[a]	7.8494[a]	0.6259
	(0.2971)	(0.1012)	(1.3048)	61
Size of the unofficial economy[1]	14.7553[a]		−3.7982	0.2482
	(2.5698)		(5.2139)	73
	6.4849[b]	−6.1908[a]	67.1030[a]	0.5187
	(2.5385)	(1.0834)	(13.7059)	73
Employment in the unofficial	19.4438[a]		−4.1103	0.3132
economy	(2.5756)		(5.9160)	46
	13.8512[a]	−4.4585[a]	41.5133[b]	0.4477
	−3.6056	(1.3918)	(17.6836)	46
Product market competition	−0.4012[a]		5.7571[a]	0.1405
	(0.1213)		(0.2511)	54
	−0.1418	0.2108[a]	3.3579[a]	0.3087
	(0.1202)	(0.0680)	(0.7749)	54

Note: [a] Significant at 1%; [b] Significant at 5%; [c] Significant at 10%.
[1]The regression on the size of the unofficial economy controls for the log of GDP per capita plus unofficial economy income (i.e., GDP per capita*(1+unofficial economy)), and not just by GDP per capita as all other regressions on the table do.

The negative results in table 10.4 should be interpreted with caution. First, some of our measures of public goods, such as deaths from accidental poisoning, are probably more relevant for poor countries, and in particular are unlikely to be influenced by entry regulation for rich countries. Accordingly, it might be more appropriate to perform the analysis separately for countries at different income levels. To this end, we divide the sample at the median per capita income and re-run the regressions in table 10.4 for each sub-sample. The data do not support the proposition that, in the sub-sample of poorer countries, heavier regulation of entry is associated with better social outcomes or more competition.

Second, an even deeper concern with the results in table 10.4 is that, despite our control for per capita income, there is important unobserved heterogeneity among countries correlated with regulation, which accounts for the results. For example, suppose that some countries have particularly egregious market failures, but also especially poor alternative mechanisms for dealing with them, such as the press and the courts. Regulation, for example, might be less infected by corruption than either the press or the judiciary. A publicly interested regulator in such countries would choose to use more regulatory procedures because the alternative methods of dealing with market failure are even worse, but still end up with inferior outcomes.

We cannot dismiss this concern with the results of table 10.4, although our later findings cast doubt on its validity. We run the regressions in table 10.4 using information on the freedom of the press from Djankov, McLiesh, Nenova, and Shleifer (2003) and find that, holding constant various measures of freedom of the press and per capita income, the number of procedures is still not associated with superior social outcomes. We also run the regressions in table 10.4 using a number of measures of citizen access to justice and of efficiency of the judiciary from chapter 5. Again, we find that, holding constant these measures and per capita income, the number of procedures is associated, if anything, with inferior social outcomes.

A direct implication of the tollbooth hypothesis is that corruption levels and the intensity of entry regulation are positively correlated. In fact, since in many countries in our sample politicians run businesses, the regulation of entry produces the double benefit of corruption revenues and reduced competition for the incumbent businesses already affiliated with the politicians. Figure 10.3 presents the relationship between corruption and the number of procedures without controlling

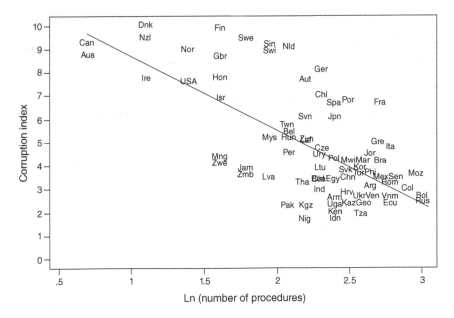

Figure 10.3
Corruption and number of procedures. The scatter plot shows the values of the corruption index against the (log) number of procedures for the 78 countries in our sample with non-missing data on corruption.

for per capita GDP[12]. Panel A of table 10.5 shows statistically that, consistent with the tollbooth theory, more regulation is associated with worse corruption scores. The coefficients are statistically significant (with and without controlling for income) and large in economic terms. The estimated coefficients imply that, controlling for per capita GDP, reducing the number of procedures by ten is associated with a reduction in corruption of 0.8 of a standard deviation, roughly the difference between France and Italy. The results using the cost and the time of meeting the entry regulations as independent variables are also statistically significant, pointing further to the robustness of this evidence in favor of the tollbooth theory.

One way to reconcile the findings in table 10.5 with the public interest theory is to argue that regulation has unintended consequences. Thus benign politicians in emerging markets imitate the regulations of rich countries with best intentions in mind, but are stymied by corruption and other enforcement failures. This theory is not entirely consistent with our earlier finding that poorer countries in fact have more entry regulations than rich countries do. A further implication of this

Table 10.5
Evidence on the Toll-Booth Theory.
The table presents the results of OLS regressions using corruption as the dependent variable. The independent variables are: (1) the log of the number of procedures; (2) the log of time; (3) the log of cost; and (4) the log of per capita GDP in dollars in 1999. Panel A presents results for the 78 observations with available corruption data. Panel B reports results separately for the subsample of countries with GDP per capita in 1999 above and below the sample median. Table 10.2 describes all variables in detail. Robust standard errors are shown in parentheses below the coefficients.

Panel A: Results for the whole sample

Independent variable	(1)	(2)	(3)	(4)	(5)	(6)
Number of procedures	−3.1811[a] (0.2986)	−1.8654[a] (0.2131)				
Time			−1.7566[a] (0.1488)	−0.8854[a] (0.1377)		
Cost					−1.2129[a] (0.1206)	−0.4978[a] (0.1285)
Ln GDP/ POP1999		0.9966[a] (0.0864)		0.9765[a] (0.1014)		0.9960[a] (0.1118)
Constant	11.8741[a] (0.7380)	1.1345 (0.9299)	11.0694[a] (0.5932)	0.0677 (1.1176)	2.7520[a] (0.2414)	−4.0893[a] (0.7867)
R^2	0.4656	0.8125	0.4387	0.7662	0.4256	0.7306
N	78	78	78	78	78	78

Panel B: Results for countries above and below the world median GDP per capita

Independent variable	Countries above median GDP/ POP1999			Countries below median GDP/POP1999		
	(1)	(2)	(3)	(4)	(5)	(6)
Number of procedures	−1.8729[a] (0.2971)			−0.7841[b] (0.3304)		
Time		−0.8135[a] (0.1762)			−0.0923 (0.2850)	
Cost			−0.5327[a] (0.1894)			−0.3408[a] (0.1021)
Ln GDP/ POP1999	1.4811[a] (0.2265)	1.5871[a] (0.2789)	1.7621[a] (0.2913)	0.3993[b] (0.1735)	0.3680[c] (0.1802)	0.2117 (0.1718)
Constant	−3.6970 (2.4628)	−5.9027[c] (2.9942)	−11.3736[a] (2.5773)	2.3246[c] (1.2849)	1.0098 (1.8813)	1.3125 (1.1136)
R^2	0.7820	0.7155	0.6728	0.2362	0.1324	0.2830
N	40	40	40	38	38	38

Note: [a] Significant at 1%; [b] Significant at 5%; [c] Significant at 10%.

theory is that regulations should have a bigger impact on corruption in poorer countries. Panel B of table 10.5 addresses this hypothesis by examining separately the relationship between entry regulations and corruption in countries with above and below world median income. The results show that regulations actually have a stronger effect on corruption in the sub-sample of richer countries.

On the second version of the unintended consequences argument, it may be impossible for a benevolent government to screen bad entrants without facilitating corruption (Banerjee 1997; Acemoglu and Verdier 2000). In countries whose markets are fraught with failures, it might be better to have corrupt regulators than none at all. Corruption may be the price to pay for addressing market failures. We turn next to the evidence regarding the political attributes of countries that regulate to disentangle the competing theories of regulation.

5   Who Regulates Entry?

In this section we focus on the political attributes of countries that regulate entry. These attributes are intimately related to the competing hypotheses about regulation. In the public interest theory, regulation remedies market failures. The implication is that countries whose political systems are characterized by higher congruence between policy outcomes and social preferences should regulate entry more strictly. In the empirical analysis that follows, we identify such countries with more representative and limited governments.

In the public choice theory, despotic regimes are more likely to be captured by incumbents and to have regulatory systems aimed at maximizing the bribes and profits of a few cronies rather than address market failures (Olson 1991; DeLong and Shleifer 1993). Such dictators need the political support of various interest groups, and use distortionary policies to favor their friends and to abuse their opponents. The dictator's choice of distortionary policies is not mitigated by public pressure, since he faces no elections. When the public is less able to assert its preferences, then, we expect more distortionary policy choices. Specifically, we expect more representative and limited government to be associated with lighter regulation of entry.

One might argue, in contrast, that dictators should pursue efficient economic policies, including light regulation of entry, if they are politically secure and can "tax" the fruits of entry and growth. One response, discussed by Olson (1991) and De Long and Shleifer (1993), is that while a few dictators are politically secure and pursue enlightened policies, most are not. Insecure dictators extract what they can from the economy as fast as they can both to prolong their tenure and to enrich themselves and their supporters while still in power. Democracy might not lengthen the horizons of politicians, but it does limit their opportunities.

We collect data on a variety of characteristics of political systems, partly because we want to be flexible regarding the meaning of "good government." Where possible, we use variables from different sources to check the robustness of our results. Our political variables fall into four broad groups. The first includes the de facto independence of the executive and an index of constraints on the executive. The second group includes an index of the effectiveness of the legislature and a measure of competition in the legislature's nominating process. The third group includes a measure of autocracy and one of political rights.

An additional variable that we focus on is legal origin. We classify countries based on the origin of their commercial laws into five broad groups: English, French, German, Scandinavian, and Socialist. As discussed in chapter 1, legal origin has been viewed as a proxy for the government's proclivity to intervene in the economy and the stance of the law toward the security of property rights in a country.

Correlations among the political variables are presented in table 10.6. Political variables tend to be strongly correlated within blocks. For example, the measure of constraints on the executive power is highly correlated with de facto independence of the executive (0.9761) and with the effectiveness of the legislature (0.9078). Yet, we report results on all three variables as each comes from a different source. Similarly, blocks of variables tend to be correlated with each other. In particular, democracy tends to be positively associated with competitive and limited executive and legislative branches. Legal origin, in contrast, is insignificantly correlated with other political variables (the exception is Socialist legal origin which has obvious correlations with democracy and limited government).[13] Income levels are positively associated with democracy as well as with competitive and limited executive and legislative branches, but not with the legal origin. The fact that countries with severe market failures have more abusive governments by itself limits the normative usefulness of the Pigouvian model.

In table 10.7, we present the results of regressing the number of procedures on a constant, each of the political variables taken one at a time, and the log of per capita income. In interpreting these regressions, we take the broad political measures of limited and representative government as being exogenous to entry regulation. It is possible, of course, that both the political and the regulatory variables are simultaneously determined by some deeper historical factors. Even so, it is interesting to know what the correlation is. Does the history that produces good government also produce many or few regulations of entry? The control for the level of development is crucial (and in fact our results without this control are significantly stronger). Market failures are likely to be both more pervasive and severe in poor countries than in rich ones. Moreover, our measures of good government are uniformly higher in richer countries. Without income controls, our political variables may just proxy for income levels. Imagine, for example, that the consumers in poor countries are exposed to a larger risk from bad firms entering their markets and selling goods of inferior quality. The Pigouvian planner would then need more tools to screen entrants in the poorer countries.

Holding per capita income constant, countries with more limited and representative governments have statistically significantly fewer procedures for entry regulation using five out of six measures of better government.[14] These results show that countries with more limited governments, governments more open to competition, and greater political rights have lighter regulation of entry even holding per capita income constant. Figure 10.4 plots the number of procedures against the autocracy score and shows that regulation is increasing in autocracy. Regulation is heavy in autocratic countries such as Vietnam and Mozambique and light in democratic countries such as Australia, Canada, New Zealand, and the U.S.

The log of per capita GDP tends to enter these regressions significantly. The interpretation of this result is clouded both because there are problems of multicollinearity with the political variables and because the direction of causation is unclear. In the public choice theory, burdensome regulation reflects transfers from entrepreneurs and/or consumers, which are likely to be distortionary and, hence, associated with lower levels of income. Countries may be poor because regulation is hostile to new business formation.

Holding per capita income constant, countries of French, German, and Socialist legal origin have more regulations than English legal origin countries, while countries of Scandinavian legal origin have about the same. The result that civil law countries (with the exception of those in Scandinavia) regulate entry more heavily supports the view

Table 10.6
Correlation Table for Political Attributes.

The table reports correlations among measures of regulation and the variables used in table 10.7. All variables are in table 10.2. Significance levels are Bonferroni-adjusted.

	Executive de facto independence	Constraints on executive power	Effectiveness legislature	Competition nominating	Autocracy	Political rights	French LO
Executive de facto independence	1.0000						
Constraints executive power	0.9761[a]	1.0000					
Effectiveness legislature	0.9210[a]	0.9078[a]	1.0000				
Competition nominating	0.8243[a]	0.8069[a]	0.8484[a]	1.0000			
Autocracy	−0.9085[a]	−0.8844[a]	−0.8514[a]	−0.7819[a]	1.0000		
Political rights	0.8440[a]	0.8448[a]	0.8485[a]	0.7191[a]	−0.8564[a]	1.0000	
French legal origin	−0.1814	−0.1814	−0.1901	−0.1985	−0.0258	0.0565	1.0000
Socialist legal origin	−0.3321	−0.2927	−0.3236	−0.3240	0.5475[a]	−0.4572[a]	−0.4169[a]
German legal origin	0.2101	0.2008	0.2023	0.1281	−0.1920	0.2444	−0.2141
Scandinavian legal origin	0.3391	0.3274	0.3378	0.2522	−0.2978	0.3109	−0.1727
English legal origin	0.2259	0.1998	0.1462	0.2412	−0.2324	0.0778	−0.4874[a]
Ln GDP/POP1999	0.6900[a]	0.6703[a]	0.7483[a]	0.6123[a]	−0.6389[a]	0.7519[a]	−0.0767[b]
Ln(number of procedures)	−0.5518[a]	−0.5234[a]	−0.5848[a]	−0.4435[b]	0.4662[a]	−0.4412[a]	0.4863[a]
Ln(time)	−0.5420[a]	−0.5204[a]	−0.5635[a]	−0.4360[b]	0.4770[a]	−0.4921[a]	0.3976[b]
Ln(cost)	−0.5070[a]	−0.4937[a]	−0.5656[a]	−0.4177[b]	0.4075[b]	−0.4588[a]	0.3472
Ln(cost+time)	−0.5700[a]	−0.5478[a]	−0.6267[a]	−0.4745[a]	0.4713[a]	−0.5085[a]	0.3870[b]

Note: [a] Significant at 1%; [b] Significant at 5%; [c] Significant at 10%.

Socialist LO	German LO	Scandinavian LO	English LO	Ln GDP/ POP1999	Ln (number procedures)	Ln (time)	Ln (cost)	Ln (cost + time)
1.0000								
−0.1479	1.0000							
−0.1192	−0.0612	1.0000						
−0.3365	−0.1729	−0.0139	1.0000					
−0.1995	0.3409	0.3133	−0.0742	1.0000				
0.1538[b]	0.0030[b]	−0.3413[b]	−0.5069[a]	−0.4745[a]	1.0000			
0.1869	−0.0640	−0.2914	−0.4291[b]	−0.5014[a]	0.8263[a]	1.0000		
0.0319	−0.0727	−0.3007	−0.2172	−0.5953[a]	0.6354[a]	0.6147[a]	1.0000	
0.0851	−0.0933	−0.2786	−0.3094	−0.6244[a]	0.7434[a]	0.7793[a]	0.9605	1.0000

Table 10.7
Evidence on Regulation and Political Attributes.
The table presents the results of running regressions for the log of the number of procedures as the dependent variable. We run seven regressions using various political indicators described in table 10.2 and (log) GDP per capita. Robust standard errors are shown in parentheses below the coefficients.

Dependent variable	(1)	(2)	(3)	(4)	(5)	(6)	(7)
Executive de facto independence	-0.1249[a] (0.0322)						
Constraints on executive power		-0.1048[a] (0.0352)					
Effectiveness of legislature			-0.3301[a] (0.0778)				
Competition nominating				-0.2763[b] (0.0999)			
Autocracy					0.0545[b] (0.0178)		
Political rights						-0.3470 (0.2185)	
French legal origin							0.7245[a] (0.0916)
Socialist legal origin							0.4904[a] (0.1071)
German legal origin							0.7276[a] (0.1363)
Scandinavian legal origin							-0.0085 (0.1733)
Ln GDP/POP1999	-0.0491 (0.0331)	-0.0634[c] (0.0352)	-0.0087 (0.0401)	-0.0902[b] (0.0358)	-0.0867[a] (0.0321)	-0.0939[b] (0.0386)	-0.1434[a] (0.0270)
Constant	3.1782[a] (0.2334)	3.2040[a] (0.2408)	2.8709[a] (0.2586)	3.3540[a] (0.2641)	2.7457[a] (0.2888)	3.1850[a] (0.2599)	2.9492[a] (0.1955)
R^2	0.3178	0.2872	0.3424	0.2475	0.2640	0.2350	0.6256
N	84	84	73	73	84	84	85

Note: [a] Significant at 1%; [b] Significant at 5%; [c] Significant at 10%.

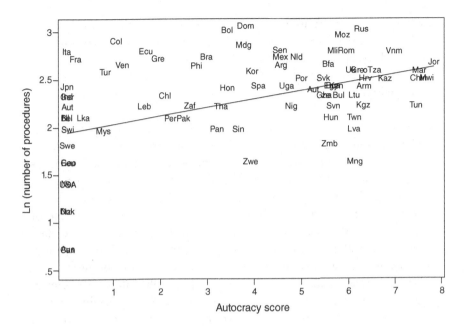

Figure 10.4
Autocracy and number of procedures. The scatter plot shows the values of the (log)
number of procedures against the autocracy score (higher values for more autocratic
systems) for the 84 countries in our sample with non-missing data for the autocracy score.

that the legal origin proxies for the state's proclivity to intervene in
economic life. Note, however, that in itself this evidence does not discriminate among the alternative theories in the same way as the evidence on democracy does: French origin countries might merely be
more prepared to deal with market failures than common law
countries.

These results are broadly consistent with the public choice theory
that sees regulation as a mechanism to create rents for politicians and
the firms they support. The public choice theory predicts that such rent
extraction should be moderated by better government to the extent that
outcomes in such regimes come closer to representing the preferences
of the public. In contrast, these results are more difficult to reconcile
with public interest unless one identifies it with political systems of
countries such as Bolivia, Mozambique, or Vietnam, where corruption
is widespread, governments are unlimited, and property rights insecure. Of course, it is possible that autocratic countries would perform
even worse in the absence of heavy regulation because market failures

are larger and alternative mechanisms of social control are inferior. Such a possibility strikes us as remote, especially since we hold the level of development constant.

6 Conclusion

An analysis of the regulation of entry in 85 countries shows that, even aside from the costs associated with corruption and bureaucratic delay, business entry is extremely expensive, especially in the countries outside the top quartile of the income distribution. We find that heavier regulation of entry is generally associated with greater corruption and a larger unofficial economy, but not with better quality of private or public goods. We also find that the countries with less limited, less democratic, and more interventionist governments regulate entry more heavily, even controlling for the level of economic development.

This evidence is difficult to reconcile with public interest theories of regulation but supports the public choice approach, especially the toll-booth theory that emphasizes rent extraction by politicians (McChesney 1987; Shleifer and Vishny 1993). Entry is regulated more heavily by less democratic governments, and such regulation does not yield visible social benefits. The principal beneficiaries appear to be the politicians and bureaucrats themselves.

Notes

Chapter 2

1. In the words of Karl Llewellyn (1951, p. 45), "[A judge is] a lawyer, and as such skilled in manipulating the resources of persuasion at his hand. A lawyer, and as such prone without thought to twist analogies, and rules, and instances, to his conclusion. More, as a practiced exponent of the art of exposition, he has learned that one must prepare the way for argument. You set the mood, the tone, and you lay the intellectual foundation—all with case in mind, with the conclusion—all, because those who hear you also have the case in mind, without the niggling criticism which may later follow. You wind up, as a pitcher will wind up—as in the pitcher's case, the wind-up often is superfluous. As in the pitcher's case, it has been known to be intentionally misleading."

2. Although our model focuses on judges, much of the discussion—particularly the sections focused on judicial bias—is applicable to juries as well. Strictly speaking, our model deals with fact-finder fact discretion.

3. In some rare instances, such as "clear error" or "constitutional facts" (Hoffman 2001), federal appeals courts review facts. The rarity and special features of these instances only justify our basic assumption of no factual review. If in addition appellate courts are biased (as in our model), it is unlikely that a review of facts reduces fact discretion.

4. If h is unknown to I, the problem becomes trivial. The analysis goes through if I is imperfectly informed about h.

5. Studying fact discretion under negligence rules would complicate the analysis because in that case precautions may jump rather than change smoothly with judicial error. We leave the study of negligence rules for future research.

6. The cost c may be interpreted as the cost for a judge of bending facts so as to avoid reversal for "clear error."

7. In this respect, one might wonder about the difference between an increase in α and an increase in the cost of fact discretion c. The following analysis shows that the key difference is that an increase in α not only reduces the bias in adjudication, but also tilts the distribution of accidents toward the less severe ones.

8. Although we do not explicitly study the effect of a higher α on welfare, we can show that this effect is ambiguous. However, as α becomes very large, social welfare approaches the first best.

9. Relaxing this assumption complicates the analysis without probably adding much insight. Because the key results of this section hinge on appellate courts' preferences being sufficiently polarized, little would change with endogenous appeals as judicial polarization is also a prerequisite for appeals to occur (section 5 formalizes this idea).

10. Appellate courts do not always follow established law and sometimes overrule precedents. We ignore overruling for two reasons. First, it is costly to appellate courts and is thus infrequent. Second, our key results are likely to hold even if overruling sometimes occurs, as it is still true that trial courts are more likely to be reversed when fact finding is inconsistent with precedents. See Gennaioli and Shleifer (2007) on the causes and consequences of overruling.

11. This assumption is consistent with Schanzenbach and Tiller (2007) who find in the context of the U.S. Sentencing Guidelines that law-oriented departures from the Guidelines concerning the kind or degree of an offense are subject to review on appeal, whereas fact determinations concerning the quantification of the offense level are not reviewed.

12. The assumption that precedents are equivalent to the biased judges' ideal points is not important for our results.

13. For simplicity, we abstract from I's choice of precautions and only study the choice of litigation vs. settlement.

14. The cost is assumed to increases in $|h_I - h_V|$ because when the parties' messages are far apart, they both likely neglect to report relevant evidence, which the judge must then identify to find out the true harm. This assumption simplifies the analysis, but our main results also hold with a fixed cost.

15. This assumption captures the idea that when the judge does not exert search effort, the parties' arguments are of higher quality than the judge's argument and thus less likely to be reversed on appeal.

Chapter 3

This essay originally appeared as "The Evolution of Common Law." *Journal of Political Economy* 115:1 (2007). Copyright 2007 by the University of Chicago. All rights reserved.

1. See also Holmes (1897), Cardozo (1921), Frank (1930), Radin (1925), Llewellyn (1951), Stone (1985), Posner (2005).

2. Some law and economics scholars are more skeptical about the efficiency of common law. Hadfield (1992) argues that it is not necessarily the case that the less efficient precedents are more likely to be challenged. Zywicki (2003) believes that common law evolution used to be efficient in the nineteenth century, but is no longer so because judges are excessively influenced by their own preferences as well as by rent-seeking pressures from litigants. Hathaway (2001) discusses how the doctrine of *stare decisis* introduces path dependence into the law that is not conducive to efficiency.

3. Klein (2002) finds that judicial attitudes matter also for appellate court decisions. Legal academics increasingly accept the importance of judicial ideologies for rulings on politi-

cally sensitive issues (e.g., Pinello 1999; Rowland and Carp 1996; Revesz 1997; Sunstein, Schkade, and Ellman 2004).

4. For instance, the court may award punitive damages. If damages are equal to harm, then O does not take over-precautions and, in addition, strict liability (rather than negligence) yields the first best. Yet, even strict liability leads to over-precautions if O does not fully internalize the dog's cost of precautions.

5. The judge is assumed to act myopically and thus does not act strategically with respect to future judges. The same qualitative results hold when judges are forward looking.

6. Trivially, the law always converges if the number of empirical dimensions defining a transaction is finite and—which is essentially the same—if transactions do not continuously change over time. This result hinges on the assumption that judges cannot introduce irrelevant dimensions into the law. In other words, the *materiality* of a dimension is a physical characteristic that even the most biased judges cannot subvert. As a result, a *stare decisis* doctrine constraining judges to distinguish the current precedent by using only material dimensions is successful in assuring convergence.

7. Because of its very informational benefit, distinguishing allows precedents to adapt to changing circumstances. Suppose that the previously immaterial dimension d becomes material to a transaction. Our model of distinguishing shows, for a given initial precedent A, *if* and *how* judges adapt the law to these changed circumstances.

8. Llewellyn (1960) and Stone (1985) argue that to implement their bias, judges sometimes distinguish precedents by using irrelevant dimensions. In our model, even if judges are allowed to introduce irrelevant dimensions into the law, the informational benefit of distinguishing is still present. This is so because judges prefer to distinguish using material rather than irrelevant dimensions. Both dimensions allow judges to bias the law optimally, but material ones yield the extra benefit of greater precision. Hence, the informational benefit remains a feature of distinguishing, at least until material dimensions are exhausted. This implies that some polarization in judicial preferences is still desirable.

Chapter 4

This essay originally appeared as "The Evolution of a Legal Rule." *Journal of Legal Studies* 39:2 (2010). Copyright 2010 by The University of Chicago. All rights reserved.

1. You may of course be able to recover the cost of repairing or replacing the windows in a suit for breach of contract or warranty.

2. An early U.S. case is *Anthony v. Slaid*, 52 Mass. 290 (1846). An important early statement of the rule is Holmes's opinion for the Supreme Court in *Robins Dry Dock & Repair Co. v. Flint*, 275 U.S. 303, 308–310 (1927), an admiralty case. The most famous case announcing the fundamental principle is *Ultramares Corp. v. Touche*, 255 N.Y. 170 (1931), which held in an opinion by Chief Judge Cardozo that an accountant owes no duty to third parties, such as lenders, to refrain from negligently causing economic injury as a result of a third party's reliance on the accountant's audit of a firm in which the third party invested or to which it made a loan. Feldthusen (2000) provides a detailed historical analysis of tort recovery for economic losses in various common law countries. The arguments for limiting recovery in tort for economic loss are analyzed in Bishop (1982), Rabin (1985), Goldberg (1994), and Posner (2006).

3. 63 Cal. 2d 9 (1965).

4. Seely actually recovered for both the repairs of the truck and lost profits under his warranty, but the case is important because it established the legal rule with respect to recovery for economic loss in tort. We discuss the role of contracts in the application of the ELR in section 4.

5. See Barrett (1989) for a discussion of early ELR cases in the construction industry.

6. Cases at the trial level are rarely decided in judicial opinions that explain the factual and legal issues fully. And opinions at the trial-court level have very limited impact on the evolution of legal doctrine, because they are not considered precedents, that is, authorities, binding courts in subsequent decisions.

7. 902 F.2d 573, 574 (7th Cir. 1990).

8. An example is the 1965 New Jersey case of *Santor v. A & M Karagheusian, Inc.*, 44 N.J. 52, in which a consumer recovered tort damages from a carpet manufacturer because the carpet had a defect. The dealer from whom he had bought the carpet had gone out of business before the consumer realized that the defect could not be fixed, so the dealer's warranty was of no value to him; and there was no manufacturer's warranty. We do not know whether the New Jersey court was moved by an alternative view of efficiency or by sympathy for the plaintiff, but it rejected the ELR.

9. A study like ours must immediately consider the effects of selection of disputes for appeal on our findings. To be specific, we must ask: is it possible that the law converges over time to efficient legal rules, but because of how cases are selected, our data reveal no convergence? We believe that the answer is no.

The selection of disputes could be a problem if we were trying to infer judicial support for the ELR from the frequency with which a plaintiff prevailed in a suit in which the ELR was invoked. For then we would have to consider the bearing of the Priest-Klein hypothesis that because uncertainty increases the likelihood that a case will be litigated to judgment and then appealed, rather than settled or abandoned, the win rates of appellants and appellees will tend to equality. We would also have to examine factors, such as asymmetric gains from litigation or asymmetric information, that refute the Priest-Klein hypothesis in numerous areas of law (Priest and Klein 1984; see also Shavell 1996; Kessler, Meites, and Miller 1996; Eisenberg and Farber 1997). But the selection effect should not distort the accuracy with which appellate decisions state the legal rules that are applied to resolve a dispute. We determine legal doctrine directly rather than inferring it from the rate of plaintiff victories.

A more subtle selection effect is suggested by Parisi and Fon (2009), who argue that plaintiffs have some information about the political predispositions of judges, and therefore cases selected for litigation tend to reflect judges' political preferences. As a consequence, the law might evolve differently in different states, with the differences determined by the politics of different state judiciaries rather than by efficiency. The implication for our analysis is that the number of suits, number of plaintiff wins, and number of idiosyncratic exceptions would all grow over time in liberal states relative to conservative ones. A finding that differences in the ELR across states in construction disputes were not explicable in efficiency terms would be consistent with the Parisi-Fon hypothesis, but would not undermine the rejection of the null hypothesis that the law converges to efficiency.

10. The fact that an exception is applied does not necessarily mean that the plaintiff can recover damages. The appellate court might return the case to a lower court to consider other defenses, assess damages, or resolve other issues essential to a final resolution of the litigation.

11. For example, we have coded fraudulent inducement as a "generally recognized exception" even though in two cases in our dataset fraudulent inducement was held not to constitute an exception. One was overruled a year later; the other was based on a statutory exception. In *Woodson v. Martin*, 663 So. 2d 1327 (Fla. 1995), the Florida court held that any misrepresentations of the defects in the house caused only economic losses. This was overruled in *Wassall v. W H Payne*, 682 So. 2d 678 (Fla. 1996) and has been disapproved in a number of other Florida cases. In *Flagg Energy Development Corp. v. General Motors Corp.*, 244 Conn. 126, 151–55 (1998), the Connecticut court dismissed the claim for fraudulent misrepresentation, but while mentioning the ELR the court actually based its decision on an interpretation of the Uniform Commercial Code. The case has not been overruled.

12. State courts vary in their application of this exception. For simplicity, we classify all applications of the other-property exception as generally recognized.

13. See *A.C. Excavating v. Yacht Club II Homeowner's Ass'n*, 114 P.3d 862 (Colo. 2005) for an example of a Colorado court holding that a builder owes a duty in tort to a homeowner association, and *Snow Flower Homeowner's Ass'n v. Snow Flower*, 2001 UT. App. 207 for a factually similar case from Utah holding that no such duty exists.

14. See, for example, *Sensenbrenner v. Rust, Orling & Neale, Architects, Inc.*, 236 Va. 419 (1988), holding that the defendant builder did not owe a duty to plaintiff homeowners. Similar cases in West Virginia (see e.g., *Sewell v. Gregory* 179 W.Va. 585 (1988)) and Maryland (see e.g., *Council of Co-Owners Atlantis Condominium, Inc. v. Whiting-Turner Contracting Co.*, 308 Md.18 (1986)) carved out exceptions for defendant builders in certain circumstances.

15. *Ferentchak v. Frankfort*, 121 Ill. App. 3d 599 (1984), was the early architect case. The similar cases from Illinois that upheld the ELR are *Illinois Housing Development Authority v. M-Z Construction Corp.*, 110 Ill. App. 3d 129 (1982); *2314 Lincoln Park West Condominium Association v. Mann, Gil, Ebel & Frazier, Ltd.*, 136 Ill. 2d 302 (1990); and *Martusciello v. JDS Homes, Inc.*, 361 Ill. App. 3d 568 (2005).

16. In 1999, the Florida Supreme Court allowed a plaintiff home purchaser to make a claim in negligence against the defendant architect-engineer who had failed to discover structural defects (*Moransais v. Heathman*, 744 So.2d 973 (Fla. 1999)). This holding conflicted with earlier Florida case law, where these duties were *not* recognized (see, e.g., *Sandarac Ass'n v. W.R. Frizzell Architects, Inc.*, 609 So.2d 1349 (Fla. 2d DCA 1992) and *Ocean Ritz of Daytona Condominium v. G.G.V. Assoc., Ltd.*, 710 So.2d 702 (Fla. 5th DCA 1998)).

17. We have considered alternative procedures for measuring convergence. For example, an alternative way of testing convergence to the middle view of efficiency would use state-by-year observations with a dummy dependent variable that measures the position of the law of each state in each year. The dependent variable would take the value 1 if the state adopts the ELR with generally recognized exceptions and 0 if the state uses idiosyncratic exceptions. Convergence to the middle view could be measured by testing whether the standard deviation across states converges to 0 over time. However, this methodology presents problems. We have a number of different idiosyncratic exceptions and, importantly, different states use different idiosyncratic exceptions. If a state uses just one of these idiosyncratic exceptions, this alternative methodology suggests that we code the position of the law in that state as 0. This may lead to problems if a state judiciary generally adheres to the middle view of efficiency but in one outlying case uses an idiosyncratic exception. The dependent variable would fail to describe the law of the state accurately. The methodology that we use in this paper tracks each case as it occurs. It is

a more direct method of addressing the issue of whether courts are increasing or decreasing their use of these different idiosyncratic exceptions.

18. We fit the lowess curve over the 461 binary observations of cases applying exceptions. The trend curve is an amalgam of 461 linear regressions around each local point using a localized subset of the data. This smoothes the data and generates a trend curve. The smoothing parameter (referred to as bandwidth) is the proportion of all observations that each regression uses. The smaller the bandwidth, the coarser the trend line appears, since individual regressions are more localized. The default bandwidth for lowess curves in STATA is 0.8 (meaning that each of the 461 regressions uses 369 observations), which we use throughout. The picture is similar with a bandwidth of 0.25.

19. Simple linear tests demonstrate that the downward trend in the use of idiosyncratic exceptions before the mid-1990s is significant ($t = -2.03$ for the period 1970–1994) and the upward trend in these exceptions in the last ten years of our sample is also significant ($t = 1.83$ for the period 1995–2005). Over the last ten years of our sample we see significant growth of idiosyncratic exceptions as a percentage of all exceptions.

20. *East River S.S. Corp. v. Transamerica Delaval, Inc.*, 476 U.S. 858 (1986).

21. Over 1983–2005, the trend for fraud is positive and significant at the 10 percent level ($t = 1.92$). In the same period, the trend for negligent misrepresentation claims is positive and significant at the 1 percent level ($t = 2.93$).

22. From 1970 to 2005, the trend for "other torts" is positive and significant at the 10 percent level ($t = 1.78$).

23. Testing for differences in the use of exceptions across regions does not yield any notable patterns. Testing for differences based on levels of economic growth in each state from 1970 to 2005 generates insignificant results, and testing for differences based on growth in the construction industry in each state from 1970 to 2005 also yields insignificant results.

24. States differ in the method by which judges are appointed and retained. We use the categories employed in Choi, Gulati, and E. Posner (2007) to divide states into four types of judicial selection method (appointed, merit-selected, partisan election, nonpartisan election). The methods by which judges are retained are highly correlated with the method of selection. The differences in the use of exceptions across states of different judicial selection methods are not significant.

25. Using a simple measure of party-adjusted surrogate judicial ideology ("PAJID") from Brace, Langer, and Hall (2000), we test whether the ideology of the Supreme Court judges in a given state can help explain the variation in the use of exceptions across states. In the cases in which the court upheld the ELR to preclude recovery, the average PAJID score was 47.20. In those cases where an exception was used, the average PAJID score was 47.46. The difference is not significant ($t = 0.1817$).

26. New York's position may reflect the prestige and continuing influence of Judge Benjamin Cardozo, the author of the *Ultramares* opinion, which continues in New York to block third-party suits against auditors, though a majority of other states have abandoned that application of the ELR.

Chapter 5

This essay originally appeared as Simeon Djankov, Rafael La Porta, Florencio Lopez-de-Silanes, and Andrei Shleifer (2003). "Courts." *Quarterly Journal of Economics*. Vol. 118(2): 453–517. Reprinted by permission of Oxford University Press.

1. We have discovered that attorneys in even the largest law firms in most countries are familiar with eviction and check collection procedures, generally because they have worked on such cases for their clients.

2. We count only the minimum number of independent procedural actions required to bring the case to completion. Thus, the appointment of a lawyer is counted only as a step if legal representation is mandatory. Notifications of interlocutory decisions that do not require further interaction between the parties and the judge or court officer (as when the clerk makes an entry into the notification book) are not counted as separate steps since they are ancillary to the decision.

3. Law firms also provide us with estimates of the minimum and the maximum amount of time in calendar days each case could take given its specifics. This request helped lawyers to focus on the average length of time and not just think about the worst or best case they had encountered.

4. We also consider the hypothesis that the influence of Catholicism, with its protection of creditors, shapes judicial formalism. Although the percentage of a country's population that is Catholic is a statistically significant determinant of formalism, this variable becomes insignificant in a horse-race with legal origin, which remains important.

5. The results in table 5.6 hold with the French and the English legal origins, and are robust to alternative measures of heterogeneity, such as religious heterogeneity from Alesina et al. (2003).

6. At the same time, the instrumental variable procedure cannot reject the hypothesis that the adverse effect of French civil law on the efficiency and quality of dispute resolution works through a channel other than formalism. For example, suppose that the transplantation of French legal rules is conducive to general state interventionism and bureaucratic inefficiency, as argued in La Porta et al. (1999), and that this channel undermines the performance of courts as well. In this case, we cannot be sure that formalism, as opposed to general interventionism, is the culprit. To assess this alternative, we repeat the analysis using in place of formalism a measure of state interventionism having nothing to do with courts per se, namely the heaviness of regulation of entry by new firms from chapter 10. That paper finds that such regulation is heavier in French civil law countries than in common law countries. When we do this analysis, we find that, indeed, the regulation of entry predicts longer duration of dispute resolution, and lower quality of adjudication, in both the OLS and instrumental variable regressions. However, the explanatory power of regulation of entry is only four to five percent, compared to the explanatory power of formalism of 18 to 20 percent. Thus, while we cannot reject the hypothesis that the channel of influence of legal origin on the quality of dispute resolution is general interventionism, the channel we have identified in this paper, namely procedural formalism, explains much more than a generic measure of interventionism.

Chapter 6

This essay originally appeared as "The Rise of the Regulatory State." *Journal of Economic Literature* 41:2, 401–425 (2003). Reprinted by permission of the American Economic Association.

1. This is not to say that there was no regulation at all. Novak (1996) gives examples of extensive regulation in nineteenth-century America, but virtually all the regulation he discusses is local, not dealing with commercial disputes, and not relying on regulatory agencies.

2. Schwartz (1981, 1989) argues that the movement from strict liability to negligence is not detectable prior to the Civil War. Our theory focuses on the post–Civil War period, where the change is clearer.

3. One may ask why the α's don't drive the β's out of business. Presumably, there are some other parts of the cost structure where the former types have higher costs, so both types coexist in the market.

4. We have also solved the case where p is endogenous. Since it yields qualitatively similar results, we focus here on the simpler scenario with exogenous p.

5. In general, some subversion costs are incurred ex ante (befriending regulators), some after the accident occurs (hiring a legal team), and some after liability is determined (bribes to reduce punishment). Our formulation avoids the credibility issues of many crime and punishment models, where the violator might not want to follow through with punishing the law enforcer (and vice versa). Our formulation also avoids the possibility of the firm bargaining with the law enforcer over the verdict and the bribe.

6. This is not so when disputes are between two entities possessing comparable abilities to subvert justice, as in the battle for the Erie railroad. In this case, a judge or a legislator can just auction off a decision, with the result that X actually scales up with S.

7. In the first volume of the A.E.R. in 1887, Henry Adams wrote: "The policy of restricting public powers within the narrowest possible limits tends to render government weak and inefficient, and a weak government placed in the midst of a society controlled by the commercial spirit will quickly become a corrupt government; this in its turn reacts upon commercial society by encouraging private corporations to adopt bold measures for gaining control of government machinery. Thus the doctrine of laissez-faire overreaches itself; for the application of the rule which it lays down will surely destroy the harmony between public and private duties essential to the best results in either domain of action."

8. The other—diametrically opposite—interpretation of the Progressive Era is that, following populism, reforms represented just a redistribution from the rich to the poor. This interpretation is inconsistent with the view that many reforms were supported not just by the poor, but by urban elites and many firms, and championed by Republican presidential candidates—Roosevelt and Taft.

9. A modern analogy illustrates this point. It is surely the case that, in the period of post-Enron investigations, investment banks and accounting firms try to shape the changes in regulation. But we would not conclude that they sought these changes in the first place to benefit themselves.

Chapter 7

This essay originally appeared as Edward Glaeser, Simon Johnson, and Andrei Shleifer (2001). "Coase vs. the Coasians," *Quarterly Journal of Economics* Vol. 116(3): 853–899. Reprinted by permission of Oxford University Press.

1. The classic reference on the incentive of law enforcers is Becker and Stigler (1974), to whose work we return below. A recent survey of public enforcement of law by Polinsky and Shavell (2000) scarcely pays attention to the incentives of the enforcers.

2. Coase (1988, p. 117–118) recognized that regulation may be preferred to judicially enforced contracts as a method of regulating some types of conduct: "There is no reason

why, on occasion, such governmental regulation should not be an improvement on economic efficiency."

3. Note that if $a > b$, the only equilibrium outcome is abuse.

4. In 1997, the EBRD gave Poland a 3+ relative to the Czech Republic's 3 on securities markets and financial institutions. We argue below that the difference should have been larger.

5. A foreign-controlled mobile phone company, Ceske Radiokomunikce, raised $134 million in 1998 by issuing Global Depositary Receipts in London.

Chapter 8

This essay originally appeared as Edward Glaeser and Andrei Shleifer (2002). "Legal Origins." *Quarterly Journal of Economics* Vol. 117(4): 1193–1230. Reprinted by permission of Oxford University Press.

1. In a study of civil procedures in 109 countries, chapter 5 identifies 42 countries in the English common law tradition and 40 in the French civil law tradition. In addition, German civil law, Scandinavian law, and socialist law prevail in parts of the world.

2. Kessler and Piehl (1998) present a more modern example of juries in a common law system undoing harsh penalties (mandatory sentencing guidelines in the United States).

3. It is sometimes argued that Henry II designed his legal system too early, and that the choice of Romano-Canon law was not available to him. Berman (1983) presents compelling evidence against this view, including the fact that one of Henry's principal advisors had previously worked for Roger II in Palermo, who chose the Roman law system for his country.

4. For a discussion of preferences of judges, see Posner (1995).

5. The king's writ did not run in the duchies, which exemplify the power of the nobles.

6. In this analysis, we obviously simplify. Even the legal systems of the United States and the United Kingdom have important structural differences (Posner 1996).

7. Incentives for prosecutors are discussed by Dewatripont and Tirole (1999) and Glaeser, Kessler, and Piehl (2000).

Chapter 9

This essay originally appeared as Casey B. Mulligan and Andrei Shleifer (2005). "The Extent of the Market and the Supply of Regulation." *Quarterly Journal of Economics* Vol. 120(4): 1445–1473. Reprinted by permission of Oxford University Press.

1. To our knowledge, all militaries have some volunteers. Hence, the question is not a volunteer versus a draft system, but whether a draft system supplements the volunteer system.

2. Some forces might lead to reductions in c. Becker and Mulligan (2003) and Peltzman (1989) conclude that regulation increases in response to its own enhanced efficiency.

3. There are three reasons to measure KB rather than pages. First, not all states have their statutes published by the same publisher (or, within publisher, in the same format), so cross-state comparisons of pages would require adjustments for each publisher's font size, formatting style, etc. Second, some states have their total statutes published irregularly, and publish only additions and retractions in the meantime. Third, bytes can be calculated (as described below) by computer and potentially be disaggregated by statute type.

4. The number of lawyers is likely to be correlated with other determinants of the number of laws. However, including this variable does not affect the estimated population elasticity because population and lawyers per capita happen to be uncorrelated. Appendix 2 explains how lawyers per capita are measured from the 1990 Census. Another measure of lawyers per capita for 2003 from the American Bar Association (2003) also does not help predict KB of law, in part because it records (unlike the Census) NY and MA as extreme outliers.

5. We are aware of only four studies that use absolute population as a determinant of regulation. Among the variables they use to predict adoption of "general incorporation code" by U.S. states, Shughart and Tollison (1985) include both aggregate population and aggregate manufacturing income (both in levels, with population measured in different years for different states). They find that populous states adopt later and states with more manufacturing income adopt earlier, so it is hard to tell from their results whether populous states adopted earlier or later (we find the raw correlation between year of adoption and log 1910 population to be –0.55). McCormick and Tollison (1981) use absolute size of legislature to predict occupational licensing, and note that Stigler (1976) used absolute population to predict the size of legislature. Davis (2006) argues that smaller jurisdictions should have fewer and more vague legal rules.

6. See appendix 2 for details on constructing the heterogeneity measures. We have also tried various measures of earnings inequality from the 1990 Census PUMS, and the fractions of income and employment in agriculture, with similar results.

7. Log seats is more correlated with log 1920 population than with log 2000 population.

8. From the annotated statutes (not used for the KB counts cited in the text) we see that Illinois has many more annotations and corrections to its criminal law than does Indiana.

9. Indiana covers coin slugs under a wider law regarding "Forgery, Fraud, and Other Deceptions" in reference to a slug that might be "deposited in a coin machine." Illinois' Coin Slug Act explicitly references "slug, washer, disc, token, string, cord or wire or by means of any false, counterfeited, mutilated, sweated or foreign coin, or by any means, method, trick, or device whatsoever not lawfully authorized by the owner of such coin box telephone, coin operated transit turnstile or transit fare box." In addition, Illinois has a "Telephone Coin Box Tampering Act."

10. Results are similar if we use statutes inclusive of annotations: Illinois has 426 drug pages while Indiana has 147.

11. Stigler did not enter occupational prevalence (total number of persons practicing the occupation divided by total labor force) in log form, but if he had, and occupation size were normalized by population rather than labor force, then his specification and ours would differ only by a log population term. Stigler's estimated occupational prevalence coefficient was statistically insignificant. Another reason we emphasize log population,

rather than log occupation size, as a regressor is that licensing may affect occupation size more readily than it affects population.

12. The ten largest states were GA, IL, IN, MA, MI, MO, NY, OH, PA, and TX. The ten smallest states were AZ, DE, ID, MT, NH, NM, NV, UT, VT, and WY.

13. Interestingly, among the 28 states with enforceable legislation, the correlation of year of first law with log total black population (black population share) is −0.26 (−0.11), respectively.

14. Botero et al. (2004) and chapter 10 have 85 countries. We exclude the former Soviet republics, Vietnam, and Lebanon, due to insufficient data on GDP for the years 1960–1990.

15. www.deathpenaltyinfo.org reports that Florida (2000 population = 16 million) and California (34 million) annually spend $51 million and $90 million, respectively, in order to have the death penalty rather than life in prison.

16. We have also used government spending GDP and the share of the population over the age of 65, and obtained similar results.

17. Those nine states are Colorado, Kansas, Louisiana, Maryland, New Mexico, Ohio, Oklahoma, Virginia, and Wisconsin. A number of states have both java and html statutes on line, including AR, CA, SD, TN.

18. A typical html page from SD statutes reads: "*32-5-10.2. Motorcycle safety education fee-Deposit in special revenue fund. The county treasurer shall remit to the department the motorcycle safety education fees collected pursuant to § 32-5-10.1. The fees shall be deposited in the state treasury in a special revenue fund for use as specified in § 32-20-14.* Statutes Menu | FAQ | My Legislative Research | Privacy Policy | LRC Menu This page is maintained by the Legislative Research Council. It contains material authorized for publication that is copyrighted by the state of South Dakota. Except as authorized by federal copyright law, no person may print or distribute copyrighted material without the express authorization of the South Dakota Code Commission," where we have italicized the actual statute. The non-italicized portion is 523 bytes, so we subtract 523 bytes per SD web page of law.

19. The only exception is VT, for which we counted statutes in effect as of 1995. Including year of statute in the regressions has no impact on the results.

Chapter 10

This chapter originally appeared as Simeon Djankov, Rafael La Porta, Florencio Lopez-de-Silanes, and Andrei Shleifer (2002). "The Regulation of Entry." *Quarterly Journal of Economics* Vol. 117(1): 1–37. Reprinted by permission of Oxford University Press.

1. In practice, the largest city coincides with the capital city except in Australia (Melbourne), Brazil (San Paolo), Canada (Toronto), Germany (Frankfurt), Kazakhstan (Almaty), Netherlands (Amsterdam), South Africa (Johannesburg), Turkey (Istanbul), and the U.S. (New York).

2. If the Company Law allows for more than one privately owned business form with limited liability, we choose the more popular business form among small companies in the country.

3. The World Competitiveness Report (2001) surveys business people on how important are administrative regulations as an obstacle to new business. Our three measures are strongly positively correlated with these subjective assessments.

4. Shleifer and Vishny (1993) distinguish corruption with theft from corruption without theft. In the latter case, the regulator must remit the official fee to the Treasury, and therefore has no interest in that fee being high.

5. In several countries, our consultants advised us that certain procedures, while not required, are highly recommended, because failure to follow them may result in signifi- cant delays and additional costs. We collected data on these procedures, but did not include them in the variables presented here because we wanted to stick to the manda- tory criterion. We have rerun the regressions discussed below including these highly recommended procedures. The inclusion does not have a material impact on the results.

6. In the calculation of time, when two procedures can be completed on the same day in the same building, we count that as one day rather than two (following the urgings of officials in several countries, where several offices are located in the same building). Our results are not affected by this particular way of computing time.

7. One objection to this finding is that entrepreneurs in rich countries might face more post-entry regulations than they do in poor countries. We have data on one aspect of post-entry regulation, namely the regulation of labor markets (see Botero et al., 2004). The numbers of entry and of labor market regulations are positively correlated across countries, contrary to this objection.

8. We have tried measures of air pollution and obtained similar results.

9. Due to reporting practices in poor countries, the second variable might better capture deaths from accidental poisoning in the poor countries, according to the World Health Organization.

10. There is a large literature detailing how regulation can drive firms into the unofficial economy, where they can avoid some or all of these regulations. See, for example, Johnson, Kaufmann, and Shleifer (1997) and Friedman, Johnson, Kaufmann, and Zoido- Lobaton (2000).

11. Using data for publicly traded firms, we have found no evidence that countries with heavier entry regulation have more profitable firms, as measured by the return on assets. These profitability numbers, however, are very crude. We also measured profitability using the return on World Bank financed projects from the World Bank Operations Evalu- ation Department. These data also yield no evidence that more regulations are associated with greater returns.

12. We have tried a number of measures of corruption, all yielding similar results. We have made sure that our results do not depend on "red tape" being part of the measure of corruption.

13. Consistent with this finding, La Porta et al. (2004) find that common law legal origin is associated with English constitutional guarantees of freedom, such as the indepen- dence of the judiciary and the accountability of the government to the law. These con- stitutional guarantees of freedom are strongly associated with economic freedoms, but less so with political freedoms.

14. Results are significant in all six regressions when we use time rather than number of procedures as the dependent variable. In contrast, results are insignificant in three regressions (competition in the legislature's nominating process, autocracy, and political rights) when using cost as the dependent variable.

References

Abrams, David, Marianne Bertrand, and Sendhil Mullainathan. 2011 (forthcoming). Do Judges Vary in Their Treatment of Race? *Journal of Legal Studies.*

Acemoglu, Daron, and Thierry Verdier. 2000. The Choice Between Market Failures and Corruption. *American Economic Review* 90:194–211.

Adams, Henry. 1887. Relation of the State to Industrial Action. *American Economic Review* 1:7–85.

Alesina, Alberto, and Enrico Spolaore. 2003a. *The Size of Nations.* Cambridge, MA: MIT Press.

Alesina, Alberto, and George-Marios Angeletos. 2005a. Corruption, Inequality, and Fairness. *Journal of Monetary Economics* 52:1227–1244.

Alesina, Alberto, and George-Marios Angeletos. 2005b. Fairness and Redistribution. *American Economic Review* 95:960–980.

Alesina, Alberto, Arnaud Devleeschauwer, William Easterly, Sergio Kurlat, and Romain Wacziarg. 2003b. Fractionalization. *Journal of Economic Growth* 8:155–194.

Allais, Maurice. 1947. Le Probleme de la Planification Economique dans une Economie Collectiviste. *Kyklos* 2:48–71.

American Bar Association. 2003. *National Lawyer Population by State.* Chicago, IL: ABA Market Research Department.

Balcerowicz, Leszek. 1995. *Socialism, Capitalism, Transformation.* Budapest, Hungary: Central European University Press.

Banerjee, Abhijit. 1997. A Theory of Misgovernance. *Quarterly Journal of Economics* 112:1289–1332.

Barrett, Sidney. 1989. Construction Claims: Recovery of Economic Loss in Tort for Construction Defects. *South Carolina Law Review* 40:891–942.

Barro, Robert, and Jong-Wha Lee. 2001. International Data on Educational Attainment Updates and Implications. *Oxford Economic Papers* 53:541–563.

Bauer, Ralph. 1933. The Degree of Moral Fault as Affecting Defendant's Liability. *University of Pennsylvania Law Review* 81:586–596.

Bebchuk, Lucian. 1984. Litigation and Settlement Under Imperfect Information. *Rand Journal of Economics* 15:404–415.

Beck, Thorsten, Asli Demirguc-Kunt, and Ross Levine. 2003. Law and Finance: Why Does Legal Origin Matter. *Journal of Comparative Economics* 31:653–675.

Beck, Thorsten, Asli Demirguc-Kunt, and Ross Levine. 2005. Law and Firms' Access to Finance. *American Law and Economics Review* 7:211–252.

Becker, Gary S. 1968. Crime and Punishment: An Economic Approach. *Journal of Political Economy* 76:169–217.

Becker, Gary S. 1983. A Theory of Competition Among Pressure Groups for Political Influence. *Quarterly Journal of Economics* 98:371–400.

Becker, Gary S., and George J. Stigler. 1974. Law Enforcement, Malfeasance, and the Compensation of Enforcers. *Journal of Legal Studies* 3:1–18.

Becker, Gary S., and Casey B. Mulligan. 2003. Deadweight Costs and the Size of Government. *Journal of Law & Economics* 46:293–340.

Berdejo, Carlos, and Noam M. Yuchtman. 2009. "Crime, Punishment and Politics: An Analysis of Political Cycles in Criminal Sentencing." Unpublished manuscript, Harvard University.

Berkowitz, Daniel, Katharina Pistor, and Jean-Francois Richard. 2003. Economic Development, Legality, and the Transplant Effect. *European Economic Review* 47:165–195.

Berman, Harold J. 1983. *Law and Revolution*. Cambridge, MA: Harvard University Press.

Bernstein, Lisa. 1992. Opting Out of the Legal System: Extralegal Contractual Relations in the Diamond Industry. *Journal of Legal Studies* 21:115–157.

Bianco, Magda, Tullio Jappelli, and Marco Pagano. 2005. Courts and Banks: Effects of Judicial Enforcement on Credit Markets. *Journal of Money, Credit and Banking* 37:223–244.

Bishop, William. 1982. Economic Loss in Tort. *Oxford Journal of Legal Studies* 2:1–29.

Botero, Juan, Simeon Djankov, Rafael La Porta, Florencio Lopez-de-Silanes, and Andrei Shleifer. 2004. The Regulation of Labor. *Quarterly Journal of Economics* 119:1339–1382.

Boycko, Maxim, Andrei Shleifer, and Robert W. Vishny. 1995. *Privatizing Russia*. Cambridge, MA: MIT Press.

Brace, Paul, Laura Langer, and Melinda G. Hall. 2000. Measuring the Preferences of the State Supreme Court Judges. *Journal of Politics* 62:387–413.

Brenner, Saul, and Harold J. Spaeth. 1995. *Stare Indecisis: The Alteration of Precedent on the U.S. Supreme Court, 1946–1992*. New York, NY: Cambridge University Press.

Brenner, Saul, and Marc Stier. 1996. Retesting Segal and Spaeth's *Stare Decisis* Model. *American Journal of Political Science* 40:1036–1048.

Bueno de Mesquita, Ethan, and Mathew Stephenson. 2002. Informative Precedent and Intrajudicial Communication. *American Political Science Review* 90:1–12.

Buscaglia, Edgardo, and Maria Dakolias. 1999. *Comparative International Study of Court Performance Indicators*. World Bank, Legal Department.

Bussani, Mauro, and Vernon Valentine Palmer, eds. 2003a. *Pure Economic Loss in Europe*. Cambridge, UK: Cambridge University Press.

Bussani, Mauro, Vernon Valentine Palmer, and Francesco Parisi. 2003b. Liability for Pure Financial Loss in Europe: An Economic Restatement. *American Journal of Comparative Law* 114:112–162.

Calfee, John E., and Richard Craswell. 1984. Some Effects of Uncertainty on Compliance with Legal Standards. *Virginia Law Review* 70:965–1003.

Callow, Alexander. 1966. *The Tweed Ring.* New York, NY: Oxford University Press.

Cardozo, Benjamin N. 1921. *The Nature of the Judicial Process.* New Haven, CT: Yale University Press.

Central Intelligence Agency, *CIA World Factbook,* (2001), published online.

Chandler, Alfred. 1977. *The Visible Hand.* Cambridge, MA: Harvard University Press.

Chang, Tom, and Antoinette Schoar. 2007. "Judge Specific Differences in Chapter 11 and Firm Outcomes." MIT Sloan Working Paper.

Chidzero, Anne-Marie. 1996. Senegal. In *The Informal Sector and Microfinance Institutions in West Africa,* ed. Leila Webster and Peter Fidler. Washington, DC: The World Bank.

Choi, Stephen J., G. Mitu Gulati, and Eric A. Posner. 2010. Professionals or Politicians: The Uncertain Empirical Case for an Elected Rather than Appointed Judiciary. *Journal of Law Economics and Organization* 26:290–336.

Coase, Ronald. 1960. The Problem of Social Cost. *Journal of Law & Economics* 3:1–44.

Coase, Ronald. 1988. *The Firm, the Market, and the Law.* Chicago, IL: University of Chicago Press.

Coffee, John C., Jr. 1996. Institutional Investors in Transitional Economies: Lessons from the Czech Experience. In *Corporate Governance in Central Europe and Russia. Volume 1,* ed. Roman Frydman, Cheryl Williamson Gray, and Andrzej Rapaczynski. Budapest, Hungary: Central European University Press.

Coffee, John C., Jr. 1999. The Future as History: The Prospects for Global Convergence in Corporate Governance and its Implications. *Northwestern Law Review* 93:631–707.

Coffee, John C., Jr. 2002. Convergence and its Critics: What are the Preconditions to the Separation of Ownership and Control? In *Corporate Governance Regimes: Convergence and Diversity,* ed. Joseph McCahery, Luc Renneboog, Piet Moerland, and Theo Raaijmakers. New York, NY: Oxford University Press.

Cooter, Robert, Lewis Kornhauser, and David Lane. 1979. Liability Rules, Limited Information and the Role of Precedent. *Bell Journal of Economics* 10:366–373.

Cooter, Robert. 1988. Punitive Damages for Deterrence: When and How Much? *Alabama Law Review* 40:1143–1196.

Coppin, Clayton A., and Jack High. 1988. Wiley and the Whiskey Industry. *Business History Review* 62:286–309.

Coppin, Clayton A., and Jack High. [1999] 2002. *The Politics of Purity: Harvey Washington Wiley and the Origins of Federal Food Policy.* Ann Arbor, MI: University of Michigan Press.

Craswell, Richard, and John E. Calfee. 1986. Deterrence and Uncertain Legal Standards. *Journal of Law Economics and Organization* 2:279–303.

Croly, Herbert. 1965. *The Promise of American Life.* Cambridge, MA: Harvard University Press.

Dal Bo, Ernesto, Pedro Dal Bo, and Rafael Di Tella. 2006. *Plato o Plomo:* Bribe and Punishment in a Theory of Political Influence. *American Political Science Review* 100:41–53.

Damaška, Mirjan R. 1986. *The Faces of Justice and State Authority.* New Haven, CT: Yale University Press.

Dari-Mattiacci, Giuseppe, and Hans-Bernd Schafer. 2007. The Core of Pure Economic Loss. *International Review of Law and Economics* 27:8–28.

Daughety, Andrew, and Jennifer Reinganum. 2000. On the Economics of Trials: Adversarial Process, Evidence, and Equilibrium Bias. *Journal of Law Economics and Organization* 16:365–394.

Davis, Kevin E. 2006. Lawmaking in Small Jurisdictions. *University of Toronto Law Journal* 56:151–184.

Dawson, John P. 1960. *A History of Lay Judges.* Cambridge, MA: Harvard University Press.

De Melo, Martha, Cevdet Denizer, and Alan Gelb. 1996. "From Plan to Market: Patterns of Transition." Background paper for the 1996 World Development Report. World Bank.

De Soto, Hernando. 1989. *The Other Path.* New York, NY: Harper and Row.

DeLong, J. Bradford and Andrei Shleifer. 1993. Princes and Merchants: European City Growth Before the Industrial Revolution. *Journal of Law & Economics* 36:671–702.

Demsetz, Harold. 1967. Toward a Theory of Property Rights. *American Economic Review* 57:347–359.

Dershowitz, Alan, and John Hart Ely. 1971. *Harris versus New York:* Some Anxious Observations on the Candor and Logic of the Emerging Nixon Majority. *Yale Law Journal* 80:1198–1227.

Dewatripont, Mathias, and Jean Tirole. 1999. Advocates. *Journal of Political Economy* 107:1–39.

Dicey, Albert Venn. 1939. *Law of the Constitution.* London, UK: Macmillan and Co.

Djankov, Simeon, Caralee McLiesh, Tatiana Nenova, and Andrei Shleifer. 2003. Who Owns the Media? *Journal of Law and Economics* 46: 341–381.

Djankov, Simeon, Edward Glaeser, Rafael La Porta, Florencio Lopez-de-Silanes, and Andrei Shleifer. 2003. The New Comparative Economics. *Journal of Comparative Economics* 31:595–619.

Easterbrook, Frank, and Daniel Fischel. 1991. *The Economic Structure of Corporate Law.* Cambridge, MA: Harvard University Press.

Edlin, Aaron S., and Alan Schwartz. 2000. Optimal Penalties in Contracts. *Chicago-Kent Law Review* 78:33–54.

Eisenberg, Theodore, and Henry S. Farber. 1997. The Litigious Plaintiff Hypothesis: Case Selection and Resolution. *Rand Journal of Economics* 28:S92–S112.

Ellickson, Robert. 1991. *Order Without Law: How Neighbors Resolve Disputes.* Cambridge, MA: Harvard University Press.

European Bank for Reconstruction and Development. 1995. *Transition Report*. London, UK: EBRD.

European Bank for Reconstruction and Development. 1996. *Transition Report*. London, UK: EBRD.

European Bank for Reconstruction and Development. 1997. *Transition Report*. London, UK: EBRD.

European Corporate Governance Network. 1997. *The Separation of Ownership and Control: A Survey of 7 European Countries Preliminary Report to the European Commission*. vol. 1–4. Brussels, Belgium: European Commisson.

Feldthusen, Bruce. 2000. *Economic Negligence*. 4th ed. Toronto, Canada: Carswell.

Fishback, Price, and Shawn Kantor. 2000. *A Prelude to the Welfare State: The Origins of Workers' Compensation*. Chicago, IL: University of Chicago Press.

Ford, Franklin L. 1953. *Robe and Sword*. New York, NY: Harper Torchbooks.

Frank, Jerome. 1930. *Law and the Modern Mind*. New York, NY: Brentano's.

Frank, Jerome. 1932. What Courts Do in Fact. *University of Illinois Law Review* 26:645–666.

Frank, Jerome. 1951. *Courts on Trial*. Princeton, NJ: Princeton University Press.

Freedom House. 2001. *Freedom of the World*. New York, NY: Freedom House.

Friedman, Eric, Simon Johnson, Daniel Kaufmann, and Pablo Zoido-Lobaton. 2000. Dodging the Grabbing Hand: the Determinants of Unofficial Activity in 69 Countries. *Journal of Public Economics* 76:459–494.

Friedman, Lawrence. 1985. *A History of American Law*. New York, NY: Simon and Schuster.

Froeb, Luke, and Bruce Kobayashi. 1996. Naïve, Biased, yet Bayesian: Can Juries Interpret Selectively Produced Evidence? *Journal of Law Economics and Organization* 12:257–276.

Galanter, Marc. 1974. Why the Haves Come Out Ahead: Speculations on the Limits of Legal Change. *Law & Society Review* 9:95–169.

Galanter, Marc. 1981. Justice in Many Rooms: Courts, Private Ordering, and Indigenous Law. *Journal of Legal Pluralism* 19:1–47.

Galbraith, John Kenneth. 1952. *American Capitalism: The Concept of Countervailing Power*. New Brunswick, NJ: Houghton Mifflin.

Gandasurbrata, Purwoto. 1980. Indonesia. Administration of Justice: Procedural Reforms on Court Congestion. In *Asian Comparative Law Series*. vol. 2. ed. Purificacion Valera-Quisumbing. Manila, Philippines: Asian Law Association of the Philippines and University of the Philippines.

Gennaioli, Nicola, and Andrei Shleifer. 2007. Overruling and the Instability of Law. *Journal of Comparative Economics* 35:309–328.

Gennaioli, Nicola. 2011 (forthcoming). Contracting in the Shadow of the Law. *Journal of the European Economic Association*.

George, Tracey, and Lee Epstein. 1992. On the Nature of Supreme Court Decision Making. *American Political Science Review* 86:323–337.

Gilligan, Thomas, William Marshall, and Barry Weingast. 1989. Regulation and the Theory of Legislative Choice: The Interstate Commerce Act of 1887. *Journal of Law & Economics* 32:35–61.

Glaeser, Edward, and Andrei Shleifer. 2001. A Reason for Quantity Regulation. *American Economic Review* 91:431–435.

Glaeser, Edward, Daniel P. Kessler, and Anne M. Piehl. 2000. What Do Prosecutors Maximize? *American Law and Economics Review* 2:259–290.

Glaeser, Edward, Giacomo Ponzetto, and Andrei Shleifer. 2007. Why Does Democracy Need Education? *Journal of Economic Growth* 12:77–99.

Glaeser, Edward, Jose Scheinkman, and Andrei Shleifer. 2003. The Injustice of Inequality. *Journal of Monetary Economics* 50:199–222.

Glaeser, Edward. 2004. Public Ownership in the American City. In *Urban Issues and Public Finance: Essays in Honor of Dick Netzer*, ed. A. E. Schwartz. Northampton, MA: Edward Elgar Publishing.

Goldberg, Victor P. 1994. Recovery for Economic Loss Following the Exxon Valdez Oil Spill. *Journal of Legal Studies* 23:1–40.

Goldman, Eric. 1947. *Rendezvous with Destiny, a History of Modern American Reform*. New York, NY: Knopf.

Gomez, Fernando, and Hans-Bernd Schafer. 2007. The Law and Economics of Pure Economic Loss: Introduction. *International Review of Law and Economics* 27:1–7.

Goodhart, Arthur. 1930. Determining the *Ratio Decidendi* of a Case. *Yale Law Journal* 40:161–183.

Greif, Avner. 1989. Reputation and Coalitions in Medieval Trade: Evidence on the Maghribi Traders. *Journal of Economic History* 49:857–882.

Grossman, Gene, and Elhanan Helpman. 2001. *Special Interest Politics*. Cambridge, MA: MIT Press.

Grossman, Herschel I. 2002. Make Us A King: Anarchy, Predation and the State. *European Journal of Political Economy* 18:31–46.

Guiso, Luigi, Paola Sapienza, and Luigi Zingales. 2003. People's Opium? Religion and Economic Attitudes. *Journal of Monetary Economics* 50:225–282.

Gwartney, James D., and Robert Lawson. 1997. *Economic Freedom of the World 1997*. Vancouver, Canada: The Fraser Institute.

Gwartney, James D., Robert Lawson, and Walter Block. 1996. *Economic Freedom of the World 1975–1995*. Vancouver, Canada: The Fraser Institute.

Hadfield, Gillian. 1992. Bias in the Evolution of Legal Rules. *Georgetown Law Journal* 80:583–616.

Hansford, Thomas G., and James F. Spriggs, II. 2006. *The Politics of Precedent on the U.S. Supreme Court*. Princeton, NJ: Princeton University Press.

Hart, Oliver, Andrei Shleifer, and Robert Vishny. 1997. The Proper Scope of Government: Theory and an Application to Prisons. *Quarterly Journal of Economics* 112:1127–1161.

Hathaway, Oona A. 2001. Path Dependence in the Law: The Course and Pattern of Legal Change in a Common Law System. *Iowa Law Review* 86:601–665.

Hay, Jonathan R., and Andrei Shleifer. 1998. Private Enforcement of Public Laws: A Theory of Legal Reform. *American Economic Review Papers and Proceedings* 88:398–403.

Hay, Jonathan R., Andrei Shleifer, and Robert W. Vishny. 1996. Toward a Theory of Legal Reform. *European Economic Review* 40:559–567.

Hayek, Friedrich A. 1960. *The Constitution of Liberty*. Chicago, IL: University of Chicago Press.

Hayek, Friedrich A. 1973. *Rules and Order*. vol. 1. Law, Legislation, and Liberty. Chicago, IL: University of Chicago Press.

Henderson, James A., Jr. 2003. *MacPherson versus Buick Motor Company*: Simplifying the Facts While Reshaping the Law. In *Torts Stories*, ed. Robert Rabin and Stephen Sugarman. New York, NY: Foundation Press.

Henisz, Witold Jerzy. 2000. The Institutional Environment for Economic Growth. *Economics and Politics* 12:1–31.

High, Jack, and Clayton Coppin. 1988. Wiley and the Whiskey Industry: Strategic Behavior in the Passage of the Pure Food Act. *Business History Review* 62:286–309.

High, Jack, ed. 1991. *Regulation: Economic Theory and History*. Ann Arbor, MI: University of Michigan Press.

Hoffman, Adam. 2001. Corralling Constitutional Fact: De Novo Fact Review in the Federal Appellate Courts. *Duke Law Journal* 50:1427–1466.

Hofstadter, Richard. 1955. *The Age of Reform*. New York, NY: Random House.

Holmes, Oliver Wendell. 1881. *The Common Law*. Boston, MA: Little Brown and Company.

Holmes, Oliver Wendell. 1897. The Path of the Law. *Harvard Law Review* 10:457–478.

Holt, James C. 1992. *Magna Carta*. Cambridge, UK: Cambridge University Press.

Horwitz, Morton. 1992. *The Transformation of American Law 1870–1960*. New York, NY: Oxford University Press.

IMD. 1997. *World Competitiveness Yearbook*. Lausanne, Switzerland.

Institute for International Management Development. 2001. *World Competitiveness Report*. Lausanne, Switzerland: IMD.

International Institute for Strategic Studies. *The Military Balance*. London, various issues.

Jaggers, Keith, and Monty G. Marshall. 2000. *Polity IV Project*. Center for International Development and Conflict Management, University of Maryland.

von Jhering, Rudolf. [1878] 1898. *Geist des Römischen Rechts auf den Verschiedenen Stufen Seiner Entwicklung, (The Spirit of Roman Law Through its Several Phases of Development)*. Leipzig, Germany: Breitkopf und Härtel.

Johnson, Simon, Daniel Kaufmann, and Andrei Shleifer. 1997. The Unofficial Economy in Transition. *Brookings Papers on Economic Activity* II:159–239.

Johnson, Simon, John McMillan, and Christopher Woodruff. 2002. Courts and Relational Contracts. *Journal of Law Economics and Organization* 18:221–277.

Johnson, Simon, Peter Boone, Alasdair Breach, and Eric Friedman. 2000a. Corporate Governance in the Asian Financial Crisis. *Journal of Financial Economics* 58:141–186.

Johnson, Simon, Rafael La Porta, Florencio Lopez-de-Silanes, and Andrei Shleifer. 2000b. Tunneling. *American Economic Review Papers and Proceedings* 90:22–27.

Josephson, Matthew. [1934] 1962. *The Robber Barons: The Great American Capitalists, 1861–1901.* New York, NY: Harcourt, Brace and Co.

Kalven, Harry, and Hans Zeisel. 1966. *The American Jury.* Chicago, IL: University of Chicago Press.

Kaplow, Louis, and Steven Shavell. 1994. Accuracy in the Determination of Liability. *Journal of Law & Economics* 37:1–15.

Kaplow, Louis, and Steven Shavell. 1996. Accuracy in the Assessment of Damages. *Journal of Law & Economics* 39:191–210.

Kaplow, Louis, and Steven Shavell. 2002. Economic Analysis of Law. In *Handbook of Public Economics*, ed. Alan J. Auerbach and Martin Feldstein. Amsterdam, Netherlands: Elsevier.

Kaplow, Louis. 1992. Rules versus Standards. *Duke Law Journal* 42:557–629.

Kaplow, Louis. 1994. The Value of Accuracy in Adjudication: An Economic Analysis. *Journal of Legal Studies* 23:307–401.

Kaplow, Louis. 1995. A Model of Optimal Complexity of Legal Rules. *Journal of Law Economics and Organization* 11:150–163.

Kasnakoglu, Zehra, and Münür Yayla. 1999. Unrecorded Economy in Turkey: A Monetary Approach in *Informal Sector in Turkey, Volume I*, ed. Tuncer Bulutay. Ankara, Turkey: SIS.

Kaufman, Andrew. 2000. *Cardozo.* Cambridge, MA: Harvard University Press.

Kaufman, Herbert. 1960. *The Forest Ranger.* Baltimore, MD: Johns Hopkins Press.

Keeton, Robert E., Lewis D. Sargentich, and Gregory C. Keating. 2004. *Tort and Accident Law.* 4th ed. St. Paul, MN: Thomson West.

Kessler, Daniel P., and Anee M. Piehl. 1998. The Role of Discretion in the Criminal Justice System. *Journal of Law Economics and Organization* 14:256–276.

Kessler, Daniel, Thomas Meites, and Geoffrey Miller. 1996. Explaining Deviations from the Fifty-Percent Rule: A Multimodal Approach to the Selection of Cases for Litigation. *Journal of Legal Studies* 25:233–259.

Klaus, Václav. 1997. *Renaissance: The Rebirth of Liberty in the Heart of Europe.* Washington, DC: Cato Institute.

Klein, David. 2002. *Making Law in the United States Courts of Appeals.* Cambridge, UK: Cambridge University Press.

Knack, Stephen, and Philip Keefer. 1995. Institutions and Economic Performance: Cross Country Tests Using Alternative Institutional Measures. *Economics and Politics* 7:207–227.

Knack, Stephen, and Philip Keefer. 1997. Does Social Capital Have an Economic Payoff, A Cross-Country Comparison. *Quarterly Journal of Economics* 112:1251–1288.

Kornai, János. 1992. *The Socialist System: The Political Economy of Communism*. Princeton, NJ: Princeton University Press.

La Porta, Rafael, Florencio Lopez-de-Silanes, and Andrei Shleifer. 2002. Government Ownership of Banks. *Journal of Finance* 57:265–301.

La Porta, Rafael, Florencio Lopez-de-Silanes, and Andrei Shleifer. 2006. What Works in Securities Laws? *Journal of Finance* 61:1–32.

La Porta, Rafael, Florencio Lopez-de-Silanes, and Andrei Shleifer. 2008. The Economic Consequences of Legal Origins. *Journal of Economic Literature* 46:285–332.

La Porta, Rafael, Florencio Lopez-de-Silanes, Andrei Shleifer, and Robert W. Vishny. 1997a. Legal Determinants of External Finance. *Journal of Finance* 52:1131–1150.

La Porta, Rafael, Florencio Lopez-de-Silanes, Andrei Shleifer, and Robert W. Vishny. 1997b. Trust in Large Organizations. *American Economic Review* 87:333–338.

La Porta, Rafael, Florencio Lopez-de-Silanes, Andrei Shleifer, and Robert W. Vishny. 1998. Law and Finance. *Journal of Political Economy* 106:1113–1155.

La Porta, Rafael, Florencio Lopez-de-Silanes, Andrei Shleifer, and Robert W. Vishny. 1999. The Quality of Government. *Journal of Law Economics and Organization* 15:222–279.

La Porta, Rafael, Florencio Lopez-de-Silanes, Andrei Shleifer, and Robert W. Vishny. 2000. Investor Protection and Corporate Governance. *Journal of Financial Economics* 58:3–27.

La Porta, Rafael, Florencio Lopez-de-Silanes, Cristian Pop-Eleches, and Andrei Shleifer. 2004. Judicial Checks and Balances. *Journal of Political Economy* 112:445–470.

Landes, Elisabeth M. 1980. The Effect of State Maximum-Hours Laws on the Employment of Women in 1920. *Journal of Political Economy* 88:476–494.

Landes, William M. 1968. The Economics of Fair Employment Laws. *Journal of Political Economy* 76:507–552.

Landes, William M. 1971. An Economic Analysis of the Courts. *Journal of Law & Economics* 14:61–107.

Landes, William M., and Richard A. Posner. 1987. *The Economic Structure of Tort Law*. Cambridge, MA: Harvard University Press.

Landes, William M., and Richard A. Posner. 2008. "Rational Judicial Behavior: A Statistical Study." *University of Chicago, Olin Working Paper* 404.

Landis, James M. 1938. *The Administrative Process*. New Haven, CT: Yale University Press.

Langbein, John. 1985. The German Advantage in Civil Procedure. *University of Chicago Law Review. University of Chicago. Law School* 52:823–856.

Leoni, Bruno. 1961. *Freedom and the Law*. Princeton, NJ: D. Van Nostrand.

Lerner, William. 1975. *Historical Statistics of the United States: Colonial Times to 1970.* Washington, DC: Bureau of the Census.

Lewis, Arthur. 1949. *The Principles of Economic Planning.* London, UK: George Allen and Unwin Ltd.

Libecap, Gary D. 1992. The Rise of the Chicago Packers and the Origins of Meat Inspection and Antitrust. *Economic Inquiry* 30:242–262.

Llewellyn, Karl N. 1951. *The Bramble Bush: On Our Law and Its Study.* New York, NY: Oceana.

Llewellyn, Karl N. 1960. *The Common Law Tradition.* Boston, MA: Little Brown.

Lloyd, Henry Demarest. 1894. *Wealth Against Commonwealth.* New York, NY: Harper and Brothers.

Lockard, Duane, and Walter Murphy. 1992. *Basic Cases in Constitutional Law.* Washington, DC: CQ Press.

Macaulay, Stewart. 1963. Non-Contractural Relationships in Business: A Preliminary Study. *American Sociological Review* 28:55–70.

McChesney, Fred. 1987. Rent Extraction and Rent Creation in the Economic Theory of Regulation. *Journal of Legal Studies* 16:101–118.

McCormick, R. E., and R. D. Tollison. 1981. *Politicians, Legislation, and the Economy.* Boston, MA: Martinus Nijhoff.

McCraw, Thomas. 1984. *Prophets of Regulation.* Cambridge, MA: Harvard University Press.

Meade, James. 1948. *Planning and the Price Mechanism: The Liberal Socialist Solution.* London, UK: George Allen and Unwin Ltd.

Mehren, Arthur T. von. 1957. *The Civil Law System.* Englewood Cliffs, NJ: Prentice Hall.

Merryman, John Henry, and Rogelio Perez-Perdomo. [1969] 2007. *The Civil Law Tradition: An Introduction to the Legal Systems of Europe and Latin America.* Stanford, CA: Stanford University Press.

Messick, Richard. 1999. Judicial Reform and Economic Development: A Survey of the Issues. *World Bank Research Observer* 14:117–136.

Milgrom, Paul, and John Roberts. 1986. Relying on the Information of Interested Parties. *Rand Journal of Economics* 17:18–32.

Moehling, Carolyn. 1999. State Child Labor Laws and the Decline of Child Labor. *Explorations in Economic History* 36:72–106.

Montesquieu, Charles de Secondat Baron de. 1984 [1748]. *The Spirit of Laws.* Birmingham, AL: John D. Lucas Printing Co.

Mulligan, Casey B., and Andrei Shleifer. 2005. Conscription as Regulation. *American Law and Economics Review* 7:85–111.

Mulligan, Casey B., Ricard Gil, and Xavier Sala-i-Martin. 2004. Do Democracies Have Different Public Policies Than Nondemocracies? *Journal of Economic Perspectives* 18:51–74.

Nagel, Mark. 1999. *Supplicants, Robber Barons, and Pocket Banks*. Ph.D. dissertation, Department of Government, Harvard University.

Niblett, Anthony. 2009. "Inconsistent Contract Enforcement." Unpublished manuscript, Harvard University.

Nonnenmacher, Tomas. 2001. State Promotion and Regulation of the Telegraph Industry, 1845-60. *Journal of Economic History* 61:19–36.

North, Douglass C. 1981. *Structure and Change in Economic History*. New York, NY: Norton.

Novak, William. 1996. *The People's Welfare*. NC: University of North Carolina Press.

Novick, Sheldon. 1989. *Honorable Justice*. New York, NY: Laurel.

Okun, Michael. 1986. *Fair Play in the Marketplace*. DeKalb, IL: Northern Illinois University Press.

Olson, Mancur. 1991. Autocracy, Democracy, and Prosperity. In *Strategy of Choice*, ed. Richard Zeckhauser. Cambridge, MA: MIT Press.

Olson, Mancur. 1993. Dictatorship, Democracy and Development. *American Political Science Review* 87:567–576.

Parisi, Francesco, and Vincy Fon. 2009. *The Economics of Lawmaking*. New York, NY: Oxford University Press.

Parisi, Francesco, Vernon Valentine Palmer, and Mauro Bussani. 2007. The Comparative Law and Economics of Pure Economic Loss. *International Review of Law and Economics* 27:29–48.

Partridge, Anthony, and William Eldridge. 1974. *The Second Circuit Sentencing Study*. Washington, DC: Federal Judicial Center.

Peltzman, Sam. 1976. Toward a More General Theory of Regulation. *Journal of Law & Economics* 19:211–240.

Peltzman, Sam. 1989. The Economic Theory of Regulation After a Decade of Deregulation. *Brookings Papers on Economic Activity* Special Issue:1–41.

Pigou, Arthur Cecil. [1920] 1932. *The Economics of Welfare*. 4th ed. London, UK: Macmillan and Co.

Pigou, Arthur Cecil. [1928] 1952. *A Study in Public Finance*. 3rd ed. London, UK: Macmillan and Co.

Piketty, Thomas. 1995. Social Mobility and Redistributive Politics. *Quarterly Journal of Economics* 110:551–584.

Pinello, Daniel. 1999. Linking Party to Judicial Ideology in American Courts: A Meta-analysis. *Justice System Journal* 20:219–254.

Pistor, Katharina, and Chenggang Xu. 2003. Incomplete Law-A Conceptual and Analytical Framework and its Application to the Evolution of Financial Market Regulation. *Journal of International Law and Politics* 35:931–1013.

Pistor, Katharina. 2001. Law as a Determinant for Equity Market Development: The Experience of Transition Economies. In *The Value of Law in Transition Economies*, ed. Peter Murell. Ann Arbor, MI: University of Michigan Press.

Plucknett, Theodore. 1956. *A Concise History of the Common Law*. Boston, MA: Little, Brown.

Poe, Steven C., and C. Neal Tate. 1994. Repression of Human Rights to Personal Integrity in the 1980s: A Global Analysis. *American Political Science Review* 88:853–872.

Poe, Steven C., C. Neal Tate, and Linda Camp Keith. 1999. Repression of the Human Right to Personal Integrity Revisited: A Global Crossnational Study Covering the Years 1976-1993. *International Studies Quarterly* 43:291–313.

Polinsky, Mitchell, and Steven Shavell. 1979. The Optimal Tradeoff between the Probability and Magnitude of Fines. *American Economic Review* 69:880–891.

Polinsky, Mitchell, and Steven Shavell. 2000. The Economic Theory of Public Enforcement of Law. *Journal of Economic Literature* 38:45–76.

Polinsky, Mitchell, and Steven Shavell. 2001. Corruption and Optimal Law Enforcement. *Journal of Public Economics* 81:1–24.

Political Risk Services. 1996. *International Country Risk Guide*. East Syracuse, NY: PRS Group.

Pollock, Sir Fredrick, and Frederic William Maitland. [1895] 1968. *The History of English Law: Before the Time of Edward I*. Cambridge, UK: Cambridge University Press.

Ponzetto, Giacomo A. M., and Patricio A. Fernandez. 2008. Case Law versus Statute Law: An Evolutionary Comparison. *Journal of Legal Studies* 37:379–430.

Posner, Richard A. 1972. A Theory of Negligence. *Journal of Legal Studies* 1:29–96.

Posner, Richard A. 1974. Theories of Economic Regulation. *Bell Journal of Economics* 5:335–358.

Posner, Richard A. 1990. *Cardozo: A Study in Reputation*. Chicago, IL: University of Chicago Press.

Posner, Richard A. 1995. *Overcoming Law*. Cambridge, MA: Harvard University Press.

Posner, Richard A. 1996. *Law and Legal Theory in England and America*. Oxford, UK: Oxford University Press.

Posner, Richard A. [1973] 2003. *The Economic Analysis of Law*. 6th ed. Boston, MA: Little Brown.

Posner, Richard A. 2006. Common Law Economic Torts: An Economic and Legal Analysis. *Arizona Law Review* 48:735–748.

Posner, Richard A. 2008. *How Judges Think*. Cambridge, MA: Harvard University Press.

Prestwich, Michael. [1988] 1997. *Edward I*. New Haven, CT: Yale University Press.

Priest, George, and Benjamin Klein. 1984. The Selection of Disputes for Litigation. *Journal of Legal Studies* 13:1–55.

Priest, George. 1977. The Common Law Process and the Selection of Efficient Rules. *Journal of Legal Studies* 6:65–82.

Rabin, Robert L. 1985. Tort Recovery for Negligently Inflicted Economic Loss: A Reassessment. *Stanford Law Review* 37:1513–1538.

Radin, Max. 1925. The Theory of Judicial Decision: Or How Judges Think. *American Bar Association Journal. American Bar Association* 11:357–362.

Ramseyer, Mark, and Eric Rasmusen. 1997. Judicial Independence in the Civil Law Regime: The Evidence from Japan. *Journal of Law Economics and Organization* 13:259–286.

Revesz, Richard. 1997. Environmental Regulation, Ideology, and the D.C. Circuit. *Virginia Law Review* 83:1717–1772.

Reynolds, Susan. 1994. *Fiefs and Vassals: The Medieval Evidence Reinterpreted*. Oxford, UK: Oxford University Press.

Reynolds, Thomas H., and Arturo A. Flores. 1989. *Foreign Law: Current Sources of Codes and Basic Legislation in Jurisdictions of the World*. Littleton, CO: F.B. Rothman.

Ross, Thomas W. 1994. Raising an Army: A Positive Theory of Military Recruitment. *Journal of Law & Economics* 37:109–131.

Rowland, Charles, and Robert Carp. 1996. *Politics and Judgment in Federal District Courts*. Lawrence, KS: University Press of Kansas.

Rubin, Paul. 1977. Why is the Common Law Efficient? *Journal of Legal Studies* 6:51–63.

Rubin, Paul. 1993. *Tort Reform by Contract*. Washington, DC: AEI Press.

Sananikone, Ousa. 1997. Burkina Faso. In *The Informal Sector and Microfinance Institutions in West Africa*, ed. Leila Webster and Peter Fidler. Washington, DC: The World Bank.

Schanzenbach, Max, and Emerson Tiller. 2007. Strategic Judging under the U.S. Sentencing Guidelines: Positive Political Theory and Evidence. *Journal of Law Economics and Organization* 23:24–56.

Schlesinger, Rudolf, Hans Baade, Mirjan Damaska, and Peter Herzog. 1988. *Comparative Law. Case-Text-Materials*. New York, NY: Foundation Press.

Schneider, Friedrich. 2000. *The Value Added of Underground Activities: Size and Measurement of Shadow Economies and Shadow Economy Labor Force All Over the World*. Mimeo.

Schneider, Friedrich, and Dominik H. Enste. 2000. Shadow Economies: Size, Causes, and Consequences. *Journal of Economic Literature* 38:77–114.

Schwartz, Gary. 1981. Tort Law and the Economy of 19th Century America: A Reinterpretation. *Yale Law Journal* 90:1717–1775.

Schwartz, Gary. 1989. The Character of Early American Tort Law. *UCLA Law Review. University of California, Los Angeles. School of Law* 36:641–718.

Schwartzstein, Joshua, and Andrei Shleifer. 2010. "An Activity-Generating Theory of Regulation." *NBER Working Paper* 14752.

Shapiro, Martin. 1981. *Courts: A Comparative and Political Analysis*. Chicago, IL: University of Chicago Press.

Shavell, Steven. 1984a. A Model of the Optimal Use of Liability and Safety Regulation. *Rand Journal of Economics* 15:271–280.

Shavell, Steven. 1984b. Liability for Harm versus Regulation of Safety. *Journal of Legal Studies* 13:357–374.

Shavell, Steven. 1987. *Economic Analysis of Accident Law*. Cambridge, MA: Harvard University Press.

Shavell, Steven. 1996. Any Frequency of Plaintiff Victory at Trial Is Possible. *Journal of Legal Studies* 25:493–501.

Shavell, Steven. 2006. The Appeals Process and Adjudicator Incentives. *Journal of Legal Studies* 35:1–29.

Shleifer, Andrei, and Robert W. Vishny. 1993. Corruption. *Quarterly Journal of Economics* 108:599–617.

Shleifer, Andrei, and Robert W. Vishny. 1998. *The Grabbing Hand: Government Pathologies and their Cures*. Cambridge, MA: Harvard University Press.

Shughart, William F., and Robert D. Tollison. 1985. Corporate Chartering: An Exploration of the Economics of Legal Change. *Economic Inquiry* 23:585–599.

Skocpol, Theda. 1992. *Protecting Soldiers and Mothers*. Cambridge, MA: Harvard University Press.

Smith, Adam. [1776] 1976. *An Inquiry Into the Nature and Causes of the Wealth of Nations*. Chicago, IL: University of Chicago Press.

Songer, Donald, and Stefanie Lindquist. 1996. Not the Whole Story: The Impact of Justices' Values on Supreme Court Decision Making. *American Journal of Political Science* 40:1049–1063.

SRI International. 1999. *International Practices and Experiences in Business Startup Procedures*. Arlington, VA: SRI.

Steffens, Lincoln. 1906. The Shame of Minneapolis. In *The Muckrakers*, ed. Arthur and Lila Weinberg. 2001. Urbana-Champaign, IL: University of Illinois Press.

Stigler, George J. 1964. Public Regulation of the Securities Market. *Journal of Business* 37:117–142.

Stigler, George J. 1971. The Theory of Economic Regulation. *Bell Journal of Economics and Management Science* 2:3–21.

Stigler, George J. 1976. The Sizes of Legislatures. *Journal of Legal Studies* 5:17–34.

Stiglitz, Joseph. 1989. *Wither Socialism?* Cambridge, MA: MIT Press.

Stone, Julius. 1985. *Precedent and Law: Dynamics of Common Law Growth*. Sydney, Australia: Butterworths.

Summers, John. 1983. The Case of the Disappearing Defendant: An Economic Analysis. *University of Pennsylvania Law Review* 132:145–185.

Sunstein, Cass, David Schkade, and Lisa Michelle Ellman. 2004. Ideological Voting on Federal Courts of Appeals: A Preliminary Investigation. *Virginia Law Review* 90:301–354.

Taelman, Piet, ed. 1994. *International Encyclopaedia of Laws-Civil Procedure*. Hague, Netherlands: Kluwer Law International.

Tarbell, Ida M. 1903. The History of the Standard Oil Company: The Oil War of 1872— How the 'Mother of Trusts' operated. In *The Muckrakers*, ed. Arthur and Lila Weinberg. 2001. Urbana-Champaign, IL: University of Illinois Press.

Temin, Peter. 1980. *Taking Your Medicine: Drug Regulation in the United States*. Cambridge, MA: Harvard University Press.

Texas A&M University, and the Real Estate Center. 2002. "State Population by Decade." Online http://recenter.tamu.edu/data/popsd/.

Troesken, Werner. 2003. The Letters of John Sherman and the Origins of Antitrust. *Review of Austrian Economics* 15:275–295.

Tullock, Gordon. 1967. The Welfare Costs of Tariffs, Monopolies, and Theft. *Western Economic Journal* 5:224–232.

Turnham, David, Bernard Salome, and Antoine Schwartz. 1990. *The Informal Sector Revisited*. Paris: OECD.

United States Census Bureau. 2001. *Statistical Abstract of the United States*. Washington, DC: Census Bureau.

United States Census Bureau. 2002. *Statistical Abstract of the United States*. Washington, DC: Census Bureau.

University of Virginia Geospatial and Statistical Data Center. 1998. *United States Historical Census Data Browser*. Online http://fisher.lib.virginia.edu.

Viscusi, Kip. 1988. Pain and Suffering in Product Liability Cases: Systematic Compensation or Capricious Awards? *International Review of Law and Economics* 8:203–220.

Viscusi, Kip. 1998. The Social Costs of Punitive Damages Against Corporations in Environmental and Safety Torts. *Georgetown Law Journal* 87:285–345.

Watson, Alan. 1974. *Legal Transplants: An Approach to Comparative Law*. Charlottesville, VA: University of Virginia Press.

Wermiel, Sara. 2000. *The Fireproof Building*. Cambridge, MA: Harvard University Press.

Wilson, Woodrow. 1913. *The New Freedom*. New York, NY: Doubleday, Page and Co.

Woloch, Isser. 1994. *The New Regime*. New York, NY: Norton.

Wood, Donna. 1986. *Strategic Uses of Public Policy*. New York, NY: Pitman Publishing.

World Bank. 1999. "Administrative Barriers to Investment in Africa: The Red Tape Analysis." Washington, D.C.: FIAS.

World Bank. 1998. "Constraints to Small Business Development in Georgia," Private Sector Assessment Study, Washington, D.C.

World Bank. 2000. *World Business Environment Survey*. Washington, DC: World Bank.

World Bank. 2001. *World Development Indicators*. Washington, DC: World Bank.

World Bank. 2002. *World Business Environment Survey*. Washington, DC: Private Sector Advisory Group, World Bank.

World Economic Forum. 1996. *World Competitiveness Report*. Davos, Switzerland.

World Economic Forum. 1999. *The Global Competitiveness Report 1999*, eds. Klaus Schwab et al. New York, NY: Oxford University Press.

World Health Organization. 1998. *Causes of Death and Life, Birth Statistics*. Geneva, Switzerland: World Health Organization.

Yildiz, Muhamet. 2004. Waiting to Persuade. *Quarterly Journal of Economics* 119:223–248.

Young, James. 1989. *Pure Food*. Princeton, NJ: Princeton University Press.

Zywicki, Todd. 2003. The Rise and Fall of Efficiency in the Common Law: A Supply-Side Analysis. *Northwestern University Law Review* 97:1551–1634.

Index

Printed in the United States
By Bookmasters